Praise for *Alexander Hamilton: A Life*

"Readable and worthy."   —*Washington Post*

"The life of Alexander Hamilton, vividly re-created. . . . A fine biography."   —*Boston Globe*

"A fresh look at the many-faceted career of one of the founding fathers."   —*BookPage*

"Hamilton's turbulent life, the dramatic birth of a nation, all against the richly evoked, gritty background of the eighteenth century—Randall's book is propelled with the page-turning intensity of an epic novel."

—Ronald Blumer, Peabody Award–winning writer

"A sturdy and readable life, in company with Randall's other portraits of the Revolutionary generation."   —*Kirkus Reviews*

"If you are interested in the founding father who made the United States functional, you cannot do better than this lively, entertaining, and informative book. Will Randall, a master biographer and renowned historian, uses his considerable skills to bring Alexander Hamilton and his turbulent times to life."

—Rod Paschall, editor,
MHQ: The Quarterly Journal of Military History

"Randall excels in describing the conflicts Hamilton created and weathered as a soldier, politician, and lawyer; his capacity for making enemies; and the peaks and valleys of his tumultuous personal and professional life."   —*St. Louis Post-Dispatch*

"Engaging. . . . Vivid."  *ers Weekly*

Nancy Nahra

About the Author

WILLARD STERNE RANDALL is Historical Scholar in Residence at Champlain College in Vermont and an expert on early U.S. history. As an investigative reporter, he received the Sidney Hillman Prize and the National Magazine Award. His book *Benedict Arnold: Patriot and Traitor* was a finalist for the Pulitzer Prize, and *A Little Revenge: Benjamin Franklin and His Son* won a Frank Luther Mott Prize. He lives in Burlington, Vermont, with his family.

Alexander
HAMILTON

Colonel Hamilton awaits signal to attack Redoubt No. 10 at Yorktown.
By Alonzo Chappell (*Hulton/Archive by Getty Images*)

Alexander
HAMILTON

A Life

WILLARD STERNE RANDALL

Perennial

An Imprint of HarperCollinsPublishers

HarperCollins books may be purchased for educational, business, or sales promotional use. For information please write: Special Markets Department, HarperCollins Publishers Inc., 10 East 53rd Street, New York, NY 10022.

First Perennial edition published 2004.

Designed by Joseph Rutt

The Library of Congress has catalogued the hardcover edition as follows:

Randall, Willard Sterne.
    Alexander Hamilton : a life / Willard Sterne Randall.—1st ed.
      p. cm.
    Includes bibliographical references and index.
    ISBN 0-06-019549-5
    1. Hamilton, Alexander, 1755–1804. 2. Statesmen—United States—
Biography. 3. United States—Politics and government—1783–1809. I. Title.

E302.6.H2 R25 2003
973.4'092—dc21
[B]   2002068674

ISBN 0-06-095466-3 (pbk.)

04 05 06 07 08 ❖/RRD 10 9 8 7 6 5 4 3 2 1

For Nan and Lucy
for their patience, love, and understanding

CONTENTS

Illustrations follow page 174.

ACKNOWLEDGMENTS

In 1993, when I published my Jefferson biography, the American Revolution Round Table summoned me to a dinner meeting at Fraunces Tavern in New York City to present my interpretation and lay out any new evidence I had uncovered about the third president. Once before I had addressed this audience of experts on America's founding era so I knew to brace for a good after-dinner grilling. To my relief, only one question came that night, but what a question: Who was right about America, Jefferson or Hamilton? The hour was late, my answer brief: Jefferson for the eighteenth century, Hamilton for more modern times.

But that one sally from a darkened corner of the tavern where British commanders had dined during the Revolution, where George Washington bade farewell to Hamilton and his fellow officers, set me off on another five-year quest. This book is that night's answer, revised and more complete, and many people, in large ways and small, have helped me to research it.

As always, Thomas V. Fleming patiently answered my questions, despite his own tireless research and writing schedule. Donald Wickman, my own former graduate student, shared his research on

Samuel Barber, Hamilton's tutor in the classics and, later, comrade-in-arms. Alan Stracke, my colleague at Champlain College, helped with his knowledge of the Caribbean. Nick Westbrook, director of the Fort Ticonderoga Museum, where many of the Schuyler family papers are housed, gave me an invaluable hint about the Hamilton-Schuyler menage. J. Robert Maguire allowed me to study his as-yet-unpublished work on painter-spymaster John André and his connections with the Schuyler sisters.

At the New York Public Library, I was able to work with more than one hundred manuscripts from the Schuyler Papers. Earlier research on Henry Knox in the Morgan Library helped to flesh out the portrait of Hamilton as aide-de-camp and fellow cabinet member. At a symposium on the 1781 Virginia campaign that included workshops on new online archival research services and techniques, I learned from Michael Plunkett, director of the Albert and Shirley Small Special Collections Library at the University of Virginia, of the recently acquired Angelica Schuyler Church Papers and, back in my Vermont office, was able to peruse them. Diane Depew, coordinator of Colonial National Park and the organizer of that first Revolutionary War symposium at Yorktown, brought together some one hundred serious scholars of military history, several of whom shared their knowledge and insights with me. Colonel William Blair, director of the Commonwealth of Virginia's Victory Center at Yorktown, led me on an extensive and detailed battlefield tour. Among fellow conferees who added to my understanding of Hamilton's military ambitions were Professor Harry Dickinson of the University of Edinburgh, Thad W. Tate, professor emeritus of history at the College of William and Mary, and Lloyd Kramer, Lafayette scholar at the University of North Carolina at Chapel Hill, who cast new light on the character of Hamilton's French connections.

The staffs of many research institutions and libraries deserve special thanks. Over the years, I have been given generous access to the collections of Princeton University Library, the Henry E. Huntington Library, the William L. Clements Library at the University of Michigan, the Historical Society of Pennsylvania, the American Philosophical Society Library, the New-York Historical Society, the New York

Public Library, the Vermont Historical Society, the Georgetown University Library, the Alderman Library of the University of Virginia, and the Library of Congress. I am grateful to the University of Vermont's Bailey-Howe Library staff for Research Associate privileges, to Lori Colburn at my hometown Fletcher Free Library, and to Tammy Miller at the Miller Information Commons of Champlain College. All have stretched the meaning of the word *overdue*.

Thanks are also due to the Belvidere Trust, the guardians of Angelica Schuyler Church's Long Island home, to the staff of the Schuyler mansion in Albany, of Valley Forge State Park and Morristown National Historic Park. Arnold A. Rogow, an earlier writer on the Burr-Hamilton duel, kindly rushed me Angelica's photo. For a dozen years now, Diann Varricchione has selflessly given up evenings, weekends, and holidays to prepare my book manuscripts. Regina McNeeley, outstanding photo researcher for several historical magazines, including *MHQ: The Quarterly Journal of Military History*, helped me to meet a virtually impossible production deadline. Friend and colleague Stephen Zeoli designed and produced the maps that help trace Hamilton's restless life. I thank my editor at HarperCollins, Carolyn Marino, for her careful and constructive criticism and editing. Jennifer Civiletto, her assistant, has consistently and competently aided in the effort.

Researching and writing any biography sooner or later depends on the kindness of friends. Ray Lincoln has been my dear friend and literary agent for nearly three decades now. Roger Perry, president of Champlain College, has encouraged and helped to support my research. But only my wife and best editor, Nancy Nahra, knows how much it takes to bring to life a biography and how carefully it must be nurtured.

Alexander
HAMILTON

ONE

"The Wish of My Heart"

Alexander Hamilton realized instantly that he would die. Before he even heard the shot, the oversize lead ball had torn into his right side just above the hip, crashed through a rib, sliced through his liver, shattering a vertebra. Pitching forward on his face, Hamilton, the first secretary of the treasury of the United States, the author of the *Federalist Papers*, George Washington's strong right hand, the financial genius who had created Wall Street, and as inspector general of the U.S. Army, launched the U.S. Navy, fell to the ground, clutching his dueling pistol. His friend and second in the duel, Nathaniel Pendleton, rolled him over, cupped him in his arms, and held him, half sitting, under a cedar tree, away from the glaring July sunlight.

"Dr. Hosack!" Pendleton yelled. "Dr. Hosack!" Waiting with the oarsman below by the Hudson shore, Dr. David Hosack rushed up the narrow path toward the dueling place atop a small granite outcropping of cliff below the waking village of Weehawken, New Jersey, that steaming Thursday morning of July 11, 1804. He brushed past Aaron Burr, vice president of the United States, shielded by his second's umbrella to conceal his face as he hastened toward a rowboat that would hurry him across to New York City.

By the time Dr. Hosack, breathless, reached him, Hamilton had slumped to the ground and was losing consciousness. But he managed to gasp, "This is a mortal wound, Doctor." Once, Hamilton had wanted to study medicine. He knew anatomy. He knew the path of his pain, that his legs no longer moved. He thought he would die on the spot. So did Dr. Hosack. When he pulled up the bloody shirt, probed for a pulse, he could not hear Hamilton breathing. Hamilton had, Dr. Hosack wrote a few weeks later, "become to all appearance lifeless. His pulses were not to be felt. His respiration was entirely suspended. Laying my hand on his heart, I considered him irrecoverably gone."

Hosack and Pendleton carried Hamilton out of the woods and down the steep path. The boatman helped wrestle him onto the barge, placing the ornate case and pistol beside him. The doctor worked over him, rubbing spirits of hartshorne over his face, lips, forehead, neck, breast, arms. The cool massage seemed to have a miraculous effect. About fifty yards from shore, Hamilton sighed, the fresh breeze on the open water helping to revive him. His eyes half open, "to our great joy," recounted Hosack, "he at length spoke: 'My vision is indistinct,'" he said. "His pulse became more perceptible, his respiration more regular; his sight returned." But when the doctor tried to press Hamilton's side, to examine the wound, the pain was too much for Hamilton.

For a while, as the oars groaned in the tholes and slapped the water, Hamilton tried to talk. He spied the pistol, lent to him by his friend John Church. It was the same hair-triggered pistol Hamilton's oldest son had used three years before when he had been killed in a duel. The sight jolted him. "Take care of that pistol!" Hamilton cried. "It is undischarged, and still cocked. It may go off and do harm." He did not realize he had fired the gun into the air when Burr's bullet had struck him. Now he tried to turn his head toward Pendleton, sitting behind him in the stern. "Pendleton knows I did not intend to fire at him." His second nodded. "Yes, I have already told Dr. Hosack that." Then Hamilton fell silent. He remained calm, his eyes closed.

Just before the boat bumped into the dock, Hamilton asked his friends to summon his wife, Elizabeth, at home with their seven children at The Grange at Manhattan's northern tip. She had no idea of the duel. "Let Mrs. Hamilton be immediately sent for. Let the event be gradually broken to her, but give her hopes."

Hamilton's old friend William Bayard was looking down at him as the boat docked. A servant had told him that Hamilton had rowed away from Bayard's dock at dawn with two other men. Now Bayard strained to see as the boat neared: he could make out only two figures. Looking down into the boat, he could see why. Bayard had known Hamilton some thirty years since Hamilton, a young artillery captain, had fortified the Bayard family home and turned it into Bunker Hill Fort at the outbreak of the Revolution. "I called [Bayard] to have a cot prepared," Dr. Hosack recorded. "He, at the same moment, saw his poor friend lying in the bottom of the boat. He threw up his eyes and burst into a flood of tears." Hamilton alone appeared tranquil and composed. "We then conveyed him as tenderly as possible up to the house."

ALEXANDER HAMILTON lasted thirty-one hours after Aaron Burr shot him. When they finally got him into a bed on the second floor of Bayard's house on Chambers Street, he was nearly comatose. The doctor undressed him and administered a large dose of a strong anodyne, a painkiller. During the first day, Hosack gave Hamilton more than an ounce of an opium and cider potion, called laudanum, washing it down with watered wine. But, Hosack noted, "his sufferings during the whole day were almost intolerable." The ball had lodged inside his second lumbar disk, which had shattered, paralyzing his legs. His stomach was slowly filling with blood from severed blood vessels in his liver. Hosack "had not the shadow of a hope of his recovery," but he called in surgeons from French men-of-war anchored in the harbor who "had much experience in gunshot wounds." They agreed that Hamilton's condition was hopeless.[1]

During the night of July 11, the sedated Hamilton "had some imperfect sleep." He knew he had little time left to live: he asked Bayard to summon the Reverend Benjamin Moore, Episcopal bishop of New York and president of Columbia College, where Hamilton had once been a scholarship boy. In recent months, Hamilton had prayed Episcopal Matins and Vespers with his family at home. He had not attended any church since the Revolution. When the bishop arrived, he refused Hamilton Holy Communion after he learned that Hamilton not only had never been baptized an Episcopalian, but had been wounded in a duel, something Moore considered a mortal sin. Instead, the bishop gave Hamilton a lecture on the meaning of communion and left him to take some "time for serious reflection." Hamilton, clearheaded and determined now, asked the Bayards to send for the Reverend John M. Mason, pastor of the Presbyterian church and son of the man who had once sponsored him for a place at a Presbyterian academy when he had arrived in New York, an orphan from the West Indies. Hamilton as a boy had undergone a strong Presbyterian conversion experience—although, as a bastard, he had not been allowed to receive Presbyterian communion. But this Reverend Mason informed Hamilton that he could only receive communion in church, at the altar, during a regular Sunday ceremony. Hamilton pleaded for Bayard to go once more to Bishop Moore and try to persuade him.

It was noontime on the twelfth, more than twenty-four hours after the duel, before Elizabeth Hamilton arrived with their seven children. No one had told her the truth. Hamilton, she believed, was suffering only from stomach cramps: he'd had digestive disorders recently. Now she learned everything. She became frantic. Hamilton had been semiconscious, his eyes closed. He opened them, saw his children. His own grief at seeing his daughter Angelica, half mad since her brother's death in a duel over his father's politics, swept over him. He closed his eyes again, only saying to his wife, "Remember, Eliza, you are a Christian." It was as if he had banished her. She left with the children, sobbing hysterically.

When Bishop Moore called again, he lectured Hamilton once more on his own "delicate" situation. He wanted to help "a fellow mortal in distress," but he must "unequivocally condemn" dueling. Hamilton agreed with him "with sorrow and contrition," Moore reported. If Hamilton survived, would he vow never to duel again and use his influence to oppose the "barbaric custom"? It was a promise Hamilton found easy to make. Would he live "in love and charity with all men"? He answered yes, he bore "no ill will" to Aaron Burr. "I forgive all that happened." He received communion "with great devotion," Moore recorded, and "his heart afterwards appeared to be perfectly at rest."

But Hamilton was now writhing in agony. He could not hear the commotion downstairs when a note arrived from Aaron Burr, asking about his condition and worrying about a rumor that Hamilton had never intended to fire at him. When Bishop Moore returned the morning of the twelfth, he stayed at Hamilton's bedside—across the bed from another grief-stricken visitor, Hamilton's sister-in-law, Angelica Schuyler Church. She did not speak, nor did Hamilton. Over the years, they had been lovers. For nearly thirty years, Angelica Church had loved Hamilton more than her own dour, money-grubbing husband. Church, an expert duelist, had fled England after believing he had killed a man, changed his identity, grown rich selling supplies during the Revolution, and then returned to take a seat in Parliament. He often had left Angelica alone in their Manhattan mansion near Hamilton's town house while Elizabeth Schuyler stayed in the country with the children. John Church's pistols had finally ended the affair. Hamilton and Angelica could say nothing now. There was nothing more to say.[2]

On July 12, 1804, shortly after noon, with his mistress and his bishop at his bedside, Alexander Hamilton died "without a groan." He was forty-nine.

———— ◆ ————

"A Short Time to Live"

I n February 1768, on the Danish-ruled Caribbean island of St. Croix, yellow fever came, as it did every year, to the narrow streets of bright-roofed houses in Christiansted, the colony's capital. It came from miasmic patches of undrained land, from recesses in the lush green sugarcane-coated hills, from pools and puddles where the larvae of mosquitoes bloomed in the splendid sunlight. Nobody understood yet that the dreaded deadly fevers came on their almost invisible wings, not, as they thought, on the hundreds of ships that plied the Caribbean, bringing slaves in chains from Africa to work and die in the brutal canebrakes. That winter, more than a century before anyone knew what caused it or what to do to prevent it, yellow fever invaded the small two-story rented house at No. 34 Company's Lane, where Rachel Hamilton lived with her two teenage sons, James, fifteen, and Alexander, thirteen. There, Rachel supported her small family by running a store, selling provisions to nearby sugar plantations.

At first, for about a week, Rachel, who had little money, tried to recover with only the aid of a nurse midwife. But when her fever raged unabated, Rachel finally summoned a physician, one Dr. Heering, on February 17. Following the accepted practice of the time, Dr. Heering bled Rachel, cutting into her with a double-bladed razor that punched holes deep in her delicate white arm, producing a dark red current that quickly filled the doctor's pan before he tightened a tourniquet to staunch it. Dr. Heering then made Rachel drink his favorite fever nostrum.

But this did no good. The next morning, he came back. This time, he administered an emetic. He gave both Rachel and her son Alexander, who had now also contracted the illness, the favored medicine. Burning with a high fever, Rachel became dehydrated as she continued to vomit and perspire in the hot, close bedchamber. She grew weaker with each visit of the doctor. Her attempt to eat—the doctor ordered a chicken from her landlord and had the nurse-midwife reduce it to broth—helped her to rally briefly. The nurse also gave frail, pale Alexander his first nourishment in days, draining some of the fire from his cheeks. The next day, on his third visit, Dr. Heering gave Rachel a different fever medicine, this time containing valerian root, with a glass of alcohol to relieve her headache. Then he bled Alexander and gave him an enema. That evening, around nine o'clock, before Dr. Heering could return, thirty-nine-year-old Rachel Fawcett Levine Hamilton died.[1]

It was less than one hour later, even as the midwife was washing Rachel's corpse before laying out her body in a shift, that the town judge knocked at the shop door. He was accompanied by the bailiff and two probate court officials, and, acting as witnesses, the landlord and his clerk. There in the crowded parlor, at ten o'clock at night in feebly guttering candlelight, as the feverish Alexander Hamilton listened nearby, the hastily summoned probate court sealed up Rachel's belongings. They applied hot wax to her trunks, her bedroom, attic doors, and two outbuildings, "after which there was nothing more to seal up except some pots and other small things." The court record showed that the few things "which remained unsealed for use in preparing the body for burial," included "6 chairs, 2 tables and 2 wash-bowls." In the storehouse out back, the magistrates found eight salted porks, three firkins of butter, a considerable amount of flour, and the remnants of another, better household, including six leather chairs, three tables, eleven cups and saucers, three stoneware platters, two candleholders, and a mirror. There also was a goat: Rachel was of French descent and, like any good French housewife, probably made her own chèvre.

Three days later, the magistrate and the court recorder were back to take a more exacting inventory. The first things they listed were Rachel's children, *three* of them. The court officials had learned in the past few days that Rachel had an older son named Peter Levine, "about 22 years old," who lived in South Carolina, and that Rachel was divorced from this son's father. The two younger sons, the recorder noted, were "illegitimate children born after the decedent's separation" from Johann Michael Levine, a German Jewish sometime planter, sometime peddler, on the island. It had not been hard to learn the legal details: the beautiful, dark-haired Rachel's marriage to the much older planter and their subsequent divorce had titillated Christiansted's whispering gossips for nearly a decade.[2]

Even as Rachel's sister and brother-in-law went around the small port city of Christiansted for the next few days arranging for her funeral, buying new shoes for the boys and black veils to hide the shame of their tears, the probate court officials busily gathered more testimony. They discovered that Rachel had inherited nine slaves, five women she rented out for income and four slave boys who had acted as her house servants. She had given two of the slave boys to her sons, one boy, Ajax, to Alexander, another, Christian, to his older brother, James. Her personal effects, it turned out, were quite scanty for a daughter of one of the island's principal families: six silver spoons, seven silver teaspoons and a pair of sugar tongs that enabled her to serve a respectable tea, a pair of chests, and a bed with a well-worn feather comforter. Evidently, the boys slept with her. Most strikingly, there were some thirty-four leather-bound books, a sizable library for the time and place. And her wardrobe was surprisingly meager: four dresses, one red skirt, one white shirt, a black silk sun hat. She left no cash but no bills more than a year old, which was considered unusual. There may have been more than this: the court noted that a seal on one of the outbuildings had been broken since the first late-night hearing.

Rachel's brother-in-law, James Lytton, a wealthy retired sugar planter, took charge of the funeral arrangements, buying eleven yards of expensive black cloth to drape the coffin. The town judge advanced the money for the boys' shoes and veils until he could reimburse himself from the proceeds of the estate auction. The landlord unsnapped his purse and bought eggs, bread, and cakes for the funeral. Young Alexander, his face even more florid than usual, recovered sufficiently to join his brother and their relatives for the bone-rattling two-mile carriage ride behind the hearse out to the Lyttons' plantation, Grange No. 9. There, on a hilltop behind Rachel's family home, under ancient mahogany trees in the burial yard overlooking the azure Caribbean, Alexander Hamilton heard the local Church of England curate intone the matter-of-fact Anglican formula: "Man that is born of woman has a short time to live and is full of misery."

Rachel died intestate. A few days later her belongings were auctioned in the yard behind 34 Company's Lane. Alexander's uncle bought Rachel's books and gave them to the youth. Her slaves, silver, and furniture fetched a considerable 1,700 rigsdalers, but this was little more than enough to cover her 1,067 rigsdalers in suppliers' bills. Because she had no will, Rachel had every reason to expect that everything would go to her two younger sons. But their small inheritance soon vanished. The Danish court left the probate open for six months to allow claims to be entered. On August 3, 1768, shortly before the probate expired, Rachel's former husband appeared. Brandishing his Danish divorce decree, he filed a claim for his ex-wife's entire estate. Under the terms of their rare Danish divorce, Rachel had been forbidden to remarry. Her second and third sons, therefore, were considered illegitimate under Danish law. Her entire, however insignificant, estate, the court ruled, went at once to her firstborn and only legitimate son, her child by Levine. Under Danish law, Alexander and James—"born in whoredom" were the words of Levine's petition—received nothing. They were left not only publicly humiliated and orphaned but penniless. As Alexander Hamilton put it some thirty years later in a long letter to his Scottish uncle, the fifth Laird Hamilton, his mother's death "threw me upon the bounty of my mother's relations." But, within little more than a year, they, too, were dead.[3]

THREE

"Twice Guilty of Adultery"

A s Alexander Hamilton put it late in his life, shortly after he helped create the United States, his bloodline entitled him to "better pretensions than most of those who, in this country, plume themselves on ancestry." But Hamilton's ancestry never gave him emotional stability or financial security. From the moment of his birth, he was surrounded by conflict—affection and abandonment, beauty and brutality, refinement and savagery.[1]

There could have been few more beautiful and romantic settings in which to begin life than the volcanic British island colony of Nevis. The bright green island took its name from one of the many fortunate mistakes of its European discoverer, Christopher Columbus, who thought a cloud hanging over its 3,596-foot-high conical peak was filled with snow and named the island Las Nieves, snow in Spanish.

Wrenched away from the Spanish by the British, the island, renamed Nevis, became a haven for French Huguenots fleeing Catholic persecution under Louis XIV. That is why Jean Faucette, renaming himself John Fawcett, sailed there in 1678 and took up the life of a sugar planter, establishing himself on an estate, Gingerland, in St. George's Parish on the southeast side of the island. At the time Fawcett arrived, Nevis, nine miles long and five miles wide at most, had ten thousand white settlers and twenty thousand black slaves, more than three times its modern population. In his 1793 *History of the West Indies*, Bryan Edwards, a Jamaican, recorded that the white settlers of Nevis lived "amidst the beauties of an eternal spring beneath a sky serene and unclouded" in surroundings "inexpressibly beautiful for it is enlivened by a variety of the most enchanting prospects in the world in the numerous islands which surround it."[2]

One English visitor in 1745 described "a kind of perpetual spring." On the hilly shoulders that sloped off toward the sea, orange and lemon trees and pepper plants "exhibited at one and the same time fruit that were full grown, half-grown, a quarter grown and even flowers and buds and, as for vegetables of all sorts, they were ever fresh and blooming." Sugar exports had fallen from one hundred thousand hundred-pound barrels in 1707 to fewer than 25,000 barrels in 1755, the year Hamilton was born. By 1751, another visiting English official reported that, far from a paradise, Nevis actually had become an unhealthy, unpleasant place. By this time there were only nine hundred whites left on the island to drive sixty-five hundred slaves.[3]

Thirty years after John Fawcett arrived from France, a Nevis census listed his son, John Fawcett IV, as a physician as well as a sugar planter living with two white females, three black males, and four black females. The maternal grandfather of Alexander Hamilton lived with Mary Uppington, Hamilton's English maternal grandmother, at common law for at least four years before he married her. According to the Common Records of Nevis, they received a deed to property as John and Mary Fawcett in 1714. Yet the parish register of St. George's lists, under marriages, "Mr. John Faussett and Mrs. Mary Uppington" but not until August 21, 1718. The term "Mrs." did not necessarily mean Mary had been married before but was the contraction for "Mistress," a term of respect for her gentry status. Alexander Hamilton's grandmother Mary Fawcett gave birth to seven children. Only two of them survived. The older daughter, Ann, married a wealthy planter, James Lytton, about 1730, meaning that she probably was the second white female living under Dr. Fawcett's roof during the Nevis census before her parents married. The second and legitimate daughter, Rachel, born in 1729, was Alexander Hamilton's mother.[4]

The Fawcett plantation sat on Nevis's red clay south slope in a house that overlooked sugary-white beaches along the dark blue Atlantic and faced nearby Montserrat's volcanic peak. The Fawcetts, like most planters, seem to have divided their time between the plantation, with its scores of slaves cultivating then hacking down the sugarcane, and the colony's capital of Charlestown, where on the principal street they maintained a solid stone house overlooking the sea. A garden wall blocked the view of anything ugly in the town's teeming, slave-filled streets. In this beautiful place, tall, dark-haired Rachel Fawcett learned from her parents what usually was reserved for boys: French literature and the ancient classics of Greece and Rome.

But her father was much older than her mother, and her parents had an increasingly unhappy marriage. In 1741, when Rachel was eleven, her mother won a Leeward Islands agreement of separate maintenance exceedingly rare for a time when divorce was impossible in the British Empire. Because she had brought a dowry to the marriage, Mary Fawcett won custody of her daughter, Rachel, an annual income of 53 pounds a year, and her share of her husband's real estate and real property, including slaves. Mary had been eager to leave Nevis since a terrifying hurricane had devastated most of the island, including her older daughter Ann's plantation. Her sister and her brother-in-law had already sailed away to St. Croix, capital of the Danish Caribbean islands, where, after her separation from Dr. Fawcett, Mary and Rachel Fawcett joined them. The arrival of a single woman with an eleven-year-old daughter did not create much of a stir in the small society of Christiansted, where Mary and Rachel lived for the next five years.

In 1745, John Fawcett IV died. He left all his money, property, and slaves to his sixteen-year-old daughter, Rachel. Practically speaking, that was leaving it all, at least until Rachel married or turned twenty-one, to his ex-wife. Mary Fawcett was now free to remarry, and she set about spending her daughter's inheritance freely to attract a new husband for herself. But a woman with a beautiful sixteen-year-old daughter in tow found it difficult to gain a new husband. So the ambitious and manipulative Mary Fawcett decided to concentrate on making a match for her young daughter, already on her way to earning Alexander Hamilton's description of "a woman of great beauty, brilliancy and accomplishment."5

Rachel was still only sixteen when Johann Michael Levine, a German Jewish merchant who had just sold his clothing-and-housewares business on Nevis, arrived on St. Croix, bought a small sugar plantation and a bright red suit, and went looking for a bride. Mary Fawcett soon introduced him to the beautiful young Rachel. More accurately, her mother, seeing an obviously well-to-do planter in a fancy suit, shoved her young daughter at the thirty-eight-year-old Levine. Levine sold his plantation, taking a quick profit, then bought a cotton plantation that he named Contentment. The plantation was on the southwest edge of Christiansted, conveniently only a mile or so from Rachel and her family at Grange No. 9. Levine's flashy apparel and business connections, which included Rachel's uncle, dazzled Rachel's mother. She thought he was rich. Levine, himself seeking a rich young wife, eagerly responded. In the same year that her father had died, Rachel married the much-older Levine and rode away with him. Contentment, she found, sat in a depression away from town and had no view of the sea. Her mother stayed close, settling in at Rachel's sister's plantation. Soon, Rachel gave birth to a son, Peter.

When Alexander Hamilton's own son John sat down to write his by-then-famous father's biography, he noted that his father "rarely" talked about his own mother, only saying that Levine had been "attracted by her beauty and, recommended to her mother by his wealth, received her hand against her [Rachel's] inclination." Later, when Rachel's firstborn son, Peter Levine, died, Alexander Hamilton wrote to his own wife that he grieved little at his half brother's death because "you know the circumstances that abate my distress." He was to learn that Peter left him nothing: "He dies rich, but has disposed of the bulk of his fortune to strangers."

Rachel's marriage to Levine was unhappy from the outset, made only worse as he spent his way through her inheritance, now at his disposal by right of marriage, and deeply into debt. Like most West Indies sugar planters, he lived on credit far beyond his income. Before the first year of the Levines' marriage was over, he owed the Danish West India Company 1,930 rigsdalers, twice what the plantation was worth. He went on ordering provisions for the slaves who worked his cotton fields, riding into Christiansted in his carriage with his bride and liveried servants, and on credit buying furniture and luxuries for his house in the expensive shops of the capital. The next year, while he managed to add 2,432 rigsdalers to his pile of debts, he no longer had enough credit even to stock a merchant's small store. He had to sell Contentment. Slipping in status, he became a plantation manager, then an overseer, a brutal job of personally whipping and driving his own African slaves to work harder under the broiling tropical sun. No longer was Levine the plantation owner with the big house and servants, but a renter. Each step down the social ladder meant less money, a smaller and less elegant house. There apparently was nothing left of Rachel's dowry by this time.[6]

Five years after they married, Levine apparently abused his wife both emotionally and physically until she tried to run away from him. Under Danish law, her husband could have her jailed. Years later, when he needed grounds for a divorce, Levine alleged that Rachel had "twice been guilty of adultery." What is more likely is that Rachel refused any longer to keep up the sham of their marriage and that, when she threatened to take their child and move out, Levine had her arrested. The language Levine used in court papers nearly ten years later when he wanted to remarry draws a picture of their tempestuous relationship: Rachel had "shown herself to be shameless, rude and ungodly" and had "completely forgotten her duty," the common phrase for no longer having sexual relations with him. He had her locked up in jail. A short stretch in St. Croix's miserable military dungeon was supposed to make Rachel repent her "ungodly mode of life" and, when she was released, make her "live with him as was meet and fitting." After her mother appealed to him, the fort's commandant, Captain Bertram Pieter De Nully, freed Rachel. But instead of running home chastened to her heavy-handed husband, Rachel, released to the custody of the island's highest-ranking officer, went to live with him on his own plantation. Yet, under Danish law, Levine had sole custody of their four-year-old son. Soon a shattered Rachel sailed back to Nevis with her mother. She never saw her firstborn child again.[7]

As beautiful as it was, Nevis was, as Rachel already knew, anything but an island paradise for the Africans who had come to the island as slaves of the English. Few white workers could be induced to leave England and brave the searing heat, the fatal fevers, the heavy labor. English farmers flocked to cooler climates like New England or, seeking riches in the tobacco trade, settled in Virginia.

LARGELY IN fear of revolts by the slaves they had imported, sugar planters in the Leeward Islands who could afford to do so moved their families to England, becoming absentee landlords. Many planters did not want their children in close contact with slaves fresh from the jungles of Africa. Among the imported slaves were Koromantyns from the Gold Coast. Coveted for their powerful constitutions and their ability to endure the hardships of slave labor, they were also feared by whites such as Alexander Hamilton's family because of these same qualities. Only the hardiest of slaves survived five years of the brutal heat, tropical disease, and hard labor. Because few African women were imported, the slave workforce had to be restocked almost annually. As the successful planters deserted their homes in the islands and moved back to England, they hired agents and overseers, often brutal and of dubious ability as managers, who cheated them or ate up their profits. The planters, going ever deeper into debt, often lost their estates. Only owners of large-scale operations could afford to leave the islands and live in England. Impoverished small-time planters left behind settled into a culture of debt.

But the fortune seekers, merchants, importers, and exporters who bought and sold everything the planters needed and produced, still came. Shortly after Rachel Levine fled her first husband and sailed back to Nevis in 1750, she met one of these merchants, James Hamilton, who was to become Alexander Hamilton's father. Born in Stevenson Parish, Ayrshire, he came from a lesser branch of a ducal Scottish family. He was the fourth of nine sons of wealthy landowner Alexander Hamilton. His great-grandfather had purchased medieval Sheni-stone Castle in 1685 and renamed it The Grange. Here, Alexander Hamilton's father had grown up. Forty years later, Hamilton would choose the same name for his New York manor house. Alexander Hamilton's father grew up in this romantic ruin, its thick stone walls, covered with ivy, only allowing shafts of light to penetrate through thin slits that had been pierced for defense. Inside the walls, for private view only, were flower gardens and high, delicate Gothic windows. One Ayrshire historian claimed that "no other castle of the 13th or 14th Century has such beautiful windows."[8]

Alexander Hamilton's grandfather had married Elizabeth Pollock, the daughter of an "ancient baronet," as Hamilton put it. Sir Robert Pollock had been created baronet of Nova Scotia in 1702. Elizabeth Pollock's family had been prominent in Scottish politics for six centuries and were staunch defenders of English monarchy. In modern terms, Alexander's grandfather collected about $250,000 a year in rents for his sheep-grazing lands. His wife brought a stunning 41,000-pound dowry (about $1.6 million in today's currency) to their marriage. But, under the English laws of primogeniture and entail, a fourth son could not expect to inherit anything at all unless all three of his older brothers died without issue. With no prospects in Scotland, James Hamilton apparently underwent some sort of counting-house apprenticeship, probably in nearby Glasgow, before being packed off to the West Indies to support himself as a merchant as best he could.

James Hamilton seems never to have had any of the qualities necessary for success in business. He was lazy to the point of indolence, generous, and according to some of his famous son's biographers, fond of drinking. "You no doubt have understood," Alexander Hamilton wrote back to the laird of the family manor in Scotland in 1797, "that my father's affairs at a very early date went to wreck, so as to have rendered his situation during the greatest part of his life far from eligible." His choice of cash-poor Nevis as a place to establish a business only confirms his unsound business judgment. But James Hamilton was handsome and warm and undemanding, attributes that certainly attracted Rachel Levine after she moved back to Nevis to escape her menacing husband.[9]

Shortly after her arrival in Charlestown, Rachel and James began living together. Hamilton was eleven years older than Rachel, who was still only twenty-one. They lived as husband and wife for fifteen years. Their informal marital arrangement, while technically adulterous at first, was not unusual in the islands. The Hamiltons, as they became known, were considered an exemplary couple, living together longer as husband and wife than many of their legally married neighbors. Under English law, seven years' cohabitation would have entitled them to be considered married at common law, were Rachel free to marry. At least that seems how the couple considered themselves. As they traveled to other islands, they introduced themselves as husband and wife. On October 1, 1758, for example, as "James Hamilton and Rachel Hamilton his wife," they stood as godfather and godmother at a christening on St. Eustatius.[10]

By this time, they had two sons of their own. According to the probate court record made on St. Croix when Rachel died, their first child, James, was born in 1753. On January 11, 1755, their second son, Alexander Hamilton, was born. According to local historians, he was born in a large house opposite St. Paul's Anglican Church on Main Street in Charlestown, which now houses Nevis's historical society on the first floor and the Nevis House of Assembly on the second. Many years later, Hamilton, in an attempt to make himself appear more the prodigy, insisted that he had not been born until 1757. But Rachel's brother-in-law, James Lytton, testified at the probate hearing about Hamilton's age. One of the most responsible men on the island, he had no reason to shade the truth. Since the orphaned Hamilton boys were about to become his charges, he was scrupulous in the testimony he gave to a court noted for its legal precision.

Even though Rachel had tried to help her consort, James Hamilton, by rolling up her sleeves, minding the store, and keeping the books, he was unable to make a go of his own business and went bankrupt. Insolvent, James, like Rachel's first husband, took jobs as a manager or chief clerk on plantations or in countinghouses on one

island after another. Fortunately, Rachel had already learned accounting, like many young ladies in the islands, in a private school as a
young girl. She believed in education and, by the time he was five,
Alexander Hamilton was attending a small Hebrew school on Nevis.
Local histories say that he was barred from any other school on the
island because he was a bastard. Learning to read and write precisely
in French from his mother and grandmother (who probably spoke
French with him at home), he also picked up some Hebrew. He
impressed neighbors when his teacher asked him, standing by her
side on a table and holding her hand, to recite the Decalogue in
Hebrew.

Alexander Hamilton grew up surrounded by the whirling wind-
mills that crushed the sugarcane. His boyhood was filled with the
fragrance of fields where gingerroot and cinnamon, nutmeg and avo-
cados grew. Hikes along goat paths took him past giant aloes and
fields that yielded yams and sweet potatoes to feast on with fresh fish
and smoked hams. He was also learning to love the romantic lore of,
to him, exotic, faraway Scotland as his father reconstructed family
castles in the air, filling young Hamilton with yearning for an aristocratic heritage he would never be allowed to share.[11]

In the spring of 1765, when Alexander Hamilton was ten, his
father took Rachel, their two sons, and their slaves on a journey from
St. Kitts, where James Hamilton was now head clerk in the mercantile house of Archibald Ingram, to Christiansted, the capital of the
Danish island of St. Croix. There, he was supposed to collect 807
pounds owed his employer. Christiansted court records show that
the debtor refused to pay the claim and that James Hamilton had to
remain on the Danish-held island until the next Court for Strangers
convened several months later. It must have been at this time that
James and Rachel learned that Johann Levine had sued her for
divorce in St. Croix in 1759, six years earlier, and nearly ten years
after she had left him. The petition in the matrimonial court, dated
February 26, 1759, alleged that she had "shown herself to be shameless, rude and ungodly," had "completely forgotten her duty and let
husband and child alone and instead gave herself up to whoring with
everyone." Such a charge against Rachel exists only in this self-

serving divorce document and has never been corroborated or sub-
stantiated. Levine had sued at such a late date because he wanted to
marry again and he learned that when Rachel returned to St. Croix
she had two sons. If Levine died, Rachel, as his widow, could claim
for her two younger sons all of their son Peter's inheritance. At the
time she was summoned to the hearing, the summons was served at
the Christiansted town fort and to its commandant's house where
she had last stayed on the island. But Rachel, drifting from island to
island with James Hamilton, never received the St. Croix summons,
and thus she never got to testify. The court ruled that her absent
silence proved the case against her and dissolved the marriage. Rachel
was to have "no rights whatsoever as to wife to either [Levine's] person or means." Rachel's "illegitimate" children by Hamilton were
denied "all rights or pretensions" to Levine's possessions. Levine was
free to marry again, which he did, but Rachel was not.[12]

Communications among the islands were poor. Each island was,
in effect, a separate country, remote fragments of rival European
empires. Only by returning to St. Croix did Rachel ever learn the full
force of Levine's wrath. She and Hamilton may have, at some point,
formalized their living arrangements in a wedding ceremony. But the
question remains whether James Hamilton knew of her earlier marriage. Levine's decree not only made her a bigamist and an adulterer
but also deprived her younger sons of all inheritance rights and formally declared them bastards. The shock of this discovery seems to
have been the final blow to Rachel and James Hamilton's relationship.
He had never been successful, never been able to provide well for his
common-law wife. In 1765, when he returned to his clerk's desk on
distant St. Kitts, he left his family behind on St. Croix. But it was
hardly a case of child abandonment, as some historians have made it.
Rachel would no longer submit to raising her children in the shabby
quarters provided for a plantation clerk. Whatever James and Rachel
told their sons, ten-year-old Alexander thought his father would
rejoin them soon. Late in life, he still wrote feelingly of the "separation between him and me when I was very young." But Alexander
Hamilton never saw his father again.[13]

* * *

IN THE last three years of Rachel Fawcett Levine Hamilton's life, James Hamilton stayed away while she struggled to set up her own business and raise their children. James, the older son, like his father, seems to have had little aptitude for business, but Alexander thrived as his mother's companion, shopkeeper's assistant, and part-time clerk, learning the merchant's business, how to mind the store and to keep the accounts and the inventory. Rachel was a better provider than James Hamilton ever had been, but she never rose above a subsistence level. When, two years after James left, Rachel's mother died, Rachel was left with nine slaves but no money to feed them. She rented out as domestic servants the five women slaves she had inherited. With this modicum of security, she rented a small house at No. 34 Company's Lane next to St. John's Anglican Church and opened up a small store. She bought salt pork, butter and flour from Dipnall, her landlord, and resold them as provisions for planters and ship's captains from the New York import-export firm of Beekman and Cruger. She settled her accounts promptly, kept proper books, and refused the help of her wealthy relatives nearby, although their presence must have helped her to obtain credit and customers. She was just beginning to furnish her house—her brother-in-law, James Lytton, gave her six handsome handmade oak chairs so that she could entertain again—when, at age thirty-nine, she died.

James Hamilton did not learn of her death until long after the funeral and then he did not come to reclaim his sons. He continued his drinking and drifting from job to job, island to island. For seven years, Alexander continued to write him regularly, and for the rest of his life, he spoke of him affectionately. In 1771, when he was sixteen, he read in the Christiansted newspaper that his father had been seriously wounded during a slave revolt on Tobago. Thirty Koromantyn slaves had set out to destroy all the island's white inhabitants. According to the *Royal Danish-American Gazette* for January 23, 1771, the slaves "attacked Mr. Hamilton's house" and "wounded three white men desperately, two of whom are since dead . . . Mr. Hamilton was shot through the thigh but is recovering."[14]

For long periods for the rest of his father's life, Alexander Hamilton did not know of his whereabouts or his welfare, but on the surface at least, he never seemed to be bitter about it. As his own fortunes soared, he was troubled that his father might be living in poverty. At the end of the Revolution, in 1783, Hamilton wrote to his brother James, who never left the islands, inquiring,

> What has become of our dear father? It is an age since I have heard from him. Perhaps, alas! he is no more, and I shall not have the pleasing opportunity of contributing to render the close of his life more happy than the progress of it. My heart bleeds at the recollection of his misfortunes and embarrassments.

And when he reopened his correspondence with his father, he urged him to come to New York and live with him. He paid all his father's debts and sent him several thousand dollars that supported him in his old age. Yet it continued to haunt Alexander Hamilton that, as he grew wealthy, his feckless faraway father remained indigent.[5]

FOUR

"I Wish There Was a War"

Sometime before his mother's death, probably at age thirteen when his father sequestered himself from his family, Alexander Hamilton went to work as a clerk in the Christiansted office of the New York–based import-export house of Beekman and Cruger. His boss was young Nicholas Cruger, junior partner in a prominent mercantile family whose operations included ships, countinghouses and warehouses in England, New York, and throughout the Caribbean. Their business interests linked all the European colonies in the New World. Young Hamilton eagerly plunged into commerce. Even though he came to hate being a lowly clerk, at first it was an exciting environment for a young boy, and he thrived.

His experiences over the next few years at this crossroad of international trade gave him a priceless grounding in business management and marked him as a prodigy. Young Hamilton was able to make himself invaluable to the Crugers' burgeoning Caribbean operations by the age of seventeen even as, once again, his family failed him. James Lytton, the wealthy uncle and patriarch of a planter family whose influence had helped procure Alexander's job, died eighteen months after Alexander's mother. The steady decline of the Lytton dynasty, once one of St. Croix's wealthiest, had gone on for four years. After Rachel Hamilton's sister, Ann—Alexander's aunt—died during a visit to Nevis in 1765, her husband, James Lytton, had sold his plantation there and ensconced himself in their luxurious St. Croix apartment. Retiring as a planter, Lytton still had substantial investments in trading firms, slaves, and ships when Rachel died. Then Lytton's son, Peter, to whom young Alexander was closer than any other family member, committed suicide. Peter had married an aged widow, sold off her plantations, speculated wildly, fled his creditors, and killed himself. Attempting to bequeath his estate to his black mistress and their mulatto son, he left nothing to Alexander.

This left Alexander only his fifteen-year-old brother and a slightly older cousin, Ann, who had married a luckless planter who also had gone bankrupt. James Lytton's death was an especial blow. Alexander's guardian died suddenly before he could change his will to provide anything for Hamilton, if he ever intended to. The only morsel of good fortune left for Alexander was that, at his mother's death, he had gone to live in Christiansted with the family of his two-years-older friend Edward Stevens, whose father was a partner in a mercantile firm trading with New York. Hamilton's formal schooling came to a halt, to all appearances permanently.

But his education was never to be confined to a classroom. After long hours on a stool in a countinghouse each day, young Hamilton dipped into the trove of his only inheritance, his mother's small library. He loved to read Alexander Pope's antimonarchical rhyming couplets and Plutarch's hero-worshipping comparisons of Greek and Roman leaders. His studies and his knowledge soon surpassed those of most of the island's full-time students. In his small room at the Stevenses, with the help of his friend Neddy, he learned mathematics and chemistry. Both boys dreamed of becoming physicians. But his real schooling, what he was to tell his children was "the most useful part of his education," was his apprenticeship on the waterfront. In the warehouses, in the ship's holds, and on the high stool of Beekman and Cruger's countinghouse in Christiansted, he learned, he said, to be at ease with financial affairs and with giving orders.

Young Hamilton's first order of business as a merchant's clerk was to learn St. Croix intimately. The nineteen-mile-long island, five miles at its widest, was crammed to the hilltops with 381 plantations mostly producing sugar but some cotton and coffee on thirty thousand precious acres. Accurate knowledge of the status of each crop became essential for Hamilton to decide when to buy and sell mules to help in the harvest, what grain to buy to bake for the slave labor force. Slaves outnumbered whites on the plantations twenty to one. He needed an intimate knowledge of Christiansted (population thirty-five hundred—three fourths slave), its merchants, bankers, lawyers, ship captains, solvent planters, and deadbeats. While the Danes officially controlled the government waterfront, faraway Dutch bankers and New York brokers like the Crugers controlled Christiansted's commerce. Seventy letters survive from Hamilton's St. Croix years. They reveal that he flourished on this bustling little island. He became thoroughly familiar with Christiansted's twenty thronged streets lined with six hundred or so seventeenth- and eighteenth-century Danish-style houses. Their gaily painted yellow, raspberry, buff, or salmon-colored overhanging balconies shaded him as he hurried along its tile-inlaid sidewalks on his master's errands.

By law, young Hamilton also had to become part of St. Croix's militia. He was required to be prepared to help stifle any slave insurrection among Christiansted's blacks. In case of revolt, each trading company's warehouse also served as a well-stocked fort. Every white male was required to be equipped with a gun, sixteen cartridges with balls, a sword or cutlass, and a lantern. When an alarm gun went off in the fort or prearranged drumbeats pounded, every white man was to race into field or street with his gun and, at night, his lighted lantern.

Young Hamilton also had to learn about tides, storms, wind, and sea, when it was safe to send precious cargoes from Christiansted's shallow harbor over the coral reef one mile offshore and when it was more prudent to send them around to smaller Fredericksted at the island's western tip. He had to learn the capacities and capabilities of each of the beamy barks, schooners, and sleek sloops that lined the great wharf, how to load and unload them. He also had to learn accounting, bookkeeping, and the art of writing all sorts of business letters.

When young Hamilton went to work for the firm of Beekman and Cruger, it was St. Croix's most important exporter of sugar and molasses to the American mainland. It was also the most reliable provider of food and supplies for its plantations. So valuable was Caribbean land for sugar cultivation that little acreage had been set aside for growing food. There were seldom enough provisions to last six months. Food and clothing for its twenty-four thousand people had to be imported constantly. With their own new sloop, Beekman and Cruger hoped to provide cargoes for other shipping firms and to arrange passage for mail and passengers among the islands and to New York. They advertised their ships' arrivals and departures in the local newspaper, the *Royal Danish-American Gazette*.

Hamilton toiled on the second floor of the firm's large building at Nos. 56–57 King's Street across from present-day Government House and next to the town's main wharf. Downstairs behind the store was a large enclosed yard where newly arrived slaves were auctioned. Buyers were kept out until the slaves were rubbed down with oil "in order to make them look sleek and handsome." The slaves then curled one another's hair, braiding it into ropes. But, as Alexander saw, little could be done to improve the appearance of the battered and half-starved slaves. In 1772, when he was seventeen, it was Hamilton's job to help sell a cargo of slaves consigned to Cruger from the Gold Coast aboard the Dutch East Indiaman *Venus*. Cruger described the 250 slaves crowding into his yard as "very indifferent indeed, sickly and thin," fetching on the average 30 pounds, less than the cost of a good Spanish mule, as Hamilton dutifully recorded the transaction. In one 1771 advertisement, the firm announced the sale "at said Cruger's Yard," of three hundred "prime slaves." The next year, the manager reported to his New York City partner, Henry Cruger, Jr., "We have a Danish Guinea man [slaving ship] just arrived with 250 Gold Coast slaves. They will sell all for half produce and half cash or bills [of exchange]." Sometimes it was Alexander Hamilton who wrote out these advertisements. In his early life especially,

Hamilton benefited from the Caribbean's slave-based economy. He learned to trade and socialize with its richest benefactors, who included not only his own relatives but all his business colleagues. Much later, Hamilton was to become a vocal public enemy of slavery. But on St. Croix, as a teenage boy, he was learning to despise the gulf between the island's white aristocrats who insisted on their fine mahogany furniture, their silks, and their imported cheeses, and the horrible living and working conditions of the vast slave majority.[1]

His patron and employer, the man who taught him the import-export business, was Nicholas Cruger, only twenty-five years old when he hired the thirteen-year-old Hamilton. A scion of one of colonial America's leading mercantile families, Cruger was also engaged to marry the daughter of Christiansted's town captain, Pieter De Nully (whose father had once released Hamilton's mother from the fort's dungeon). The New York–born Cruger was a third-generation American merchant. His grandfather had emigrated from Germany, become mayor of New York City, and with his sons established the Cruger firm on the Caribbean islands of St. Croix, Curacao, St. Kitts, St. Eustatius, and Jamaica, as well as in England. The New York branch had its own Manhattan wharf jutting from Pearl Street into the East River. There it shipped and received cargoes from its English and Caribbean factors. English navigation laws and chilly foreign relations made it impossible for British-American colonies to trade directly between England or its colonies and islands belonging to its commercial rivals, France and Spain. But trade could move through the neutral Dutch and Danish ports and the Cruger warehouses on Dutch Curacao, Danish St. Croix, and British Jamaica. The St. Croix branch also imported and distributed slaves from West Africa and smuggled mules from the Spanish Main colonies of Cuba and Puerto Rico to work in the sugarcane harvest. Nicholas Cruger, Hamilton's young boss, had inherited his uncle John's St. Croix business interests. Rachel Hamilton's tragic death inadvertently cemented her son's connection with one of colonial America's most enterprising families.

HAMILTON'S BOYHOOD friendship with Edward Stevens and his generous family had helped him to survive a four-year ordeal of family disasters. But then in 1770, two years after Hamilton's mother died, his best friend traveled fifteen hundred miles to New York City to attend a preparatory school before taking premedical studies at King's College (present-day Columbia University), a prospect that Hamilton now thought beyond his possibilities. As they parted, Stevens later recalled, they renewed "those vows of eternal friendship which we have so often mutually exchanged." In what may have been his first letter to anyone other than his errant father, the fourteen-year-old Hamilton responded to a letter from Stevens that announced that he would soon be coming home to St. Croix for a visit. Stevens's father and sister had just sailed for New York to meet him—"for whose safe arrival I now pray"—and he no doubt meant it literally.

In stilted adolescent prose, Hamilton told his friend he truly "wished for an accomplishment of your hopes" of "having soon the happiness of seeing us all." He missed his erstwhile playmate, yet he was nervous about his return. Had his friend, soon to enter college, become too grand to still be the companion of a mere countinghouse clerk? Hamilton did not know whether he could "still be present" in the Stevens household. "To confess my weakness," he confided, "I [despise] the groveling and condition of a clerk to which my fortune condemns me." He vowed that he "would willingly risk my life" if he could only "exalt my station:"

> I'm confident, Ned, that though my youth excludes me from any hopes of immediate preferment, nor do I desire it, but I mean to prepare the way for my futurity. I'm no philosopher, you see, and may be justly said to build castles in the air. My folly makes me ashamed, and [I] beg you'll conceal it yet, Neddy, we have seen such schemes successful when the projector is constant. I shall conclude [by] saying, I wish there was a war.

Frustrated by his indefinite sentence as a lowly clerk, fearing that his loss of social status, in a place and time when that was all-important, would preclude any further education or possibility of advancement, young Hamilton was determined to find an opening for his ambition. He refused to be a stoic about his lot—"I am no philosopher." He refused to accept the fact, as many others would have, that the deaths of his mother and cousins and his father's desertion of him might permanently reduce him to a career on a stool in a warehouse. He was all youthful optimism, but he also was striking a chord that he would play again and again until his dying day. He believed that, by boldness and courage, if by no other avenue, he could benefit from combat. This was not too farfetched a notion in the contentious eighteenth century. There rarely had been a long interval of peace among the European colonial powers.[2]

Unwilling to await an opportunity for advancement to come his way, Hamilton instinctively set out to attract public attention. Once again, he exaggerated his age when he began to submit attempts at poetry to the *Gazette*. Stating that he was "about seventeen" and admitting that his efforts were "presumptuous," he nevertheless submitted two poems. The first was a pastoral, employing as a poetic device shepherd boy meets shepherd girl and extolling marriage as a means to gain more abundant sexual pleasure. Both poems were bolder and franker than the forms he imitated. He signed them "A.H." Years later, a middle-aged Hamilton was still proud of his early effusions, boasting to his children that he had "always had a strong propensity to literary pursuits." He stepped into the public eye for the first time at age sixteen with such lines as these:

> *In yonder mead my love I found*
> *Beside a murm'ring brook reclin'd:*
> *Her pretty lambkins dancing 'round*
> *Secure in harmless bliss.*
> *I bade the waters gently glide*
> *And vainly hushed the heedless wind,*
> *Then, softly kneeling by her side*
> *I stole a silent kiss.*

In a racy companion piece, Hamilton displayed a playful ribald wit:

Coelia's an artful little slut;
Be fond, she'll kiss, et cetera—but
She must have all her will;
For, do but rub her 'gainst the grain
Behold a storm, blow winds and rain,
Go bid the waves be still.[3]

Young Hamilton enjoyed his newfound notoriety. He plunged back into print with another, more serious submission for the next week's *Gazette.* Called "Rules for Statesman," this effort purportedly was penned by a correspondent in London to the Christiansted newspaper. So precocious, Hamilton was introducing what was to become the major theme in so many of his later works: the need for centralized public responsibility. In a small-town royalist Danish-American newspaper, the author praised the British system of governing by cabinet ministers under the control of "a prime minister like a commander in chief. I think this wise regulation a wholesome restraint on the people, [whose] turbulence, at times, requires a dictator." Hamilton had obviously been reading the writings of Machiavelli. Donning the mantle of the mature scholar, he cited "some years of gleaning from Machiavelli." He advised his readers to consider "by what means a premier may act most to the honor of his Prince and the enlargement of his own power." If, indeed, young Hamilton did write these lines, he could not have more succinctly prophesied his own turbulent struggle for power or the political philosophy that underpinned it. After so much disappointment, Alexander Hamilton was learning not to rely on people. So many people had already let him down. He was on his way to a belief in institutions, in the need to create them and to imbue them with sufficient power and then to depend on them more than on their constituents. He groomed his first beliefs in the practical school of a Caribbean countinghouse.[4]

IN OCTOBER 1771, Alexander Hamilton's employer, Nicholas Cruger, became seriously ill and had to go home to New York suddenly. He felt confident in turning over management of the firm's St. Croix operations to his sixteen-year-old clerk. Hamilton had long since graduated from the clerical stage of making copies of outgoing letters. For some time, Cruger had entrusted delicate errands to his youthful apprentice, who was widely known on the island as "Cruger's young man." But now, the slight, five-foot-seven, red-haired youth with milk-white complexion and ruddy cheeks must have amused ships' captains and waterfront toughs when he began giving them orders and writing commanding letters. Hamilton quickly made it clear that he was unimpressed by the merchants and mariners around him. Skillfully, smoothly, maturely he appropriated to himself Cruger's authority. Only once in the five months of Cruger's absence did Hamilton appeal for assistance to another merchant who held Cruger's power of attorney.

As soon as Cruger sailed, Hamilton began to assert himself. He sent off a letter to an agent to New York, instructing him to collect a debt in "joes" (Johannes, a Portuguese coin worth about $200 in modern times). Learning firsthand how to deal with money at an early age, Hamilton could see that the American colonies were hamstrung for lack of their own currencies. With each ship's sailing for New York, Hamilton sent off a letter recounting in detail his activities to Nicholas Cruger. He wrote Cruger as often as every five days at first, even when the letters contained no news. But the letters grew less frequent—eight days passed, then fifteen. As winter sailings to New York became more treacherous, Hamilton did not write Cruger for more than six weeks. He sent Cruger no letter at all in December 1771.

He also lost no opportunity to remind other members of the Cruger trading network that he was the diligent young gentleman busy at his crucial St. Croix post during this family emergency. He wrote to Jacob Walton, a prominent New York merchant and Nicholas Cruger's brother-in-law; he fired off letters to John Harris Cruger on Jamaica. Thomas Willing, the leading merchant in Philadelphia, was among those who learned the name of Hamilton.

Strangely, it was fully a month before Hamilton informed Nicholas's brother on Curacao that Nicholas had gone home sick. Hamilton was at his most formal and pretentious in this November

16, 1771, letter in which he introduced not only himself but *Thunderbolt*, the sluggish new sloop built by Cruger's partners:

> She has on board a parcel of lumber for yourself, sundry articles on account of her owners as per enclosed bill of lading and, when you have disposed of them, you'll please to credit each party for one third of the proceeds.

Hamilton worried to the verge of obsession in his letters about obtaining a cargo of mules in time to help with the harvest. Routinely, the Crugers smuggled the animals from the Spanish Main. The Spanish Guarda Costa, Hamilton reported, "swarm upon the coast." Hamilton took it upon himself to order *Thunderbolt*'s captain, William Newton, to arm the vessel at St. Croix. Then, to Nicholas Cruger's brother, he criticized the family's choice of a ship's captain:

> Give me leave to hint to you that you cannot be too particular in your instructions to him. I think he seems rather to want experience in such voyages.

He also faulted the ship's captain for the careless way he had loaded the ship. A cargo of barrel staves "are stowed promiscuously among other things." This meant time wasted in sorting, unloading, and reloading the ship.[5]

To the ship's captain, sixteen-year-old Hamilton was stern and patronizing. In his letter of instruction for the Curacao run, he ordered the older man to "proceed immediately" and even follow directions on shore: "You must follow [them] in every respect":

> You know it is intended that you shall go from thence to the [Spanish] Main for a load of mules and I must beg if you do, you'll be very choice in quality of your mules and bring as many as your vessel can conveniently contain. . . . Remember, you are to make three trips this season and unless you are very diligent, you will be too late, as our crops will be early in. Take care to avoid the Guarda Costas.[6]

As the weeks passed, Hamilton made bold decisions. *Thunderbolt* would have lost precious sailing time if he had followed the Crugers' instructions. He ordered Captain Newton to unload quickly:

She landed here only
23 hogsheads Indian [corn] meal
6469 staves
20 barrels apples
300 boards—inch & half
21 kegs bread [water biscuits]
646 ropes onions.

"All the rest of her cargo," he wrote to the senior New York partner, "I think must turn out better at Curacao than here, or at any rate not worse." He would have liked to unload the "superfine flour" but the captain had stowed it "so promiscuously" at Philadelphia "that to get at it would take some time."[7]

In self-serving and increasingly infrequent reports to the ailing Nicholas Cruger, Hamilton showed he was not afraid to criticize his superiors. "Your Philadelphia flour is really very bad." It was "swarthy" and "very intractable." Opening several barrels, "I have observed a kind of worm very common in flour about the surface, which is an indication of age . . . It could not have been new when 'twas shipped." The Christiansted market was overstocked with flour so Hamilton on his own authority decided to mark the price down. He designated the weevily flour for consumption by slaves.[8]

Six weeks later, when the next cargo arrived from New York City, it carried presents from Cruger for Hamilton to deliver: china plates and silk stockings for Cruger's fiancée, wheels of cheese for her mother and for a fellow merchant. Cruger sent Hamilton a gift of apples and cheese for himself. By now, one day short of seventeen years old, Hamilton was so confident that he had become an expert in the Caribbean market that he assured Cruger the entire cargo would sell for high prices. So cocky had Hamilton become that he wrote to his employer, "I am a good deal hurried just now" and promised a letter with "more minute detail" at some later time. He assured Cruger he was keeping pressure on creditors—"Believe me, Sir, I dun as hard as is proper."[9]

When the vessel again lagged into Christiansted, Hamilton wrote with disgust that it carried only forty-one starving mules fit only to be put out to pasture. Furious, Hamilton wrote a blistering letter of instruction to Captain Newton:

> Reflect continually on the unfortunate voyage you have just made and endeavor to make up for the considerable loss. . . . Furnish the vessel with four guns . . . This is all I think needful to say so. . . . [10]

The self-assured teenager left his employer's brothers speechless with his highhandedness. To Henry Cruger in New York he complained, "Your mahogany is of the very worst kind." The ship's captain carrying this letter of rebuke also came in for a knuckle-rapping. "His cargo was stowed very hickledy-pickledy." One of Cruger's partners hadn't been able to raise his share of the cash required for a cargo "and God knows when I shall be able to receive Mr. Burling's who is so long winded."[11]

In spite of a brief bout of illness, Hamilton managed Nicholas Cruger's interests from October 1771 to early March 1772, when Cruger returned from New York. Upholding all Hamilton's dealings, Cruger was especially pleased that his youthful deputy's bullying of Captain Newton had resulted in healthier cargoes. *Thunderbolt* sailed one last time that winter to New York loaded with fresh-harvested sugar and cotton, bringing a solid profit to the firm. Hamilton had held the frayed network together. Their Caribbean operations would have been seriously damaged without his Herculean efforts, which the family never forgot. Once again sent back to his stool as Cruger's assistant, Hamilton watched Cruger cheat the Danish customs authorities, instructing one agent to enter highly taxed rye flour on his books as low-duted corn meal, "and give the [tide] waiter a fee, which hint you must give the Captain." Hamilton would remember such bribery

and deception years later when he became the first Continental collector of customs for the Port of New York and then founder of the
United States Customs Service.[12]

AFTER MONTHS of round-the-clock responsibility, Hamilton now
found time for a new interest. At exactly this propitious moment, a
learned clergyman landed on St. Croix. In the Reverend Hugh Knox,
the newly hired forty-seven-year-old minister of Christiansted's first
Presbyterian church, Hamilton finally found someone who recognized his intellectual promise. A warmhearted man who had undergone a rocky journey before washing ashore on St. Croix that spring,
Knox was to play a pivotal role in launching Hamilton's career. Son
of a Scottish Presbyterian minister from Northern Ireland, Knox had
been classically educated in Scotland. He arrived in America in 1751
and earned an undergraduate degree from Yale College.

"Remarkably prepossessing [in] personal appearance and manners,"
Knox then founded a small academy in Delaware and preached in
churches at St. George's and Middletown. A popular schoolmaster, he
thought it judicious to flee his post after he mimicked the Sunday sermon of a noted clergyman in a tavern. Enrolling for postgraduate
study at the College of New Jersey (now Princeton), he studied theology with its founder and first president, the Reverend Aaron Burr,
grandfather of the third vice president of the United States. Considered a radical, he was called by only one church, the Dutch Reformed
Church on the trackless island of Saba, five miles south of St. Maarten
in the Dutch West Indies. Knox arrived on the island by surfboat,
married the daughter of its governor, and lived for seventeen years in
the crater of an extinct volcano. Ministering to Saba's eighteen hundred inhabitants, he conducted a voluminous correspondence with
churchmen in Europe and America. While many of his sermons were
published and kept in print for decades, except for the fine library of
books he accumulated, he was intellectually about as isolated as he
could possibly be. After visiting St. Croix twice in the autumn of 1771,
he was offered his own church and a handsome raise.[13]

Soon after Reverend Knox's arrival, he met young Hamilton, who
became a regular at Knox's evangelical revival services. Hamilton may

have heard him when he spellbound listeners with his fiery fundamentalism during his first visit. After years of loss and rapid change, at seventeen Alexander Hamilton may have undergone a powerful religious conversion. At least that is the impression he gave that spring, as the Great Awakening swooped down on St. Croix.

All over English America, young people were joining evangelical churches where, a few years before, only gray hair could be seen from the pulpits. The revival movement known as the Great Awakening mixed fire and brimstone with a revolutionary new doctrine of free will that discredited the old Puritan notion of predestination. The Great Awakening was America's first youth movement. Older, more conservative clergymen worked hard to suppress it, pressing colonial legislatures to ban its street and open-field preaching. For the first time, Americans turned out in crowds to hear unofficial, unsanctioned, antiestablishment speakers. The style of preaching Hamilton heard for the first time,

> seems not so much to inform men's judgments as to terrify and affright their imaginations and, by awful words and frightful representations, to lift the congregation into hideous shrieks and outcries ... In every place where they come, they represent that God is doing extraordinary things in other places and that they are some of the last hardened wretches that stand out; that this is the last call they are likely to have, that they are now hanging over the pit of eternal damnation and just ready this moment to fall into it, that Hellfire now flashes in their faces and that the Devil now stands just ready to seize them and carry them to Hell. They oftentimes repeat the awful words, "Damned! Damned! Damned! Damned!" This frequently frightens their tender mothers and sets *them* to screaming, and by degrees spreads over the congregation ... And all screaming together make such an awful and hideous noise as will make a man's hair stand on end![14]

This religious revolution led to major political changes that split communities and colonies. The awakened, many of them young and poor like Hamilton, broke with officially established religions to form separatist churches that called themselves New Lights. The New Lights believed that to oppose their religious revival movement was to fight against God. Gradually, New Light political factions emerged in several colonies. They objected to every measure they felt commingled church and state. When the Reverend Knox brought the Great Awakening to the Caribbean, he instantly won over young Alexander Hamilton to its born-again ranks.

Hamilton's potential seemed at once obvious to Knox, who gave him the run of his extensive library. (There is no surviving record of what Knox owned or Hamilton read.) Knox prided himself, in his often-published sermons, on his special calling to spot and encourage youthful talent. In one sermon, he praised Maecenus, the patron of Virgil, Horace, and Livy, for "drawing these incomparable geniuses out of obscurity." To Knox goes the credit for discovering Hamilton amid the money-grubbing opulence of St. Croix's sugar planters, liveried slaves, and fashionable shops.[15]

As a youngster, Hamilton had been surrounded by extremes of great wealth and hardscrabble struggle in islands full of slaves and wealthy masters, merchants and lawyers, litigation, speculation, and ruin. He had never seen or heard a man of Knox's erudition before, never sat enthralled by the classically grounded rhetoric of a gentleman-scholar. Young Hamilton reveled in the world of ideas Reverend Knox brought to the island. Knox initiated Hamilton into the egalitarian thinking of the Scottish Enlightenment that was spreading from Edinburgh to America, fueled by the revolutionary political writings of John Locke. Hamilton was especially swayed by Knox's belief that free will had replaced predestination as the central tenet of evangelical Presbyterianism. Young Hamilton had been exposed to three versions of Calvinism so far—the Scottish through his father, who no doubt believed that, because he was of noble birth, he was among the elect and predestined for salvation, no matter his misdeeds; the French, through his Huguenot mother; and the Dutch, through his employer, Nicholas Cruger. Hugh Knox embodied the two cardinal beliefs of evangelical Calvinism—the virtue of hard work, and the ability to rise through education. Knox told him that

his destiny was in his own hands. Rejecting his father's decadent way
of life, Hamilton embraced the charming man of letters.

Few people in Hamilton's lifetime matched Knox's influence over
this precocious—and rudderless—young man. Knox probably gave
Hamilton bound volumes of his printed sermons to read, infusing
him with piety and exposing him to strong religious arguments
against the slavery and alcoholism of his father's generation, all around
him. Some of Hamilton's later government policies, such as imposing
federal excise taxes on whiskey, may be traced to this seed time. There
are also echoes of Knox's prose in Hamilton's early writings. Knox's
felicitous line, "Our duty is written, as it were, with sun beams," contains the germ of one of Hamilton's mighty lines he wrote three years
later in his first Revolutionary pamphlet, *The Farmer Refuted*:

> The sacred rights of mankind are not to be rummaged for
> among old parchments . . . They are written, as with a sunbeam,
> in the whole volume of human nature by the hand of Divinity
> itself.

Some of Knox's writings seemed pointed right at the brash young
Hamilton. In writing to another clergman, Knox urged him to

> instill into the opening mind the principles of piety [and]
> integrity . . . Who can conceive the good of which such a child
> may be made the instrument, or the degrees of happiness and of
> glory to which it may be advanced?

Knox never tired of urging education on young men like Hamilton:

> The mind is as much delighted by the discoveries of knowledge
> and truth as the body is with animal refreshments.

> But Knox realized that there was a limit to how much he could
> help his student. Young Hamilton must leave the islands to get a
> thorough education.[16]

*   *   *

FIVE MONTHS after Nicholas Cruger's return to St. Croix, Alexander Hamilton was hard at his Knox-directed after-hours studies on Monday night, August 31, 1772, when the worst hurricane in the island's history struck. Except for one brief lull, it blew wildly for six hours. Tides fourteen feet higher than normal swamped Christiansted, tearing loose all the ships in the harbor and dashing them onshore. The *Gazette* listed only the white casualties: thirty killed, many more badly injured. All the island's crops were uprooted: losses were estimated at close to $40 million in today's currency. Hamilton attended a public meeting the Sunday following the storm where he heard Knox recount his own experiences and exhort the crowd to take the tempest as a divine comment on the islanders' morals. Deeply moved, Hamilton went home and wrote his own account. A few days later, Alexander Hamilton wrote a letter describing the maelstrom to his father on St. Kitts, then showed a copy to the Reverend Knox.

On October 3, the *Gazette* carried Hamilton's letter with an introduction by Reverend Knox:

The following letter was written by a youth of this island to his father; the copy of it fell by accident into the hands of a gentleman who, being pleased with it himself, showed it to others to whom it gave equal satisfaction and who all agreed that it might not prove unentertaining to the public. The author's modesty in long refusing to submit it to public view is the reason of its making its appearance as late as it does now.

What Knox depicted as modesty may be explained by the fact that, as well as being powerfully written, the letter was self-revealing. It could be read by people who knew his family's stormy recent history as a young man who, buffeted by his fate, was lashing out at his absent father. Addressed "Honoured Sir," the letter, young Hamilton wrote, recounted "one of the most dreadful hurricanes that memory or any records can trace":

It began at dusk, at North, and raged very violently 'till ten o'clock. Then ensued a sudden and unexpected interval, which lasted about an hour. Meanwhile the wind was shifting 'round to the southwest . . . it returned with redoubled fury and continued so 'till near three o'clock in the morning. Good God! What horror and destruction. It's impossible for me to describe or you to form any idea of it. It seemed as if a total dissolution of nature was taking place. The roaring of the sea and wind, fiery meteors flying about it in the air, the prodigious glare of almost perpetual lightning, the crash of the falling houses, and the ear-piercing shrieks of the distressed were sufficient to strike astonishment into angels.

A great part of the buildings throughout the island are leveled to the ground, almost all the rest very much shattered, several persons killed and numbers utterly ruined, whole families running about the streets unknowing where to find a place of shelter; the sick exposed to the keenness of the water and air without a bed to lie upon or a dry covering to their bodies; and our harbors entirely bare. In a word, misery, in all its hideous shapes, spread over the whole face of the country . . .

Then Hamilton added "my reflections and feelings on this frightful and melancholy occasion." His "self-discourse" echoed Knox's born-again rhetoric. This segment of the letter was unmistakably angry. It could be read as pointing an accusatory finger at his "honoured father."

Where now, oh! vile worm, is all thy boasted fortitude and resolution? What is become of thine arrogance and self-sufficiency? Why dost thou tremble and stand aghast? How humble, how helpless, how contemptible you now appear. And for why? The jarring of elements—the discord of clouds? Oh! impotent presumptuous fool! . . . Death comes rushing on in triumph, veiled in a mantle of tenfold darkness . . . On his right hand sits destruction, hurling the winds and belching forth flames: calamity on his left threatening famine, disease and distress of all kinds. And oh! thou wretch, look still a little further. See the gulf of eternal misery open. There mayest thou shortly plunge—

the just reward of thy vileness. Alas! whither canst thou fly? Where hide thyself?

Then young Hamilton hurled a parting shaft at the entire planter class of St. Croix, "ye who revel in affluence."[17]

This letter, Hamilton's longest youthful literary production, proved to be one of his more fruitful efforts. It liberated him from the devastated island. Knox found Hamilton's display of youthful piety beneficial to his own efforts to rally public generosity to help hurricane victims. But he also set to work arranging a scholarship to send Hamilton to New York City for an education. Knox wrote to his protégé a dozen years later, at the end of the American Revolution, that "I have always had a just and secret pride in having advised you to go to America and in having recommended you to some of my old friends there." Wealthy merchants who had observed Hamilton's business acumen now pledged contributions. Among donors were Nicholas Cruger and Cruger's associate, Cornelius Kortright, the St. Croix partner of Kortright and Company of New York, to whom the Crugers agreed to consign four annual "cargoes of West India produce" to be "sold and appropriated to the support of Hamilton." In three years' time, this was to amount to two consignments of sugar. Among other contributors were the father of his young friend Edward Stevens, the probate judge who had seized Rachel Hamilton's effects, and the town captain whose father had locked up Hamilton's mother. In all, Knox arranged pledges of 400 pounds, his estimate of the cost of four years' tuition, board, and transportation to mainland America.[18]

Hamilton's sponsors probably had differing expectations of this young man. Knox, also a licensed physician and apothecary, expected Hamilton, like his friend Neddy Stevens, to take premedical studies before going on to study at Edinburgh, the best medical school in the British Empire. Hamilton's grandfather had, after all, been a physician, and Hamilton had watched helplessly as a poorly trained doctor had bled and purged his dying mother. But Knox also could see from Hamilton's writing that there was something more to the boy, and he wrote strong letters of recommendation to close friends in New York and New Jersey.

Alexander Hamilton had little time to make up his mind. The last safe sailing to the North Atlantic was imminent; on the American mainland, the school year was starting. His opportunity would be lost for a year, if not forever. The pledges of tuition had come so quickly, but he must decide at once or they might melt away. He penned one more poem that would not appear in the *Gazette* until after he sailed: "Ah! whither, whither am I flown/A wandering guest in worlds unknown?" But he did not hesitate. He was eager to go, to be "translated to this happy place," which must be happier, wherever it was, than the one he was leaving behind. He lugged his books and his best clothes aboard ship and left St. Croix. In early October 1772, only a few days after Hamilton's vivid portrait of hurricane and self-portrait of his personal conversion appeared in St. Croix's newspaper, but weeks after Knox had taken it around to Hamilton's admirers, the youth's benefactors saw him off for the long ocean voyage to America. He never saw his father, his brother, or, for that matter, Hugh Knox again. He did not return, and he never expressed a wish to see the searing beauty of the Caribbean again.[19]

———— ◆ ————

FIVE

"A Wandering Guest in Worlds Unknown"

B y the third week of October 1772, seventeen-year-old Alexander Hamilton had survived a fire at sea and landed safely in Boston. He had been lowered over the side of the sailing ship with a bucket to pass up water to help extinguish the blaze. Landing at Long Wharf, shaken after a dangerous three-week ocean voyage— only a few weeks before he arrived, a ship on the same run had been boarded and robbed by a French privateer—he hoisted his trunk crammed with books to his shoulder and stepped down the gangway, eager to explore the crowded, hilly New England port town. His first task was to place a plea for disaster relief for hurricane-ravaged St. Croix in the *Boston Gazette* for October 26. Then he had time on his hands. He had to wait nearly a week before the biweekly stagecoach to New York City, and he used it to meander through the busy port where he had sent so many cargoes and letters in the past few years. Everything was fresh to him. October days along Back Bay were cold and blustery; he had never seen autumn leaves.

Hamilton was stunned to find Boston an armed camp with redcoated British soldiers everywhere and townspeople seething with resentment at their treatment as a captive, conquered people. In the seventh year of chronic protests against tightening British control, the town of ten thousand was occupied by some two thousand Redcoats. A deepening confrontation between colonists and Crown-appointed officials had been punctuated by riots and mass meetings that had spread down the Atlantic Coast through all the mainland American colonies. The spark that had ignited the tinder in Boston was a seemingly trivial stamp tax. The hated stamps had to be affixed to newspapers, all legal documents, licenses, ships' papers, almanacs, pamphlets, insurance policies, diplomas, even playing cards and dice. It was the first direct tax ever imposed on English colonists in America by a Parliament far away in London. Historically, each colony had raised its own revenues to pay for its government and defense, each colony's elective assembly deciding how and whom to pay.

A loose network of protesters who styled themselves the Sons of Liberty had sprung up in virtually every English-American town since 1765, but in few places were the protests more violent than in Boston. The stamp tax had been repealed, but only one year later, Bostonians had taken to the streets again when Parliament imposed new customs duties on glass, lead, paper, paint, and tea to defray "the charge of the administration of justice and the support of civil government." Bostonians howled that this violated their royal charter, which guaranteed them the power of the purse to wield against unpopular officials. Boston's merchants now joined forces with artisans, lawyers, and consumers to boycott all British imports until the new duties were repealed. In retaliation, Parliament established an American Board of Commissioners of the Customs with headquarters at Boston—for the first time moving customs collections onto American soil and enforcing them with naval warships.

More new laws turning the appointment and pay of colonial officials over to the British home government appeared imminent even as young immigrant Alexander Hamilton landed in Boston. He watched as Bostonians, demanding they be allowed to continue to choose their own governor and judges, marched in protest to Faneuil Hall for a special town meeting. Letters of protest had appeared in the *Boston Gazette* on October 12. The newspaper was posted broadside in chophouses and taverns where young Hamilton could easily read it. During Hamilton's brief maiden visit to Boston, "a mob of upwards [of] a thousand people," its anger fanned by the indignant speeches at Faneuil Hall, surged through the streets, caught a customs informer, tarred and feathered him, and dragged him in agony around the town in a cart.[1]

Yet the observant young Hamilton could also see that not all Bostonians were ready to abandon unqualified devotion to royal government. On October 25, Hamilton's last full day in Boston, Colonel John Hancock donned his gold-braided red militia uniform and led His Excellency's Company of Cadets as it marched ahead of the colony's royal Train Band of Artillery on the Commons in a parade that celebrated the thirteenth anniversary of King George III's accession to the British throne. The *Gazette* for November 2 reported

> The company being under arms and in uniform dress made a very fine and respectable appearance ... They were exercised on the Common until noon and, having refreshed themselves at the Colonel's, they marched into King Street where, after firing three volleys, they performed a variety of evolutions.[2]

It was the first time Hamilton had seen either British redcoats or American militia. He could see clearly that, as they faced off in the spreading imperial confrontation, both were wearing the same uniform.

BOARDING THE biweekly Boston–New York stagecoach on October 26, 1772, Hamilton bumped along the Post Road in "the first stage coach that ever was improved on this road" for a full week before he reached New York City. Getting a glimpse of the towns and terrain where he would spend so much of the rest of his life, he arrived, sore but exhilarated, at the southern tip of Manhattan Island on November 2. Among his first stops was King's College, perched on a bluff overlooking the Hudson between Barclay and Murray Streets. There his closest friend, Neddy Stevens, was a premedical student. They had not seen each other since Neddy's last home visit nearly three years earlier.

Neddy saw, beaming before him, a freckled, ruddy-faced, sandy-haired young Hamilton, his violet-blue eyes flashing with happiness. While Hamilton would later mourn that "I am not handsome," his air of self-confidence in his own intelligence added an acuity that enhanced mere physical appeal. He had no singularly good feature. His forehead was high but sloped to eyes almost too close set, crowding the pinched bridge of his nose. His mouth was small, his cheekbones high, his chin almost bulbous and protruding. His shoulders were uncommonly narrow, his frame light, giving the deceptive appearance that he was shorter than he really was. At five-foot-seven, he was taller than the average for his time. But it was his overall avidity and brightness that created the aura of a charismatic figure.[3]

His intelligence, energy, enthusiasm, and wit obliterated any trace of the suffering, loss and hardship he had so abundantly endured. And people just liked to have him around. Stevens was overjoyed to see him, to show him the college. So was his favorite cousin, Ann Lytton Venton, who lived in the city. Hamilton had already done her many favors, getting her advances against her father's estate, and now she was eager to help him to get an education.

Hamilton carried a letter of recommendation to Kortright and Company, the firm that had helped underwrite his scholarship and that was to sell the consignments of St. Croix sugar earmarked to help pay Hamilton's expenses. Presenting himself at their countinghouse, he was ushered in to meet the senior partner, Lawrence Kortright. Kortright, in turn, introduced Hamilton to his partner's younger brother, the aptly named Hercules Mulligan. A jovial, thirty-two-year-old giant, Hercules Mulligan was to act as Hamilton's guardian, manage his funds, and smooth his way for him. The two hit it off immediately.

Formerly a clerk at his father's countinghouse, Hercules Mulligan, born in County Antrim, Ireland, had set up in business for himself as a custom tailor and haberdasher catering to New York's wealthiest. His home on Water Street adjoined Philip Rhinelander's china store on the edge of the East River wharves. Mulligan, a graduate of King's College, was a bachelor engaged to marry Elizabeth Sanders, a member of the elite Livingston clan. An elegant walking advertisement for his wares, Mulligan prided himself on his shopful of finery, including "gold and silver lace with some half laces for hats," as well as "gold and silver buttons and loops" and "gold and silver treble French chain." One day he would furnish President Washington with the "resplendent black velvet suit" that he wore for diplomatic and state receptions. New York City's society haberdasher was to become Hamilton's surrogate father for the next several years. Mulligan summoned his carriage, took Hamilton home with him, and showed him to his room. The bustle and noise of a nearby waterfront were familiar to Hamilton, and he happily began to blend into the Mulligan household.[4]

For the next several days, Mulligan escorted Hamilton around a town larger than any he had ever seen. Rapidly challenging Philadelphia as the largest seaport in America, New York had a population of twenty thousand, greater than all of St. Croix. Mulligan introduced him to Hugh Knox's circle of churchmen, to whom Hamilton presented Knox's glowing letters of recommendation. Over the years, Mulligan would prove to be one of Hamilton's most durable friends. An organizer and leader of New York's radical Sons of Liberty, as he showed his young ward around the town's tree-lined streets Mulligan had much to tell him about his own exploits in the turbulent world of New York pre-Revolutionary politics.

In the shadow of Fort George, the British Army's headquarters for all mainland America, New York was sharply divided over the proper reaction to England's tightening grip on its trade. Five times Mulligan had joined the crowds of the Sons of Liberty as they erected Liberty Poles on the Bowling Green; five times out-of-uniform British soldiers, sailors, and pro-government Loyalist civilians had chopped them down. When the British Parliament in London demanded that New York build barracks for the redcoats at taxpayers' expenses, the New York Assembly, pressured by Sons of Liberty in the streets, had refused. Parliament indignantly dissolved the assembly and ordered new elections. Backing down, the newly elected New York Assembly acceded to British demands and built the barracks. Fresh outcries came from the Sons of Liberty. The stocky haberdasher took young Hamilton to meet his close friend Alexander McDougall, founder of New York's Sons of Liberty, who had just papered the town with a broadside addressed, "To the Betrayed Inhabitants of the City and Colony of New York" and signed by "A Son of Liberty." While the Loyalist-dominated New York Assembly fumed, soldiers and Sons of Liberty clashed.

The Liberty Pole on the common became the scene for repeated nighttime brawls. On the Saturday night of January 13, 1770, Mulligan and the Sons were caught off-guard when redcoats swarmed out of Fort George and attempted to blow up the Liberty Pole with a large charge of gunpowder. The pole refused to fall, so the soldiers took out their frustration by attacking Montayne's Tavern, headquarters of the Liberty Boys on the West Side waterfront. The soldiers tried again to dislodge the pole two nights later, again failing. On the third attempt, they succeeded in cutting up the pole and stacking it in the form of a pile of firewood at Montayne's front door. That led, on Friday night, January 19, 1770, to the so-called Battle of Golden Hill. Isaac Sears led the Sons of Liberty (this time made up not only of angry merchants like Mulligan but sailors brandishing cutlasses and workingmen swinging clubs) into combat with forty bayonet-wielding out-of-uniform British soldiers on Golden Hill, a wheatfield at the crest of John Street near William. The first head-on clash of the American Revolution left many men on both sides badly injured and one seaman dead, run through by a bayonet. Officers managed to order the troops back into barracks but scuffles continued for days, leading to another large-scale clash before the city council restored order. Hercules Mulligan, recounting the events to an admiring Hamilton, made it clear he had emerged as one of the conspicuous heroes of the encounters. The youth's meeting with McDougall, organizer of the New York Sons, led to Hamilton's determination to one day join their ranks, if only secretly. Hamilton's admiration for the rough-cut McDougall grew when he learned that McDougall had been arrested and charged with seditious libel for writing the broadside that had triggered the riot. Refusing to post bond, McDougall had remained in jail for three months. Finally released on bail, he was rearrested, tried by the New York Assembly for contempt, and jailed for another five months.

The next man Knox had singled out to arrange Hamilton's schooling was the Reverend John Rodgers, the very preacher Hugh Knox had mocked in a Delaware tavern so long ago. Hamilton and Mulligan rode around to meet Dr. Rodgers at the Wall Street Presbyterian Church, where he was pastor. This zealous New Light preacher, trained in the classics at Harvard, had worked in Virginia as a missionary until that colony's House of Burgesses, at the request of Church of England clergy, had him expelled. Rodgers had long ago forgiven the mocking Knox and recommended him for graduate studies. In his turn, Knox was now asking Rodgers for a Princeton recommendation, this time for Alexander Hamilton.

Hugh Knox had made it clear in his letter to Rodgers that Hamilton's sponsors on St. Croix wanted him to go through Princeton, the college founded in 1748 by the burgeoning Presbyterian Church in America. Few people could help Hamilton better than Rodgers, who had been instrumental in choosing Princeton's current president, but he worried that Hamilton would fail Princeton's rigorous entrance examination. The youth, he discovered, had never had any formal schooling, never studied the requisite classical Greek or Latin, and his knowledge of mathematics did not go beyond arithmetic and keeping accounts. He would need, Rodgers opined, to be sent first to a preparatory school, one where he would be allowed to take accelerated studies instead of slogging along with boys several years his junior for the normal three to four years, consuming all his scholarship funds before he reached college. In his letter, Knox argued that Hamilton was a quick study. The simplest course would have been to hire private tutors, but Hamilton's meager fund came sporadically and unpredictably. King's College, Hamilton's choice, had a preparatory program, but it took three years, and Hamilton could not afford to live in New York City for even a year of tutoring. Rodgers decided that Hamilton must attend the one school able to tailor its teaching to Hamilton's needs and still pass muster with Princeton. He wrote Hamilton letters of recommendation to the Presbyterian-run Elizabethtown Academy, across the bay in Elizabethtown, New Jersey, one of colonial America's best schools and, in effect, the preparatory school for the College of New Jersey. Hamilton already carried letters of introduction to two of Hugh Knox's friends who happened to be on this school's board of trustees.

Sailing with Mulligan from the Battery to Elizabethtown Point, Hamilton got his first glimpse of the prosperous village of some eight hundred, already a century old and one of New Jersey's oldest towns. Except for a few houses of brick or stone, its 150 solid, trim houses wore weathered gray cedar shingles on their sides and roofs and were arranged on split rail fenced plots along five shade tree–lined streets. Embellishing each house was a large garden and an apple orchard. A New England town plunked down in northern New Jersey, it had grown up around two conflicting churches, the tall-steepled, redbrick St. John's Anglican Church and the wooden First Presbyterian Church, Hamilton's destination that raw November day. Both churches boasted fine bells that competed in clangor, echoing over the water and the surrounding countryside. Swedish botanist Peter Kalm, a recent visitor, wrote that "in and about the town are many gardens and orchards, and it might be said that Elizabethtown is situated in a garden."[5]

As the stagecoach passed the wharves where merchants moored their sloops and ferries, young Hamilton jounced across the Old Stone Bridge, passed the belfried courthouse and the militia's parade ground. He debarked at the house of Francis Barber, headmaster of Elizabethtown Academy and its Greek master. A strong friendship bloomed that day between Hamilton and Barber, only five years his senior, that lasted until Barber's tragic death ten years later. At Barber's side, Hamilton got his first look at the place where he would spend at least the next year; at his side, he would one day storm a British redoubt at Yorktown. The likable young West Indian immigrant was rapidly making lifelong friendships in a new land where no one knew of his shadowy origins.

Hamilton could not have had better or more radical sponsors than his New York and Elizabethtown wards, and they exerted a decisive influence over him. Mulligan took him around to meet Mulligan's soon-to-be in-law William Livingston. The scion of New York's wealthiest family, Livingston had just retired from his New York law

practice to build a sprawling mansion called Liberty Hall on the outskirts of Elizabethtown and devote full time to radical politics. They
then crossed the street to meet Elias Boudinot, a wealthy member of
the academy's board of trustees who had recently endowed the academy with financial aid for "a number of free scholars." Both men
eventually contributed personally to Hamilton's schooling and became
lifelong political supporters. While young Hamilton paid the requisite
fees for tuition, room, and board at the school, in effect he became
the long-term houseguest of these two generous sponsors, spending
most of a year living room-and-board free at Boudinot's commodious
house. As a result, Livingston and Boudinot, only a few years later
the leaders of New Jersey in the American Revolution, molded young
Hamilton and made him their protégé.

It would turn out that his Elizabethtown mentors and their kin
could not have given him more important connections in colonial
America. Livingston was the third son of the proprietor of the vast
Livingston Manor on the Hudson, a forest empire that included thousands of acres between Poughkeepsie and Albany. A natural conservative forced into radical politics by his convictions, this leader of the
land-rich Livingston clan had used his Yale education and his skill as
a writer to attack the other powerful family faction in New York politics, the DeLanceys. Livingston had helped to launch a radical weekly
newspaper, the *Independent Reflector*, in New York City in the 1750s.
He regularly assailed the DeLancey-led Anglican party in the New
York legislature in the biting English journalistic style of Joseph Addi-
son and Richard Steele. Using his quill and his talents as a behind-
the-scenes political organizer, Livingston emerged as the chief
advocate of the separation of church and state. This put him squarely
at odds with New York's Anglican establishment, which was using
the support of the royal government and the colonial assembly to
raise funds to build King's College as an adjunct to New York City's
Trinity Church, the unofficial cathedral of the Church of England in
America. Writing under the pseudonyms "American Whig," "Sen-
tinel" and "Watch Tower," Livingston outspokenly defended American religious liberty, becoming the major Presbyterian supporter of
religious pluralism.

By the time the lucky young immigrant was ushered into his unfinished new parlor, Livingston was openly rejecting all British efforts to strip the American colonies of their independent legislatures and make them over into economic and financial provinces subordinate to the British Parliament. He warned that King's College would serve as the base for establishing Anglican bishops over America who in turn would be de facto members of the House of Lords and, as such, America's only and unelected representatives in Parliament. Although his fears were legitimate, Livingston's years of emotional, highly charged attacks on his political and religious enemies had drained him. Because of his retirement to Elizabethtown, his Liberty Hall was to become the unofficial Revolutionary capital of New Jersey, and when the Revolutionary War broke out, he became the first governor of the new state. His political support of Hamilton proved a key to Hamilton's success in national politics.

While Hamilton spent his leisure hours with his wealthy new patrons, he gave over most of his days to the command of schoolmaster Barber, his first real teacher. Born on a farm in Princeton, Barber had attended Elizabethtown Academy and then gone on to Princeton, where he earned a master's degree in the classics. An expert on meeting Princeton's entrance requirements, he founded a Latin school at Newbridge near Hackensack, teaching there three years before his alma mater, Elizabethtown Academy, hired him. The school's wealthy Presbyterian backers had built the two-story cedar-shingled frame academy, surmounted with cupola and schoolbell, at the "upper end of the burial yard lot" (the southwest corner of Broad Street and Caldwell Place), and attracted many promising students, including, only a few years before Hamilton, Aaron Burr, son and grandson of Princeton presidents.

The academy's Board of Visitors advertised for students in the *New York Gazette*, touting Barber's performance as teacher and headmaster:

The Visitors have been well informed that those of his pupils who have been sent to our colleges were found well fitted ... From the experience they have already had of his abilities and attention to business, they cannot but look upon this school to be now under as great advantages as it has ever enjoyed. To render the education here more extensively useful, peculiar attention will be paid to reading and pronouncing English.

Teaching Scots-Irish pupils to pronounce English properly, the school also required them to learn writing, English literature, geography, arithmetic, Latin, Greek, "epistolary composition in which they are duly instructed, particularly as to orthography [and] punctuation, acquirements in which too many grown scholars are notoriously deficient."[6]

Two members of the Board of Visitors, pastors of the town's churches, supervised two full-time teachers and tutored students for an hour on alternating days and every quarter administered oral and written examinations. One Visitor was Anglican theologian Thomas Bradbury Chandler, who became a leading Loyalist pamphleteer in the Revolution. The other, the Presbyterian, who was to become Chandler's mortal enemy, was the Reverend James Caldwell. An emotional preacher who often brought tears to the eyes of his listeners with his powerful sermons, Caldwell became famous as the "Fighting Parson" after a British grenadier shot and killed his wife. Tearing up hymnals from his church to make wadding to steady the lead balls in their muskets, in the Battle of Springfield he ordered militiamen to "Give 'em Watts, boys."

Alexander Hamilton was several years older and more mature than most of Elizabethtown's students. He was not expected to take the usual three to four years' course to prepare for college. He was free to concentrate on his deficiencies, mathematics and classical languages. To gain entrance to the College of New Jersey, he would need to pass rigorous written and oral examinations in Latin prose, be able to sight-translate Virgil, Cicero, and the Greek gospels and demonstrate a thorough grounding in Latin and Greek grammar. He was lucky to have Barber, a noted Greek scholar, as his teacher. All through the winter of 1772 and spring of 1773, Barber drilled Hamilton on his conjugations, vocabulary, and his prose style.

Setting to work with his usual verve, seventeen-year-old Hamilton was up early. He became a familiar sight in the early mornings as he leaned against a headstone in the graveyard next door reading a book or pacing, as he recited and memorized, conspicuously riveting his lessons into his memory by saying them aloud. All the rest of his life, he would stroll and read or recite aloud, eventually annoying a great number of people. For now, he only impressed his teachers and sponsors with his diligence as he crammed from six in the morning until midnight. In one year, he covered the work of three, demonstrating what Barber called his "genius" during examinations by the Visitors in February, May, and August 1773.

While he was to become adept at business, Hamilton, the man who was to found America's financial system, as a schoolboy had to struggle with mathematics. Elizabethtown's mathematics teacher, James Conn, taught Hamilton accounting according to the Italian double-entry system. Conn, who built on Hamilton's natural practicality, gave instructions not only in mathematics but geography, navigation, and drawing. Fifteen years later, Hamilton would use a study he began at Elizabethtown of the geography of North and South America in an important law case in New York City. Conn also taught Hamilton how to draw maps and charts "either plain, mercator, spherical or conical." What money Hamilton was able to save by accepting invitations to dinner, he appears to have spent on tutoring and books. He studied the Bible with Reverend Caldwell, who visited the school regularly. He learned by writing commentaries on the Books of Genesis and Revelations, the first and last things.

It was away from the schoolhouse that Hamilton made his deepest impression. He became a fixture at the home of lanky, long-nosed William Livingston. As Hamilton fell in with the local Whig circle, he caught the eyes of Livingston's lively daughters. When the Livingstons moved into Liberty Hall, Hamilton joined their busy social circle. It included not only many members of the burgeoning Scots-American aristocracy centered around Livingston Manor on the Hudson, but members of the Beekman family of New York City—business partners of the Crugers—and the Schuylers of Albany, next to the Livingstons and the DeLanceys the wealthiest of fourteen river-baron clans who

virtually owned the Hudson Valley from New York City to Lake
Champlain. It was here at Liberty Hall that Hamilton met many of
the people who would become his staunch supporters in his meteoric
political career. They included John Jay, one day to be the first chief
justice of the United States; Benjamin Rush, America's foremost physician and a Revolutionary leader; and Livingston's brother-in-law,
William Alexander, the manufacturer of illegal iron who styled himself Lord Stirling. It was here, too, that Hamilton began to flirt with
the daughters of America's aristocrats. Realizing that by chance he'd
had the unbelievable luck to stumble into the inner sanction of the
middle colonies' greatest concentration of money, power and influence, he learned quickly to mine it to his advantage.

From the Livingstons, Hamilton got good meals and important
introductions; at Boxwood Hall, the nearby spread-eagled mansion of
portly philanthropist Elias Boudinot, he found riches of another sort.
A deeply yet bearably spiritual man, Boudinot could not help making
money and friends. He was part of a Huguenot refugee network that
had married into New York and New Jersey's leading families—the
Stocktons of Princeton, the Rushes of Philadelphia, the Sylvesters of
Shelter Island, and the L'Hommedieus of Long Island. By the time
Hamilton became part of Boudinot's intimate fireside family,
Boudinot was an influential member of Princeton's trustees, a leader
of the Presbyterian Church in America, and an early abolitionist,
using his lawyer's skills to defend slaves in court without fee. His sis-
ter, Annis, had married Boudinot's former law preceptor, Richard
Stockton, who would sign the Declaration of Independence.
Boudinot shared a family love of poetry. In years to come, while
Boudinot presided over the Continental Congress, his sister would
write flirtatious letters to George Washington and strew flowers in
his path as he rode to his inauguration as America's first president.
Hamilton frequently amused the couple with doggerel he composed
and recited at their family gatherings. He also became terribly fond of
the Boudinots' daughter, Anna Maria, seven months old when he
began to dandle her on his knee. In long evenings at Boxwood Hall,
a few minutes' walk over from the academy, Hamilton gave and
received affection for the first time in many years.

Among other frequent guests at the two manor houses who became Hamilton's friends he met Livingston's former law partner, William Peartree Smith, who lived across the street from the Boudinots. Also a Visitor to the academy, Smith became one of many fathers beginning to think of a match of a daughter with this newly arrived islander of mysterious but highborn origins. Smith encouraged Hamilton to keep company with his fifteen-year-old daughter, Caty. On Saturday nights, they could go to a play put on by the British officers at the Elizabethtown barracks. While Hamilton was still a student at the academy, he wrote a verse prologue and an epilogue and heard English officers recite them. On Sundays, after three-hour sermons at the Presbyterian church, Hamilton found ample distractions. In the winter, there was sledding or skating on frozen ponds or on the river. The laughing, rosy-faced Hamilton took sleigh rides in the bitter cold with the Boudinots over to their farm at Basking Ridge where they visited Lord Stirling's palatial estate and his flirtatious daughters. In spring and summer, Hamilton went along on horseback rides out to Liberty Hall on the outskirts of town to see the Livingstons' new house and their gardens being set out. There he could lose himself in the five-hundred-volume library or go fishing or watch Livingston building wren houses in his workshop or planting exotic varieties of seeds sent to him from all over the world or go for rides with one of Stirling's vibrant daughters.

It was in William Livingston's lively drawing room that Hamilton met so many of the young people who would become important to him. There he first experienced unattainable love. At seventeen, he fell helplessly in love with Catherine Livingston—"Lady Kitty"—the twenty-three-year-old daughter of his host, worshipping her unrequited. At the dinner table, around the fire, at picnics and on sleighing parties, he idolized her unnoticed, surrounded by the Livingstons' ever-expanding tribe of cousins and in-laws constantly visiting Liberty Hall from New York and New Jersey. At Liberty Hall, he met John Jay, who was courting Livingston's daughter Sarah. Jay found he had much in common with the ten-years-younger Hamilton. Both were descendants of French Huguenot refugees. Jay's grandfather had escaped imprisonment in the fortress at St. Malo and hidden on a ship to America. Young John Jay became a pious Presbyterian who distrusted both the Catholic Church and the French aristocracy that had persecuted his grandfather. By wealth, power and politics he was a natural ally of the Livingstons. Jay's mother was Mary Van Cortlandt. The Jays, Van Cortlandts, and Livingstons formed a phalanx of New York aristocrats who became Revolutionaries along with the Schuylers, another clan of Hudson Valley land barons who frequently visited Liberty Hall. It was at Liberty Hall during the Schuylers' summer visit in 1773 that Hamilton first met his future wife. Amiable yet shy, dark-eyed, fifteen-year-old Elizabeth was the daughter of General Philip Schuyler, a hero of the French and Indian Wars.

In this heady company, Alexander Hamilton saw and grasped the wealth and power of the American country gentry before most other Americans were aware of its existence. His first year in America had a profound impact on him and made him yearn for membership in this new aristocracy. The company of the rich, the convivial, the witty, and the well-educated only whetted his ambition. Determined to complete his schooling as fast as possible, Hamilton developed the lifelong capacity to plow through great amounts of work quickly. Turning eighteen, he plunged into his studies of the Bible, mathematics, elocution, Greek, and Latin. He sailed through Homer's *Iliad*, translating the Greek into English and making detailed notes on the geography of the eastern Mediterranean. Several times a week he trooped to the gray-shingled Presbyterian meetinghouse to hear rousing sermons and join in the stirring hymn singing. His willing subjection in his little spare time to the pious preoccupation of Elias Boudinot with the Bible and with doing good works for the slave, the Indian, and the orphan all make it obvious that Hamilton was sincere at this stage in his zealous embrace of radical fundamentalist Presbyterianism.

If he had an open mind on religion, as few devout young people do, it was because across from Elizabethtown's imposing Presbyterian church stood the handsome redbrick Anglican Church of St. John, with brilliant controversialist Thomas Bradbury Chandler in its pulpit. Chandler was, in every way, a fascinating contrast to Reverend Caldwell, the dour Scottish pastor of Elizabethtown's Presbyterian church. Born a Connecticut Puritan, Chandler had gone, like Livingston, to Yale, but he had come out facing the opposite direction. Embracing the Church of England, in print and in sermons he campaigned tirelessly for the creation of bishops for the American colonies. Eventually, after the Revolution, after fleeing the newborn United States, he would be appointed the first bishop of Nova Scotia.

From his Loyalist point of view, Chandler believed that there had to be Anglican bishops in America to stem the growth of anti-Episcopal—and therefore anti-English—sects like his neighbors, the Scottish Presbyterians. After he decided to become a priest, Chandler had served for years as a missionary at St. John's in Elizabethtown, saving up the money to sail to London to take holy orders: there was no bishop in America to ordain him. He was one of 332 Anglican missionaries the Society of the Propagation of the Gospel in Foreign Parts sent to the American colonies to make inroads against other Protestant sects. The number had become so large and conspicuous that it alarmed American Dissenters like William Livingston. Even more disturbing was the fact that Chandler and other leading Anglican clergymen denied there was any barrier between church and state. To Anglicans, the established Church of England was part of the English state and therefore inseparable from it. Any other church was a potential enemy of the state.

Years of violent contention that ended only with the Revolution fostered in pastoral New Jersey a climate of riot and menace which bred in young Alexander Hamilton a lifelong dread of the mob. The Sons of Liberty became especially strong in Elizabethtown. They erected a gallows near the Essex County courthouse to intimidate anyone opposing them. Reverend Chandler tried to reason again and again with his parishioners and with other townspeople to avert violence. At the same time, in his letters to church officials and the British home government in England, he advised leniency in enforcement of British laws in the American colonies. But by now there were few moderates left on either side of the Atlantic. "Such an opinion of oppression prevails throughout the colonies as I believe was scarcely ever seen on any occasion in any country on Earth," he warned. Zealous in any cause, no matter how unpopular, Chandler, like Hugh Knox, strongly influenced young Hamilton through his eloquent sermons and his biweekly lectures at the academy. But in Elizabethtown, where both were outsiders, Hamilton heard much denunciation of Chandler from people he otherwise admired. Receiving a doctor's degree from Oxford University for his campaign for an American bishopric, Chandler assembled at Elizabethtown some forty Anglican clergymen from Connecticut, New York, New Jersey, and Pennsylvania. Soon their essays began to appear in newspapers throughout the colonies, thoroughly alarming anti-Episcopal Presbyterians such as William Livingston, who counterattacked in print.[7]

It was this same controversy over Anglican bishops that brought America the most vehemently anti-Episcopal clergyman in all Great Britain, the bombastic head of the Popular Party in Scotland, the Reverend John Witherspoon. For years, he had been distinguished in the Kirk of Scotland for fiery sermons attacking Anglican churchmen for meddling in politics. In Edinburgh, he had the reputation of opposing stage plays or nearly any other source of pleasure. Witherspoon quickly turned Princeton into a mecca for strict anti-English Presbyterians from all over North America. At the same time, he made the college an un-English university. He introduced the lecture to replace tutorials. He himself introduced a new course called moral philosophy, which included science and, among other things, duplicated Benjamin Franklin's scientific experiments. By the time of Hamilton's arrival in New Jersey, as the pace of Revolutionary protests quickened, students at Princeton, undoubtedly with Witherspoon's knowledge and quite likely with his consent, took the forefront in open resistance to British policies. They burned in effigy merchants, royal governors, and members of Parliament. With royal Governor William Franklin, ex officio member of the board of trustees, sitting on the dais, to dramatize their embargo of British goods they showed up for graduation in homespun American garb instead of the customary imported (and boycotted) English academic gowns. Even valedictory addresses, delivered in Latin, became defiant displays of American patriotism. Witherspoon counted among his devoted alumni young lawyers, teachers, and Presbyterian clergymen who were at the core of the radical movement in America.

In his position as president of the one college in colonial America that served several regions, Witherspoon exerted powerful influence. He traveled and preached widely. Recruiting students from the South and from the West Indies, he quickly doubled the college's endowment. Rivaling Yale in the last five years before the Revolution, Princeton produced more graduates (about twenty-five a year) than in its entire earlier history. Some seventy-seven were graduated between 1769 and 1776 and became chaplains in Revolutionary regiments. Only two graduates took the British side. Witherspoon's fire-and-brimstone evangelical preaching and his successful linkage of anti-Episcopal Presbyterianism with republican liberties unified the New and Old Lights in the middle colonies and put Witherspoon at the pinnacle of a united Presbyterian Church in America. This, in turn, propelled him into the Continental Congress when the Revolution came, where he cast the tie-breaking vote for independence.

IN EVENINGS at Liberty Hall, William Livingston's son, Princeton student Brockhulst Livingston, and his classmate Belcher Smith regaled their young friend Hamilton with recitations of Reverend Witherspoon's radical lectures. Hamilton had crammed three years' studies into one, reading voraciously. He could now boast twenty-seven books on ancient and medieval history and philosophy in his personal library, his list roughly corresponding with gifts from his cousin, Ann Lytton. On May 3, May 26, and June 3, she drew a total of 75 rigsdalers, the proceeds of selling fifteen hogsheads of sugar from her Lytton inheritance, to help her favorite cousin with his expenses. Twenty years later, Hamilton would repay her with his personal loyalty and support her when she was old, alone, and ill. As soon as Hamilton successfully passed his final quarterly examinations, he boarded the ferry for Manhattan and told Mulligan he wanted to apply at the last minute to enter the College of New Jersey that fall of

1773: Mulligan was a graduate of the Anglican-supported King's College, its bitter rival. He said he preferred that Hamilton attend King's nearby and live with him. But Hamilton persuasively argued with him, Mulligan wrote forty years later:

> Before he had been there [at Elizabethtown] one year, he told me—and I was also informed of the same by a letter from the teacher [Francis Barber], that he was prepared to enter college. He came to New York and told me he preferred Princeton to King's College because it was more *republican*.

Hamilton certainly knew what he was talking about. Since opening in 1754 with eight students over the objections of William Livingston and other radical New Yorkers—and after a long and bitter legislative battle—King's College had come to represent the extension of royal power into America and the ascendancy of the Church of England over the colonies. With a faculty of Anglican clergy, it, too, was attracting students from distant colonies. Among its other early graduates was Hamilton's friend John Jay.

Hamilton marshaled solid reasons for insisting on Princeton. His mentor Hugh Knox and his masters at Elizabethtown were Princeton graduates. Boudinot was a Princeton trustee. William Livingston and his collaborator on the radical *Independent Reflector*, William Peartree Smith, were also on Princeton's board. So was Knox's mentor, the Reverend Rodgers, the man who had steered Hamilton to Elizabethtown Prep. The entire raison d'être of Elizabethtown Academy and of Hamilton's acceptance into the elite Presbyterian society of the town was the school's connection with the Presbyterian holy-of-holies at Princeton. And Hamilton could point to a growing percentage of West Indies boys among Princeton's eighty-five students: his sponsors were, after all, influential in the islands. Who would dare oppose him? Under the persuasive younger man's barrage, the good-natured Mulligan acquiesced.

ROLLING DOWN the King's Highway toward Princeton one day late in summer 1773, Hamilton and Mulligan could make out the college on a rise in the distance above the low-lying slash pine and scrub oak forest. The largest single building in the British American colonies, its main brownstone building (now called Nassau Hall), was 176 by 50 feet with a domed central pavilion. The two visitors probably dismounted at the Hudibras Tavern at the southeast corner of present-day Nassau Street and Washington Road. The tavern was the haunt of Princeton's students, faculty, and townspeople—and the only place they could get a drink or a good meal at the Presbyterian college. The Scottish president, Witherspoon, was notorious for providing meals heavy on turnips raised in his own garden while he pocketed the high charge to parents for more generous meals. Many students ran up considerable tabs for meals at the nearby Hudibras, which, a short time after Hamilton's visit, burned in a mysterious fire that destroyed all records of their indebtedness.

Hercules Mulligan had agreed to take Hamilton to his examination by President Witherspoon, "with whom I was well acquainted." Since Mulligan was Hamilton's guardian and bursar of his scholarship funds, his company was more than a courtesy. The two men walked up the pathway past young sycamore trees planted in 1769 to celebrate the repeal of the Stamp Act and knocked at the door of the president's house—now the residence of the college's dean. The beetle-browed Dr. Witherspoon ushered them into his study. "Introduced Mr. Hamilton to him and proposed to him to examine the young gentleman," Mulligan recalled, "which the Doctor did to his entire satisfaction." Hamilton, now eighteen, was accepted to Princeton on the spot. To Witherspoon, the only question now was at what level, first or second year. There were students who had prepared at Princeton's own Latin school but were a year or two younger. Benjamin Rush had entered the college at age thirteen. But the decision was entirely up to President Witherspoon, who was not noted for being flexible with students. But Alexander Hamilton had heard only accolades from Witherspoon's admirers. He had no reason for caution, now that Witherspoon had examined him. With characteristic audacity, Hamilton applied a condition to *his* acceptance of Princeton. Hercules Mulligan still remembered the scene, some thirty years later, after Hamilton's death:

Mr. Hamilton then stated that he wished to enter either of the two classes to which his attainments would entitle him but with the understanding that he should be permitted to advance from class to class with as much rapidity as his exertions would enable him to do. Dr. Witherspoon listened with great attention to so unusual a proposition from so young a person and replied that he had not the sole power to determine but that he would submit the request to the trustees, who would decide.

To Hamilton, the request did not seem as brash as it did to Witherspoon. Hamilton had, after all, been allowed this same dispensation at Elizabethtown Academy. He not only was older than most of his would-be peers but had nearly five years' experience in business and several published pieces of writing to his credit. More mature, Hamilton was impatient to complete his studies and might have been anxious about the continued generosity of his benefactors, who had fitfully provided only enough support to last for four years of study. Four years of Princeton after the expensive year behind him at Elizabethtown gave Hamilton sufficient grounds for anxiety.

But he completely misgauged Dr. Witherspoon, who was not unduly impressed by Hamilton's intellect or willing to be completely candid in his response. It was entirely up to Witherspoon whether he granted Hamilton's request. The college actually had no policy that prevented accelerated study. After all, Benjamin Rush, who personally had recruited Witherspoon in Scotland, had been allowed to complete his undergraduate studies in one year. More recently, so had James Madison, who was personally admitted by Witherspoon after his Virginia fund-raising tour. Madison had just completed his studies in only two years. There must have been something about Hamilton that Witherspoon did not like, something that made him unwilling to accept the pushy protégé of so many Princeton graduates and trustees. To refuse on the spot would have irked too many prominent Princetonians. Witherspoon stalled—and then refused Hamilton in writing. Whether he ever polled his board of trustees cannot be known. If there ever was a record, it has disappeared. But Witherspoon at least had given Mulligan the impression he came away with, that Hamilton's acceptance "was done" before they left that day.

Two weeks later, Witherspoon wrote to Hamilton, informing him the trustees had turned him down. Mulligan wrote:

> About a fortnight after, a letter was received from the President stating that the request could not be complied with because it was contrary to the usage of the college and expressing his regret because he was convinced that the young gentleman would do honor to any seminary at which he should be educated.[8]

Hamilton could easily learn, from Boudinots and Livingstons and other friends, that Witherspoon was shading the truth. After all, Benjamin Rush was a Livingston in-law and a frequent visitor to Liberty Hall.

More than thirty years later, the question still lingered. Mulligan, writing his memoirs shortly after Hamilton's death, apparently felt compelled, out of all the important events of Hamilton's life, to explain why Witherspoon had rejected Hamilton. What does not appear in Mulligan's account can only be deduced from a more careful scrutiny of Witherspoon's own prejudices than Mulligan was able or prepared to make. Witherspoon may have simply believed that he should not make exceptions to the Scottish Presbyterian belief that bastards should be denied Holy Communion. At this very moment, Witherspoon was the implacable foe of the royal governor of New Jersey, William Franklin, who was, as was well known, the illegitimate son of Benjamin Franklin. In only a few years, Witherspoon would order Governor Franklin's arrest and imprisonment. At the hearing of a Revolutionary tribunal, Witherspoon personally slurred Benjamin Franklin's bastard son to his face for his "distinguished birth." Like all colleges of the time, Princeton required its students to attend chapel services. The question is whether Witherspoon had any way of knowing about the circumstances of Hamilton's birth. It is entirely possible that his illegitimacy had become the subject of gossip in the small community of New Jersey's Presbyterian elite. It may have arrived in the now-lost letters of recommendation Mulligan provided him. It is also a tantalizing fact, that, when John Witherspoon had been a radical young preacher in Scotland, vehemently attacking pro-English Scottish aristocrats, his first parish assignment had been near the Hamilton family seat in Ayrshire. In any event, stunned by his first major rejection, Alexander Hamilton understandably felt betrayed. He turned his back on Princeton and headed for the enemy camp. He applied at once to King's College, where he took the same risk, proposing accelerated study. This time, his proposal was accepted. Four years later, he would come back to Princeton—with cannon.[9]

SIX

"Americans Are Entitled to Freedom"

His audacious plan to rush through college frustrated, the resilient Alexander Hamilton, a few months shy of nineteen, rebounded quickly from his first rejection, hauled his portmanteau of prized books aboard a ferry, and turned his back on the pious controversies of Elizabethtown, returning to New York City in the autumn of 1773. He could see on the Hudson riverbank above him a burgeoning town where people went about their business briskly, noisily. From Hercules Mulligan's waiting carriage, Hamilton studied his new home. Scarcely penetrating a mile up Manhattan island, America's second largest town was crammed with twenty-five hundred buildings. In less than a square mile, he could see docks, warehouses, solid brick town houses, a dozen inns, more churches than theaters (there was only the part-time John Street Playhouse). Lapped by water on three sides, Manhattan extended from the bristling cannon of Fort George at its southern tip to "the Fields"—City Hall Park—its northern limit at present-day Chambers Street in Greenwich Village. Driving north along Broadway, Hamilton could pass quickly out of town to the countryside, to the manor houses of wealthy merchants, and, just beyond, to well-cultivated farms.

Hamilton's arrival in New York was a turning point in his life. Had he been admitted to Princeton on his own terms, his career might have been altogether different. Though Princeton students caught the Revolutionary spirit, Hamilton would have been fifty miles out of the way of the critical events in New York City in which he took part as a student at King's College, an interplay that he helped to shape as it shaped him. He would no doubt have made lasting friendships in either place, but not necessarily with the Revolutionary leaders who became his steadfast political allies. He most likely would have completed college in about three years and been drawn to Philadelphia, where his timing and setting could have proven less advantageous for him and the new nation. At Princeton, he would have been surrounded by like-minded radical Presbyterians, his reactions to unfolding events mere abstractions. In New York City, King's College President Myles Cooper was, as his student Robert Troup put it, "a most obnoxious Tory" to radical Patriots. Hamilton's fellow students, steeped in royalist Church of England views, provided him the whetstone for sharp encounters with Loyalist Americans who took the king's side in what was rapidly becoming a civil war.[1]

Alexander Hamilton found the New York City of the 1770s a fascinating place. For the rest of his life, he never expressed a desire to live anywhere else. Challenging Quaker Philadelphia as the leading commercial center of colonial America, New York grew rapidly as both port of entry and export outlet for northern New Jersey, southern Connecticut, western Massachusetts, the Hudson River and its tributaries. One in six colonial Americans was engaged in its commerce. Its warehouses bulged with furs traded with Indians, West India sugar, rum, and indigo; and tea from India. Its broad harbor was rarely frozen, and shiploads of cargo clearing New York harbor had increased fivefold in a single generation, from 140 a year in 1750 to 700 by 1775. New York–based vessels plied the North Atlantic (principally to London and Holland), the Caribbean, and the Mediterranean. Its shipyards produced fast oceangoing vessels such as the Crugers' *Thunderbolt* for Dutch as well as English masters. Barter for New York's goods fetched Madeira wine from Lisbon, mahogany from Honduras, flaxseed from Ireland. It was also the headquarters of the British Army in North America.

A young immigrant of mixed French, Scottish, and English stock himself, Hamilton fit right into the rich ethnic mosaic of a city already the most cosmopolitan in America. Dutch and Walloons, Scots and Irish refugees, Jews, Germans, black slaves and freedmen on Manhattan; New England Puritans on Long Island; and French Huguenots in New Rochelle all helped to assure fewer social barriers than other colonial American towns. Scottish-born New York Lieutenant Governor Cadwallader Colden reported that there were many New Yorkers who "have risen suddenly from the lowest rank of the people to considerable fortunes"—mostly, and this was the point of his observation, from illicit trade. The city abounded in rough-cut men of new wealth. "New York," wrote Judge Thomas Jones,

consists principally of merchants, shopkeepers and tradesmen, so [it] sustains the reputation of honest, punctual and fair dealers. With respect to riches, there is not so great an inequality as is common in Boston and some other places [in America] ... Every man of industry and integrity has it in his power to live well, and many are the instances of persons who came here distressed by their poverty who now enjoy easy and plentiful fortunes.[2]

With a curl of his lip, John Adams of Boston liked to point out that

with all the opulence and splendor of this city, there is little good breeding to be found ... At their entertainment, there is no conversation that is agreeable. There is no modesty, no attention to one another. They talk very loud, very fast, and all together.[3]

What Alexander Hamilton saw was quite different. From any angle of approach to New York by water, the low-lying town was surrounded by a forest of ship's masts. At Manhattan's southern tip,

120 cannon protruded from the fourteen-foot-high walls of Fort George. The Battery was a favorite place for promenades. As Mulligan's carriage rattled by, Hamilton could look across Bowling Green toward the imposing new equestrian statue of classically garbed King George III. Rounding the green, dodging horses and wagons as they crossed Broadway, he saw the town houses of wealthy merchants and caught a glimpse of King's Arms Tavern, where the town's posh society danced at subscription assemblies in an upstairs ballroom. Amid painted brick houses, left from seventeenth-century Dutch rule, he saw blacksmiths' forges and carpenters' shops and the massive eight-story Rhinelander sugar warehouse. Next door, Mulligan's carriage passed his fashionable tailor shop, then stopped at the recently married haberdasher's handsome new residence on Queen Street, one block back from the East River waterfront.

After Hamilton unpacked, Mulligan escorted his young ward west along Robinson Street across town to the campus of King's College. The cupola-capped four-story gray stone college building, by far the largest in the city, sat perched on a bluff 150 feet above the Hudson River. One English traveler, the Reverend Andrew Burnaby, described the campus as "the most beautifully situated of any college, I believe, in the world." Its president, Oxford-educated Myles Cooper, in his best academic recruiting prose, wrote, just before Hamilton's arrival, that the first building of what is now Columbia University commanded

from the eminence on which it stands a most extensive and beautiful prospect of the opposite shore and country of New Jersey, the city and island of New York, Long Island, Staten Island, New York Bay with its islands, the Narrows, forming the mouth of the harbour . . . and being totally unencumbered by any adjacent buildings and admitting the purest circulation of air from the river and every other quarter, has the benefit of as agreeable and healthy a situation as can possibly be conceived.

It had been only seventeen years since New Yorkers had seen their first academic procession that had ended with a "very elegant dinner" at the Province Arms Tavern on Broadway, a speech in Latin, and the toast of "Health to his Majesty and success to his arms." Hamilton's Presbyterian mentor William Livingston had lobbied hard against the creation of the Anglican college for nearly ten years, but now Hamilton was leaving his Presbyterian friends behind him. He climbed the stairs and offered his allegiance—once again on his own terms—to King's President Cooper.[4]

This time, Hamilton had better luck. Oxford-educated Cooper, the second president of King's, was, as King's pre-Revolutionary royal charter required, "a member of and in communion with the Church of England." Morning and evening, he was in the habit of personally intoning Matins and Vespers while his students chanted responses from the *Book of Common Prayer*. Cooper, handpicked by the archbishop of Canterbury, head of the Church of England, because he was "very well affected to the [British] government," seemed bent on making King's a little Oxford on the Hudson. He was exactly the sort of self-confident proselytizer Livingston had warned Hamilton against. He would "put a new face upon the religion and affect the politics of the country" while "tincturing the minds of the students with [the] sentiments of the [Anglican] sect." After a King's College education, dyed-in-the-wool King's men would, Livingston warned, become New York's aristocrats and "fill all the offices of the government."[5]

Putting Livingston's cautions aside, Hamilton saw before him an attractive role model who could transform a provincial youth into an English gentlemen. The handsome Cooper, who had learned the gentlemanly arts at Queen's College, Oxford, and had taken Anglican orders in his early twenties after mastering the classics, had elegant manners. Urbane, convivial Cooper was a lifelong bachelor who kept a well-stocked wine cellar and put on meals so sumptuous for his students and faculty that his girth was showing the effects. At table, he recited poetry, including his own London-published love poems. His lusty verses suited Hamilton's taste, and Hamilton suited Cooper. After quizzing the applicant and scanning the letters of introduction presented by King's alumnus Mulligan, President Cooper promptly approved Hamilton's request for self-paced tutoring for a year so he could quickly take the entrance examination, then enter the college as a sophomore. He welcomed a beaming Hamilton to a student body of twenty-four undergraduates and six medical students.

Dr. Cooper and other professors tutored Hamilton during their leisure hours. As roommate, Hamilton drew Robert Troup, who openly admired him. Troup recalled after Hamilton's death that he "was studious and made rapid progress in the languages and every other branch of learning to which he applied himself." Hamilton set to work making up for his scholastic deficiencies; studying Latin and Greek that fall, he translated Homer's *Iliad*, beginning with book twelve. His Latin translations were literal, not free. He had to struggle, relying constantly on a dictionary. Because he still wanted to study medicine, he was "regular in attending the anatomical lectures" of Dr. Samuel Clossy, who had been trained at Trinity College in Dublin. Like any other student, Hamilton simply paid a fee at the door. Hamilton closely followed Dr. Clossy's "Anatomical Predilections." He probably attended the lectures with his St. Croix friend Neddy Stevens, whom Troup called Hamilton's "particular associate" for the next few years.

By early 1774, the nineteen-year-old Hamilton had completed the first part of the anatomy course as advertised in the *New York Gazette*, "Osteology and Muscling." At Clossy's eleven o'clock lecture on Monday morning, January 10, 1774, Dr. Clossy promised to begin his "pneumatical optical lectures" of "the Properties of Air and Light" by which "the primary use of respiration and the visual operations are wont to be illustrated." In subsequent anatomy lectures, Hamilton heard Clossy explain "the Distribution of the Arteries, Veins and Nerves and the Structure of the Viscera." He also attended the chemistry lectures of Dr. James Smith. That first year, Hamilton also became close friends with two other upperclassmen, Samuel and Henry Nicoll of New Haven. They formed themselves into a literary society that met weekly, presented their writings, and debated them. A sixth member, Nicholas Fish, who had left Princeton to become a law clerk, soon joined the sessions, which met until the Revolution.[6]

For once, Hamilton was content, happy to be an exemplary student. He scrupulously followed the college's rules and routines.

That meant being in his room on the college's first floor by nine o'clock at night in winter and ten in summer. He could not "convene with persons of bad fame," like the prostitutes a block away on Robinson Street, gamble (even at cards or dice), or do anything that would require Dr. Cooper to break down his door during one of his random inspections. He could not pass through the college gates after the porter locked them or enter or leave over the fence. One reason Hamilton adhered to all Dr. Cooper's transplanted rules was that any student with an unblemished record each year was entitled "in the most honorary manner and publicly" to receive presentations of books bought with the steep fines paid by less obedient students. More than half of Hamilton's classmates paid the fines or carried out punishments: "Translate into Latin 4 Pages of Dr. Chandler's Charity Sermon . . . Translate the 4th Section of the third Chapter of Pufendorf . . . Translate Numbers 255 [and] 256 of [Addison and Steele's] Spectator into Latin."[7]

Thriving not only intellectually, Hamilton, so recently on short rations in St. Croix, ate better than most college students before or since, if the steward's stated bill of fare can be trusted. On Sundays, the midday dinner was "roast beef and [Yorkshire?] pudding"; on Thursdays, corned beef and "mutton pye"; on Fridays, "leg mutton and soup." Breakfasts followed the continental plan: tea or coffee, bread and butter; suppers the same, but with cheese. Hamilton seems to have spent little time dawdling at table. He could be seen on mild days pacing back and forth under the tall trees on Dey Street, talking to himself, memorizing, practicing speeches. On any day, he could be found in King's magnificent library. English benefactors had shipped over fifteen hundred books. Hamilton raced through the natural rights writings of John Locke, Grotius, Pufendorf, Montesquieu, Burlamaqui, Hobbes, Blackstone, and Hume; Thomas Hutchinson's *History of Massachusetts Bay*; the eleven-volume *New and General Biographical Dictionary*; recent parliamentary acts; colonial charters; New York's laws; Samuel Johnson's dictionary; and biographies of Peter the Great of Russia and Holy Roman Emperor Charles XII. While none of these works was required of him, they stood him in good stead when he studied for the bar a decade later.

Another new student arriving at King's that summer of 1773 was George Washington's stepson, John Parke Custis, up from Virginia. Young Custis was secretly engaged to be married. After only four months he dropped out to go home to Mount Vernon. In a letter to his mother, Martha Washington, he left probably the best surviving portrait of a student's quarters and the King's College way of life:

I have a large parlour with two studies or closets, each large enough to contain a bed, trunk, and a couple of chairs. One I sleep in, and the other, Joe [Custis's slave valet] calls his. My chamber and parlour are papered with a cheap tho' very pretty paper; the other is painted. My furniture consists of six chairs [and] two tables with a few paltry pictures. I have an excellent bed and, in short, everything very convenient and clever.

I generally get up about six or a little after, dress myself and go to chapel . . . [After] a little breakfast, to which I sit down very contentedly, and after eating heartily, I thank God—go to my studies, with which I am employed till twelve, then I take a walk and return about one, dine with the professors and after dinner, study till six, at which time the bell always [rings] for prayers. They being over, college is broke up, and then we take what amusement we please.[8]

Just what "amusement" the students pleased may have been perfectly innocent. On a hot day, a favorite pastime was to stroll along the top of the Battery of Fort George on Manhattan's southernmost tip to catch any breeze coming off the bay. But more than one visitor worried about the corrupting influence of nearby Robinson Street. A Scotsman who visited King's at this time reported that the college made "a fine appearance" but

One circumstance I think is a little unlucky. The entrance to this college is through one of the streets where the most noted prostitutes live. This is certainly a temptation to the youth that have occasion to pass so often that way.[9]

The favorite play of New Yorkers in the 1773-74 season was William Shakespeare's *The Tempest*, the bard's only play inspired by America. The shipwreck on Bermuda of a fleet bound from London to Virginia was the perfect prologue to the furious reaction of many Americans to England's continuing incursions into colonial affairs. Theater buff Hamilton undoubtedly saw it at the John Street Playhouse.

Outside the walls, prostitutes; inside, compulsory prayers. Dr. Cooper enforced his rigid set of rules, personally noting each infraction in the "Book of Misdemeanors." Since Hamilton's name does not appear once, it suggests he never disobeyed a college rule—or at least was never caught. Cooper's rules included, as young Custis wrote his mother, not only prayers between five and seven o'clock in the summer and six and eight in winter, but afternoon and evening prayers and church twice on Sundays. According to Hamilton's roommate, Robert Troup, Hamilton still took his religion undiluted. Which religion he was following at the moment is hard to tell. A staunch Presbyterian in Elizabethtown, he apparently about-faced briefly and became devoutly Anglican at King's. Chambermate Troup recalled:

Whilst at college, [he] was attentive to public worship and in the habit of praying upon his knees both night and morning. I have lived in the same room with him for sometime and I have often been powerfully affected by the fervor and eloquence of his prayers. [He] had [already] read most of the polemical writers on religious subjects and he was a zealous believer in the fundamental doctrines of Christianity.[10]

Yet Hamilton did not make so profound an impression in some other subjects. He had difficulty with chemistry. When he formally matriculated in May 1774, he abandoned pursuit of a medical career. Next to Hamilton's name in the registry of "Admissions Anno 1774," Dr. Cooper did not note the requisite "S.M." for a student of medicine. To help with math, Hamilton hired a tutor, forty-five-year-old Robert Harpur, the college's Scottish-born professor of mathematics and natural philosophy. When Harpur learned Hamilton was a scholarship student he waived his customary fee. Hamilton appreciated Harpur's rigorous lessons, even if other students jeered the Scottish mathematician. Also an accomplished astronomer, Harpur had devised ingenious methods for teaching commercial mathematics that would prove critical to Hamilton in his military, banking, and government careers. Hamilton made rapid progress in calculating simple interest, commercial applications of discounting in partner's shares, and currency exchange, Harpur's specialty. Hamilton came to value Harpur's advanced mathematics instruction so highly that, after the Revolution shut King's College and threw Harpur out of a job, Hamilton gave the threadbare Harpur a generous gift of five guineas, about $250 today.

ONLY THREE months after Alexander Hamilton began his studies in New York, a riot in Boston polarized America, making it difficult for any colonist to remain completely disinterested in the confrontation with England. When ships owned by the British East India Company arrived off Boston in December 1773, the Sons of Liberty prevented their unloading. Sons organizer Sam Adams, a brewer who feared cheap English tea would prove too tempting to Bostonians, called for a "tea party." On December 16, 1773, eight thousand men cordoned off the wharves while fifty blanket-wrapped armed men with painted faces gave a war whoop and boarded the tea ships. For three hours, they passed 342 black-lacquered Chinese crates of tea topside, smashed them open, and dumped them into the harbor. Paul Revere took the news quickly down the Post Road to New York's Sons of Liberty headquarters at Montayne's Tavern on Broadway across from the commons, where they called a mass protest meeting. A broadside posted overnight all over the city warned that tea importers were the enemies of America and any harbor pilots who guided the tea ships up the harbor would be dealt with harshly. The consignees of the tea all promptly resigned. Within days, on December 29, 1773, inside Fort George, the Governor's House burned to a smoldering shell in a fire some said was deliberately set, destroying not only house and furniture but many official documents—including papers implicating radical leaders. When the tea ship *Nancy* arrived off Sandy Hook on

April 18, 1774, a committee of Sons of Liberty, including Hercules Mulligan, most likely with Hamilton at his side, marched to the waterfront offices of the tea consignees and warned them not to permit the ship to come up to the city. At a rally at Murray's wharf, Hamilton, Troup, and Mulligan joined in the cheering as the tea merchants knuckled under and sent the ship back to England. Hamilton and his young friends were on hand when a second tea ship, the *London*, arrived. Her skipper denied he had tea aboard, but several Sons remembered he had been the captain who had delivered the hated tax stamps in 1765. After a persuasive visit to Captain Gordon's ship by a large number of the Sons of Liberty, the captain admitted he had eighteen crates of tea on board for sale as his own private business. When the Sons printed "invitations" to their own "tea party," Hamilton and his friends eagerly posted them around Manhattan. "To the Public," the broadsides reported, the Sons had conveyed to Captain Gordon "the sense of the city." They were determined that, "at his departure, he should see with his own eyes their detestation of the measures pursued by the Ministry and the India Company to enslave this country." Summoning all citizens to a "Convention of the People," the Sons left no doubt that "every friend to this country will attend" the farewell planned for the tea ship's captain: "The bells will give the notice about an hour before [Captain Gordon] embarks from Murray's Wharf."[11]

Imitating their Boston coconspirators, a contingent of the Sons dressed as Mohawks, but this time the large crowd of protesters could not be controlled. Surging onto the *London*, they "broke the cases and started to throw contents into the river." The captain and his crew were happy to escape with their lives. The sight of an out-of-control mob at work horrified Hamilton, and he would later deny he had taken any part in it. In his essay *The Farmer Refuted*, published ten months later in Rivington's *New York Gazetteer*, Hamilton, defending himself against a Loyalist pamphleteer's charge that he had been active in Sons of Liberty protests, insisted "that you are entirely mistaken." He had every reason to believe he would lose his college scholarship or be expelled from King's College if it became known that he was personally involved. But Hamilton was developing the lifelong habit of working in secret. In his room late at night, he was synthesizing his learned readings and his analysis of current events into anonymous writings calculated to sway everyone around him to his privately held Revolutionary point of view.[12]

Completing his first year of studies at King's College in April 1774, at exactly the same time as New York's tea party, Hamilton no sooner matriculated as a sophomore than he decided to challenge the college president's Tory views outside the classroom in the radical press. A later King's graduate, DeWitt Clinton, reported that, up to this time, Hamilton had been an outspoken monarchist who had sided with President Cooper and the Loyalists' point of view. Now adopting a stock Patriot line of reasoning, Hamilton argued that the king, not Parliament, was the legitimate ruler of his empire, but that Parliament, by meddling in American domestic affairs, had usurped the king's authority. But while President Cooper remained unswervingly and unquestioningly pro-British, in anonymous pamphlets based on his own research Hamilton began to elaborate for less well-educated New York newspaper readers distinctions between the rights and powers of Parliament and those of the king.

THE AFTERSHOCKS of the tea parties struck New York in waves. The first came when New York's conservative provincial assembly on January 20, 1774, created a committee of correspondence to coordinate opposition to the Tea Act with other colonies. That committee became the first public body in America to suggest convening a continental congress. Then, early in June 1774, shortly after Hamilton's sophomore year at King's began, angry crowds gathered when a royal mail packet boat arrived from London with news that an indignant Parliament by four to one vote had carried out King George III's personal wish that Boston be severely punished for its destruction of tea. Parliament authorized the king to close and reopen Boston's port for trade only when the India Company was compensated for its 10,000-pound losses. As a tidal wave of disciplinary acts by Parliament swamped Boston harbor, New Yorkers shuddered. Massachusetts courts were put under Crown control. Its royal charter was suspended. Members of the Massachusetts elective council henceforth would be appointed by the king, as were the attorney general, sheriffs, judges, and justices of the peace. Parliament banned town meetings, the basis of New England's unruly democracy. They could be convened only with the written approval of the royal governor. Finally, Parliament replaced Massachusetts's native-born governor with a military governor. Sir Thomas Gage, a tough veteran of the French and Indian Wars, sailed for Boston from New York City to the command of this new headquarters of all British forces in North America. Stunned, every American colony but Georgia convened emergency congresses that summer to choose delegates to send to the First Continental Congress in Philadelphia.

When New York proved to be the most conservative of all colonies in choosing delegates to Congress, on June 15, 1774, New York's Sons of Liberty carried effigies of Lord North, the head of the British ministry, and of other English officials through the streets and burned them at City Hall Park. The Loyalist-controlled assembly appointed a standing Committee of Fifty-one made up principally of pro-British public officials and businessmen who preferred to petition London through the royal governor and refused to allow any popular voice in nominating congressional representatives. When the Sons of Liberty's leader Alexander McDougall applied to the standing committee on July 4, 1774, for a voice for the Sons in choosing delegates, his motion was voted down twenty-four to thirteen. A second motion, for the Committee of Fifty-one to nominate five delegates to be approved by the "freeholders and freemen of the city," passed. The Sons tried to nominate former privateersman McDougall and radical lawyer John Morin Scott but their nominations were blocked. The Committee of Fifty-one announced its lopsidedly conservative slate of delegates would be ratified at a public meeting at City Hall on July 7. Before the committee could meet again, the Sons of Liberty distributed handbills throughout the city calling a mass protest meeting "in the Fields" at the Liberty Pole outside City Hall for the night before. It was here that Alexander Hamilton made his public political debut.

When the crowd gathered in City Hall Park at six o'clock, Hamilton stood with Mulligan and his young friends. McDougall,

arriving with his usual retinue of about 150 muscular sailors, laborers, and artisans, inveighed against "the dangerous tendency of the
numerous vile arts used by the enemies of America" and proposed
passing a series of anti-Parliament resolutions. As he described the
"alarming state of the liberties of America," Hamilton explained in a
low voice to the people around him in detail just how explosive the
crisis had become. Spontaneously, his listeners urged him forward
toward the makeshift stage. There, in a self-deprecating, faltering
voice at first, he laid out the arguments for supporting all nine resolutions McDougall had read to the crowd. Holding his audience, surprised by his youthful appearance, spellbound by his passionate
reasoning, Hamilton denounced the Boston Port Act for causing
"our brethren" so much "suffering in the common cause of these
colonies." He insisted that the colonies had the right to unite to
resist unconstitutional taxation by Parliament. He demanded that all
American imports and exports to Great Britain be halted until the
British reopened the port of Boston. Nothing less, Hamilton contended, could check the "fraud, power and most odious oppression"
that would otherwise "rise triumphant over right, justice, social
happiness and freedom." No newspaper reporter was on hand to
take down Hamilton's first speech verbatim, but thirty years later,
his roommate, Robert Troup, there that night, could still vividly
remember it.[13]

THE ARGUMENTS that this intense, boyish-looking collegian—now nearing his twentieth birthday—marshaled to inspire a crowd of merchants,
mechanics, sailors, lawyers, and bartenders to vote unanimously for
all the Sons of Liberty's resolutions were hardly spontaneous. Hamilton had been rehearsing them in his murmuring undertone during
strolls around the city, refining them in debates with his classmates,
and writing them anonymously to New York newspapers. The surprise discovery that day for many of New York's fledgling activists
was that it must have been this unassuming college boy who had
been so skillfully laying out the colonial position in Holt's *New-York
Journal*.

There is no direct evidence that Hamilton, alternately using the pennames "Americanus" or "Monitor," wrote frequently in the Patriot Holt's paper. But the style was unmistakably his. The arguments housed the germs of many of Hamilton's later ideas and policies. King's College President Cooper refused to believe it was anyone so young as Hamilton. He thought it was an earlier King's student, John Jay. But Jay knew it was not Jay: as he wrote from the Continental Congress in Philadelphia to Alexander McDougall in December 1775, while Hamilton was still a student, "I hope Mr. Hamilton continues busy. I have not received Holt's paper these three months and therefore cannot judge of the progress he makes."[14]

In the *New-York Journal* for December 16, 1773, Hamilton, who would never give up defending the legitimacy of father figures, still upheld the king's authority even as he denied Parliament's. "The very charters which confirm our liberty reserve to him a sovereign authority." Britain's American colonies were "distinct independent states." The series of parliamentary acts restricting American manufacturing and trade and imposing new taxes were "an unwarrantable exercise" of "arbitrary power unknown to the British constitution." Hamilton supported the Continental Congress as a "union of counsel" to oppose British tyranny. He recommended that it become permanent as "an annual congress." "Americanus's" recitation of history and systemic cataloguing of pertinent laws foreshadow arguments later used by Hamilton. In successive articles in the *Gazette* "Monitor" described parliamentary economic policy as a "scheme to enslave this country and eat up the fruits of our industry in the endless train of taxes."[15]

UNMASKED BY his "Fields" speech as a champion of colonial rights, Hamilton found it harder to maintain his neutrality at King's College. His public speaking and writings brought him to the attention of the leading radicals, merchant McDougall; one-eyed John Lamb, the rabble-rousing son of a deported burglar; prominent lawyer Thomas Randall; and flamboyant Hudson River aristocrat Peter Livingston. Through Hercules Mulligan, McDougall supplied Hamilton with the books, newspapers, and pamphlets he needed to construct his carefully reasoned letters to the press, materials he would not find in the

Anglican college's library. In an apparent attempt to silence him, another student, probably Loyalist, broke into Hamilton's room, coming in through a window and stealing irreplaceable books and papers. Hamilton was reluctant to report the burglary to McDougall. In a recently discovered undated letter, Hamilton wrote McDougall "with the utmost chagrin" that

> I am not able to return you all your pamphlets and what is still worse, the most valuable of them is missing. I beg you will not impute it to carelessness . . . I put your pamphlets in the case with my other books, and some person about the college got into my room through the window, broke open my case and took out the "Friendly Address," Bancroft's treatise, two volumes of natural philosophy and a Latin author.

Always short on cash as he waited for dilatory payments of his allowance from his St. Croix sponsors, Hamilton could hardly afford to replace the books, but he had "taken all possible pains" to recover or replace them. His efforts "have been fruitless." Admitting "no small uneasiness" that he had lost the volumes, Hamilton dared not reveal to Loyalist students as he carried on his campus probe just who had been "Americanus" and "Monitor."[16]

IN EARLY September 1774, a sad event pulled Hamilton away from King's College and back to Elizabethtown. There, two-year-old Anna Maria Boudinot, whom he had first dandled on his knee when she was seven months old, died. Her death hit Hamilton hard. When he learned she was dying, he hurried to catch the ferry to New Jersey and the stagecoach to Elizabethtown. He sat up all night, holding her lifeless body. Back at his college room, he put aside Revolutionary pamphleteering long enough to write one of his more sensitive poems to the "sweet babe" he had so doted on in long, happy months with the Boudinots. He missed her "prattling in my happy arms," the "embryo meaning" of her "imperfect accents" which her "speaking looks" could "still display":

Thou'st gone, forever gone—yet where,
Ah! pleasing thought, to endless bliss.
Then, why indulge the rising tear?
Canst thou, fond heart, lament for this?

Let reason silence nature's strife,
And weep Maria's fate no more;
She's safe from all the storms of life,
And wafted to a peaceful shore.[7]

TWENTY YEARS old and looking still younger, ruddy-faced, sandy-haired, and slight, Alexander Hamilton became the darling of New York's radicals. He returned from his brief New Jersey interlude to roll up his sleeves in the newspaper war against British imperial policy. While appearing in classes at King's College as a mere schoolboy, he pursued a secret life as a Revolutionary pamphleteer.

When he had taken up residence with Hercules Mulligan on Water Street, little more than a year earlier, he had outspokenly supported loyalty to England. In classes at King's and over the breakfast table at Mulligan's, he had argued hotly in defense of England's right to tax its colonies. When someone, probably Mulligan, asked him point-blank after the English shut the port of Boston, which side he would be on in case of war, he answered, "on the side of England." But eyewitnesses remembered an overnight conversion. The next morning, after a night of tossing and turning, Hamilton announced that he believed the colonies were right. In December 1774, after the First Continental Congress met in Philadelphia, Hamilton published his first pamphlet, *A Full Vindication of the Measures of Congress.* Congress had adopted a nonimportation agreement boycotting all exports to the British Isles and West Indies until Parliament reopened the port of Boston.

Congress's sanctions evoked a sharp attack from Dr. Samuel Seabury, an Anglican priest in Westchester County, New York, using the pseudonym "A Farmer." In *Free Thoughts on the Proceedings of the Continental Congress,* Seabury, a leading advocate of an American bishopric in New York and one of King's College President Cooper's closest friends, accused Congress of betraying the colonies as well as their king. He called the boycott an "abominable scheme" that would incite riots and provoke the British to crush American resistance with military force. "You had better trust to the mercy of a Turk" than to this "parcel of upstart lawless committeeman," wrote Seabury. "If I must be devoured, let me be devoured by the jaws of a lion and not gnawed to death by rats and vermin."[18]

Seabury was part of a loose alliance of colonial politicians and clergy loyal to the Crown who set about denigrating Congress and disparaging the characters of its delegates. Alexander Hamilton, supplied with books and pamphlets by Sons of Liberty leader McDougall, stepped into the political arena to defend Congress against the Loyalists whenever they broke into print.

His first salvo, A Full Vindication, printed December 15, 1774, mocked the "impotence" of Seabury and his Loyalist friends. He called them "restless spirits" violently opposed to the "natural rights of mankind," who preferred the "absolute sovereignty of Parliament." He derided the Anglican clergymen for trying to persuade Americans that it was their "Christian duty to submit to be plundered of all we have." Hamilton insisted that America and Great Britain were already separate. The central question was "whether the inhabitants of Great Britain have a right to dispose of the lives and properties of the inhabitants of America." No human being had the right to "power or pre-eminence over his fellow creatures" unless they voluntarily gave it to him. "Americans have not by any act of theirs empowered the British Parliament to make laws for them."

Here Hamilton was invoking Scottish philosopher John Locke's natural-rights doctrine of government by consent of the governed. Defending the Continental Congress boycott, he argued that England could not tax Americans without their consent in a body that represented them. He argued for bold economic resistance:

> We can live without trade of any kind. Food and clothing we
> have within ourselves. Our climate produces cotton, wool, flax
> and hemp which, with proper cultivation, would furnish us

with summer apparel . . . We have sheep which, with due care in improving and increasing them, would soon yield a sufficiency of wool. The large quantity of skins we have among us would never let us want a warm and comfortable suit . . .

That Hamilton would devote so much of his pamphlet to the sources of clothing must have made some of his radical friends chuckle. From his guardian Mulligan, he had learned a great deal about fine clothing; indeed, he was always outfitted and fed far beyond a scholarship student's means by his benevolent landlord.

A few weeks short of twenty-one, Alexander Hamilton was formulating his basic political philosophy. Building upon a foundation of rich natural resources, through free trade America could prosper without the approval of Europe.[19]

Soon after Hamilton published his *Full Vindication*, Seabury unleashed a more scathing denunciation of Congress, admitting he was responding to Hamilton, whose identity he still did not know. "If the author of the *Vindication* has any teeth left, here is another file at his service." This time, Hamilton waited nearly two months to respond while he conducted extensive research and surreptitiously wrote by candlelight behind a locked door inside what had become the enemy camp, King's College. Hamilton took delight that Seabury, King's President Cooper, and other leading Loyalists believed the author of his pamphlets was Jay, a New York delegate to the Continental Congress. He refused to be goaded into publishing prematurely. When he learned from the printer that "The Farmer" was going to attack him in print, he read a leaked set of his rival's galley proofs, obtaining them without Seabury's knowledge. A brief rejoinder, "A Card," appeared in Rivington's *New York Gazetteer* on December 22, 1774, two weeks before Seabury could respond to his *first* salvo. This time styling himself "Friend to America," Hamilton was sure that what he wrote would never change Loyalists' minds:

The intellectual eye of every advocate for despotism is too much blinded to perceive the force of just argumentation.

Ridiculing Seabury, Hamilton delivered a finger-wagging pseudo-academic discourse, throwing in some bad poetry that produced gales of laughter among Sons of Liberty reading it in their taverns. He "burlesqued his antagonists in doggerel rhyme with great wit and humor," wrote roommate Robert Troup years later.[20]

Between the 1774 and 1775 sessions of the First Continental Congress, one of Hamilton's former tutors at Elizabethtown Academy, Reverend Chandler, joined the pamphlet war over Congress's actions. President Cooper of King's College and the Reverend Charles Inglis, assistant rector of Trinity Church in New York City, joined the learned array of "ministerial champions," as his roommate Robert Troup phrased it. Chandler's *What Think Ye of Congress Now?* predicted that American actions would bring on armed British vengeance, and encouraged Loyalists to resist Congress. Repeatedly menaced by the Sons of Liberty, Chandler finally left Elizabethtown with only a few "articles of necessary apparel." He escaped by boat at night to New York City, where he hid in the home of Attorney General William Smith until the New York City Sons of Liberty tracked him down. This time he escaped in a rowboat to a British man-of-war in the harbor.

Hamilton's writings, stirring Patriots and smoking out Loyalists, systematically rebutted Loyalist pamphleteers, Troup noted,

in a way which manifested such a fund of information and such maturity and strength of mind as to confer the credit [on] Mr. Jay. I remember that in a conversation I once had with Dr. Cooper about [Hamilton's *Farmer Refuted*] he insisted that Mr. Jay must be the author of it, it being absurd to imagine that so young a man as [Hamilton] could have written it.[21]

After his papers and books were ransacked in his college room, Hamilton wrote *The Farmer Refuted* at Hercules Mulligan's house—"part in my presence," Mulligan later attested—"and read some pages to me as he wrote them." Hamilton's second pamphlet made clear his maturing belief that private interest was the glue that would hold American society together and make it succeed. Just as long as Americans learned to rein in their impulse toward unbridled greed

and could control, channel, and regulate their prosperity for the public good, they would be invincible even against English military
might.[22]

Declaring that moral obligation preceded the law of nations,
Hamilton asserted that colonial rights flowed from "the law of nature
and that supreme law of every society—its own happiness." Borrowing from Locke's *Second Treatise on Government*, he sounded the note
"the pursuit of happiness" a year and a half before Thomas Jefferson
penned the Declaration of Independence. It was the inherent right of
American colonists, Hamilton argued, to govern themselves through
their own legislatures. In perhaps his most radical declaration,
Hamilton explicitly rejected the traditional Whig idea that only a
mixed government, such as one including both king and Parliament,
was free.

He distinguished between freedom and slavery in the most radical
form of any Patriot of the time:

> In the former state, a man is governed by the laws to which he
> has given his consent, either in person or by his representative:
> in the latter, he is governed by the will of another. In the one
> case, his life and property are his own; in the other, they
> depend upon the pleasure of a master . . . The foundation of the
> English constitution rests upon this principle, that no laws have
> any validity or binding force without the consent and approba-
> tion of the people, given in the persons of their representatives,
> periodically elected by themselves.

The difference between freedom and slavery to Hamilton was not
theoretical. Hamilton had done his homework. He had found that in
the first charter of an English colony in America, King James I in
1606 had guaranteed Virginia the right to its own legislature. Every
person who lived within any of the English colonies should have the
same liberties as if residing in England. The claim of Parliament to
govern American colonists, therefore, by arbitrary laws was "unconstitutional, unjust and tyrannical."[23]

Hamilton's twin pamphlets, totaling some sixty thousand words, laid out a comprehensive colony-by-colony, grievance-by-grievance brief in defense of the Continental Congress and against Parliament. He wrote each pamphlet in about two weeks following five or six weeks of careful research.

IN FEBRUARY 1775, when the Loyalist-dominated New York Assembly refused to choose delegates to the Second Continental Congress, the colony's legal government collapsed. A newly formed revolutionary Committee of Sixty assumed power and called for a mass meeting at the Exchange Coffee House, at Broad and Water Streets, to select its own congressional delegates. Hamilton was no doubt in the crowd as his friend Mulligan, a member of this committee, led the Sons of Liberty, "trumpets blowing, fifes playing, drums beating and colors flying," to the latest Liberty Pole, an eighty-foot ship's mast a team of oxen had dragged to City Hall Park from the East River waterfront, then on to the exchange. There, hundreds of citizens loudly shouted their "ayes" to resolutions that endorsed the Committee of Sixty's proposal: citizens from every county should vote in a special election for representatives to a provincial convention that would convene at the exchange in mid-April. The Revolutionary New York Provincial Convention first met on April 20, 1775, and selected a delegation to the Second Continental Congress. The old New York Assembly adjourned and never met again.[24]

Putting teeth in the Committee of Sixty's powers of enforcing the trade boycott imposed by Congress, the Sons of Liberty began a systematic purge of Loyalists opposed to a provincial convention and sympathetic to England. On April 15, 1775, New York's radical leaders called another mass meeting at the Liberty Pole in City Hall Park, then, four hundred strong, marched to the home of Ralph Thurman, a merchant who, ignoring the colonists' boycott of English goods, was shipping military goods to the British in Boston. They attempted to tar and feather him, but he fled.

Three days after the Revolutionary Provincial Convention met for the first time on April 20, a weary rider, Israel Bissell, whipped his panting horse down the Great Post Road into Manhattan and handed Alexander McDougall a countersigned letter from Massachusetts.

Fighting had broken out in Lexington. The Revolutionary War had begun. The fighting outside Boston prompted Alexander Hamilton to transform his literary discussion club at King's College into a militia company. With his friends Robert Troup and Nicholas Fish, he enlisted under a retired British officer, Major Edward Flemming, former adjutant of a British regiment. "Immediately after the Battle of Lexington," Fish recalled, "[Hamilton] attached himself to one of the uniform companies of militia then forming . . . He devoted much time and zeal." Troup remembered that Flemming, who had married into the prominent DePeyster family, was "an excellent disciplinarian" who became "ardently attached to the American cause." He formed "a volunteer company consisting of young gentlemen in New York" and taught them "the manual exercise." They drilled every morning in the churchyard of St. George's Chapel, on the northwest corner of Beekman and Cliff Streets, in snappy short green coats. They wore leather caps with the inscription "Freedom or Death" on the front and a cockade on one side. They described themselves as "The Corsicans," referring to a recent failed revolution on the Mediterranean island. All over Manhattan, volunteer companies were drilling.

Noting that several companies were well armed, Lieutenant Governor Cadwallader Colden wrote to Lord Dartmouth in London, "The spirit of arming and military parade runs high in the city." Hamilton, recalled Troup, "was in constant attendance and very ambitious of improvement. He became exceedingly expert in the [military] exercise." With less time now for pamphleteering, Hamilton also took a keen new interest in mathematics. His math tutor, Robert Harpur, taught him gunnery.[25]

But Hamilton's time for drilling was brief. On April 16, 1775, the Sons of Liberty, rallying at the Liberty Pole, followed Isaac Sears, John Lamb, and Marinus Willett downtown to the East River docks and forced their way aboard two British munitions ships. Next raiding City Hall arsenal, they took away six hundred muskets plus bayonets and cartridge boxes. Little more than a week later, on April 24, a crowd of eight thousand—virtually everyone who had not already fled—jammed City Hall Park. Hamilton was almost certainly in the crowd at the elbow of his mentor Mulligan, a member of this new radical ruling body. This latest committee now crossed the line from resistance to revolution. It voted to form a new Provincial Congress to control the colony. It then voted to turn over the city to a Revolutionary Committee of One Hundred that would move quickly to defend the city against the expected British attack. Isaac Sears, a former privateersman, led 360 armed Sons of Liberty as they seized the keys to the Customs House and declared the port of New York closed. For the next few weeks, radical Sears and his coalition of sailors and waterfront shopkeepers were the only effective government in New York. Sears reigned from his house on Queen Street and kept order in the city on his own terms with the help of his Sons of Liberty, taking over the town watch, patrolling the streets all night.

New York's deposed British officials felt powerless to do anything but grumble. Former Attorney General William Smith, Jr., confided to his diary on April 29:

It is impossible fully to describe the agitated state of the town. At all corners, people inquisitive for news, tales of all kinds invented, believed, denied, discredited, the taverns filled. Little business done in the day. The merchants are amazed and yet so humbled as only to sigh or complain in whispers. They now dread Sears' train of armed men.[26]

Another Loyalist called it a "total revolution." New York City was ruled by "a parcel of the meanest people, children and Negroes." With no police or troops at his command, Lieutenant Governor Colden retreated to his country house in Flatbush. He wrote to London that "Congresses and committees are now established in this province and are acting with all the confidence and authority of a legal government."[27]

While Loyalists clung to hope of relief from England, they thronged the road and ferries out of Manhattan, taking their families and valuables to country houses outside the city. In April 1775, more than twenty-two thousand residents had crowded Manhattan. Only five thousand remained one year later.

* * *

LATE AT night on May 10, 1775, Alexander Hamilton was dozing in his room on the ground floor of King's College, a great gray building on the bluff over the Hudson, when he became aware of a growing roar. As he shook off sleep, he could make out shouting. Jamming his feet into his shoes, he pulled on his green militia jacket and grabbed his hat. By now, his roommate, Robert Troup, was awake, too. Together they peered out of their window toward the torches and the yelling. It was all too evident to Hamilton what had awakened them: there were distinct voices now yelling for "that damned Tory"—the Reverend Myles Cooper, president of King's College.

Shouting to another student to run and wake President Cooper and get him out a back way, Hamilton and Troup dashed out the front door. By now, some of the Liberty Boys had scaled the iron fence. They began rocking it until it collapsed. Surging toward the front doors, a crowd of about four hundred halted abruptly. A thin young man was yelling at them and trying to block their path. He was familiar-looking to many who had heard his recent speech at City Hall. A few could make out the motto on his uniform hat: "Freedom or Death." This was obviously a fellow Patriot.

President Cooper had already fled the college once before. Within a week of the Battle of Lexington, a very menacing open letter had appeared in New York's coffeehouses and taverns, distributed by the Sons of Liberty. Dated "Philadelphia, April 25th, 1775," it was addressed to five leading citizens of New York, including Lieutenant Governor Colden, Speaker of the Assembly Stephen Delancey—and Reverend Cooper. Signed "Three Millions," it laid at the door of these leading British sympathizers England's warlike preparations, especially blaming them for giving assurances to British officials that New York would remain loyal to the Crown and defect from Continental ranks. It also blamed them "for all the calamities of towns in flames, a desolated country, butchered fathers and weeping widows and children" in Massachusetts. Cooper had been shaken when he read:

Executions of villains in effigy will now no longer gratify their resentment. The blood of your unfortunate British and American fellow-subjects, who have already fallen in Massachusetts Bay, calls to Heaven for vengeance against you. The injury you have done to your country cannot admit of a reparation. Fly for your lives or anticipate your doom by becoming your own executioners.[28]

Cooper had taken refuge for several days aboard the British frigate HMS *Kingfisher* in New York harbor until, he believed, tempers had cooled, then returned to his teaching duties.

But now, on the night of May 10, 1775, a crowd had gathered at the King's Arms and heard, Lieutenant Governor Colden reported to London, that Cooper was the Loyalists' most effective apologist:

The odium excited against [Dr. Cooper] is for his warm attachment to Government and his being a supposed author of almost every piece that was published on that side of the question.

Or, as Hercules Mulligan later wrote, "Dr. Cooper was a Tory and an obnoxious man and the mob went to the college with the intention of tarring and feathering him or riding him upon a rail." Troup said later that Hamilton feared worse than that would happen if the mob got their hands on the college president: "If Dr. Cooper should be taken hold of by the mob his life would be endangered, as he was a most obnoxious Tory."

As the crowd clambered over the fence and pushed up close to Hamilton, Troup, who said later he stayed by Hamilton's side, was struck by Hamilton's courage and his eloquence:

When the mob approached the college, Hamilton took his stand on one of the stoops and proceeded with great animation to harangue [it] on the disgrace it would bring on the cause of liberty, of which they avowed themselves to be the champions.

Dr. Cooper did not help matters when, aroused by one of Hamilton's young friends, he leaned out a window. Troup wrote to Timothy Pickering years later that Hamilton "diverted their attention until the affrighted clergyman who, at first imagining [Hamilton] was exciting the mob, exclaimed from an open window, 'Don't listen to him, gentlemen, he is crazy, he is crazy!'" Cooper could not hear what his student was saying. He imagined that Hamilton, whom he knew by now was an ardent Patriot, was inflaming "a murderous band." When someone explained to the clergyman that Hamilton was trying to stop the mob from seizing him, Cooper finally escaped out a back door, climbed over the fence, and guided by "a heaven-directed youth," fled down a path to the Hudson riverbank. Together they picked their way north in the darkness to the house of New York's attorney general. The crowd had finally shoved past Hamilton and Troup and, pushing into the college, battered down the door to Cooper's empty apartment. Lieutenant Governor Colden reported that Cooper had "escaped, only half dressed, over the college fence" and "found shelter in the house of Mr. [Peter] Stuyvesant." Hamilton overtook the rescue party and guided Cooper along the riverbank. They stumbled in the dark to the Stuyvesant country house at present-day First Avenue and Fifteenth Street. The next night, they rowed Cooper out to the HMS *Kingfisher*. A week later, he sailed for England with Hamilton's former tutor, Reverend Chandler. Neither man ever returned to America.[29]

Frustrated in their attempt to seize Cooper, the Sons of Liberty had regrouped and rushed on to the shop of the man they believed was Dr. Cooper's printer, James Rivington, publisher of the *New York Gazetteer*, on Hanover Square. Rivington had tried unsuccessfully in his newspaper to convince the Patriots that he was not the printer of Loyalist tracts. In fact, it was true that he was not Cooper's publisher, but he was Chandler's. He had printed the odious *What Think Ye of Congress Now?* and had printed Loyalist placards, handbills, broadsides, pamphlets, and newspaper essays. But he also had published Alexander Hamilton's pamphlets. His promise in print not to do anything that would offend the Patriots did not save him. As Lieutenant Governor Colden reported to the Colonial Office in London:

Mr. Rivington the printer of one of our newspapers was attacked by the same mob and rescued out of their hands by the resolution of one or two friends. He has since taken refuge on board of the man-of-war [*Kingfisher*] and will not yet venture to return to his house. His crime is only the liberty of the press.

Rivington returned, only to be mobbed again six months later. This time, in November 1775, eighty armed Sons of Liberty, recruited by now-Captain Sears in Connecticut, rode from New Haven into New York to round up Loyalists including Reverend Seabury, Hamilton's principal antagonist in the pamphlet wars, in Westchester County. Joined by eighty New York members of the Sons, they sent their Westchester prisoners back to New Haven, then rode on to Manhattan. They arrived at noon on November 23. With bayonets fixed, they "drew up in close order before the printing office of the infamous James Rivington," the *New England Chronicle* reported, while a contingent smashed Rivington's presses and strewed his type through the streets as they rode off. According to Hercules Mulligan, who, as a prominent member of the city's Sons of Liberty, doubtless was on hand, Hamilton again tried to talk a mob out of its mischief. The Sons "then marched out of town to the tune of 'Yankee Doodle.'" A crowd of New Yorkers cheered the column as it crossed the Coffee House Bridge.[30]

RAIDS ON the houses and businesses of suspected Loyalists by the Sons of Liberty now became more frequent. "Last Tuesday," the *New York Journal* reported on December 28, 1775,

about four hundred of the militia of [Kings] county assembled and proceeded in good order and regularity in quest of Tories, a considerable number of whom had entered into a combination and agreement not to comply with any Congress measures. About forty, we hear, are taken, most of whom have recanted, signed the Association and professed themselves true sons of liberty, being fully convinced of their error. Two or three who remain incorrigible are to be sent to Congress to be dealt with.[31]

Just how the Sons of Liberty could deal with incorrigible Loyalists appeared in the first issue of the *Journal* for 1776. Thomas Randolph, a cooper,

> had publicly proved himself an enemy to his country by revil-
> ing and using his utmost endeavors to oppose the proceedings
> of the Continental and Provincial Conventions and committees
> in defense of their rights and liberties.

Randolph's sentence was tarring and feathering.

The ritual of tarring and feathering by now was familiar to every good Son of Liberty. A fresh barrel of pine tar had been broken open and heated in an iron cauldron until it was bubbling hot and thin enough to spread with brushes. The Sons then applied it to the writhing, squirming Randolph's head, face, body, arms, legs, groin, and feet until they had liberally covered all of his skin, which began to burn and blister and crack, giving off a rancid-smelling steam into the cool air. Randolph screamed and prayed and pleaded for mercy. The Sons had ransacked his house for incriminating papers and had dragged out his down-filled mattress, which they now slit open with their knives. Dancing and cheering at Randolph's grotesque form, they sprinkled soft feathers over his roasting stinking flesh. If, as usual, a few of the feathers were ignited by the sizzling tar, the flames could be beaten out readily enough, even though, by this time, the slightest touch made Randolph scream in agony. So that every Loyalist could witness his humiliation and every good Patriot hear him recant, Ran-dolph was "carried in a wagon publicly 'round the town," the *Journal* reported. "He soon became duly sensible of his offense, for which he earnestly begged pardon and promised to atone as far as he was able." After half an hour of this, the Sons released Randolph "and suffered him to return to his house." The patriotic *Journal* pointed out that "the whole was conducted with that regularity and decorum that ought to be observed in all public punishments."[32]

As a boy in the West Indies, Hamilton had witnessed rough jus-tice over recalcitrant slaves. He never became callous to such brutality and had instead become horrified by the spectacle of even the most controlled mob action. The memory of a slave insurrection in which his father was seriously wounded combined with the years of watching torchlight militia drills to fill him with abhorrence when he saw the Sons of Liberty, augmented by resentful sailors rendered unemployed by the anti-British boycott, surging through the streets of Manhattan at night after their latest Loyalist quarry. Three days after Isaac Sears's raid on Rivington's press in New York City, Hamilton wrote to John Jay, now a New York delegate to the Second Continental Congress, to object to this "evil":

I cannot help disapproving and condemning this step. In times of such commotion as the present, while the passions of men are worked up to an uncommon pitch, there is a great danger of fatal extremes. The same state of the passions which fits the multitude, who have not a sufficient stock of reason and knowledge to guide them, for opposition to tyranny and oppression, very naturally leads them to a contempt and disregard of all authority. The due medium is hardly to be found among the more intelligent; it is almost impossible among the unthinking populace.

Hamilton knew Jay from the Liberty Hall circle, and he knew his reputation for prudence. He was sure Jay would agree with him that when people's minds were becoming "loosened from their attachment to ancient establishments," they would "grow giddy" and could "run into anarchy." From reading and experience, Hamilton believed it was up to men "of public affairs" to "keep men steady and within proper bounds." Hamilton averred that he was "always more or less alarmed at everything which is done, of mere will and pleasure, without any proper authority." The "irregularities" of mob action were "dangerous and ought to be checked." The Sons of Liberty had to be reined in because they would cherish a spirit of disorder at a season when men are too prone to it of themselves."

Hamilton feared that raids by New England Patriots into New York would only revive "ancient animosities" that already made New Yorkers reluctant to join Massachusetts radicals against the British.

Worse, it would send a message to the English that New Yorkers were not part of the "American cause." Hamilton did not doubt that some means had to be found to "owerave" the Loyalists. Instead of mobs and raiders, he suggested that militia be sent into New York from Philadelphia or New Jersey—anywhere but New England—to keep order and support the Revolution.[33]

HAMILTON'S LETTER to Jay was his first attempt to make his voice heard by Congress. Already, many members had read his anonymous writings: now there would be a name with his voice. Hamilton's strong letter brought an equally strong rebuke to the Sons of Liberty from Jay, writing in Congress at Philadelphia on December 4, 1775, to Sons of Liberty leader McDougall. The son of a Scots milkman, McDougall had become rich as a privateer. His two ships had raided French commerce for years as he built up a mercantile house in Manhattan that, among other things, sold the loot his crews plundered. He had become "the first martyr of the Patriot cause" for his libelous writings against the British government after the Stamp Act crisis and had presided over the July 1774 meeting in the "Fields." It was he who had primed Hamilton's lethal pen with books and pamphlets from his library. To McDougall, Jay was blunt, even sarcastic:

> The valorous expedition against Rivington gives me pain: I feel for the honor of the colony and most sincerely hope [the Sons of Liberty] will upon this occasion act a part that may do some little credit to their spirit as well as prudence.[34]

In a postscript, the congressman asked McDougall to "be so kind as to give the enclosed to young Hamilton." That letter has been lost but it is obvious from Hamilton's answer to Jay on the last day of 1775 that the congressional delegate had asked Hamilton to become his regular correspondent, keeping him informed on events in New York. Hamilton was thrilled and flattered. It comes across in his tone: "I shall be at all times ready to comply with your request of information concerning the state of the province or any matters of importance that may arise." He "embraced" the opportunity to do "anything that may conduce to the public service." He had found a new patron in the ten-years-older Congressman Jay, and he pledged earnestly to do whatever "may serve as a testimony of my respect to you." And then he plunged into his next analysis of New York politics: the Loyalists were contemplating "stealing a march on us" by calling a new assembly. If the Patriots were too distracted by their "new institutions, Congresses, committees," the Loyalists would have an opportunity to "elect their own creatures." This would cause "divisions and ferments injurious to present measures." Hamilton warned his new mentor that the Loyalists were "very artful and intriguing":

It behooves us to be very vigilant and cautious. I have thrown out a handbill or two to give the necessary alarm and shall second them with others.

Yet Hamilton was confident that the Patriots had "a large majority of the people" behind them. But, he boldly added, Jay needed to come home at once to organize support for Congress:

If you approve the hint, I should wish for your presence here. Absence, you know, is not very favorable to the influence of any person, however great.

Hamilton's stock was high among Loyalists at King's College and among merchants, including his old mentors, the Crugers, after his courageous protection of Reverend Cooper. He was in an excellent position to gather and feed intelligence to Jay to pass along to Congress. He was quite correct in his assessment of Loyalist motives and intentions. Loyalist opposition to the new Provincial Congress was well organized and vigorous. Some Loyalists thought the moment had come to restore the old assembly to power. On January 2, 1776, only two days after Hamilton's reply to Jay, the royal governor dissolved the old assembly and signed writs calling for a new royal assembly election. A new assembly met on February 14 but accomplished nothing because the majority of members elected to it were also members of the Provincial Congress.

At the same time, New York's Patriots carried out the plan Hamilton had suggested to Jay, electing four men suggested by Hamilton, including Jay, as delegates to the new Continental Congress. Meanwhile, Hamilton directed a steady stream of information to Jay in Philadelphia, sending him the latest newspapers and his comments on them. A few chin whiskers short of twenty-one, Alexander Hamilton was already a valuable adviser to Congress. He apparently was the first to tip off Jay that the royal governor was trying to revive the old assembly. He repeated his warning that the Loyalists "give out that there will be no opposition" to the Provincial Congress "but I suspect this is an artifice to throw the people off their guard." Hamilton was clearly worried that the radical leaders of the Sons of Liberty on the scene were no match for the experienced Loyalists and royal government officials. "I should be glad to see you here with all convenient dispatch."[35]

In June 1775, the Continental Congress in Philadelphia chose Colonel George Washington, a delegate from Virginia, as commander-in-chief of a Continental army surrounding British-occupied Boston. Hurrying north, Washington spent only one day in New York City. There, on Sunday, June 25, 1775, Alexander Hamilton saw him for the first time. Hamilton and his Corsicans joined eight other companies of militia at the foot of Wall Street at four in the afternoon. The thrilled young officer braced at attention for Washington to inspect his troops before the general and his entourage hurried north. The British had fought a bloody battle with patriots at Bunker Hill. Washington gave orders to fortify Kingsbridge on the Hudson River, erecting artillery batteries on either bank of the Hudson with the aid of three thousand recruits.

IT WAS only two months later that Alexander Hamilton experienced his first action under fire. By then, freed from his studies by the summer break, he was immersed in the preparations for war. Alexander McDougall personally raised the First New York Regiment, composed chiefly of workingmen, the first of five regiments authorized by Washington. Militiamen like Hamilton were soon drilling daily in the fields and patrolling the streets at night while laborers threw up barricades and breastworks and dug trenches. The fear of anarchy among moderate Revolutionaries intensified when the last hundred British troops in the Fort George garrison withdrew from the city, going aboard the sixty-four-gun man-of-war *Asia*. As this remnant of the Royal Irish Regiment marched down Broad Street, the Sons of Liberty intercepted them. Their leader, Marinus Willett, insisted that the soldiers had received permission from the city's radical Committee of One Hundred to leave, but with only a musket apiece. The Sons commandeered a wagon train loaded with muskets, ammunition, and the regiment's personal baggage. Next, the Sons of Liberty raided the royal munitions storehouse at Turtle Bay, defying orders from the Provincial Congress. In July, a crowd burned a supply barge from the *Asia*.

At eleven o'clock on the night of August 23, Captain John Lamb gave the orders for his artillery company, supported by Captain Flemming's Corsicans and Colonel John Lasher's light infantry, to seize the two dozen cannon that lined the Grand Battery beneath Fort George. The *Asia*'s captain had been informed by Loyalists that the Patriots would raid the fort that night: he posted a patrol boat with redcoats aboard, who spotted Hamilton, Hercules Mulligan, and their comrades shortly after midnight as they tugged on ropes they had attached to the heavy guns. The redcoats opened a brisk musket fire from the barge. Hamilton and the militiamen returned the fire: they killed one redcoat. At this, the *Asia*, anchored at the mouth of the Hudson, hoisted sail and began working in close to shore, firing a tattoo of single cannon. Hercules Mulligan long remembered the scene that night when, under fire, he struggled to pull away a cannon from British muskets and the *Asia*'s guns:

I was engaged in hauling off one of the cannons, when Mister Hamilton came up and gave me his musket to hold and he took hold of the rope . . . Hamilton [got] away with the cannon. I left his musket in the Battery and retreated. As he was returning, I met him and he asked for his piece. I told him where I had left it and he went for it, notwithstanding the firing continued, with as much concern as if the [British] vessel had not been there.[36]

One reason Mulligan remembered the incident three decades later may have been that he was far larger and far more powerful than Hamilton. That night, Hamilton conspicuously distinguished himself for his reckless bravery under fire. His display of raw courage helped to inspirit the men around him: they got away with twenty-one of the Battery's twenty-four guns, dragged them uptown to City Hall Park, and drew them up around the Liberty Pole, where Hamilton's unit jealously guarded them. As Hamilton and his comrades hauled away the guns, the man-of-war *Asia* fired a thirty-two-gun broadside of solid shot into the sleeping town: one cannonball pierced the roof of Fraunces Tavern at Broad and Pearl Street, a mile from the waterfront.

Hamilton's role as political analyst under the guise of college student ended on January 6, 1776; the New York Provincial Congress ordered that an artillery company be raised to defend the colony. Hamilton leaped at the opportunity. He applied for the command.

Working behind the scenes to advance his candidacy, Hamilton seemed unfazed by the fact that virtually all other commissions were going to native New Yorkers of wealth and social position. Here was a bastard, a newcomer who had arrived as an orphaned immigrant little more than three years earlier. But he was a nova whose writing, speaking, and fighting talents had dazzled more timid men with better claims on command. Winning the support of John Jay, Alexander McDougall, and William Livingston, in the next two months he waged his first political campaign. His mathematics teacher at King's could vouch for his mastery of the necessary trigonometry, and Captain Stephen Bedlam, a skilled artillerist, furnished a certificate that "he has examined Alexander Hamilton and judges him qualified." On March 14, 1776, the Provincial Congress ordered him "appointed Captain of the Provincial Company of Artillery of this colony." He took his last quarter's scholarship money from his St. Croix sponsors to have his friend Mulligan's tailor shop make him a blue coat with buff cuffs and facings and the best white buckskin breeches. He would not need the money to finish college. He never did. He had no more time to be a schoolboy.[37]

SEVEN

"Men Go to Those Who Pay Them"

While Alexander Hamilton awaited approval of his artillery captain's commission from the New York Provincial Congress, Elias Boudinot wrote from Elizabethtown to dangle a post as brigade major in the newly formed New Jersey Militia. Hamilton would probably be the youngest major in the Revolutionary armies. Boudinot, now a leader of New Jersey's Provincial Congress, out of his own pocket was buying up gunpowder and shipping it to General Washington in Massachusetts. Chafing at the New York Congress's slow pace in commissioning him, Hamilton mulled Boudinot's offer of serving as aide-de-camp to Lord Stirling, commander of New Jersey's troops. He knew Stirling well: Stirling was brother-in-law to William Livingston and a member of the Board of Governors of King's College. Appointed by Washington to take command of defending New York City, Stirling was trying to fortify Manhattan Island.

Hamilton had first met Stirling at his New Jersey estate during vacations from Elizabethtown Academy. He admired the wealthy, handsome Scotsman, whose claim as sixth earl of Stirling had been disallowed by the English House of Lords, a particularly touchy point for Hamilton, illegitimate son of a Scottish laird.

About this time, Nathanael Greene, a logistical genius who was leading his brigades south from Massachusetts to defend Long Island, also invited Hamilton to become aide-de-camp. In either case, Hamilton believed, he would serve fine military commanders, but he himself would not be able to lead troops into combat. Making his first military decision, he declined both offers of promotion to remain in command of his own contingent of troops, a choice more significant to his future than he could imagine. Had he joined either general's staff, he might never have distinguished himself in battle. His restraint now was to catapult him a few months later to prominence in the Revolution.

Instead, Hamilton set about recruiting the thirty men required for his company. The very first afternoon, Hercules Mulligan, who helped him, later remembered, "We engaged 25 men." The persuasive pair signed up lieutenants, sergeants, corporals, bombardiers, and gunners, but couldn't get beyond that number because, as Hamilton complained in writing to the Provincial Congress, he could not match the pay offered by Continental Army recruiters. On April 2, 1776, two weeks after Hamilton's commission finally arrived, the Provincial Congress ordered Hamilton and his fledgling artillery company to relieve Alexander McDougall's First New York Regiment. They were to guard the colony's official records, which were being shipped by wagon from New York's City Hall to the abandoned Greenwich Village estate of Loyalist William Bayard to keep them out of reach of counterattacking British forces.[1]

The New York Congress chose Hamilton's provincial company because it cost less than paying Continental troops for guard duty. Hamilton took this as a springboard for campaigning for higher pay for his militia men. By late May 1776, only ten weeks after becoming an officer, Hamilton was boldly addressing his first long letter to the Provincial Congress, in session in New York's City Hall. He argued the "considerable importance to the future progress" of recruiting of granting parity in pay for his company. He impatiently urged a "speedy" reply from Congress. Citing the pay rates spelled out in the Continental Congress's own journal, he contrasted them rank by rank to his own payroll:

> You will discover a considerable difference. My own pay will remain the same as it is now, but I make this application on behalf of the company, as I am fully convinced such a disad-vantageous distinction will have a very pernicious effect on the minds and behavior of the men. They do the same duty with the other companies and think themselves entitled to the same pay.

His men did not accept the argument that they were being used only on the defensive. They would "willingly leave the colony and take the offensive." Captain Sebastian Bauman of the Continental artillery was offering Hamilton's men higher pay, and "men will naturally go to those who pay them best." While he was at it, Hamilton wanted to be able to offer expense accounts to recruiters to fan out over the countryside and sign up more men. Evidently, the supply of unem-ployed sailors willing to use their gunners' skills in New York's artillery was about exhausted. One further request: he wanted to be able to buy his men loose-fitting frocks for summer fatigue duty as they dug trenches and built gun emplacements. He argued that this would spare their heavy uniforms harder wear, making them last "much longer." The day the Provincial Congress received Captain Hamilton's hardheaded, practical missive, it capitulated to all his requests. His first siege had been a complete success. Inside three weeks, the indefatigable young officer's company strength was up to sixty-nine better-paid men, more than double the requirement.[2]

Two months later, he was back again. This time, he demanded better rations for his men. He had taken matters into his own hands, ordering far more food from his commissary, Cornelius Roosevelt, than the Provincial Congress allowed. This time, Congress papered over Hamilton's complaint that his men were allotted less money for food than Continental or other provinces' militias by lending his company to General John Morin Scott's Continental brigade, acceding to Hamilton's demands without parting with New York funds. By hectoring New York Revolutionary leaders, overnight young Hamilton in effect became a captain in the Continental artillery.

But Hamilton's most important crusade as a newly minted officer was to have far more lasting effects. It was Hamilton who broke with the age-old tradition of appointing only gentlemen as officers and never promoting them from the ranks of enlisted men. When one of his lieutenants was promoted to captain of one of Benedict Arnold's row galleys on Lake Champlain, it opened up a slot for a lieutenant. Only five weeks after the new nation was born on the Fourth of July, 1776, Hamilton, in an August 12, 1776, letter to the convention of the newly proclaimed State of New York, raised the question of democratically rewarding the exemplary service of an enlisted man with promotion to an officer's rank:

> I would beg the liberty warmly to recommend to your attention Thomas Thompson, now first sergeant in my company, a man highly deserving of notice and preferment. He has discharged his duty in his present station with uncommon fidelity, assiduity and expertness. He is a very good disciplinarian, possesses the advantage of having seen a good deal of service in Germany [during the Seven Years' War], has a tolerable share of common sense and is well calculated not to disgrace the rank of an officer and gentleman . . . His advancement will be a great encouragement and benefit to my company . . . and will be an animating example to all men of merit . . . [3]

The New York Convention sent Colonel Peter R. Livingston to meet with Hamilton and study his proposal. On August 15, the convention promoted Thompson to lieutenant, establishing a precedent for American armed forces that broke with European custom. Perhaps it should be noted that Hamilton's stroke of genius at making the infant American army democratic was repaid symbolically on the two hundredth anniversary of his birth, when his artillery company, the oldest unit in the United States Army, fired its guns in salute to their founding father.

Hamilton took Revolution as a carte blanche opportunity for change. He reexamined the very nature of a company of soldiers, and he went on establishing precedents in his year and a half as an artillery officer. When a cannon exploded and one of his matrosses, William Douglass, lost his right arm, Hamilton again wrote to the New York Convention. This time, he urged that the state pay the man a disability pension just as the Continental Congress paid "for all persons disabled in the service of the United States." He insisted that, in all matters, the individual states' soldiers and sailors had the same rights as Continental troops, and when some of his men deserted to a Continental warship where they could receive a share of any loot captured at sea, he obtained the convention's permission for a state officer—himself—to lead a boarding party onto the Continental ship, search it, and haul back the miscreants for flogging.[4]

At the outset of a revolution, Hamilton repeatedly showed his innovative genius in analyzing a need and ignoring his own status in pushing for reform. Illegitimate, an immigrant of an unknown family, he audaciously dismissed birth and social status as requisites for winning a revolutionary war. To many other Revolutionaries, his suggestions seemed not only reasonable but vital. America had many men and few officers. Everything he urged helped the common cause. As he ignored rank and privilege, he quickly made himself known to Revolutionary leaders and became an inspiration for the enlisted men.

To fill out his company, he took men who knew nothing about artillery. With the help of a few skilled gunners, he taught them everything he could about artillery, including what each piece was and how it was supposed to work. Hamilton could expect no new weapons since the English had banned the manufacture of iron in the colonies. Guns had to be stripped from ships at anchor in the harbor or seized from British forts. Among the pickup lot of guns left over from England's and France's past colonial wars, Hamilton could find two basic kinds: guns with relatively long barrels fired solid shot, usually of three, six, nine, or the rarely found eighteen pounds, and mortars with short barrels threw shells at high elevations. Fieldpieces were mounted on wheeled carriages drawn by horses; heavier siege guns usually were mounted on fixed gun emplacements but sometimes could be maneuvered on the battlefield on carriages. There were mortars of various sizes that were used especially for sieges of fortified positions. Usually aimed at a fixed elevation of forty-five degrees, they could be adjusted by wedges, called quoins, placed under the barrel. Cannon were typically made of cast iron, but superior guns were made of stronger bronze. Mortars were always bronze. Small mortars were called cohorns, a corruption of the name of the Dutch military engineer Baron Menno van Caehoorn, who introduced them. Somewhere between guns and mortars and with barrels of intermediate length were the howitzers, which, like mortars, fired shells at a high angle.

Neophyte artilleryman Hamilton had to learn about the three types of ammunition. Solid cast-iron shot—cannonballs—weighed from three to forty-two pounds. Fieldpieces were generally three- or six-pounders, siege guns eighteen- to twenty-four pounders. Light cannonballs fired from fieldpieces usually were aimed at enemy soldiers, the heavier projectiles at fixed defenses. Guns, especially fieldpieces, also fired scatter ammunition, either grapeshot, a cluster of grape-size small shot packed into a cloth bag, or canister shot, made up of mixed small shot and nails and bolts enclosed in a can, used especially to shred sails. Scatter shot was used as a particularly vicious deterrent of infantry or cavalry charges.

Shells or bombs were explosive and were made of hollow cast iron filled with gunpowder through a small hole in which the fuse, a small hollow wooden plug several inches long, was inserted. A fine priming powder was tamped into the fuse, which was wider at one end in the shape of a cup, which, in turn, was filled with a fine powder dampened with alcohol. The wooden fuse was trimmed to determine the timing of the explosion: it projected from the shell by a quarter inch. To ignite the fuse, the bombardier touched it with a "slow match" made of strands of cotton rope soaked in chemicals: it burned at the rate of four inches an hour.

During the American Revolution, the range of a cannon was only about a mile, the accurate range even less. Mortars had a greater effective range than guns with solid shot: they were aimed by varying the powder charge. Most cannon had such short ranges because the black powder was so weak, made up of six parts saltpeter (potassium nitrate) to one part of charcoal and sulfur. When this noxious concoction burned, it freed three hundred times its volume in smoky gases, quickly enveloping a battlefield in a choking dark fog. But in the smog of war, the artilleryman was a particular target. Alexander Hamilton had chosen the state-of-the-art weaponry but probably the most exposed and dangerous duty.

HAMILTON DID not have to wait long to go to war. The war came to him. In his first flying visit to New York City in June 1775, General Washington had ordered an offensive against Quebec province under the command of Major General Philip Schuyler. In an attempt to bring Canada into the United States by conquest, in September 1775, an army of New York and New England troops had invaded Quebec province. But the aging Schuyler was ill. His successor, Richard Montgomery, captured Montreal in November. An in-law of William Livingston and a veteran British officer, Montgomery joined forces with Benedict Arnold, who had led 1,060 men through the woods of Maine, for a winter assault on the walled city of Quebec. Montgomery was killed by cannon fire at point-blank range in the opening assault on the Canadian capital. Of fourteen New York officers with Montgomery as he charged the blockhouse the last day of 1775, only one, Montgomery's aide-de-camp Captain Aaron Burr, survived. McDougall's First New York Regiment, which Hamilton had freed from garrison duty for the Canadian campaign, suffered heavy casualties. One of McDougall's sons was killed, the other taken prisoner; both were friends of Hamilton. John Lamb's artillerymen and their cannon had bogged down in snowdrifts. New York's few remaining artillery officers became precious commodities. Captain Alexander Hamilton drilled his new artillery company in New York City even longer and harder each day.

The first of 479 British warships—52 men-of-war and 427 troop transports—sailed into New York harbor and began to disgorge thirty-nine thousand troops—the largest expeditionary force in English history—onto Staten Island on July 4. Through his telescope atop Bayard's Hill, Captain Hamilton watched the forest of ship masts growing ominously to the east. On July 9, 1776, five days after its adoption in Philadelphia, the Declaration of Independence arrived in New York City. At six o'clock that evening, Captain Hamilton and his Corsicans stood to attention on the commons to hear it read aloud from the balcony of City Hall. Then the soldiers roared off down Broadway to the Bowling Green where a crowd had pulled down and smashed to bits the only equestrian statue of King George III in America. Later that afternoon, a cavalcade of horse-drawn carts began to haul the four thousand pounds of shattered lead fragments off to Ridgefield in the Berkshire hills of Connecticut, where scores of women melted them down to mold 42,088 lead bullets. The head of the statue they mounted on a stake at Blue Bell Tavern at present-day Broadway and 181st Street, at the northern approach to the city. There was no more time to celebrate.

It took nearly six weeks before Washington began to move the major portion of his army south from Boston to respond to the British landings. He detached his second-in-command, Major General Charles Lee, who let everyone know he thought the situation hopeless. Lee, a former British lieutenant colonel, had served in the French and Indian Wars and in Poland against the Turks. To counter the expected British landings, Lee was supposed to erect forts at strategic points across Manhattan island and at Brooklyn Heights on Long Island. Lee believed that, while the American army could not hold New York City, it could slow down a British invasion that "might cost the enemy many thousands of men to get possession of it."[5]

When Washington arrived on April 13, he found that Lee had done little before Congress ordered him to South Carolina. Washington pressed servants, slaves, and every able-bodied man into building fortifications. Fourteen new batteries with a total of 120 cannon took shape on Manhattan, Governors Island, Red Hook, and Paulus Hook on the New Jersey shore. By midsummer, ten thousand American troops transformed New York City into an armed camp.

Two huge bivouacs took shape, crammed with tents, shacks, wagons, and mounds of supplies. At one of them, on present-day Canal Street in Greenwich Village, just outside town along the Post Road, Hamilton and his company dug in. Atop Bayard's Hill, he built heptagonal Fort Bunker Hill at the intersection of present-day Canal and Mulberry Streets, the highest ground overlooking the city. Hamilton ordered his men to rip apart fences and cut down the stately trees for which the city was famous to build barricades and provide wood for cook fires. All over Manhattan island, other American officers were commandeering homes, warehouses, and loft buildings belonging to Loyalists. King's College became an army hospital. Its library books, so long the grist for Hamilton's literary labors, were hauled away in carts. They turned up nearly a century later in a nearby church basement. In the country houses of Loyalists, soldiers propped their muddy boots on damask furniture, ripped up parquet floors to fuel the fireplaces, tossed their garbage out windows, and turned their horses loose to graze in the gardens and orchards. One Loyalist watched in horror as army woodcutters, ignoring his protests, chopped down his peach and apple orchards on Twenty-third Street. Despite a curfew, drunken soldiers caroused and prostitutes thrived in the brothel-lined streets around Trinity Church.

At five o'clock every morning Hamilton and his men reported for duty to draw their tools and receive instructions for the day's digging. They labored in summer heat and humidity until sunset, stopping only long enough for drills and inspections. Hamilton's men signed the pay book with English names, some Irish and Scottish, a few Dutch. Many of the rank and file were illiterate, making their marks as they drew their pay. Hamilton had been assigned to construct the commanding redoubt in a line of earthworks that reached halfway across Manhattan island. His friend Nicholas Fish described Fort Bunker Hill as "a fortification superior in strength to any my imagination could ever have conceived." When Washington inspected the works with its eight nine-pounders, four three-pounders, and six cohorn mortars in mid-April, he commended Hamilton and his fatigue parties "for their masterly manner of executing the work."[6]

One of Washington's soldiers wrote in his diary that it seemed "all London was afloat." On July 12, Hamilton's battery went into action the first time. The British commander, Lord Richard Howe, probed the American shore defenses by detaching two vessels, the forty-four-gun *Phoenix* and the twenty-eight-gun *Rose*, from his forest of ships to sail up into the Hudson. The captain of the *Rose* coolly sipped claret on his quarterdeck as the two vessels glided past the Battery at Fort George—where an ill-trained American gun crew immediately blew itself up. The two British ships sailed unmolested up the Hudson to Tarrytown and back as Washington's men abandoned their posts to watch. Appalled, Washington fumed to the New York Provincial Congress, "Such unsoldierly conduct gives the enemy a *mean* opinion of the army." As the two British ships passed within cannon range of Hamilton's company at Fort Bunker Hill, Hamilton ordered his nine-pounders to fire. The British warships returned his fire. In the brief skirmish, one of Hamilton's cannons burst, killing one man and severely wounding another.[7]

On August 8, Hamilton tore open orders from Washington. Washington believed the main British attack would come on Manhattan. Hamilton and his company were to be on round-the-clock alert on Bayard's Hill, Manhattan's northernmost outpost, where Washington believed the British would strike first:

> The movements of the enemy and intelligence by deserters give the utmost reason to believe that the great struggle in which we are contending for everything dear to us and our posterity, is near at hand.

Hamilton was to give the alarm at the approach of British transports to the Manhattan shore: "A flag in the daytime, or a light at night . . . with three guns fired quick but distinct [as] a signal for the troops to repair to their posts and prepare for action." Hamilton was to order all the camp's drums to be beaten. The men were to keep enough food ready for two days and their canteens filled.[8]

The long weeks of suspense ended early the morning of August 27, 1776. Hamilton watched, helpless, as everything went wrong. The British ferried fifteen thousand troops over from Staten Island, not to Manhattan island but to Long Island, in a single morning. There was little American resistance as Hessians quick-marched inland from the British beachhead, which stretched all the way from Flatbush to

Gravesend. Israel Putnam, the American commander, had only 2,750 men in four makeshift forts spread too thinly over four miles of Gowanus ridge, which ran like a wooded spine west to east. Each outpost roadblocked a pass. But Lord Cornwallis moved to Flatbush on the American east flank where only a mounted patrol of five young militia officers, including Hamilton's college roommate, Robert Troup, guarded Jamaica Pass. British dragoons easily captured them, enabling ten thousand redcoats to march stealthily at night around behind the Americans. The Americans tried to turn and fight, but the American riflemen had no time to reload before German jaegers were on them. Cut off from retreat by an eighty-yard-wide swamp, twelve hundred Americans died in the rout, many of them drowning.

From his Manhattan hill fort, Alexander Hamilton watched the debacle. According to his friend Hercules Mulligan, Hamilton huddled with Mulligan and the Reverend John Mason over dinner at Bayard's Fort and hastily formulated a plan that led to Washington's miraculous night retreat. By rowboat, barge, sloop, skiff, and canoe in a howling northeaster, a regiment of New England fishermen ferried Washington's surviving ninety-five hundred men across to Manhattan. According to Mulligan, it was he who had crossed to Washington's headquarters during the Battle of Brooklyn and handed a letter proposing the plan of escape to Colonel Samuel Blachley Webb, Washington's chief aide-de-camp. Mulligan stood waiting while Webb read it. He left assured that Webb would take Hamilton's plan to Washington. Whether Mulligan was gilding Hamilton's laurels posthumously, the decisions Washington and his staff made in the next few days left Hamilton and his company in peril. Mulligan never made it back to Bayard's Fort to tell Hamilton whether he had delivered the plan: on his way toward the ferry landing, he was recognized as a member of the Committee of Sixty by a Loyalist and captured by British dragoons.

At a September 12, 1776, council of war, Washington asked his generals whether New York, if the American army evacuated it, ought "to stand as winter quarters for the enemy?" The Continental Congress had resolved that the city be spared but Rhode Islander Nathanael Greene, Washington's second-in-command, argued that "the city and island of New York are no objects to us." He contended that "a general and speedy retreat is absolutely necessary" and insisted that "I would burn the city and suburbs." Most of the property, Greene argued, belonged to Loyalists. The council of war decided to split the army into three divisions and spare the city.[9]

The British attacked again before the Americans could evacuate their guns and supplies. They attacked at Kip's Bay, on the East River between present-day Thirtieth and Thirty-fourth streets, two miles above Hamilton's hill fort. Hamilton's company, along with the rest of Henry Knox's artillery and John Morin Scott's New York infantry brigade, were now cut off and in danger of being captured by the British. Washington sent Putnam with his aide-de-camp, Captain Aaron Burr, to lead their rescue. They reached Fort Bunker Hill on Bayard's Hill just as American militia from lower Manhattan began to stream past Hamilton up the Post Road (now Lexington Avenue). At Kip's Bay, Howe's troops blocked the Post Road, but they had stopped for tea on the east side of a peach orchard. Hamilton had received orders from the chief of Continental artillery General Henry Knox to rally his men for a stand at the hill fort, but Burr, carrying Washington's express order to evacuate the city, countermanded Knox. Burr knew a concealed path that would lead them safely to Bloomingdale Road and on up the west side of the island. As Burr guided Hamilton and his men, clouds of dust from tramping feet and horses' hooves shrouded their escape. Hamilton had to leave behind at the fort virtually everything he owned: books, papers, clothing, everything but the uniform on his back and his horse as he dragged two cannon up Manhattan island.

It was dark before Hamilton's company reached the freshly dug entrenchments of Harlem Heights. Here, according to some historians, Hamilton met Washington for the first time. He impressed Washington as he kept his exhausted troops hard at work throwing up makeshift defenses in the dark. With all his picks and shovels left behind in his escape, Hamilton had his men pull up corn plants with mud-caked roots and stack them to look like ramparts through an enemy's spyglass. According to legend, Washington invited Hamilton to his marquee tent. At best, it was a brief meeting interrupted by aides riding in all directions with fresh orders.

* * *

THE BRITISH celebration after taking New York City was short-lived. As they paused fully four weeks to build defenses across northern Manhattan, someone set fire to New York City. The fire, fanned by high winds, broke out at midnight on September 20 in a frame house along the waterfront near Whitehall Slip. Only a shift in the wind kept the flames from engulfing the entire town: as it was, 493 houses between Broadway and the Hudson River—one fourth of the city's buildings—were destroyed before British soldiers and sailors and the townspeople put out the flames. The British accused Washington of ordering the fire set, but no proof has ever been found. Washington would only comment, in a letter to his brother at Mount Vernon, "Providence, or some good honest fellow, has done more for us than we were disposed to do for ourselves."[10]

In mid-October, the American army had withdrawn north from Harlem Heights to White Plains. There, on October 28, the British again overtook them. Behind hastily built earthworks atop 180-foot-high Chatterton's Hills, Alexander Hamilton's artillerymen crouched tensely as Hessians built a bridge of felled trees and fence rails across the flooded Bronx River and unleashed a bayonet charge up the wooded slope. Hamilton, his gunners flanked by Maryland and New York troops, repulsed the assault, causing heavy British casualties. Crossing a ford downriver and marching north, the British again attacked up the heights. Despite dogged resistance by Hamilton and his artillerymen, the British ignored his grapeshot and finally drove back the Americans.

Breaking off the fighting, the British went into winter quarters in basements and tents amid Manhattan's smoldering ruins. Cold weather pinched the toes and numbed the fingers of Hamilton's soldiers as they dug embankments. His pay book shows that he was desperately trying to round up enough shoes for barefoot frostbitten men. But the expected British attack to the north did not come. Instead, Howe's redcoats and Hessians stormed the last American stronghold on Manhattan island, Fort Washington, and present-day 181st Street on the Hudson River shore, where some 2,818 besieged Americans surrendered. Four days later, the British force crossed the Hudson and stormed Fort Lee on the New Jersey shore. This time, the Americans escaped, evacuating the fort, useless for controlling the Hudson without Fort Washington. In their pell-mell retreat they left behind 146 precious cannon, 2,800 muskets, and 400,000 cartridges.

Three days later, on November 10, Captain Hamilton and his artillery company were sent up the Hudson River to Peekskill, when he received orders to join Lord Stirling's retreating column. He was to cross the river to Haverstraw, then march ahead of the main army's vanguard through the Clove, a gap in the Palisades. He was then to go on to Hackensack, New Jersey, where Washington would overtake him with fifty-four hundred "much broken and dispirited" men.[11]

Hamilton hitched the horses to his two remaining six-pound guns and went on ahead. Managing to stay out front, Hamilton marched his gun crews twenty miles in one day to the Raritan River. Rattling through Elizabethtown, he passed the academy where, only three years earlier, his greatest concern had been studying Latin and Greek. School seemed so long ago. But nothing now mattered as much as the shimmering bayonets of British grenadiers so close behind him.

Oddly, at this point the British pursuit stalled for a full week to allow time for the commander-in-chief, Howe, to overtake his fast-moving army and plan the winter's deployments. During this unexpected breather, the main American army waited for reinforcements by New Jersey militia that never came. At Hackensack, Captain Hamilton dug in near Washington's headquarters. He was startled when his old friend, Hercules Mulligan, showed up on November 20. Because the English considered Mulligan a gentleman, he had been entitled to be released and placed on his parole of honor not to leave New York City. Violating his parole and risking imprisonment, he managed to slip by boat across the Hudson. He overtook Hamilton five miles west of Fort Lee. After their overjoyed reunion, Hamilton evidently suggested to Mulligan that he return to New York City and act, as Mulligan later put, as a "confidential correspondent of the commander-in-chief"—a spy. Hamilton knew not only that Mulligan outfitted British and Loyalist officers but that his brother Hugh, as a ship's chandler and wholesale merchant, was in constant touch with British officials and supply officers who would know troop movements and strengths. But there was no time now to formulate a plan.

Finally, the British, now twice the Americans' numbers, resumed their onslaught. Hard on Hamilton's heels at the Raritan River, the British arrived at noon, November 29. From the opposite bank, Hamilton and his guns kept up an incessant hail of grapeshot at British and Hessian grenadiers, shielding American troops as they tore up the planks of the New Bridge. Under Hamilton's valiant covering fire, Washington and his army were able to slip away toward Princeton. Halfway there, Washington dispatched a brief message by express rider to Congress in Philadelphia: "The enemy appeared in several parties on the heights opposite Brunswick and were advancing in a large body toward the [Raritan] crossing place. We had a smart cannonade whilst we were parading our men."[12]

The smart cannonade came from Hamilton. On the high west bank a few hundred yards above the Raritan, he had deployed his field pieces. Again and again, the slight, boyish-looking captain yelled, "Fire! Fire!" to his gun crews, ordering them to ram home bags of grapeshot and touch the matches, then quickly reposition the jumping, recoiling guns. Even after his slashing grapeshot repulsed the British attack, Hamilton kept up a steady fire for several hours, lobbing solid shot at the stalled British column until Washington was safely away—so far away that he had lost contact and had no idea if Hamilton, his Horatio at the bridge, had survived. Washington's step-grandson Daniel Parke Custis later wrote that Washington was "charmed by the brilliant courage and admirable skill" of the twenty-one-year old Hamilton. On the march toward Princeton, Washington sent one of his aides to find out just who it was who had halted his pursuers. A veteran officer, observing Hamilton shortly afterward, recorded that he had

Noticed a youth, a mere stripling, small, slender, almost delicate in frame, marching, with a cocked hat pulled down over his eyes, apparently lost in thought, with his hand resting on a cannon, and every now and then patting it, as if it were a favorite horse or a pet plaything.

Another officer later recalled that day when Hamilton's company marched into Princeton:

It was a model of discipline; at their head was a boy, and I wondered at his youth, but what was my surprise when he was pointed out to me as that Hamilton of whom we had already heard so much.

Hamilton overtook Washington and the main army at Princeton the morning of December 2.

After losing all of New Jersey to the British, Washington ordered his army ferried across the Delaware River by every boat and barge along the Delaware River for sixty miles. A shivering Hamilton and his gunners crossed the river in a Durham ore boat, joining artillery ranged along the western riverbank. Whenever British patrols ventured too near the water, Hamilton's artillery repulsed them with brisk fire. As it grew steadily colder, British commander Howe said he found the weather "too severe to keep the field." His redcoats returning to New York City, he posted a Hessian brigade for the winter at Trenton.[3]

In command of Trenton, the British strongpoint nearest the Americans, Howe placed Colonel Johann Gottlieb Rall, whose troops had slaughtered Americans as they tried to surrender on Long Island, and at Fort Washington on Manhattan island. Rall's regiments had a reputation for plunder and rape. One day an American patrol on the Pennsylvania riverbank heard a group of women calling for help. Rowing over to New Jersey, the American soldiers learned that all of the women, including a fifteen-year-old girl, had been raped that morning by the invaders. While the American patrol dared not retaliate at once, they passed the word to headquarters, where American officers would later be in a position to retaliate. Hessian brutality succeeded where all Washington's appeals had failed. Jersey farmers, who until now had refused to help the American army, formed marauding militia bands that ambushed Hessian patrols and British scouting parties whenever they ventured outside Trenton. "We have not slept one night in peace since we came to this place," a Hessian officer moaned.[14]

For weeks, Washington had been using spies to cultivate the myth of his army's impotence. One member of his fledgling secret service was John Honeyman, who had been conscripted to serve with the British in the French and Indian Wars and had been bodyguard to General James Wolfe, conqueror of Quebec in 1760. Honeyman was eager to provide vital information to Washington. Posing as a cattle dealer and butcher, on December 22, he walked into a woods inside the American lines. Cracking his bullwhip as if chasing cattle, he attracted the attention of an American patrol that took him into custody and delivered him to headquarters. Honeyman gave the commander-in-chief detailed information on the deployments and route inside Trenton. Washington then handed Honeyman a key to the guardhouse where he was to be locked up.

The Americans had to attack quickly before the enlistments of the last Continental troops expired at midnight December 31. On Christmas Eve, Dr. Benjamin Rush rode out to visit Washington. He found him scribbling on small pieces of paper. Rush picked one up and read, "Victory or Death." It was the watchword for the all-out Christmas Day attack on Trenton while its garrison slept off the effects of its Christmas celebration. A victory, even over a small outpost, would inspire lagging Patriots, cow the Loyalists, encourage reenlistments, drive back the British—in short, keep the Revolution alive. Defeat could mean death for the American cause. The main assault force was made up entirely of toughened veterans including Hamilton's battle-tested New Yorkers. Henry Knox, Nathanael Greene, James Monroe, John Sullivan, and Alexander Hamilton, the future leaders of America's republic, huddled around a campfire at McKonkey's Ferry the frigid afternoon of December 25, 1776, to receive their marching orders. Hamilton and his men wore capes made out of their blankets as they hefted the two heavy six-pounders and their cases of shot and shells onto the nine-foot-wide, sixty-foot-long Durham iron-ore barges they had commandeered, then pushed and pulled their horses aboard. Nineteen-year-old James Wilkinson noted in his journal that footprints down to the river were "tinged here and there with blood from the feet of the men who wore broken shoes." Jut-jawed Marblehead ship captain John Glover ordered the first boatloads to push off at two o'clock in the morning into the storm. By then, the wind was rising and clouds were beginning to blot out the moonlight. Snow and sleet stung Hamilton's eyes.[5]

Tramping past darkened farmhouses for twelve miles, Hamilton with his artillery company led Nathanael Greene's division as it swung off to the east to skirt the town. One mile north of Trenton, Greene halted the column to allow John Sullivan's column time to reach its destination. At precisely eight in the morning, Hamilton's advance guard attacked the Hessian outpost. At three minutes after eight, Hamilton heard the firing to his right. The Americans poured into the town. Driving back the few Hessian pickets with their bayonets, they charged into the old British barracks and woke the groggy Hessians at gunpoint. Some Hessians in nearby houses attempted to regroup in the streets and counterattack. At the west end of King Street, Hamilton and his guns were waiting for them. Firing in tandem, Hamilton's cannon cut the Hessians down with murderous sheets of grapeshot. The Hessians sought cover behind houses but were driven back house by house by Virginia riflemen, who stormed into the houses and fired down from upstairs windows. Hessian artillerymen managed to get off thirteen rounds from two brass fieldpieces before Hamilton's gunners killed them. Riding back and forth behind the guns, Washington this time saw for himself the brutal courage and skillful discipline of this youthful artillery captain as he stood up to the deadly Hessian fire and repulsed repeated enemy charges.

The Hessian's best regiments, the Rall and the Lossberg, surrendered. But one Hessian regiment, the Knyphausen, escaped to warn the British at Princeton. The Americans had to march swiftly to Princeton and attack them or slog back upriver with 948 prisoners, their vital supplies and weapons, including sixty precious cannon. But the Americans were too battle-weary. As they recrossed the Delaware, it was so cold that both the Americans and their prisoners had to stomp their feet in time in the boats to break up the ice that was forming. Five men froze to death.

Stung by the Trenton defeat, the British field commander, Lord Cornwallis, raced across New Jersey with battle-seasoned grenadiers to retaliate. The Americans, $10 gold reenlistment bonuses in their pockets, recrossed the Delaware to intercept them. The British drew up their lines across from the American camp along a three-mile stretch of Assunpink Creek just outside Trenton. Washington ordered a rear guard to continue all night digging noisily within the hearing of British pickets and to pile firewood on their roaring campfires while his main force slipped away.

At one in the morning on January 2, 1777, Hamilton and his artillerymen hitched up their horses and guns. Their numbers reduced from sixty-nine to twenty-five men by death, desertion and expired enlistments, they wrapped rags around the wheels of their cannon to muffle the noise on the frozen road. Avoiding the main route (now Mercer Street) into Princeton, the advance division followed a new and unmapped road, strewn with tree stumps, through darkened woods. After picking their way all night, they emerged at sunrise on the south end of Princeton—right into a corps of British light infantry. The two forces raced for the high ground. General Hugh Mercer fell with seven bayonet wounds. The Americans broke before a British bayonet charge. When Washington galloped onto the battlefield with his division and surrounded the British, about two hundred redcoats ran to Nassau Hall, the main building at Princeton College. The British had begun firing from its windows by the time Alexander Hamilton arrived with his two cannon. It had been a little more than three years since Hamilton had sought admission on his own terms to Princeton and been rejected. Now he came with field artillery—and promptly opened fire on the rear of the four-story red sandstone edifice. College tradition holds that one of Hamilton's six-pound balls shattered a window, flew through the chapel, and beheaded a portrait of King George II. Under Hamilton's unnerving cannonade, the British quickly surrendered.[16]

* * *

ONE EFFECT of twin victories at Trenton and Princeton in only ten days was that militia volunteers began to swarm to the American standard, far more than could be fed, clothed, or armed, despite all the captured Hessians' munitions. Washington realized that his staff, short-handed, was ill-equipped to coordinate logistics and state militia. A shortage of experienced officers on his headquarters staff had plagued him since he took command. In four months since the British onslaught had begun, three hundred American officers had been killed or captured. "At present," Washington complained,

> my time is so taken up at my desk that I am obliged to neglect many other essential parts of my duty. It is absolutely necessary for me to have persons [who] can think for me as well as execute orders.

Washington explained what he expected in an aide:

> As to military knowledge, I do not expect to find gentlemen much skilled in it. If they can write a good letter, write quick, are methodical and diligent, it is all I expect to find in my aides.

Washington explained to the president of the Continental Congress that his letters were "first drawn by my secretaries and aides-de-camp." But judging from the variety and sheer volume of correspondence at headquarters, Adjutant General Timothy Pickering was probably closer to the mark when he said that "not only the composition, the clothing of the ideas but the ideas themselves originated generally with the writers," in particular Hamilton who was "scarcely in any degree" Washington's amanuensis. An aide's letters usually contained some variant of the tagline, "composed for the General's signature." But the letters all had to represent the thought and temper of the commander. Until an aide proved his adeptness at this art form, he worked from a dictated memorandum or a set of scribbled notes. One longtime aide, Colonel Tench Tilghman, observed that "the weight of the whole war lay upon the commander's shoulders." After months of fighting and marching and fighting again, the army swelling and shrinking, starving and freezing while politicians cut and ran, Washington's other staff officers were vigilant for bright, young, battle-tested officers who could help them deal with congresses, contractors, spies, doctors, militias—all the myriad intermediaries who must be coordinated from a headquarters on wagon wheels. The paperwork was only going to get worse as the war dragged on. "Winter quarters," Tilghman wrote to his friend Robert Morris, brings "an increase in business in the way of papers, pens and ink."[17]

As early as the summer of 1776, Nathanael Greene, assessing New York's defenses before the British invasion, had noticed Alexander Hamilton briskly drilling his company. Again, as the Americans dug in for the futile last-ditch defense of Manhattan, Greene had noticed Hamilton, who may or may not have suggested a way out of the British trap on Long Island. At Trenton and Princeton, Greene watched Hamilton adjust the guns and, sword slashing, line up infantrymen to protect his gunners as they went about their deadly, methodical work until more than two hundred Hessians were killed in less than ten minutes. Impressed by Hamilton's bearing under fire, shortly after the army was led into winter quarters at Morristown, New Jersey, in January 1777, Greene sent a messenger to invite him to dinner at Washington's headquarters. There, other Continental officers, including artillery chief Henry Knox, paid their compliments to the boyish Hamilton, who had just turned twenty-two.

Washington need an aide with good connections in New York. In January 1777, he invited Hamilton to join his headquarters staff. The appointment carried a promotion from captain to lieutenant colonel. While Hamilton had earlier turned down two appointments as aide-de-camp, this time he did not hesitate. Because he knew what to expect, he would not give up his battle commission to be an aide to anyone less than the commander-in-chief. He had the imagination to see that he would be at the center of a great and dramatic struggle. As he made himself a central figure in planning and executing campaigns, he would also make himself invaluable both as Washington's assistant and, in designated areas, as his proxy, a role he had already learned in a St. Croix countinghouse. He would become Washington's personal liaison with his generals in battle. He would be called upon not only to convey orders but to carry out special missions requiring judgment and diplomacy. He also would be in a position to work closely coordinating American intelligence-gathering operations: it was at this time that he made Washington aware of Hercules Mulligan and his value as an American mole inside British lines in New York City.

Hamilton must have been aware that the men so close to power could play central roles in a new nation once—and if—independence was secured by battle. But Alexander Hamilton was not merely opportunistic. He was dedicated to an ideal, a revolution that was already obviously changing the rules of American society. Or how else could the bastard son of a bankrupt merchant, an immigrant with no wealthy family connections but only his skill as a writer, his daring, and his panache in whatever society he found himself, presume to join the official "family" of a commander-in-chief? But he had found himself in battle. For the next four years, Hamilton would help to win a revolution, then he would help to make a nation. On March 1, 1777, Hamilton turned over the command of his artillery company to Lieutenant Thompson, the sergeant he had dared to make an officer, and joined Washington's headquarters staff.

For the next four years, he would excel at particularly delicate and discreet tasks that would, a few years later, propel him to one of the highest offices in the land. When Timothy Pickering first met Hamilton at camp, he considered him "a very extraordinary young man." Many years later, the prickly Pickering declared Washington's great good fortune to recognize Hamilton's talents when he was so young—and then to harness them throughout most of their joint careers:

> During a long series of years, in war and in peace, Washington enjoyed the advantages of Hamilton's eminent talents, integrity and felicity, and these qualities fixed [Hamilton] in [Washington's] confidence to the last hour of his life.[18]

Hamilton, the impecunious abandoned son, Washington the patriarch without a son, had begun a symbiotic relationship that, except for a few months of misunderstanding, would endure for nearly a quarter century, years corresponding to the birth, adolescence, and coming to maturity of the United States.

ALEXANDER HAMILTON still—always, in fact—looked younger than his age. For some unexplained reason, he contributed to this image of his youthfulness by lying about it, understating his age by two years. While it is difficult to know when he began this practice, as he reached his time of majority, he stepped into his new role with an ease that amazed the young aristocrats around him. From his first winter at Morristown, as one visiting Pennsylvania officer described it, Hamilton

> presided at the General's table, where he dined ... in a large company where there were several ladies, among whom I recollect one or two of the Miss Livingstons. He acquitted himself with an ease, propriety and vivacity that gave me the most favorable impression of his talents and accomplishments.

As one of a half dozen headquarters staff officers, the twenty-two-year-old Alexander Hamilton settled into an always difficult, sometimes dangerous routine that proved a continuation for another four years of the spartan life he had always led but with infinitely more responsibility. In all, thirty-two aides were to pass through headquarters in eight years, but few were more loyal and durable than Hamilton—or turned out to be more valuable. It was a touchy business. Working closely with Washington was no fun.[19]

"I give in to no kind of amusement myself," wrote Washington, "and consequently those about me can have none." If he allowed "the same relaxation from duty" to his staff as other officers had, they would not get so much done. The commander asked aides to "have the mind always upon the stretch, scarce ever unbent, and no hours for recreation." For an ambitious young officer like Hamilton who wanted to stretch his mind, the great man's notice and approval was usually compensation for the relaxation he rarely allowed himself anyway.[20]

As one of his colleagues put it, writing home to a father concerned that his son would pursue pleasures that damaged his health,

> You need be under no apprehension of my losing it on the score of excess in living. Vice is banished from the General's Family. We never sup but go early to bed, and are early up.[21]

But there Hamilton found other forms of pleasure. He loved to read and study. The quartermaster general always commandeered the best house in any region as headquarters, often one with a well-stocked library. Hamilton was able to indulge this particular passion, as he always had, while others slept.

Fortunately, he also made friends easily. His closest new friend was volunteer aide-de-camp John Laurens of South Carolina, who limned this sketch of a day and a night at headquarters for his father, president of the Continental Congress Henry Laurens, from "a small noisy crowded room":

> Between copying and composing I have inked a great deal of paper and it begins to be time for me to join my snoring companions, who are extended before the fire in the style which we practiced formerly in the interior parts of South Carolina.[22]

But, after months of frigid nights in tents or in open air, even this intimate form of camping must have seemed luxurious to Hamilton, especially after a long day of what he called the "hurry of business." Just as often, in the fighting seasons, sleep came in a tent after a day of writing on a portable desk.

There were breaks. When Martha Washington arrived at camp each winter, she organized the other officers' wives into a closely knit society that put on cotillions. Hamilton, never to be outdone, once danced with Mrs. Nathanael Greene for a full three hours. Mrs. Theodorick Bland, a Virginia officer's wife visiting Morristown that winter, noticed one aide in particular. Colonel Hamilton was "in our riding party generally." She described Hamilton as "a sensible, genteel, polite young fellow, a West Indian." Because of his avidity, both in battle and in society, Hamilton had already earned from his fellow officers the nickname "The Little Lion." It would stick. But Martha Washington had a more oblique way of letting it be known that she had noticed Hamilton's singular attentiveness to women. At headquarters, she found a tomcat that constantly pursued the females of his species. She named it Hamilton. As well as Washington and his staff there were often official visiting members of Congress. After a meager meal, whenever young ladies were visiting, Hamilton and his fellow officers liked to take them into the nearby village of Morristown, ostensibly for tea.[23]

EVENTUALLY, HAMILTON, like any other new staff member, decoded exactly what the general expected of him, often learning it from conversations with sympathetic colleagues. Washington did not make his wishes explicit: it was not until more than twenty years later, when he, as ex-president, was reorganizing the army, that he wrote down what he sought in a staff officer:

> The variegated and important duties of the aids [sic] of a commander in chief or the commander of a separate army require experienced officers, men of judgment and men of business, *ready pens* to execute them properly and with dispatch. A great deal more is required of them than attending him at a parade or delivering verbal orders here and there, or copying a written one. They ought, if I may be allowed to use the expression, to possess the Soul of the General, and from a *single* idea given to them, to convey his meaning in the clearest and fullest manner.[24]

While Washington here was downplaying the importance of attending him on parade, he had always been fastidious about his uniform and demanded proper attire from his staff. Fellow aide John Laurens wrote that an aide was supposed to wear suitable clothing to "contribute to the propriety of the commander-in-chief's family." Hamilton, like Laurens, had "but one pair of breeches that are wearable." He was to order fabric and buttons to have made up by a tailor in time for "the opening of the campaign" in spring: "blue and buff cloth . . . lining [and] double gilt buttons sufficient to make me a uniform coat . . . besides corded dimity for waistcoats and breeches." In addition, Hamilton would need gold epaulettes, gloves, hair powder, pomade, and a comb plus the aide-de-camp's blue sash. Hair could be pomaded and powdered, but no American officer wore a wig: that would be too aristocratic, too English. A revolution was taking place and the attire of the general's staff had symbolic importance. To help him dress each day and to tend to his horse, Hamilton was assigned an orderly from the ranks. Yet Hamilton, like Laurens, had difficulty outfitting himself from his meager pay, and he had no wealthy kinsman to write home to. However, there is no hint that, at first at least, Hamilton felt at a disadvantage.[25]

EIGHT

"We Shall Beat Them Soundly"

Alexander Hamilton's first assignment as confidential writing aide to George Washington came March 3, 1777. It dealt with the treatment of prisoners of war, which was to be one of his major endeavors over the next four years. Gradually, Washington virtually put Hamilton in charge of coordinating all prisoner exchanges. Hamilton showed deep personal interest in the subject: after all, his two closest friends, Robert Troup and Hercules Mulligan, had been captured at Brooklyn Heights. While they were alive and unhurt, both were on their parole of honor not to leave New York City until they were exchanged for British prisoners of equal rank or until the war was over.

Hamilton's duties as prisoner negotiator assumed added urgency when British dragoons captured Major General Charles Lee, the American second in command. Returning from the South, he was supposed to lead troops from the New York Highlands to reinforce Washington during his retreat across New Jersey. Pausing at a tavern at Basking Ridge, New Jersey, he was breakfasting leisurely when British dragoons surrounded the tavern. The British refused to release him on parole, contending he was not a prisoner of war but, as a former British officer, a traitor, to be hanged.

The Continental Congress still had no fixed policy for the treatment of prisoners and the British commander, unwilling to accord the Americans legal status, had no authority from London to deal with rebels. A captured British officer who was also a member of Parliament, Lieutenant Colonel Archibald Campbell of the Seventy-first Regiment, complained that he and five Hessian officers taken at Trenton were being treated harshly. Congress refused to ameliorate their treatment despite the fact that, while the Americans held only fifty British officers, the British held three thousand Americans. Setting to work on the knotty problem in his first letter as a staff officer, Hamilton wrote compassionately to Colonel Campbell, "I shall always be happy to manifest my disinclination to any undue severities towards those whom the fortunes of war may chance to throw into my hands." In time, Hamilton would help negotiate a general agreement for the exchange of prisoners, working with his old Elizabethtown mentor, Elias Boudinot, the American commissary of prisoners and the man who saw they were supplied with food and clothing.[1]

Working from a few hasty notes he scrawled in a brief meeting with Washington conveying his tone, Hamilton tackled each delicate assignment. Washington ordered him to upbraid Major General Horatio Gates for failing to keep track of the number of troops receiving recruiting bonuses and bounties and deserting from the army, only to "enlist" again. He next dealt with the flamboyant General Benedict Arnold, who was itching to attack the British garrison of Newport, Rhode Island. Washington did not like to second-guess field officers on the scene but he approved what Hamilton wrote:

Unless your strength and circumstances be such that you can reasonably promise a *moral certainty* of succeeding . . . relinquish the undertaking and confine yourself, in the main, to a defensive operation.

Over the next few years, Hamilton would have the delicate task of dealing repeatedly with the feisty Arnold. Congress for the second time had passed over Arnold for promotion. Hamilton assured Arnold that Washington was working to remedy the "error" and that, in a typical Hamiltonian flourish, "My endeavors to that end shall not be wanting." In consoling the disgruntled Arnold when Congress promoted two former subordinates over him, Hamilton wrote Arnold a self-revealing letter:

> If smaller matters do not yield to greater, if trifles, light as air in comparison of what we are contending for, can withdraw or withhold gentlemen from service when our all is at stake and a single cast of the die may turn the tables, what are we to expect? It is not a common contest we are engaged in. Success depends upon a steady and vigorous exertion.[2]

Another sensitive matter at headquarters was the Continental Army's relationship to state legislatures, which were jealous of their authority over their own militias. Hamilton's former New York artillery company was now so under strength, behind in pay, and destitute of qualified officers that, Hamilton argued, it could no longer be of any use to New York State. He recommended that it be transferred intact to the Continental service. The New York Congress sent a delegate, Gouverneur Morris, with a resolution that followed Hamilton's advice. Morris, witty, cynical, aristocratic scion of a wealthy New York family, was deeply impressed with Hamilton at this first meeting. The two men, both French speakers with Huguenot mothers, hit it off instantly. Morris returned to the New York Congress and recommended that Hamilton become the state's confidential military liaison between headquarters and its own Committee of Correspondence. The New York Congress agreed. This time writing for himself, Hamilton said that he was pleased, even if it meant extra duty without pay:

> With cheerfulness, I embrace the proposal of corresponding with your convention . . . and shall from time to time as far as my leisure will permit and my duty warrant, communicate such

pieces of intelligence as shall be received and such comments upon them as shall convey a true idea of what is going on in the military line.

Hamilton was stepping for the second time into the New York political arena—and deciding what the state's politicians should be told of Continental military affairs. But he was not seduced by the compliment. He never allowed his attachment to his adopted state to take precedence over his primary loyalty to the national interests. Born outside any of the American states, from this early time he gave his principal allegiance to the Continental cause. He was also careful to write that he was speaking only for himself. His opinions were "to be considered merely as my private sentiments." They were "never to be interpreted as an echo" of Washington's, which, of course, as everyone knew, they were.[3]

Giving New York the benefit of his first military analysis, Hamilton wrote that the British couldn't attack until at least May 1: the roads were too muddy, their reinforcements from England too tardy. They would probably try to capture Philadelphia in a combined land and sea campaign. They would follow the "well-grounded rule in war to strike first at the capital towns and cities." Hamilton's intelligence sources had proved amazingly accurate.[4]

Yet as Hamilton gradually widened his correspondence with New York leaders to include politicians in other states, it became clear that he did not agree with Washington on everything. He worried about the British attack on Philadelphia, "a place of infinite importance," while Washington was opposed to allowing Pennsylvania to form its own army to defend itself. Hamilton also disagreed on how harshly Loyalists should be treated. Washington dealt severely with all suspected Loyalists. When New Jersey Revolutionaries rounded up leading Loyalists and herded them to headquarters at Morristown for questioning, Hamilton played a prominent part in their interrogation. He had tried to ascertain

Who of them were subject to a military jurisdiction and who came properly under the civil power; also, to discriminate those who were innocent or guilty of trivial offenses from those whose crimes were of a capital or heinous nature.

In part because of Hamilton's influence, the board of inquiry persuaded Washington to release passive Loyalists and only send "daring offenders" to Governor Livingston for punishment, leaving to the civil authority their disposition. Hamilton wrote he wanted to keep clear of "the least encroachment either upon the rights of the citizen or of the magistrate."

This time, the sentiment as well as the words were more Hamilton's than Washington's. He went even further. Confiscation of the estates of Loyalists "is not cognizable by martial law." Instead of wholesale arrests and confiscations, Hamilton urged the New York Congress to carry out "an execution or two, by way of example," that would "strike terror and powerfully discourage" other Loyalists while not encouraging "wicked practices" such as public whippings. "Corporal punishment," he warned, would only create sympathy among fence-sitting citizens and was "apt to excite compassion and breed disgust." When the New Jersey Loyalists were still held in irons at Morristown without trials, Hamilton wrote to his schooldays mentor, now New Jersey Governor Livingston, to caution him not to be unduly severe. "Private pique and resentment" had caused the arrests of "some innocent persons." Hamilton knew that he was reflecting public opinion in New Jersey when he so boldly lectured Livingston on the dangers of appearing to persecute innocent citizens.[5]

Offering advice that the New York Congress did not solicit, the twenty-two-year-old aide-de-camp provided that august body with a brilliant analysis of New York's new constitution. There was "a want of vigor" in the office of governor. The choice of a chief executive "cannot be safely lodged with the people at large," but there could be stable government if there was a truly representative democracy:

When the deliberative or judicial powers are vested wholly or partly in the collective body of the people, you must expect error, confusion and instability. But a representative democracy, where the right of election is well-secured and regulated, and the exercise of the legislative, executive and judiciary authorities is vested in select persons, chosen *really* and *nominally* by the people, will in my opinion be most likely to be happy, regular and durable.

Hamilton worried that New York's two-house legislature would result in "delay and dilatoriness":

Your senate, from the very name and from the mere circumstance of its being a separate member of the legislature, will be liable to degenerate into a body purely aristocratical. And I think the danger of an abuse of power from a simple legislature would not be very great in a government where the equality and fullness of popular representation is so widely provided for as in yours.[6]

As everyone waited for the 1777 spring campaign to open, New York's politicians sought Hamilton's expert opinion of cannon produced from iron manufactured by a fellow New Yorker, Colonel Robert Livingston. Hamilton responded that one cannon, weighing precisely 227 pounds, had been fired as fast as possible twenty times and that that had satisfied Washington. But Hamilton felt it should have been fired fifty times for a truly adequate field trial that, if passed, would prove "beyond a doubt" her value to be "immense."[7]

Not all of Hamilton's letter writing was official. He found time to write to Hugh Knox in St. Croix, who had become a staunch admirer of the Revolution. Knox was helping to edit the island's newspaper. He wrote back to praise Hamilton's now-missing letter as "a more true" account of the Revolution "than all the public and private intelligence we had received here." Ever cheering his protégé on, the schoolmaster-cum-preacher urged him to become

the analyst and biographer as well as the aide-de-camp of General Washington and the [historian] of the American war! I hope you will take minutes and keep a journal! This may be a new and strange thought to you but if you survive the current troubles, I aver few men will be as well qualified to write the history of the present glorious struggle![8]

On August 26, 1777, on a hill a few miles south of Newark, Delaware, Alexander Hamilton sat on his horse beside Generals Washington and Greene and the Marquis de Lafayette, and gazed down at the sprawling white canvas bivouac of Sir William Howe's seventeen-thousand-man invasion force. In the last two weeks, it had become plain that the British fleet that had left New York early in August was heading for the Chesapeake to land an army to attack the capital at Philadelphia from the south. Hamilton's intelligence sources inside New York City had never been more valuable. His contacts in the New York Assembly, alarmed at the new British invasion from Canada, were certain that the British Army in New York City intended to sail north up the Hudson and link up with the British Northern Army at Albany in a giant pincers movement that would sever rebellious New England and probably end the Revolution. Indeed, this had been the British ministry's plan. But Hamilton's sources inside New York City, undoubtedly funneling reports from Long Island and from spies in Manhattan through Hercules Mulligan by boat to New Jersey, told him otherwise. Details came from scores of sources. American wives of Loyalist officers transmitted their observations of unusual boat-building activity on Long Island. At his tavern on Pearl Street, Samuel Fraunces eavesdropped on British officers' meetings. Orders for provisions, tackle, and fodder for a large number of horses coursed from the East River waterfront to Hercules Mulligan, who sent coded messages across the Hudson from the Fulton Street ferry landing to the New Jersey shore. Mulligan's slave Cato made countless nighttime crossings through the British naval patrols. Hamilton constantly updated Washington as, in makeshift lookout towers in coastal saltworks all along the New Jersey shoreline, American telescopes watched for the British fleet. First feinting northward toward the Hudson to confuse the Americans, the British fleet came about and sailed out to sea, disappearing for six days. While it was still at sea, Washington, deciding to depend on his spies, made one of his greatest gambles. Keeping his army split instead of marching north to reinforce Gates against the British assault from Canada, Washington shifted the bulk of his army south through Philadelphia to defend against a British attack from the south. Never had the fledgling American intelligence network scored so vital a coup. A sixteen-thousand-man American army had marched south from Morristown, New Jersey, through Philadelphia to oppose the invasion.

Hamilton and other American officers had ridden out, as he wrote to Gouverneur Morris, his New York correspondent, to reconnoiter "Howe's coming into Chesapeake Bay":

> He still lies there in a state of inactivity, in a great measure, I believe, from the want of horses to transport his baggage and stores. It seems he sailed with only about three weeks' provender and was six at sea. This has occasioned the death of a great number of his horses and has made skeletons of the rest. He will be obliged to collect a supply from the neighboring country before he can move.[9]

Based on information he had received from Hercules Mulligan and other New York operatives over the past few months, Hamilton had correctly assumed that Howe would follow a classical military formula and attack city after city instead of following the wiser course of sailing up the Hudson to link up with a second British army that was slow-marching south from Canada. When the British feinted an attack up the Hudson, Hamilton knew from Mulligan's network that the ships were destined for a more southerly climate. He had urged Washington to race south, not north, to the horror of New York Revolutionaries who still believed the British were heading north and that all of Washington's army should be joining in their defense. Now Hamilton was ready to reassure them. The danger from an intercepted message was past.

There was something almost mocking of Howe in the tone of Hamilton's confidential report, sped by courier to the infinitely relieved New York Congress. The "enemy will have Philadelphia if they dare make a bold push for it," Hamilton predicted, "unless we fight them a pretty general action." Washington had adopted a Fabian policy of trying to wear down the British by arm's-length resistance and deprivation of supplies. Hamilton disagreed with his policy. He thought the American army should put up a fight for Philadelphia even if it meant risking all-out battle: "I opine we ought do it," Hamilton wrote Morris, "and that we shall beat them soundly if we do" while the army was "in high health and spirits." While Hamilton played the dutiful sycophant around the commander-in-chief, in his secret correspondence with Morris, once again he disagreed with Washington.[10]

Washington tried to halt the British advance at Brandywine, the border between present-day Delaware and Pennsylvania. The opposing forces at Brandywine were about even. As soon as Washington retreated behind prepared earthworks at Chadd's Ford the morning of September 11, 1777, Howe sent five thousand Hessians against the center of the American lines while seventy-five hundred redcoats marched around the American right flank. Amazingly, once again the British blew their chance for total victory by hesitating for a late lunch, giving the Americans a chance to reinforce their right wing. With Hamilton and Lafayette and two regiments of reinforcements, Washington arrived in time to line up behind a stone wall as the English wiped off their chins. Hamilton was directing the unlimbering of field artillery when the British lunch hour ended. The Americans now absorbed a terrible pounding from heavier British guns and withstood bayonet charges for more than an hour. Washington, Hamilton, and Lafayette trotted up and down the line, swinging their swords and cheering on the men. Lafayette fell from his horse, shot through the thigh; Hamilton helped to drag him to safety.

Hamilton was eager for another fight to erase the embarrassment of the Americans' technical defeat at Brandywine. He was busy for days in mid-September at temporary headquarters set up at Yellow Springs, Pennsylvania, writing orders requesting reinforcements from the northern army. Typically, Congress, instead of sending blankets for Washington's shivering soldiers, provided rum to warm them. As the nights grew chill, he grew disgusted with the Continental Congress. The supply problem only worsened as winter approached, consuming Hamilton's efforts as the British seized or destroyed one American depot after another abandoned by the retreating Continental Army. One British raid on Valley Forge yielded "3800 barrels of flour, soap and candles, 25 barrels of horse shoes, several thousand kettles and entrenching tools," Hamilton reported. To keep even more supplies out of British hands, Washington assigned Hamilton the odious duty of destroying flour mills at Deviser's Ferry on the Schuylkill River. Hamilton rode out with Henry "Light-Horse Harry" Lee and his Virginia cavalry to carry out the scorched-earth mission. Hamilton's detachment had barely set fire to the mills before guards they had left on a hilltop fired shots warning of approaching British dragoons. Fortuitously, Hamilton had brought ashore a flat-bottomed boat: with four men and their horses, Hamilton shoved off just as the dragoons galloped up and opened fire. The British volley killed one of Hamilton's oarsmen, wounded another, and crippled Hamilton's horse.

A breathless Hamilton returned to headquarters, picked up his quill, and dashed off a warning to John Hancock, president of the Continental Congress inside Philadelphia:

> If Congress have not yet left Philadelphia, they ought to do it immediately, . . . without fail, for the enemy have the means of throwing a party this night into the city.

In his hasty escape, Hamilton had been forced to abandon another boat that could make it possible for the British to ferry fifty men at a time across the Schuylkill to carry out a raid on Congress. "In a few hours," he warned Hancock, they may have forded dragoons "perhaps sufficient to overmatch the militia who may be between them and the city." Hamilton was not forgetting General Lee's capture by dragoons. "This renders the situation of Congress extremely precarious." Congress, heeding Hamilton's warning, fled Philadelphia.[11]

But the British, instead of marching directly into Philadelphia, marched up the Schuylkill and away from the city. Congressman John Adams, shaken out of his bed, cursed Hamilton for a false alarm and wrote to Abigail that "Philadelphia will be no loss to us." When

Howe did not cross the Schuylkill, Hamilton, in effect, was called on the congressional carpet. A few days later, Hamilton's warning did prove correct when Howe suddenly laid pontoon bridges across the Schuylkill at its lower fords at night and, eluding Washington, marched the entire British Army across the river and on toward Philadelphia.[12]

In the last few days before the British took control of the capital, Hamilton went on a dangerous mission inside Philadelphia trying to commandeer blankets, clothing, shoes, and horses, all badly needed if the remaining American soldiers were to survive winter outside the city. A Virginia officer with Washington, John Marshall, reported that, in Hamilton's attempts to garner goods from Philadelphia merchants, "this very active officer could not obtain a supply, in any degree, adequate to the wants of the army." Yet Hamilton managed to round up enough military stores and send them by boat up the Delaware River and out of British reach "with so much vigilance that very little public property fell, with the city, into [British] hands." Hamilton had carried out his breathless raid on the city's munitions in only two days under the noses of Cornwallis's battalions as they took up positions in the capital.[13]

Increasingly, Washington drew on Hamilton for assistance and advice in coordinating the Philadelphia campaign in the winter of 1777–78. The next American objective was a lightning strike on the British at Germantown before the British could consolidate their hold on Philadelphia. Only three weeks after his failure at Brandywine, the Americans counterattacked. There were only eighty-five hundred unsuspecting British at the main British encampment at Germantown, eight miles north of Philadelphia. At five-thirty the morning of October 4, the lead American regiment, the Sixth Pennsylvania, trotted with bayonets fixed into a British outpost. In bloody hand-to-hand fighting, the Pennsylvanians pushed back the British. For the first time in the Revolution, Americans heard a British bugler sound retreat.

Through his spyglass, Hamilton could dimly make out Cliveden, a fortresslike stone house surrounded by broad lawns. By this time the Americans were firing volley after volley into a ground fog thickened by gunsmoke. As an aide, Colonel Timothy Pickering, rode back from delivering a message, he came under fire from Cliveden. He found Colonel Thomas Proctor, an artillery officer, and told him to bombard the house, then hurried to inform Washington. The main American attack had already swept past Cliveden. A heated debate ensued inside Washington's headquarters. Hamilton and Colonel Pickering wanted to surround the house with a regiment of reserves to keep the British from escaping and press onward with the main army. Artillery chief Henry Knox objected: a castle in the rear was a real threat. By the logic of European warfare, it must be reduced by artillery. Washington accepted Knox's argument, as he did so often, over Hamilton's objection, insisting on sending an officer with a flag of truce. But a sharpshooter inside Cliveden only saw a soldier's moving form and shot him. The American artillery bombardment of Cliveden merely shattered the shutters and doors. Deadly fire from inside the stone mansion tore into infantry Washington ordered into the siege. Eighteen New Jersey Brigade troops storming the massive oak front door were bayoneted. Another seventy-five Jersey men lay dead or dying on the grounds as American artillery opened fire from the opposite side of the house. American gunners blasted away at each other, the cannonballs passing through the house and striking more Americans than Englishmen. The sounds of heavy artillery fire halted the American advance corps, which marched back to Cliveden and opened fire from the south. Now American guns blazed away at Cliveden from all four sides. In the smog of war, Virginians and Pennsylvanians blasted away at each other until they were out of ammunition. Yelling for more ammunition, they gave away their positions to the British. Hamilton, his advice to bypass the fortified house ignored, watched in horror as the Americans retreated pell-mell, throwing away their victory.

IN LATE November 1777, Washington finally began an eleven-day march, safely moving his army into winter quarters at Valley Forge, twenty-five miles west of Philadelphia. The British made no attempt to follow. In the six months between September 1777 and March 1778, fully one half of Washington's troops were killed, captured, or wounded, froze to death on patrols, died of camp contagions, deserted, or resigned. An estimated three thousand men died of typhoid or smallpox in American field hospitals, while two thousand more died as prisoners of war inside unheated buildings in Philadelphia. The Continental Congress, on the run first to Lancaster and then to York, 140 miles west of Philadelphia, was able to provide very little in the way of shoes, bread, meat, blankets, or pay for the freezing, starving American soldiers at Valley Forge. The army's privations did not so much result from shortages in the land, but reflected inefficiency in arranging supplies and the outright meddling of politicians. That winter, Congress's ineptitude nearly wrecked the Revolution.

A crisis over who should command the American army had been developing since early autumn 1777. A deep schism within American ranks developed after the British advanced down Lake Champlain, forcing the abandonment of woefully undermanned Fort Ticonderoga. As regional jealousies flared, New Englanders blamed a New York general, Philip Schuyler, commander of the Northern Department, for the loss of the fortress, which left the New England backcountry dangerously exposed. He then incurred the wrath of Samuel and John Adams of Massachusetts for siphoning off troops from Massachusetts to defend New York. Hamilton had tried, with Washington's approval, to bind the wounds among Revolutionaries, but, uniquely, the Northern Department came under the direct jurisdiction of Congress.

There was little Hamilton could do. When Congress demanded an investigation of the fall of Ticonderoga, it stripped Schuyler of his Northern command and ordered Washington to choose a successor, but Washington insisted the choice, like the responsibility, must be Congress's. Samuel Adams promptly nominated Horatio Gates, a former British officer. In a pair of major battles near Saratoga in the autumn of 1777, Gates had stayed in camp safely behind his defense lines and ordered Benedict Arnold, his most experienced field commander, to stay in his tent. After a bitter quarrel, Gates had taken away Arnold's command. Arnold had defied Gates's orders and led a successful assault on a key Hessian redoubt and was severely wounded. Gates claimed full credit for the victory, not even mentioning Arnold in his official report to Congress.

When news of the victory reached Washington's camp at Whitemarsh on October 29 shortly after the fiasco at Germantown, a council of war decided to draw down twenty regiments from Gates at Albany for an all-out attack on Philadelphia. Hamilton wrote to Congress that the council of war could not "conceive that there is any other object now remaining that demands our most rigorous efforts so much as the destruction of the enemy in this quarter [Philadelphia]." Hamilton left unwritten the delicate position Washington was now in: in the eyes of Congress and many American and European observers, he had not done enough to defend Philadelphia, while Gates had scored a major victory.[14]

ON OCTOBER 28, 1777, James Wilkinson, a twenty-one-year-old aide to Gates, stopped at Reading, Pennsylvania, en route to Philadelphia from Saratoga with the official report for the Continental Congress of the great victory at Saratoga. Wilkinson repeated to one of Lord Stirling's aides a cutting remark about Washington that he had heard before he left Gates's headquarters in Albany. The mere fact that Wilkinson was heading for Congress *before* delivering Gates's report to the commander-in-chief at Washington's headquarters suggested that Gates was deliberately snubbing his commanding officer. Wilkinson revealed to Stirling's aide that Brigadier General Thomas Conway, while serving under Washington in Pennsylvania, had been secretly corresponding with Gates at Albany. Lord Stirling, loyal to Washington, wrote immediately to him: "In a letter from General Conway to General Gates, he said, 'Heaven has been determined to save your country, or a weak general and bad councilors would have ruined it.'" Washington had little regard for Conway. An Irish soldier of fortune married to a French countess, Conway had lobbied Congress over Washington's head to be promoted to major general over all the more senior brigadiers. The tone and intended confidentiality of the letter suggested that Conway believed Gates agreed with him.[15]

When he received Stirling's note, Washington immediately had Hamilton send Conway a stiff rebuke. By dispatching his letter to Conway through normal channels in his headquarters, Washington was guaranteeing that all his officers knew its contents. Even in peacetime, Washington did not take criticism easily. But in wartime, such a written comment about the commander-in-chief by one of his own subordinate generals smacked of mutiny. That Gates had remained safely behind the lines at Saratoga while Benedict Arnold fought the battle and that Gates had wrongly taken full credit were facts that Washington and his staff had only just learned from New York Governor George Clinton. To the outraged Washington, trained, like Gates, as a British officer, the note Lord Stirling sent him gave Washington what he considered evidence that at least two of his generals were plotting to overthrow him, something he considered not only disloyal but possibly treasonous. Even worse, Gates had kept a large army intact around him. By not reporting his troop strengths to the commander-in-chief as part of his official dispatches, for two weeks he had been hampering Washington's efforts to consolidate the American victory by combining forces and driving Howe out of Philadelphia.

Immediately after confronting Conway, Washington summoned a council of war in the oak-paneled library at Emlen House in Whitemarsh. Now, what would be the appropriate follow-up strategy to Saratoga? The generals agreed that Gates should send twenty regiments of his best troops at once to reinforce Washington. Washington summoned Hamilton the next morning and told him to draw up his own orders. Hamilton was to ride as fast as possible to Gates's headquarters at Albany and persuade him as delicately as possible to forward the reinforcements as quickly as possible.

Washington gave Hamilton extraordinary discretionary as well as diplomatic powers. He was to act as Washington's proxy. He was to assess the military situation in New York and to gauge whether Gates had a feasible plan for using his troops or was merely stalling and withholding aid to Washington for some other motive. Hamilton wrote in his own orders that he was to

Lay before him the state of this army and the situation of the enemy... Point out to him the many happy consequences that will accrue from an immediate reinforcement being sent from

the Northern Army ... in the clearest and fullest manner ...
[This] will in all probability [defeat] General Howe ...

If Gates had in mind "some expedition" that would more greatly benefit "the common cause," Hamilton was not to interfere with it. But
if his plan was vague or insignificant, Hamilton must insist he reinforce Washington with most of his troops. It would be up to Hamilton to decide what strategy was more appropriate. Washington had
so much confidence in Hamilton, a twenty-two-year-old member of
his staff for only eight months, that he made it clear by signing the
orders that he trusted Hamilton more than Gates.[16]

With a bodyguard, Captain Caleb Gibbs of Washington's Life
Guards, Hamilton rode an incredible 150 miles in three days. Reach-
ing New Windsor on the Hudson the second day, Hamilton met
General Daniel Morgan, who was already marching south from
Saratoga with his riflemen to reinforce Washington. He assured
Hamilton "that all the Northern Army were marching down."
Hamilton, relaying this happy news to Washington, wondered if
there was any reason for "going any farther." But at Fishkill a few
hours later they learned from a former aide that Gates was sending
no one. In fact, he was keeping all four Continental brigades at
Albany and building barracks for them. Arriving in Albany, Hamilton found his old college roommate, Major Robert Troup, who had
recently been released in a prisoner exchange and was now an aide
to Gates. Troup told Hamilton confidentially that General Putnam at
Peekskill also refused to release his Continentals to Washington.
Invoking Washington's authority, Hamilton ordered Putnam to send
several regiments of New York militia with only a month left on
their enlistments south to Washington at once, even if, he wrote
Washington, his orders did not include any militia. Hamilton took
this bold step "because of accounts here that most of Clinton's, [the
British commander at New York City] troops" had gone to reinforce
Howe at Philadelphia. "As so large a proportion of the Continental
troops have been detained [by Gates] at Albany, I concluded you
would not disapprove." Taking the initiative when Hamilton found

Putnam was also disregarding Washington's plea for help, Hamilton again cut his own orders. He sent New York and New Jersey troops south and asked Washington to second his orders in writing to the troops' commanders.[17]

By November 5, Hamilton was back at Albany and ready to confront Gates, who was basking in his newfound glory. Each day seemed to bring Gates fresh laurels. Congress called for a national day of thanksgiving to honor him and ordered a gold medal struck for him. Some generals and congressmen were writing him congratulatory notes that contrasted his victory to Washington's failures. In a bid to replace Washington with Gates, Congressman James Lovell of Massachusetts declared, "Thousands of lives and millions of property are yearly sacrificed to the inefficiency of the commander-in-chief. Two battles he has lost for us by two such blunders as might have disgraced a soldier of three months' standing. Our [hope] springs all from the northward, and about all [of] our confidence." In a congressional vote of confidence, Washington retained his command by only a single vote. There were foreign critics. Washington was "too slow, even indolent," opined the recently arrived French Baron de Kalb.[18]

In Albany, meanwhile, Horatio Gates, twice Hamilton's age, certainly was unprepared for the cool, analytical, probing questions by Washington's young proxy, Hamilton. When Hamilton presented Washington's request for reinforcements, Gates was, Hamilton reported on November 6 to Washington, "inflexible" that the two brigades Washington had requisitioned should remain at Albany. Clinton might come up the Hudson and raid Albany's arsenals, Gates argued. And until the roads froze, Gates argued, it was impossible to move artillery. Weakening his force could make it impossible to retake Ticonderoga. Hamilton was "infinitely embarrassed" to report that Gates would release only one brigade. For the moment, Hamilton accepted Gates's terms and gave the appearance of preparing to leave.[19]

In his confidential report, Hamilton cautioned Washington that he was finding that "General Gates has won the entire confidence of the [New England] states." He has "influence and interest elsewhere [in

Congress]; he might use it, if he pleased, to discredit the order to reinforce Washington." Hamilton stopped off for four days at Philip Schuyler's house at Albany, where the old general, a stout Washington defender, filled him in on the political as well as the military ramifications of the plotting at Gates's headquarters. In his expense report to Washington, there is a four-day gap when he may have been staying with Schuyler. Here, too, once again, he encountered Schuyler's twenty-year-old daughter, Betsy. Catherine Schuyler, the youngest of five daughters, insisted in her unpublished memoir, *A God-Child of Washington*, that this visit was the first time Hamilton and Elizabeth Schuyler met. But it may have been the first time the Schuyler sisters noticed Hamilton, a teenage boy the last time they had met during Hamilton's Elizabethtown school days. Catherine, not yet born when Hamilton appeared in the winter of 1777 on his intelligence-gathering mission, wrote years later, probably after collecting family memories into a composite family portrait:

> Shortly after the surrender of Burgoyne, a young officer wearing the uniform of Washington's military family, accompanied by an orderly, left the ferryboat. [He] exhibited a natural yet unassuming superiority; his features gave evidence of thought, intellectual strength and a determined mind. [His] high expansive forehead, a nose of the Grecian mold, a dark bright eye and the lines of a mouth expressing decision and courage completed the contour of a face never to be forgotten. His figure of the middling height strongly framed and muscular gave the appearance of strength and activity.[20]

Philip Schuyler was famous for his hospitality: he had recently entertained Burgoyne and twenty of his top officers before the defeated British were packed off to Boston to be shipped home. After days on the road and in rough taverns, an exhausted Hamilton welcomed a reason to visit The Pastures, the Schuyler mansion, a large rose-red house bookended between tall Dutch chimneys, a distinctive balustrade wrapped around white-trimmed third floor dormer windows.

After a series of huddles with the general, refreshing meals with the large family, and restorative nights of sleep, Hamilton had to rush off. He soon learned, probably from his confidant Troup, that Gates, instead of sending a fighting-trim brigade of some fourteen hundred men, was releasing only an anemic understrength brigade with only six hundred men fit for duty, "by far the weakest here." Reversing his acceptance of Gates's terms, Hamilton refused in writing in his most courteous prose while making clear his authority:

> I cannot consider it either as compatible with the good of the service or my instructions from His Excellency General Washington, to consent, that that brigade be selected from the three, to go to him; but I am under the necessity of requiring, by virtue of my orders from him, that one of the others be substituted . . . and that you will be pleased to give immediate orders for its embarkation.

After his first meeting with Gates, Hamilton had learned from other officers at Albany that Gates had no good reason to retain the Continental brigades Washington needed. Again, Hamilton demanded the stronger corps. This time, Gates caved in. Over the next two days, twenty-two hundred Continentals headed south. An exuberant Hamilton wrote to Washington that he had "finally prevailed" after "having given General Gates a little more time to recollect himself."[21]

An angry Gates the same day wrote two letters to Washington—and decided not to send the first. Hamilton's demands had "astonished" him. He was dejected "that all hopes of ever possessing Canada vanishes with the troops taken from hence." But Gates decided not to tell Washington of his secret plan to invade Canada. Instead, he accused Washington of ruining "every good effect" of his victory over Burgoyne. He also decided not to question Washington's requirement that a general give "direct implicit obedience to the verbal orders of aides-de-camp in action." To Gates, Hamilton seemed arrogant. Gates was dumbfounded at Hamilton's pertinacious insistence on all of Washington's demands. "I believe it is never practiced to delegate that dictatorial power to one aide-de-camp sent to an army 300 miles distant," he wrote in a first draft. But Gates eliminated this slap at Washington. He knew he had failed to follow protocol when he notified Congress before Washington of his victory at Saratoga and his own plans, making it necessary for the commander-in-chief to dispatch an aide to carry out talks before he gave a direct order. To Gates, it was insulting that Washington sent an aide-de-camp: he might have sent a higher-ranking officer. But there was little Gates could do, eventually, except accede to Hamilton's terms. It was Hamilton's whipsaw authoritative tone that had offended him. In his final-drafted face-saving letter, a chastened Gates wrote Washington that "Colonel Hamilton will report everything that I wish to have you acquainted with." But there might have been a darker motive for Gates's pique at Hamilton. Later, he would insist that Hamilton had secretly been ushered into his office by an aide (Troup?), had rifled Gates's files, and had found Conway's original letter to him, a charge that Hamilton vehemently denied but that probably was true.[22]

Beginning his return trip to Valley Forge, Hamilton, to his disgust, found at New Windsor that Israel Putnam had not honored his pledge to rush reinforcements to Washington:

> I am astonished and alarmed beyond measure to find that all his Excellency's [Washington's] views have been hitherto frustrated and that no single step of those I mentioned to you has been taken to afford him the aid he absolutely stands in need of . . . by delaying which the cause of America is put to the utmost conceivable hazard . . . I speak freely and emphatically because I tremble at the consequences of the delay.[23]

Emboldened by his success with Gates, Hamilton tongue-lashed the sluggish "Old Put," three times his age and a French and Indian Wars hero: "How [your] noncompliance can be answered to General Washington you can best determine." Ignoring his own youth, invoking Washington's authority, Hamilton gave a written "positive order" to march "all the Continental troops under your command" immediately to reinforce Washington. Then Hamilton covered his tracks by writing Washington that he was "pained beyond expression" to find all his earlier arrangements "deranged by General Putnam." The old Indian fighter had argued that he planned to attack New York City. Hamilton called this Putnam's "hobby horse," adding that Putnam had paid "not the least attention" to his earlier orders "in your name" because "everything is sacrificed to the whim of taking New York."

Having cleared his throat, Hamilton took control, arranging with Governor George Clinton to borrow money to pay Connecticut troops who, in a "nigh mutiny," refused to march any farther on Putnam's "farcical parade against New York." Hamilton pleaded with Washington to recall Putnam from command: his "blunders and caprices are endless." (He could not know that Congress had already relieved Putnam and ordered him to report to Washington.) But Hamilton was making enemies, especially among New England officers close to Gates and Putnam who, from habit, distrusted New Yorkers almost as much as Virginians. It may have been at this time that whispers of Hamilton's illegitimacy began to spread among Puritan New England officers who were looking for a reason to bring the cocky little colonel down a peg.[24]

Two exhausting weeks in the saddle and in anxiety over his confrontations with unreliable senior officers had taken their toll on Hamilton. He reported to Washington that he was "very unwell" with "a fever and violent rheumatic pains" all over his body. After two days' bed rest in an inn during which he insisted on firing off a long report to his commander, Hamilton crossed the Hudson on November 13 and became seriously ill. He did not have the strength to write again for fully five weeks. Never was he so ill as he was as a result of this grueling mission in the winter of 1777 in the Hudson Valley. He was apparently suffering from a severe attack of rheumatic fever that for several days, according to a physician rushed to his bedside by Governor Clinton, made it seem Hamilton was "drawing nigh his last." Was this a recurrence of the fever that had felled him as a boy in St. Croix as his mother lay dying? Nursing him through his long illness, Washington's bodyguard, Captain Gibbs, keeping track of his expenses, bought Hamilton a bed and provided the best foods he could find: mutton, chicken, eggs, quail, partridge, and fruit juice laced with liquor. It undoubtedly helped Hamilton's recovery when he received a letter from Washington:

> I approve entirely all the steps you have taken and have only to wish that the exertions of those you have had to deal with had kept pace with your zeal and good intentions.[25]

Hamilton railed at his own inability to speed along reinforcements but he was far too weak to travel. The frail Hamilton, Colonel Hugh Hughes wrote to Gates sarcastically on December 5, "who has been very ill of a nervous disorder at Peekskill, is out of danger, unless it be from his own sweet temper."[26]

BY THE time Hamilton was well enough for the long winter ride to Valley Forge, the Conway Cabal had come to a head. On November 14, 1777, while Hamilton was carrying out his probe in Albany, Conway had sent his resignation to Congress. The affair would have ended there but Congress referred it to its newly coined Board of War, whose chairman, Thomas Mifflin, a former aide to Washington, was an active partner in the Conway plot to depose the commander-in-chief. With secret guidance by Mifflin, several members of Congress now began to beat the drums to promote Conway to inspector general of the army. Pennsylvania radicals joined congressional critics in denouncing Washington. Washington's congressional critics wanted Gates to take over the army and have Washington shunted to a lesser command. Hamilton and other Washington supporters countered by lobbying Congress to make Conway a staff officer with no authority to give orders to other officers.

As the cabal coalesced in Congress, Mifflin, on information supplied by Gates, had accused Hamilton, still ailing at Peekskill, of having rifled Gates's files. Gates believed he could discredit Washington by disgracing his aide Hamilton. After all, Washington had sent Hamilton north with extraordinary powers. To Conway, Gates anxiously wrote, "I intreat you to let me know which of the letters was copied off. It is of the greatest importance that I should discover the person who has been guilty of that act of fidelity. I cannot trace him out unless I have your assistance." When his own aide, Wilkinson, returned to Albany, Gates told him, "I have had a spy in my camp since you left me." Hamilton, Gates said,

> purloined the copy of a letter out of that closet . . . Colonel Hamilton was left alone an hour in this room during which time he took Conway's letter out of that closet and copied it, and the copy has been furnished to Washington.

In early December, Gates wrote Washington that Conway's letter had been "stealingly copied." Washington brushed aside Gates's attempt to smear Hamilton. He responded that Gates's admission in a letter to Mifflin that he knew about the note from Washington to Conway was a serious breach of security. It suggested that he had known all along that the disclosure had come from his own office *before* Washington told him where it had come from. Gates feigned surprise at Washington's reaction. Then he accused his own former aide, Wilkinson, of stealing the letter and leaking it to Hamilton.[27]

Horrified, Wilkinson challenged Gates to a duel. Their aides intervened to stop the duel just as nine brigadier generals sent a written protest about Conway's incompetence to Congress. In an attempt to absolve himself of complicity in the plot, Gates rode all the way from Albany, New York, to the temporary American capital at York, Pennsylvania, in the pit of winter to appeal to influential friends in Congress, especially the delegates from New England who had lionized Gates as the hero of Saratoga. Gates made the mistake of showing Conway's original letter to the new president of Congress, Henry Laurens. Laurens promptly wrote to headquarters at Valley Forge that it was "ten times worse" than the small quote Wilkinson had leaked. The Conway Cabal collapsed like a soufflé in a winter wind.[28]

Hamilton's value to Washington had only grown from his success in flushing out the Conway circle. He returned to Valley Forge just in time to help revamp the bickering army and to help whip it into readiness to counterattack the British inside Philadelphia. Washington's generals could not forgive Conway for making a bad winter at Valley Forge so much worse. Pennsylvania's militia commander General John Cadwalader challenged him to a duel and shot him in the face. Conway survived, but he resigned and returned to France. Hamilton emerged from the episode firmly identified as Washington's indispensable intelligence officer and stout defender of his continuance as commander-in-chief. He also became the enemy of Gates's friends and Washington's critics. Save for Hamilton's intelligence gathering, Washington could well have fallen from power. The consequences for the Revolutionary cause could not have been more grim.

NINE

"A System of Infidelity"

S hortly after his return to active duty in January 1778, Alexander Hamilton set to work on a thorough critique of the Continental Army demanded by the Continental Congress. After the blunders at Brandywine and Germantown, Washington asked the general officers at Valley Forge to suggest reforms in army regulations and training techniques. Hamilton now interviewed fellow officers and edited their complaints into a white paper report for the commander-in-chief and Congress, adding his own unsolicited—and often scathing—observations. "There are still existing in the army so many abuses absolutely contrary to the military constitution," Hamilton began, "that [unless] a speedy stop is put to them, it will be impossible even to establish any order or discipline among the troops." Hamilton aimed his sharpest criticisms at the debacle called the Paoli massacre. Shortly before dawn the morning of September 20, 1777, nearly two hundred Pennsylvanians in the army's advance guard had been killed in a surprise bayonet and cavalry attack. The few guards supposedly on duty at the camp twenty miles west of Philadelphia had inadvertently silhouetted themselves against cook fires as they ate breakfast, affording the British easy targets in the dark. "Nothing," Hamilton insisted, "is more disgraceful to the service nor dangerous for the army than for the advanced posts to be surprised by the enemy."

In preparing for his critique, Hamilton investigated abuses throughout the American army. He went about the task of devising reforms systematically. Many officers, he found, were overstaying their home leaves; they were removing too many enlisted men from the ranks and using them as personal servants. Hamilton could not account for many weapons and uniforms presumably being sold for cash to buy extra rations and liquor. Each regiment, he urged, had to be regularly inspected, its weapons and uniforms counted and its men held accountable for them. "Great quantities of arms and ammunition have been destroyed by being in the possession of men who do not use them in time of action." Many of the dragoons' horses were missing, ridden off on errands by soldiers following orders from unauthorized officers. So acute was the shortage of horses that the headquarters staff couldn't even send messages. All horses should be returned at once and henceforth be used only to carry the orders of generals.

Hamilton drew up detailed instructions for the makeup and behavior of guards, dragoons, and provosts. He proposed that sick or wounded soldiers in hospitals and private homes be tallied regularly and their regiments either brought up to full strength or disbanded. Washington accepted Hamilton's reformed regulations and turned them over to an investigating committee of the Continental Congress visiting Valley Forge. Most of all, Washington concluded from Hamilton's report that Congress needed to appoint a skilled inspector general to police and retrain the army before the next season of war began in June.[1]

The British defeat at Saratoga in October 1777 led, by February 1778, to a formal alliance between France and the American Revolutionaries against the British. The British consequently decided to shift their strategy to a worldwide naval war, putting their armies in America on the defensive. London sent its American commander orders to evacuate Philadelphia and retreat to New York City. Ecstatic at the prospect of open French aid, the ragged remnant of an American army at Valley Forge was nevertheless ill-prepared to exploit the British retreat. Unless the American army could be entirely reorganized, rearmed and retrained before spring, the decisive moment would be lost.

One glaring problem was that the Continental Army, with few experienced officers, had to rely on foreign mercenaries. European officers from twenty countries had flocked to America to fight, some from principle in a revolution against monarchy; others, like the nineteen-year-old Marquis de Lafayette, whose father had been killed by the English in the last war, seeking revenge against the British for the humiliation of their fathers' generation in the Seven Years' War. Still others were just out of work: there was no war in Europe at the moment. Some even proved helpful. They were a mixed lot, including Czechs, Poles, Hungarians, Greeks, Danes, Swedes, Italians, Bohemians, Dutch, Germans, Scots, Irish, Scots-Irish, Swiss, French, Africans, Indians, Protestants, Catholics, and Jews. Alexander Hamilton, a Scottish-French Huguenot West Indian, did not particularly stand out. By 1776, some three hundred thousand Scots-Irish had come to the mainland English colonies. Among them, Patrick Henry became the first governor of Virginia, Henry Knox, chief of artillery. Scots-Irish were only slightly more numerous than German immigrants. So many unemployed French officers had come over that the American mission in Paris became an unemployment office for, as one French chaplain put it, men who had already lost their reputations and replaced them with debts. Lafayette was one of the few wealthy Frenchmen who volunteered to fight in the American army. Defying the orders of King Louis XVI, he had chartered a ship and sailed to America with seven other French volunteer officers, assuring Congress he would serve at his own expense. Given a general's commission, he attached himself to the elegantly mannered, French-speaking Hamilton and became Washington's poodle, always at his side.

Regardless of their origins or motives, by the second week of February 1778, there was no meat at all for Washington's soldiers for four days. From their log huts, Hamilton could hear, as he passed by, the chant, "No meat, no meat." Washington warned Congress of "a general mutiny." On average, twelve men deserted every day. Many American officers, out of money and unable to sustain themselves any longer, simply went home, disgusted as foreign officers were promoted over their heads. In a February 1778 letter to Governor Clinton of New York, Hamilton complained about Congress lavishing "an absurd prodigality of rank to foreigners [as a result of] the impudent importunity of vain boasting of foreign pretenders."[2]

Washington wrote to the Continental Congress that in his army's camp he had "not a single hoof of any kind to slaughter and not more than twenty-five barrels of flour." The army had been in camp at Valley Forge for three weeks before it was possible to issue a four days' supply of fresh provisions. A lack of wagons and drivers—combined with bad roads, deep snows, and flooding on the Susquehanna River to the west—delayed the arrival of most cargoes that survived British raids and the red tape of congressional committees. The army did not even have enough horses to fetch what supplies were available. Without hay and grain and with snow covering pastures, the artillery and baggage horses were dying in such numbers that, twice a week, fatigue parties had to be dispatched to bury them. This wrought even more hardship on men already suffering terribly from the cold. Of nine thousand men reporting "present" by early February 1778, nearly 40 percent were too scantily clad and ill-shod to report for duty. When a soldier was detailed to work or assigned to guard duty, his cabinmates pooled their clothing to outfit him. By March 25, 1778, more than eleven hundred American soldiers, nine in ten of them foreign born, deserted, slipping through the British lines into warm and cozy Philadelphia.

Yet it was the arrival of one more mendicant European officer, spouting profanity in several languages with his hand out, that finally lifted the spirits as well as the fighting ability of the diehard, blanket-wrapped, disease-and-desertion-ridden little army at Valley Forge. One of the last foreigners to volunteer, Frederick Steuben, calling himself Frederick Wilhelm August Heinrich Ferdinand, Baron von Steuben, presented to Congress a letter of introduction from Benjamin Franklin in the American mission at Paris. Much of what Franklin claimed about Steuben was untrue. He had not been a lieutenant general in the army of the King of Prussia. He had been a captain. He was not of noble birth. He did not own a great estate in Swabia. But he did know how to train soldiers, and he was offering his services as an unpaid volunteer. After the American fiascoes at Brandywine and Germantown, his timing could not have been better.

Morale at Valley Forge was at ebb on February 23, 1778, when Washington, Hamilton, and Lafayette rode out of camp to greet Steuben. While Steuben had not been born a noble, Frederick the Great had awarded him the Baden-Durlach Order of Fidelity and the lifetime courtesy title of *Freiherr*, or baron, for his services while leading a *Freikorps* on dangerous raids during the Seven Years' War. He was companionable and urbane. Hamilton instantly liked him, and they became devoted friends. While Washington and Hamilton and a few other trusted aides knew that Steuben had embellished his record, the inescapable truth was that the Continental Army needed someone with exactly Steuben's ability to discipline and lead irregular troops. Leading an entourage of three aides assigned him by Congress and by twenty-five of Washington's Life Guards, Steuben made a splendid entrance into the austere Valley Forge encampment, riding between the rows of snow-topped log-and-wattle huts with their tattered occupants standing at attention as he passed. He may have noticed that some, lacking shoes, were standing on their hats to keep their feet out of the snow.

The openhanded Steuben quickly ingratiated himself to both officers and men. He fed the guards posted outside his cabin door from his general's rations and gave dinners for officers, many of them as hungry as their men. In part with money he borrowed from Hamilton, Steuben hosted a feast to which he invited only guests whose breeches were ragged.

With the help of Hamilton and Nathanael Greene, Steuben developed a plan for training the entire army in the two months that remained before the 1778 campaign began. Steuben brimmed over with suggestions that Hamilton had to translate for him. (Among Hamilton's official duties was to speak and to write to French officers in their own tongue. At the time, he was one of two fluent speakers of French among the American officers.) One was that the Americans pounce on the British if they retreated across New Jersey. Hamilton wrote Steuben in French that the Americans had enough boats "to transport our army across the Delaware," as they had at Christmas 1776, "in very little time." But boats were not the main problem. What if they caught up with the enemy? Maneuvering under fire with strict discipline once they overtook the British was a far greater problem. Hamilton, invoking his own experience training artillerymen, recommended that the Prussian take advantage of the American soldiers' eagerness to learn. Steuben, recognizing the Americans' unusual insistence on explanations by their own officers, availed himself of three German-speaking sub-inspectors, one of them Major Francis Barber, Hamilton's erstwhile teacher at Elizabethtown Academy. To avoid confusion, Steuben standardized training, discarding all three drill books then in use. With Hamilton's help, he designed a simplified manual of arms with only ten basic commands; with Hamilton, he also began writing a new set of regulations for every detail of camp life. The Steuben-Hamilton manual, eventually published as the *Regulations for Order and Discipline of the Troops of the United States*, was the basis for IDR, the Infantry Drill Regulations, still used by the U.S. Army.[3]

Then, with Hamilton's help, Steuben selected a model company of one hundred of the army's best soldiers and attached them temporarily to Washington's Life Guards as an elite training unit. They personally trained this unit day after day, requiring all the regimental officers to observe and spread the instructions in a sort of mathematical projection throughout the army. The first hundred men were dispatched to help train other units as Steuben, Hamilton, and their staff personally trained the second hundred, then the third, and so on. They taught the soldiers an easy, natural step halfway between the European slow march and British quick-time. Practicing loading and firing, the men overcame their reluctance to use the bayonet and mastered basic foot maneuvers. In less than a month, the whole army, drilling by regiments each morning and inspected by brigades each afternoon, mastered the new manual of arms. Each brigade major set his pocket watch according to the adjutant general's, whose timepiece was set by the headquarters clock. Noncommissioned officers who did not set an example of punctuality and personal cleanliness were broken to the ranks. Privates in rags were expected to shave, to wash their faces and hands, and to clean up the mess around their cabins, where they had been pitching their trash and garbage all winter.

Steuben pressed the brigade commanders to submit regular tallies of all arms, accouterments, and uniforms to him personally, as Hamilton had long urged. By April 1778, Washington, who had watched in amazement as his entire army improved in skill and spirit, recommended to Congress that Steuben be appointed inspector general with the permanent rank of major general. Not waiting for Congress to act, he had Hamilton compose a general order requiring that all officers and men regard Steuben as such.

For nearly two decades, Hamilton and Steuben were to remain close friends. After the war, Hamilton repeatedly helped Steuben to pay his debts. By the end of 1789, Hamilton had advanced 661 pounds (about $25,000 today) for Steuben, sometimes lending him large amounts of cash, sometimes cosigning notes for him, sometimes paying off Steuben's loans from other officers. The two men remained close until Steuben's death. As secretary of the treasury, Hamilton helped his spendthrift German friend obtain a $2,500-a-year pension from the new federal government in 1790 rather than trust him with a lump-sum payment. Then he helped Steuben to obtain a mortgage on advantageous terms for sixteen thousand acres in the Mohawk Valley, near Utica, where Hamilton often visited him in the summer.

DURING HIS investigations of army abuses at Valley Forge, Hamilton had become convinced that much of the blame for the army's suffering lay within Congress itself. In December 1777, a congressional committee had arrived at Valley Forge to study conditions there. Here, Hamilton first met Congressman Gouverneur Morris of New York, an outspoken conservative, and like-minded Robert Morris, a wealthy Philadelphia merchant and financial wizard. Here, too, he formed his first opinion of congressional ineptitude, imbibing much of it from the caustic comments of the flamboyant Gouverneur Morris. The two men had been corresponding for more than a year by this time. Both men shared the view that Congress was now made up of delegates, as Morris had put it back in May 1777, "perhaps not the best qualified." More than a Congress, Morris believed the state needed a "vigorous manly executive." Both men obviously believed General Washington should be given more power.[4]

While Congress studied the army, Hamilton studied Congress. In February 1778, in his capacity as liaison between headquarters and New York State, Hamilton wrote another critique, this time harsher, sending it through Gouverneur Morris to the state's first governor, George Clinton, who had helped Hamilton during his long illness a year earlier. In this secret letter, Hamilton reminded Clinton that "you and I had some conversations when I had the pleasure of seeing you last about the existence of a certain faction" in Congress. Factions, another word for political parties, were, Americans believed at the time, dangerous, indeed evil. Congress and the common cause were supposed to be unanimous, synonymous. In the historical memory of the times, factions had pulled apart the parliamentary forces in the English Revolution of the seventeenth century, leading to a restoration of monarchy and despotism. "Since I saw you, I have discovered such convincing traits of the monster [faction] that I cannot doubt its [extensive] reality." Hamilton by now counted among Washington's—and therefore his own—opponents in Congress all of Horatio Gates's supporters: Samuel and John Adams, Dr. Benjamin Rush of Philadelphia, Richard Henry Lee of Virginia, and two of Washington's former personal aides, Thomas Mifflin and Joseph Reed, both now radical Pennsylvania politicians.

Again excoriating Congress in a letter he routed through Gouverneur Morris in a February 13, 1778, letter to Clinton, Hamilton unleashed the opening salvo of a lifelong critique of Congress. The new nation's governing body was no longer made up of the likes of earlier delegates such as Washington, Jefferson, and Jay. At twenty-three years old, Hamilton had already fathomed that Congress would not always, not usually, be made up of men of the caliber of the Founding Fathers. There was now "a degeneracy of representation in the great council of America," the "effects of which we daily see and feel, that there is not as much wisdom in a certain body as there ought to be, and as the success of our affairs demands":

Folly, caprice, a want of foresight, comprehension and dignity characterize the general tenor of their actions. Of this, I dare say, you are sensible, though you have not, perhaps, so many opportunities of knowing it as I have. Their conduct with respect to the army especially is feeble, indecisive and improvident. We are reduced to a more terrible situation than you can conceive.

Congress's false notions of economizing had led it to withhold vital provisions for the army. This, in turn, was causing "carelessness and indifference" among the officers themselves. "They have disgusted the army by repeated instances of the most whimsical favoritism in their promotions."

The commissary department, appointed by Congress to feed and clothe the army, was exposing the army "to the danger of dissolution from absolute famine":

At this very day there are complaints from the whole line of [going] three or four days without provisions. Desertions have been immense and strong features of mutiny begin to show themselves . . . If effectual measures are not speedily adopted, I know not how we shall keep the army together. I omit saying anything of the want of clothing.

The greatest problem, Hamilton believed, lay in the disreputable character of many of the delegates to Congress by late winter of 1778:

America once had a representation [in Congress] that would do honor to any age or nation. The present falling off is very alarming and dangerous. What is the cause? How is it to be remedied? . . . The great men who composed our first council— are they dead, have they deserted the cause, or what has become of them? Very few are dead and still fewer have deserted the cause . . . They are either in the field or in the offices of the respective states. The only remedy is to return them to the place where their presence is infinitely more important.

This was Hamilton's first impassioned plea for the states to give back power and leadership to form a strong central government, a cry that would become his mantra. Each state had reclaimed "its best members" to "conduct its own affairs." America's first statesmen were "fonder of the emoluments and conveniences" of being nearer home in wartime. But these strong local attachments were "falsely operating" to make them watch out more for the interests of their own states "than for the common interests of the confederacy." Hamilton considered this a "most pernicious mistake" that "must be corrected."

Hamilton could not have chosen a less fitting recipient for his criticism than the ultimate Anti-Federalist, George Clinton. It might have been this, Hamilton's first venture into criticizing congressional politicians, that kindled a decades-long clash between Hamilton and this states'-rightist New York governor. It was as if he were blindly personally attacking Clinton and New York:

> However important it is to give form and efficiency to your interior constitutions and police, it is infinitely more important to have a wise general council. Otherwise, a failure of the measures of the Union will overturn all your labors and ruin the common cause. You should not beggar the councils of the United States to enrich the administration of the several members.

Hamilton was careful to point out, however, that he risked this analysis of Congress's weakness in writing only because he believed Governor Clinton agreed with him. Hamilton cautioned Clinton that his views "are not fit for the vulgar ear." But it was "time that men of weight" should "take the alarm" to purge Congress of "weak, foolish and unsteady hands" to avoid "the consequences of having a Congress despised at home and abroad." Hamilton's last bit of advice to Clinton was to "counterplot the secret machinations of [Washington's] enemies." All "true and sensible friends to their country and of course to a certain great man" must rally to purge Congress according to the "proper remedy."5

Believing, apparently, that Hamilton was speaking for Washington, Clinton wrote back that he shared Hamilton's disgust with Congress. "I wish the defects of a certain great body were less apparent." Their "want of wisdom" was "too evident." At best, Congress enacted empty resolutions. "Could our soldiery subsist on resolves, they would never want food or clothing." Clinton ended his letter: "I take for granted that military men [are] burning confidential letters for fear of accidents as soon as they are read." Obviously Hamilton did not burn this one. It still survives among Hamilton's papers.[6]

Hamilton was encouraged that the governor of his adopted state had agreed to enter into a secret correspondence with him and he continued to write to him, through Gouverneur Morris, his blunt critiques of Congress. The "defects of a certain synod" were not just the cause for idle speculation but required an immediate remedy because they were structural. Hamilton's "most melancholy" fear was that, unless men of influence like Clinton, Jay, and Schuyler stepped in, "the weakness of our councils will, in all probability, ruin us." Delays in rebuilding the army were "astonishing." Congress was passing "*ex post facto* laws or, rather, violating all law." One congressional resolution legalized drafting British prisoners of war into the Continental Army, Hamilton, the expert on prisoners of war, wrote Morris. In this instance, Congress was violating the surrender terms of the Saratoga Convention as well as international law. Burgoyne's surrendered army was supposed to have been shipped by the British Navy from Boston back to England. Congress had nitpicked the agreement, Hamilton argued. Under the surrender agreement, all British arms were to be surrendered. But when only 658 of 4,991 troops turned in their empty cartridge boxes, Congress deemed that they had not surrendered all their arms. When British troop ships had arrived off Boston in December to take Burgoyne's army home, Congress barred them from entering the port until the king could be consulted and personally ratified the convention. Months later, George III sent written orders for the new British commander to ratify the convention. This time Congress took the position that the orders might be a forgery. Congress insisted on a witness who had seen the king sign them. Only Burgoyne and two of his staff were permitted to return to England. The remaining 4,988 prisoners were marched to Virginia, then to Frederick, Maryland, where they were to remain prisoners for the rest of the war.[7]

*　*　*

CONGRESS'S HIGH-HANDED bungling made Hamilton's duties as a commissioner of prisoner exchanges all but impossible. He wrote indignantly to Governor Clinton of Congress's "system of infidelity":

> They have violated the Convention of Saratoga. . . . Lately, a [party with a] flag [of truce] with provisions and clothing for the British prisoners with G.W.'s [Washington's] passport was seized at Lancaster [Pennsylvania] with circumstances of violence and meanness that would disgrace Hottentots. Still more lately, [Washington's] engagements with General Howe for an exchange of prisoners have been most shamefully violated.

Hamilton was especially irate because Congress had resolved that it would not ratify a general cartel for an exchange of prisoners that Hamilton and his friend Boudinot had been trying to negotiate for months with British emissaries, until all accounts for food and necessities on both sides were tabulated, and any outstanding balance due Congress was paid in cash. This process could take many months while thousands of prisoners on both sides suffered and died. Congress also stipulated that it would not honor any prisoner agreement until England negotiated with the United States as a separate and equal power, that is, until England acknowledged United States independence. Since the British held twice the number of prisoners as the Americans, "we shall without doubt be in Mr. Howe's debt." But Congress's resolves had "put off an exchange perhaps forever":

> Whatever refined politicians may think, it is of great consequence to preserve a national character . . . To violate its faith whenever it is the least inconvenient to keep it [will] unquestionably have an ill-effect upon foreign negotiations and tend to bring Government at home into contempt . . .
>
> I would ask whether, in a republican state and a republican army, such a cruel policy as that of exposing those men who [were] foremost in defense of their country to the miseries of hopeless captivity can succeed? For my own part, I have so

much of the milk of humanity in me that I abhor such *Neroian* maxims, and I look up on the old proverb, that *honesty is the best policy*, to be so generally true that I can never expect any good from any systematic deviation from it.

At the end of his long, confidential letter to Governor Clinton, Hamilton passed along a terse piece of military intelligence, garnered by spies inside Philadelphia, that may have sent a chill down Clinton's back. "Some accounts say the enemy are preparing to evacuate Philadelphia." That meant that the British army and navy would be returning to New York, where, once again, they would be strong enough to menace the Hudson Valley. [8]

Hamilton's detestation of the confusion, incompetence, and outright meddling of committees and boards of the Continental Congress during the bleak winter of 1777–78, more than any other experience, explains why, when he became the first secretary of the treasury and chief architect of the federal government between 1789 and 1795, he would insist that each department have a single strong executive reporting only to the chief executive, the president of the United States.

JUST BEFORE the Battle of Brandywine in the autumn of 1777, twenty-three-year-old John Laurens of South Carolina, dashing son of Henry Laurens, the new president of the Continental Congress, joined Washington's headquarters staff as a volunteer aide. French-speaking, he had been educated at Geneva, Switzerland, where he had imbibed the revolutionary writings of Voltaire and Rousseau. Laurens became Hamilton's closest friend in the army, making up a French-speaking mess table threesome with the Marquis de Lafayette. Tall, muscular, handsome, and a resplendent dresser, Laurens was also hot-blooded and no doubt taught Hamilton the code of dueling. Together, on and off the field of honor, they set themselves up as Washington's champions, challenging anyone who insulted their chieftain.

The two young aides soon discovered they had much in common. Both had grown up surrounded by slaves. Working at first together on the problem of treatment of prisoners of war in captivity, they had gradually turned their minds to the condition of permanent captivity—slavery. For many Americans, the greatest moral dilemma of the Revolution was that whites were fighting for freedom from the British while holding blacks in slavery. Every state in the new nation tolerated slavery. In Europe, after studying the writings of the Enlightenment, Laurens had come to despise slavery. For his part, West Indian–born Hamilton was to become an early member, with his friends John Jay and Hercules Mulligan, of the New York Society for Promoting the Manumission of Slaves and was to pay numerous visits with his friends to the homes and shops of freed blacks. In New York City he had become accustomed to seeing self-reliant, prosperous African Americans. As a member of the New York Assembly, he would support a bill for gradual emancipation. Laurens, stirring Hamilton's imagination, challenged his father, the president of the Continental Congress, to free his many slaves. If he did, young Laurens vowed, he would forgo his inheritance, which was largely based on slave labor. Hamilton and Laurens worked out a plan to offer freedom to slaves in South Carolina who would risk their lives fighting the British and their Loyalist allies.

As the Revolution progressed, Hamilton and Laurens became conspicuous among American officers for speaking out against slavery. Since slavery proponents rationalized their behavior by declaring that Africans were of a lower order of being, Hamilton and Laurens decided to approach the problem pragmatically. Especially when the war shifted to the South after 1778, the Americans needed the slave-owners to fill out their depleted ranks to fight off the British and the many Loyalists, but many Southerners would not leave their farms to join the American army because they did not trust their slaves, who, in South Carolina, greatly outnumbered whites. They feared the slaves would revolt in their absence, killing white wives and children and burning their plantations. In January 1779, Rhode Island officers had suggested replenishing their undermanned battalions with slaves. Washington tacitly approved, sending their proposal on to officials in Rhode Island. In February, the state legislature voted that slaves who enlisted would receive their freedom. The state, in turn, would compensate slaveowners. Despite the slaveholders' generally held racial prejudices, Hamilton and Laurens could now point to proof of the normal capacities of blacks who had been freed to fight at a critical time in the Continental Army.

By August 1777, there was an average of fifty-four freed blacks in each of seven Continental brigades. That autumn, in the battle for the Delaware River forts, Rhode Island's freed slaves fought valiantly—and successfully. Many more were being hired from their masters as laborers who worked under extremely dangerous conditions. In addition, many freed blacks had volunteered to fight in state navies and aboard privateering ships, even though, if they were captured, they were sold as prizes of war by British ship captains and sold into slavery to plantation owners in the West Indies.

In early 1778, when president of Congress Laurens visited Valley Forge, Hamilton and Laurens's son arm-twisted the elder Laurens to urge the South Carolina legislature, of which he was a leading member, to form a regiment made up of slaves led by white officers. Young Laurens would himself be its commander. The slaves would fight the British on the promise of emancipation at war's end. "Those who fall in battle will not lose much," he reasoned. "Those who survive will obtain their reward."[9]

Fully one year later, John Laurens, like Hamilton desperate for a field command, wrote to his father to release his "able-bodied slaves instead of leaving me a fortune." With those slaves, he believed he could train an entire black regiment in time for the next campaign. The senior Laurens, even though he had endorsed the principle of emancipation in the giddy days right after the Declaration of Independence was read aloud in Charleston in 1776, now told his son that, of the three hundred slaves that were his son's inheritance, many were women and children and only forty men were fit to fight. Henry Laurens added that his son's scheme was motivated only by his ambition for fame and was pointless. "For now, I will undertake to say there is not a man in America of your opinion."[10]

The president of Congress reckoned without Alexander Hamilton. Laurens rode to Philadelphia to present their scheme in person to Congress. By now, Hamilton's old friend John Jay of New York was presiding over Congress. To Jay, Laurens carried Hamilton's written assurance, in one of his most important letters, that he considered the plan "most rational" and the only solution in South Carolina, where blacks made up the majority and many whites were Loyalists. Otherwise, Hamilton could not see "how a sufficient force can be collected in that quarter." Hamilton warmly recommended his friend Laurens to Jay for his "zeal, intelligence and enterprise."

Writing from headquarters in New Jersey on March 14, 1779, Hamilton told Jay he thought that, now that much of the fighting had shifted to the South, to arm the slaves against the British was the "most rational" expedient Congress could adopt:

> Indeed, I hardly see how a sufficient force can be collected in that quarter without it. The enemy's operations there are growing infinitely serious and formidable.
>
> I have not the least doubt that the Negroes will make very excellent soldiers with proper management. I frequently hear it objected to the scheme of embodying Negroes that they are too stupid to make soldiers. This is so far from appearing to me a valid objection that I think their want of cultivation (for their natural faculties are probably as good as ours) joined to that habit of subordination which they acquire from a life of servitude, will make them sooner become soldiers than our white inhabitants. Let officers be men of sense and sentiment and the nearer the soldiers approach to machines, the better.

Hamilton correctly foresaw strong resistance to emancipation in Congress "from prejudice and self-interest":

> The contempt we have been taught to entertain for the blacks makes us fancy many things that are founded neither in reason nor experience. An unwillingness to part with property of so valuable a kind will furnish a thousand arguments to show the impracticability or pernicious tendency of a scheme which requires such a sacrifice. But if we do not make use of [the slaves] in this way, the enemy probably will. The best way to counteract the temptations they will hold out will be to offer them ourselves. An essential part of the plan is to give them

their freedom with their muskets. This will secure their fidelity, animate their courage and, I believe, will have a good influence upon those who remain [enslaved] by opening a door to their emancipation. This circumstance, I confess, has no small weight in inducing me to wish the success of the project, for the dictates of humanity and true policy equally interest me in favor of this unfortunate class of men.[11]

Practical, cynical, compassionate all at once, Hamilton, who had antagonized many New England congressmen in the Conway cabal, now took on the Southern slavery advocates in Congress—unsuccessfully. South Carolina, which had scuttled Jefferson's antislavery clause in the Declaration of Independence by threatening to drop out of the Continental union unless it was deleted, ignored the Laurens-Hamilton proposal. Soon afterward, in a massive British invasion, Charleston and then the rest of the state fell. The British did what Hamilton predicted, offering freedom to slaves in exchange for military service. Thousands accepted, and left with the British at war's end, settling in the Caribbean as free men.

IT WOULD be weeks before Hamilton was free to send another message to Jay in New York. Washington had appointed Hamilton one of the four principal American prisoner of war negotiators. The British commander provided Hamilton with a pass to go through enemy lines to Germantown, where the talks took place. Hamilton carried Washington's authority to propose terms "on principles of justice, humanity and mutual advantage and agreeable to the customary rules and practice of war among civilized nations." But according to Hamilton's spies inside Philadelphia, Howe was being replaced. Especially with the French entering the war as America's allies, Hamilton questioned whether either commanding general, British or American, had the authority to make a binding agreement.

When the prisoner talks moved to Newtown in Bucks County, outside the British lines, on April 11, 1778, Hamilton prepared seventeen "Questions Concerning a Proposed Cartel for the Exchange of Prisoners of War," and took the official notes on the negotiations for the American side, which were used later for a conference among the American commissioners. He then drafted "A Treaty and Convention for the Exchange and Accommodation of Prisoners of War." It became a model for future prisoner exchanges. Among its features, principles and numerical values for exchanges were spelled out. "Those first captured shall be first exchanged," it began. Officers were to be exchanged for officers of equal rank. When that was impossible, "two or more inferior officers shall be given for a superior." The commander-in-chief was calculated to be worth 192 ensigns (second lieutenants today). If there remained any officers who could not be exchanged, five privates could be given for one ensign. Exchanges were to be made every two months. No officer or soldier was to be "thrown into dungeons" or any other kind of "unnecessarily rigorous confinement." Among the first to be exchanged were to be Major General Charles Lee, a prisoner in the so-called Congress Hall cellblock at the Provost Prison in New York City, and Lieutenant Colonel Ethan Allen of Vermont, who had been held in a castle dungeon in Wales. Allen, captured in an abortive attempt to capture Montreal in 1775 after he and his Green Mountain Boys had seized Fort Ticonderoga, had been treated especially harshly during his nearly three years as a British prisoner. Clapped into handcuffs and leg irons, unable to lie down for six weeks as he was transported in the filthy hold of a ship, he had been shunted from Canada to England to the Caribbean and back to Canada and then to New York, where he had been held in solitary confinement until his exchange. No longer, under the covenant Hamilton cowrote with Elias Boudinot, could captives be transported across the Atlantic for imprisonment.

Now that a general prisoner exchange appeared imminent, Hamilton took an even more prominent role. Washington deferred to him more frequently because of his tact and finesse as a diplomat (which was assisted by his fluent French). He became Washington's most trusted deputy. He made more suggestions than anyone else on the headquarters staff, but then he also relieved Washington of more numerous burdens by writing and acting on his own orders, with only a nod or a flourish of the quill needed from the busy commander-in-chief.[12]

In late May 1778, British General Howe sent word that he was ready to exchange 790 American prisoners in Philadelphia, all that survived of more than 2,000 who had been captured the previous fall. When British commissary of prisoners Joshua Loring brought this offer to Valley Forge, Washington turned the negotiations over to Hamilton. He was "to do definitively whatever may be necessary towards the execution of a general exchange of prisoners," Washington wrote Hamilton, "and I hereby assure you that your proceedings in this instance will be ratified by me." He authorized Hamilton to round up wagons to meet the British just outside the city to bring the released prisoners, many of them seriously ill and near death, to Valley Forge or to nearby houses for medical treatment.[13]

HAMILTON'S GROWING friendship with Lafayette soon led to another bold scheme: French and American troops should fight side-by-side against the British, not as separate commands. "Some considerable time previous to the arrival of the French Army," Hamilton's friend Nicholas Fish later told Hamilton's widow, "Hamilton had conceived the idea." Hamilton proposed an integrated (Franco-American) force under Lafayette's command operating independently of the American chain of command, in which Hamilton would lead the American troops. When Hamilton broached the idea to Lafayette, he embraced it enthusiastically. Using family connections in Paris, Lafayette submitted the idea to French military authorities and won their approval.[14]

Just how good Hamilton's timing was became apparent when, after five months of the cold, sick depression at Valley Forge, news reached America that the French would definitely intervene in the Revolutionary War on the side of the Americans, as unlikely as a monarchy supporting revolution against another king now seems. In a carefully planned celebration at Valley Forge, the general order for May 6, 1778, the day of jubilation, concluded, "Long live the friendly European powers. The last discharge of 13 pieces of artillery will be given, followed by a general running fire and huzzah [for] the American states." Hamilton joined Washington and his generals and inspected the troops in a grand review. Wheeling to the right by platoons, the brigades marched in five columns to the parade ground, where they trimmed their lines quickly and precisely.

Amid the fireworks, cannon salutes, and speeches, Hamilton privately sounded an anxious note. Writing to the new quartermaster general, Nathanael Greene, in a letter signed by Washington, Hamilton worried that French intervention should not "justify the least relaxation." American efforts must "be continued in their fullest vigor." Lack of preparedness against British counterattack "might be fatal." America more than ever needed "a powerful army well-furnished with every apparatus of war." Hamilton had a hard time believing at first that the British, after so much bloodshed and expense, were peacefully abandoning the American capital of Philadelphia. He wrote in Latin to Governor Clinton, "*Sed credat Judaeus Apella, non ego.*" Freely translated, "But let Congress believe it, I wasn't born yesterday." Hamilton feared a trap.¹⁵

In a last letter before leaving Valley Forge, Hamilton wrote to William Duer, a New York delegate to the Continental Congress (and Lord Stirling's son-in-law), sending it off with Baron Steuben. He warned that his friend Steuben, while he "deserves to be considered as a valuable man," possessed "a fondness for power and importance" that would make him seek more prerogatives as inspector general than the office warranted. "Be on your guard," Hamilton wrote Duer. Especially, Steuben sought the power not only to train and inspect but to give orders and mete out punishment outside the chain of command. He had already purged Washington's Life Guards of thieves and looters and replaced them with Germans who could not fraternize with American troops. Any more power "would inflame the whole army." Each officer from captain to commander-in-chief jealously guarded his own rights. And Steuben did not seem to know how many toes he had trampled. This part of the letter would have seemed to Steuben duplicitous, had he been able to read it. He evidently thought he was carrying Hamilton's strong letter of recommendation. Then, while Hamilton had Duer's attention, he launched into a general critique of the army's shortcomings. Lack of discipline was the result of the "skeleton state" of many regiments that had too many "superfluous" officers but few troops. "In the present condition of our regiments, they are incapable even of performing their common exercises without joining two or more together. We have no prospect of seeing the regiments filled. We should reduce them." Once again, Hamilton used his unique position as liaison to New York State to make his views known where they might influence reform. The question is whether Washington ever knew about it.[16]

THE REMOVAL of British artillery batteries around Philadelphia on June 17, 1778, made it certain that the British were evacuating the American capital. The British decision to abandon the hard-won city caught the American command by surprise. Early that morning, when Washington learned from his scouts that the British guns were gone, he asked Hamilton to prepare a question he could submit to his generals in a hastily convened council of war:

> In case this army overtake the enemy on their march, will it be prudent, with the aid which may reasonably be expected from the Jersey militia, to make an attack upon them, and ought it to be a partial or a general one?[17]

The generals were badly split. Charles Lee, recently exchanged by the British, opposed an all-out attack, as did Steuben and Du Portail, the chief French engineer. Greene, Lafayette, Wayne, and Cadwalader favored a general engagement. The Americans now had the superior force, thirteen thousand well-trained men.

Fearing interception by a French fleet, the British were forced to retreat overland, but by what route? To confuse the Americans, for four days the new British commander, Sir Henry Clinton, maneuvered with ten thousand men, but there was no way to conceal some fifteen hundred baggage wagons containing vast quantities of loot. They threw up clouds of dust on the sun-baked roads. Some three thousand fleeing Loyalist refugees and all their portable possessions were also gridlocked in an enormous traffic jam of carriages, carts, and wagons stretching over five miles. A large number of camp-following women trudged along on foot. The heat was taking its toll on the British soldiery, softened by a comfortable winter in Philadelphia and weighed down under personal belongings and all the booty they could carry. It took the British six days to cover only thirty-four miles in muggy ninety-six-degree heat and drenching downpours.[18]

On June 18, Washington dispatched Lee with an advance corps to harry the British rear. Lee, a former British Army major, considered himself Washington's rival. Years after the Revolution, documents were found establishing that in 1777, while a British prisoner in New York, Lee had turned traitor against the Americans. He had written a plan for the British military conquest of the colonies and had submitted it to General Howe. The British chose to ignore it. But in June 1778, Washington knew nothing of this. To be sure, he had heard, somewhat to his dismay, Lee's vitriolic discourses on the poor quality of the American soldier, who, Lee maintained, could not stand up to British bayonets. But because Lee was the second-highest ranking Continental officer, Washington automatically had to give him command of the right wing, the post of honor commanding the best troops.

Alexander Hamilton was never more vigorous or more enterprising in more different roles than during the Battle of Monmouth. Ordered by Washington to take a mounted troop and find out where the British Army was going, he spent four days and nights in the saddle, keeping Washington apprised of every British movement and troop disposition. According to the diary of Hamilton's friend James McHenry, the American pursuit of Clinton's army began exuberantly. The first rainy night, the headquarters staff stopped off at the home of Jonathan Fells in Doylestown, Pennsylvania. There Hamilton frolicked with "a pretty, fullfaced, youthful, playful lass" until he had to go to work writing out Benedict Arnold's orders as the new military governor of Philadelphia. The next day, Saturday, June 20, the "rapid morning's march" in "excessive hot" weather was more than some soldiers, so recently freezing, could bear: "Some of the soldiers die suddenly," Hamilton reported. Hamilton was at Washington's side when they crossed the Delaware River at Coryell's Ferry at noon on Sunday, June 21. "Here are some charming girls," recorded the long-imprisoned McHenry. A drummer with the Life Guards was "more a favorite than Hamilton with the local farmgirls," wrote his jealous friend. But Hamilton was busy taking notes of another kind for a warning letter from Washington to Horatio Gates on the Hudson: the British might be coming his way. Then Washington dispatched Hamilton on a reconnaissance mission. Hamilton was to find out why the British had halted at Allentown, New Jersey. Were they trying to lure the Americans into battle? Hamilton rode off toward Princeton to put out feelers to his spies in the towns the British might pass through.[19]

He had scarcely returned when, at yet another council of war, Charles Lee argued that they should let the British cross New Jersey unmolested. Even superior American numbers, he contended, were no match for European professionals. Wait for the French to do the fighting when they arrived. Hamilton, just back from reconnoitering, recorded the proceedings, but he was too low-ranking to vote. He could only fume and take the minutes of the council's decision to remain on guard. Risking a few thousand troops to harass the British flanks "would have done honor to the most honorable society of midwives, and to them only," he wrote. Under Lee's influence, the generals voted to "keep at a comfortable distance from the enemy [while making] a vain parade of annoying them." After the council met, Hamilton later revealed, Lafayette and Greene pleaded privately with Washington to ignore the vote and attack. Hamilton, in his eulogy to Greene eleven years later, made public how thoroughly he had despised the timidity of Washington's generals in "those impotent councils."

A formal vote decreed an undisturbed passage to an enemy retiring from the fairest fruits of his victories to seek an asylum from danger, disheartened by retreat, dispirited by desertion, broken by fatigue, retiring through woods, defiles and morasses in which discipline was useless, in the face of an army superior in numbers, elated by pursuit and ardent to signalize their courage.[20]

Bowing to the cautious Washington, Hamilton wrote orders for detachments of New Jersey militia and Virginia riflemen to gall the British flanks—but no more.

Gradually, however, Washington began to heed reports that Hamilton brought back from daily reconnaissances. He convinced Washington that the British were taking the shortest possible route to the

Atlantic coast and would escape completely unless he attacked. Finally, Washington sent Hamilton ahead with Lafayette. Hamilton was to urge Lee to yield his command of the forward units to the young Frenchman. Hamilton later recounted Lee's "truly childish" refusal in citing his seniority over "a young volunteering general." The command seesawed back and forth three times until Washington "grew tired of such feeble behavior and ordered the marquis to proceed." Yet still Lee demanded that he, not Lafayette, be given the post of honor. Washington, to silence him, finally gave Lee command of the whole five-thousand-man advance corps, more than one third of the army, but he demanded that Lee cooperate with Lafayette. Hamilton was to act as liaison between Washington and Lafayette.

On June 25, 1778, Hamilton rode ahead with a detachment of cavalry over the sandy roads of the Pine Barrens, gathering intelligence and keeping both Lafayette and Washington posted. To be absolutely sure of Clinton's route, Hamilton rode ahead for a second solid night in the saddle to locate the spearhead of the British column. At nine that night, he sent a courier from the village of Cranbury to Lafayette with word that the British had turned onto the Monmouth road. Their rear guard was strung out over five miles and vulnerable. Lafayette should hurry to Cranbury, rendezvous there with New Jersey Continentals and the New Jersey militia. Hamilton was riding off in the darkness to round up. Lafayette was to forward this urgent message to Washington.[21]

Based on Hamilton's timely reconnaissance, Washington now quick-marched his main force to Cranbury in heavy rain. There, Hamilton reported to Washington he had just learned that Lafayette could go no farther without food. Not only were Lafayette's troops in "extreme distress" for "want of provisions," but Wayne's force "is almost starving" and would not go on "till they are supplied." The British troops, well fed, were marching briskly, getting away. "It is evident the enemy wish to avoid, not to engage us," Hamilton told Washington. Clinton had put three brigades of redcoats behind his precious baggage wagons. The daring Hamilton had ridden close enough to the enemies to make out the brigades' insignia in his telescope, he noted. Lafayette once again signaled that he was prepared to strike, but Washington quickly sent back word with Hamilton to Lafayette that he was to avoid a premature engagement. Food was on the way: first, let the troops rest and recover from the heat.[22]

When Hamilton sent Washington his next report from Robins Tavern, eight miles east of Allentown, it was clear how close he had come to the enemy. The British, he warned, were headed toward Perth Amboy on Raritan Bay where they could ferry across to Staten Island under protection of British warships. "Their march today has been very judiciously conducted—their baggage in front" with "a rear guard of 1,000 men about 400 paces from the main body." But if Lafayette came up quickly, the Americans would catch the enemy rear off guard. When Washington again ordered a disappointed Lafayette to remain in reserve and support the main army under Lee, Hamilton, disgruntled, set to preparing New Jersey militia for the attack.[23]

Hamilton, Lafayette, and Washington met at Englishtown at dawn on June 27. Hamilton informed Washington that the American vanguard under Lee was nearing the British rear guard at Monmouth Courthouse and "they would soon engage." Hamilton urged Washington to send off his right wing to outflank the British and send his left wing under Hamilton to join Lee. Washington liked Hamilton's advice. Hamilton had begun to fire off the necessary detailed orders as they rode forward, when suddenly they began to encounter frightened soldiers running back *toward* them. The night before, Hamilton had carried to Lee Washington's order to attack the next morning as soon as the British left Monmouth. But now Lee and the whole five-thousand-man advance force were retreating!

By ten A.M., American troops under Lee had overtaken the British rear guard. Even though outnumbered, the British turned and attacked. After only a few feeble volleys, Lee ordered the American vanguard to retreat. Clinton promptly ordered the British to pursue and destroy the Americans. Lee issued a few more halfhearted orders to the Americans, only to give contradictory commands almost at once. As these senseless orders passed down the chain of command, one unit advanced while the next retreated. If treachery was Lee's objective, the confusion must have delighted him. Soon Lee's whole division was in pell-mell retreat, the men staggering toward the rear in the searing heat.

Counting house where Hamilton clerked, St. Croix.
(*From* Intimate Life of Alexander Hamilton, *1910*)

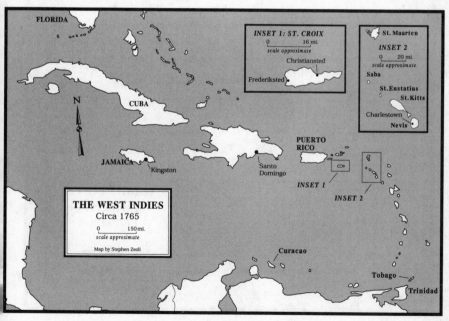

The West Indies.

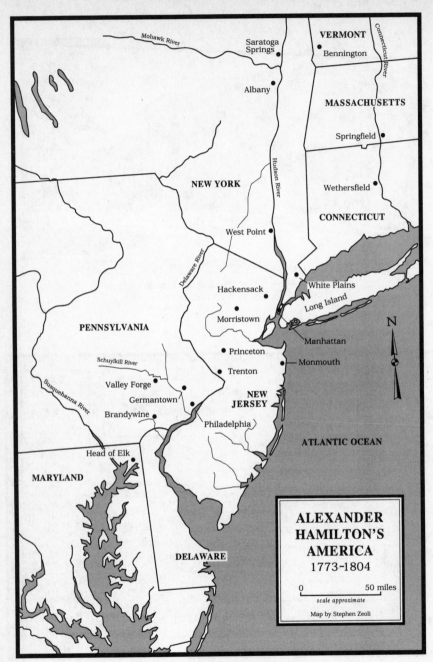

Alexander Hamilton's America.

Hamilton (*right*) meets
Washington at Bunker Hill Fort
in Manhattan in 1776.
By Alonzo Chappell.
(*National Archives*)

Alexander Hamilton (in hat) and Lafayette (wearing wig) charge into
battle behind Washington at Monmouth Courthouse, June 1778.
By Emmanuel Leutze. (*Monmouth County Historical Association*)

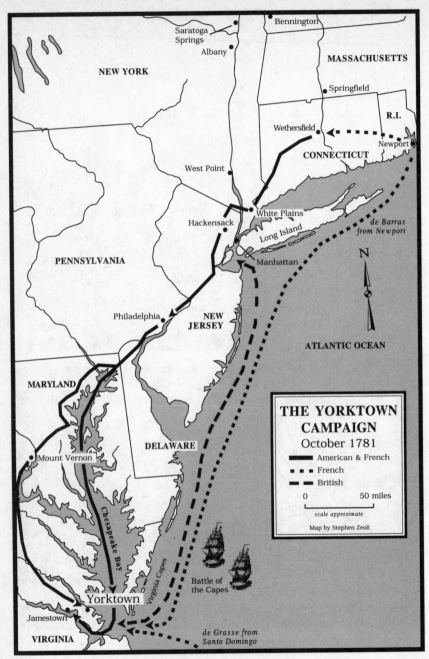

The Yorktown Campaign.

Storming of Redoubt No. 10 at Yorktown. By Eugene Louis Lami.
(Senate of the Commonwealth of Virginia, courtesy of Library of Virginia)

Surrender of Cornwallis at Yorktown (Hamilton stands beside horse on right).
By John Trumbull. *(U.S. Capitol Art Collection, Architect of the Capitol)*

Hamilton confers with Benjamin Franklin at signing of the Constitution.
By Howard Chandler Christy.
(*Courtesy U.S. Capitol Art Collection, Architect of the Capitol*)

Alexander Hamilton and Thomas Jefferson in cabinet meeting with Washington.
By Constantino Brumidi. (*Courtesy U.S. Capitol Art Collection, Architect of the Capitol*)

Elizabeth Schuyler Hamilton.
(*National Archives*)

Angelica Schuyler Church.
By John Trumbull.
(*Courtesy Belvidere Trust*)

Pistols used by Hamilton and Burr.
(*From* Intimate Life of Alexander Hamilton, *1910*)

Philip Hamilton at the age of twenty.
(*From* Intimate Life of Alexander
Hamilton, *1910*)

Aaron Burr. By John Vanderlyn.
(*Courtesy National Archives*)

There they ran into Hamilton, who tried desperately to stem the American retreat, waving his sword and bellowing orders as he tried to redeploy the fleeing men and place field artillery. Hamilton then deployed newly arrived companies of Rhode Island and New Jersey Continentals to protect the exposed American artillery. As he galloped back and forth yelling commands, a British .69-caliber musket ball struck his horse. The horse went down on Hamilton, pinning him. Rhode Island troops pulled him free and dragged him, badly injured, to safety, but he was out of action for the rest of the battle. Propped against a tree, he could only watch and listen as the Americans and British fought to a stalemate in the fierce heat. Finally, the mauled British escaped to New York City.

ONLY THREE days after the battle, Hamilton was back at his desk at headquarters, dashing off his first letter to his friend Boudinot, now an influential member of Congress from New Jersey. He could not help "saying something" about a battle that was "the finest opportunity America ever possessed." It had been "fooled away by a man in whom she has placed a large share of the most ill-judged confidence—I mean General Lee." Hamilton suspected Lee's motives. "This man is either a driveler," he wrote, "or something much worse." Disguising this backchannel report to Congress as a personal letter, Hamilton detailed Lee's "truly childish" behavior, contrasting it to Washington's "good sense and fortitude":

> Other officers have great merit in performing their parts well but [Washington] directed the whole with the skill of a master workman. He did not hug himself at a distance and leave an Arnold to win laurels for him [an obvious reference to Horatio Gates's behavior at Saratoga] but, by his own presence, he brought order out of confusion, animated his troops and led them to success.

Praising Washington, panning Lee, Hamilton was treading heavily on the tender toes of Boudinot, who had sided with Gates in the Conway affair and had openly accused Washington of retreating across New Jersey too precipitately in 1776. Hamilton heaped praise on Rhode Islanders who were with him when he "got my horse wounded and myself much hurt by a fall." He noted that their friend, former Elizabethtown schoolmaster and now Major Francis Barber, "received a ball through his side" but would probably recover. Hamilton's letter brimmed with excitement at the Americans' dramatically improved skill. "The artillery acquitted themselves most charmingly. Our troops, after the first impulse from mismanagement [by Lee], behaved with more spirit and moved with greater order than the British troops." It was the first time Hamilton ever praised the American army. But his real purpose was to damn Lee's "monstrous" conduct.

One week after the Battle of Monmouth and after two insulting letters to Washington, Charles Lee got what he demanded, a court-martial. The key witness turned out to be the bruised Hamilton, who testified that Washington had indeed ordered Lee to attack. Unfortunately, Hamilton in his haste had failed to write out or save a copy of the order, a loophole Lee managed to squeeze through. But the court-martial believed Hamilton and remanded his case to Congress, which stripped Lee of command and suspended him from the army for one year. In the course of his blunt testimony, Hamilton managed to make yet another new enemy. One of Lee's brigade commanders, Lieutenant Colonel Aaron Burr, sat grimly through the hearings.[24]

Shortly after the hearing, Hamilton's friend John Laurens challenged Lee to a duel for insulting Washington. Laurens asked Hamilton to act as his second, presupposing that Hamilton had a detailed knowledge by this time of the rules and customs of dueling. Laurens, Lee, and their seconds met at a well-known dueling ground at Point No Point, four miles south of Philadelphia. Laurens shot Lee, slightly wounding him in the side. Lee demanded another round, but, Lee's second concurring, Hamilton stopped the duel. Both Laurens and Lee considered satisfaction received. Hamilton's role in the duel, as well as Hamilton's outspoken criticism of Lee to Congress and at the court-martial, confirmed once again that Hamilton was the outspoken champion of Washington who, one way or other, would try to eliminate any rival.

Hamilton himself drew the praise of Continental Army officers for his performance in the Battle of Monmouth. Not only had he, in the emergency, proposed troop dispositions to both Washington and Lee but, by his skillful use of American artillery, he had prevented the routed vanguard from being overrun. "Your friend Hammy," wrote McHenry to Boudinot, "was incessant in his endeavors during the whole day—in reconnoitering the enemy and in rallying and charging." Hamilton "seemed to court death," McHenry added, "and triumphed over it as the face of war changed in our favor." The badly bruised Hamilton, McHenry reported, had been with Washington's staff as "night set in and we, failing in our attempt to turn the enemy flank, composed ourselves to sleep behind the line of battle under a large tree."[25]

AFTER RETREATING across New Jersey in June 1778, the British bottled themselves up in New York City, redirecting their sporadic offensive operations to the South. Congress ordered the American army to blockade the British inside the city. Increasingly, runaway inflation, lagging recruitment, and acute supply problems kept the Continental Army inactive in the North for two years.

As the Revolution settled in the North into a long stalemate and the Americans waited to coordinate their campaigns with the French, they turned to deal with Indians who were ravaging the frontiers. The Six Nations Iroquois had aligned themselves with the British. Loyalists from the Mohawk Valley in New York had escaped to Fort Niagara on Lake Erie at the beginning of the Revolution. With Loyalist rangers the Iroquois raided white settlements along hundreds of miles of frontier, pillaging, burning, and scalping. Early in June, 1778, a Loyalist-Indian force out of Fort Niagara traveled more than three hundred miles and destroyed settlements in the Wyoming Valley near present-day Wilkes-Barre, Pennsylvania, taking 227 scalps. More joint Loyalist-Indian expeditions raided German Flats on the Mohawk River (below Utica) in September 1778 and struck Cherry Valley, only fifty miles west of Albany, in November.

In the spring of 1779, Washington put Hamilton to work on drawing up detailed plans and orders for a punitive campaign against the

Iroquois. A large force of Continentals bolstered by state militias was
to invade the Iroquois homelands around the Finger Lakes and the
Genesee Valley of western New York. They were to destroy their
homes and crops and force the Iroquois to fall back on the British at
Fort Niagara and deplete their rations. "The immediate objects are
the total destruction and devastation of their settlements," wrote
Hamilton, who played a prominent role in the detailed planning of
the campaigns of 1779. "[The Indian country] may not be merely
overrun, but destroyed." Major General John Sullivan of New Hampshire, a frontiersman and experienced Indian fighter, was to lead
twenty-five hundred Continentals from Easton, Pennsylvania, on the
Delaware. General James Clinton, brother of the governor of New
York, was to march from Albany with fifteen hundred New York
Continentals. A third column was to set out from Fort Pitt in south-
western Pennsylvania (the former Fort Duquesne) with six hundred
Continentals. In all, Washington detached forty-six hundred Continentals, nearly one third of his regulars. Sullivan was also to take
along artillery. The Iroquois, in all of America's century-long wars
with European colonists, had never faced cannon fire. All along their
route, the New York troops put the torch to Anglican churches and
Indian log houses that had stone chimneys and glass windows. Fields
full of corn, beans, squash, and pumpkins either fed the hungry
American troops or were totally destroyed.[26]

After a brief battle with American artillery at Newtown, the terrified Iroquois never again stopped to put up a fight. Sullivan's unop-
posed army burned a swath from Elmira—where the men cut down
eighteen-foot stalks of corn—to the St. Lawrence River and then
southwest into the Genesee country. Detachments raided and burned
Indian settlements in the Mohawk Valley, on the west side of Seneca
Lake, and on both sides of Cayuga Lake. The army collected an
immense amount of corn, packed it into "very large and elegant"
houses, and then burned it all. At Aurora, they girdled and destroyed
fifteen hundred peach trees, some of them species never seen before
or since. In all, Sullivan's army of four thousand Americans destroyed
forty villages and an estimated 160,000 bushels of corn as well as
immeasurable quantities of other vegetables and fruits.

TEN

"Treason of the Blackest Dye"

B y the summer of 1779, as the sixth year of Revolution began, Continental currency had depreciated so badly that Alexander Hamilton could not afford to buy a horse. His old gray horse had been wounded at Monmouth—and army regulations he himself had written barred him from borrowing one except for military use. Hamilton had scratched together the money to buy a mare but she had to be left behind with her colt at Middlebrook, New Jersey, when Hamilton moved with Washington's headquarters, first to Pompton, then to Morristown. As Washington put it, even "a rat in the shape of a horse is not to be bought at this time for less than £200."[1]

That was about $40,000 in depreciated Continental currency. Hamilton was paid only $360 Continental for the six-month period between June and December 1779, or $60 Continental a month. Hamilton had invested a small inheritance from kin in St. Croix in privateering ships and he was subsisting on the shelter and rations provided by the army, taking all his meals at Washington's mess table. That winter, the price of a season ticket for the dancing assembly at winter headquarters was $400 Continental. Hamilton decided to buy the dancing ticket. It would have been a lonely winter, surrounded as he was by the sons of wealthy Americans, had he not.

What made his loneliness more acute was that his best friend, John Laurens, had gone home to South Carolina to try to advance his scheme of arming and leading slaves against the Loyalists. The two exchanged sometimes very personal letters. Hamilton had just learned, and not from Laurens, that before the Revolution, Laurens had married in London. He had fathered a daughter and left both mother and child behind, never to see them again. To cushion Laurens's embarrassment at the discovery and his own shock at this news, Hamilton wrote Laurens a long, witty, and remarkably intimate letter about his idea of a perfect wife:

> I empower and command you to get me [a wife] in Carolina ... Take her description: she must be young, handsome (I lay most stress upon a good shape); sensible (a little learning will do); well bred ... chaste and tender (I am an enthusiast in my notions of fidelity and fondness); of some good nature; a great deal of generosity (she must neither love money nor scolding for I dislike equally a termagant and an economist).
>
> In politics, I am indifferent what side she may be of: I think I have arguments that will safely convert her to mine. As to religion, a moderate stock will satisfy me. She must believe in god and hate a saint. But as to fortune, the larger stock of that, the better. You know my temper and circumstances and will therefore pay special attention to this article of the treaty. Though I run no risk of going to Purgatory for my avarice, yet as money is an essential ingredient of happiness in this world, as I have not much of my own and as I am very little calculated to get more, it must needs be that my wife bring at least a sufficiency to administer to her own extravagancies.
>
> If you should not readily meet with a lady that you think answers my description, you can only advertise in the public papers and doubtless you will hear of many competitors for most of the qualifications required who will be glad to become candidates for such a prize as I am. To excite [them], it will be

necessary for you to give an account of the lover—his *size*, make, quality of mind and *body*, achievements, expectations, fortune, etc. In drawing my picture, you will no doubt be civil to your friend. Mind you do justice to the length of my nose and don't forget that I _____ . [Words evidently scratched out by Hamilton's son and biographer.]

After reviewing what I have written, I am ready to ask myself what could have put it into my head to hazard this *jeu de follie*. Do I want a wife? No—I have plagues enough without desiring to add to the number that *greatest of all*. And if I were silly enough to do it, I should take care how I employ a proxy.

As a postscript, he added, "You will be pleased to recollect in your negotiations that I have no invincible antipathy to the *maidenly beauties* and that I am willing to take the *trouble* of them upon myself." Translation: he preferred a maiden, a virgin.[2]

When the British finally sallied from their ever-more-elaborate defenses and sailed from New York City on December 26, 1779, to besiege Charleston, South Carolina, they left behind a garrison of Hessians and Loyalists to hold the city. In April 1780, after a four-month siege of Charleston, fifty-four hundred Americans, including virtually all the South's Continentals, surrendered in the worst American defeat of the war. Among the captives was Hamilton's friend Laurens. It took weeks before Hamilton could find out if his friend was dead or alive. The old agony of loss once again afflicted him. At the same time, Hessians and Loyalist forces crossed over from New York City and attacked New Jersey. Loyalist guides pointed out Hamilton's alma mater Elizabethtown Academy and Presbyterian Church to the British. They burned both. Nearby, in the Battle of Springfield, Hamilton's onetime teacher and, more recently, intelligence source, the Reverend James Caldwell, and his entire family were killed.

The British paroled John Laurens to Philadelphia. He gave his word of honor not to fight until he could be exchanged for a British officer of equal rank. But because his father was the president of Congress and because he was able to speak French, Congress appointed him in December 1779 as secretary to the American legation in Paris. But he refused the appointment. Instead, Laurens nominated Hamilton, whose French also was impeccable:

> I thought it incumbent on me in the first place to recommend a person equally qualified in point of integrity and much better in point of ability [but] unhappily they could not agree on Colonel Hamilton . . . I am sorry that you are not better known to Congress. Great stress is laid upon the probity and patriotism of the person to be employed in this commission.[3]

In fact, Hamilton was already too well known for his criticisms of Congress, his loyalty to Washington, and his implacable hostility to Congress's favorite generals, Lee and Gates. At least once, he had threatened to challenge a member of Congress to a duel for criticizing Washington.

In July 1779, at an informal meeting of Revolutionary leaders in a Philadelphia tavern, Congressman Francis Dana of Massachusetts, a close friend of Sam and John Adams, said that "many persons in the army were acting, under a cloak of defending their country, from principles totally incompatible with its safety." Hamilton's friend and Baron Steuben's former deputy, Lieutenant Colonel John Brooks, had insisted that Dana, one of the leading members of Congress, name names:

> He fixed at length on Colonel Hamilton, who he asserted had declared in a public coffeehouse in Philadelphia that it was high time for the people to rise, join General Washington and turn Congress out of doors. He further observed that Mr. Hamilton could be in no ways interested in the defense of this country, and therefore was most likely to pursue such a line of conduct as his great ambition dictated.

By mid-1779, Hamilton had emerged as Washington's principal aide, in effect his chief of staff and one of a handful of his most trusted advisers. As Colonel Brooks put it, he occupied "so highly dignified a station." Hamilton's growing prominence only made Congressman Dana's charge more devastating. Even friends like Brooks could not believe that a congressman could dare savage Hamilton's reputation without some basis in fact. Brooks wrote to Hamilton to ask if he had ever shown any "want of that honor and regard to truth so eminently necessary in the patriot and statesman."[4]

Dana knew Hamilton well. He had spent five months at Valley Forge in the winter of 1777-78 as chairman of the committee working with Hamilton to reorganize the army. Hamilton wrote to assure Brooks that Dana's accusation was "absolutely false and groundless." But he went further. If Congressman Dana had actually said what Brooks attributed to him, its "personal and illiberal complexion" could trigger "a very different kind of competition": a duel. Dana, no soldier, ducked the implied challenge, but he responded to Brooks that, if Hamilton had suggested what would have been a military coup, he "ought to be broke [discharged] whatever his particular services may have been." He also brought up Hamilton's foreign birth. Love of country, Dana argued, could be no brake on Hamilton's ambition. When Brooks sent Hamilton Dana's response, Brooks added more details: Dana had accused Hamilton of being one of those "dangerous designing men" whose schemes "would be fatal to the liberties of this country." Brooks told Hamilton, "The words *desperate fortune* were more than once applied to you." And Brooks provided the names of two colonels who had also heard these slurs.[5]

Infuriated, Hamilton wrote Congressman Dana that only a written positive denial of his charges could avert a duel. Hamilton also threatened to fight a duel with the Reverend William Gordon, a Congregationalist minister and self-styled historian who had repeated to Dana the hearsay of someone else who supposedly had overheard Hamilton, thus bringing on the entire incident. Higher officials became embroiled. General Artemus Ward, Washington's predecessor as commander-in-chief, said that Brooks's account stemmed from a conversation on a boat crossing the Charles River in Boston after two Massachusetts officers, disgusted with Congress's neglect of the army, threw down their guns and went home.

As weeks and months of threats and counterthreats passed

between Hamilton and his antagonists, Reverend Gordon scolded Hamilton, slurred him over his illegitimate birth, and, when Hamilton challenged him to a duel, delivered a homily against dueling. "Duels do not in general produce more than the honorable settlement of a dispute, yet they may be the unhappy cause of the public's losing good and useful members, and upon the principles of religion I am totally averse to them." When Hamilton demanded to know who had disparaged his name, Gordon countered that a gentleman did not have to reveal his sources. But he would give Hamilton the name of his informant if Hamilton withdrew his demand for a duel.

In five weeks of fuming after first hearing Dana's slur, Hamilton traced the "calumny" to its "inventor," the Reverend Gordon, who would go on to write an early history of the United States. Gordon urged Hamilton to refer the matter to Congress.[6]

In one of his angriest and most sarcastic letters, Hamilton excoriated the cleric, twice his age, for his condescension and his "officious zeal for the interests of religion and for the good of society." Gordon's slander required "an act of justice": Hamilton now berated the clergyman in a homily of his own:

It often happens that our zeal is at variance with our understanding. We do not live in the days of chivalry. The good sense of the present times has happily found out that, to prove your own innocence, or the malice of an accuser, the worst method you can take is to run him through the body or shoot him through the head.[7]

The standoff sputtered on for a year and a half, leaving Hamilton writing to his friend Laurens:

Pleasant terms enough! I am first to be calumniated and then, if my calumniator takes it into his head, I am to bear a cudgeling from him with Christian patience and forbearance.

Hamilton finally chalked up the matter to the Conway cabal. But his enemies in Congress once again denied him the coveted diplomatic posting to France, where he would have served beside Franklin and Adams. By outspokenly defending Washington, Hamilton had made lasting enemies of Washington's critics. Now he was making enemies of his own.[8]

So scarce were supplies at the Continental Army's encampment at Morristown in the winter of 1779–80 that the commissary's storehouse could provide room for dancing. General and Mrs. Washington appeared in black—the color of Revolution, their way of signaling the side they were on. The French officers wore elegant white uniforms bedecked with yards of gold lace and bushels of medals. More importantly, from Hamilton's point of view, as many as fifty daughters of Revolutionary officers and local gentry appeared in brocades, decorously black and white, to honor the Franco-American alliance, their hair heavily powdered and piled fashionably high. The daughters of Abraham Lott, whose house in Morristown became one of Washington's 284 temporary headquarters, were fairly typical. Nathanael Greene described them as "of delicate sentiments and polite education."[9]

Rekindling his yearnings of adolescent visits to Liberty Hall in Elizabethtown, Hamilton was pursuing at these dances "Lady Kitty" Livingston, who may have been his first and idealized love. He had been seventeen then, an awkward boy; now he was a resplendent aide to Washington at age twenty-five, feeling the twenty-three-year-old Kitty more within his reach. He whirled with her at the dancing assemblies, bundled in bearskins beside her on sleigh rides, strolled with her at picnics, but there was always a long line of eager swains— Tench Tilghman and John Laurens, his fellow aides; Colonel Robert Troup, his former roommate—all wealthier, more eligible for the hand of Governor Livingston's daughter. From Morristown, he wrote to her in desperate supplication that her sister, Suky, had asked him to make "an advance towards a correspondence with you." He held out as bait his interest in politics, one that matched hers. He had obviously pumped Suky for some hint of common ground with Kitty. To fulfill her "relish for politics," he contended that his post "qualifies me better for gratifying" this than his rivals. But he did not want to be "limited to any particular subject":

> I challenge you to meet me in whatever path you dare. If you have no objection, for variety and amusement, we will even sometimes make excursions in the flowery walks and roseate bowers of Cupid. You know I am renowned for gallantry and shall always be able to entertain you with a choice collection of the prettiest things imaginable.

Hamilton's letter was frank, bold, a blunt proposition to become the lover of the daughter of the wealthy and powerful governor of New Jersey. Touting himself as a gallant—an explicit eighteenth-century term for a man noted for his sexual prowess—Hamilton was offering himself either as a literary correspondent or as something even more intimate. Take your pick, Lady Kitty, he was saying, but in some form, take me.

But to protect himself in case Miss Livingston thought his advances only outrageous, he added that he was only following the advice of "connoisseurs" on the subject of women.

> According to them, Woman is not simple, but a most complex, intricate and enigmatical being. After knowing exactly your taste and whether you are of a romantic or discreet temper as to love affairs, I will endeavor to regulate myself by it. If you would choose to be a goddess and to be worshipped as such, I will torture my imagination . . . You shall be one of the graces, or Diana or Venus.[10]

Fully a month passed before Kitty replied, and then only when Hamilton was "almost out of patience and out of humor with your presumptuous delay." Fearing that Kitty had succumbed to the blandishments of a rival, Hamilton wrote her that he had shown a copy of his letter to her to his most feared rival, probably his best friend, the dashing John Laurens. And when Kitty did respond, Hamilton showed him her letter and then wrote her:

To give, at once, a mortal blow to all his hopes, I will recount what passed on this occasion. "Hamilton!" cries he, "when you write to this divine girl again, it must be in the style of adoration: none but a goddess, I am sure, could have penned so fine a letter."

In her letter, now lost, Kitty had obviously ignored his offer of a physical relationship; she would settle for news and a literary dalliance. He wrote back to accept her terms, adding with a flourish, "*ALL FOR LOVE* is my motto."[11]

FOR SEVERAL weeks that winter, even as he left his fate in the hands of Kitty Livingston, Hamilton paid such avid attention to another Morristown belle, Cornelia Lott, that he was talked about at headquarters. Fellow aide-de-camp Samuel Blachley Webb took up his pen and wrote about his lovesick friend Hamilton:

> *To Colonel Hamilton*
> *What, bend the stubborn knee at last,*
> *Confess the days of wisdom past?*
> *He that could bow to every shrine*
> *And swear the last the most divine;*
> *Like Hudibras, all subjects bend,*
> *Had Ovid at his finger's end;*
> *Could whistle every tune of love,*
> *(You'd think him Ovid's self or Jove)*
> *Now feels the inexorable dart*
> *And yields Cornelia all his heart!*[12]

To refer to Ovid was to liken Hamilton to some cynic who knew how to pick up women. Webb's muse prodded him to even greater heights of doggerel: Cornelia was "a beautiful brunette." Webb's ink was hardly dry before Hamilton bent his knee to another lass, one Polly, then broke her heart, too. Hamilton, according to Webb's doggerel, was usually "one who laughs life's cares away" but that was only on the surface, and that was about to change.

On February 2, 1780, Steuben's aide-de-camp, Major Benjamin Walker, wrote him that Elizabeth Schuyler, the second daughter of Major General Philip Schuyler, had just arrived at headquarters in Morristown. Steuben replied that he was not especially interested in the twenty-three-year-old Betsy. He had written to her father in Albany, but it had been to procure some wolf skins. Schuyler, baron of a fourth-generation lumber- and flax-producing and fur-trading empire with vast holdings along the Mohawk River and around Albany, had been unable to fill his request: the snows were too deep that winter. Schuyler sent the news to Steuben with Betsy and hoped that the "most gallant men about Morristown" would "strive to take her hand ... I mean at a dance." Walker was too embarrassed to meet Schuyler's daughter and escort her to the house of her aunt, Mrs. John Cochrane, near Morristown because his uniform coat was falling apart.

Elizabeth Schuyler's arrival at the headquarters assemblies with her beautiful married one-year-older sister, Angelica, brought back pleasant memories to another of Washington's aides, Tench Tilghman of Maryland. Tilghman had met them five years earlier when he had served on General Schuyler's staff in Albany, and when Betsy was eighteen. "I was prepossessed in favor of this young lady the moment I saw her":

> A brunette with the most good-natured, lively dark eyes that I ever saw which threw a beam of good temper and benevolence over her whole countenance ... Mr. Livingston informed me that I was not mistaken in the conjecture that she was the finest-tempered girl in the world.

Betsy was a strong, outdoors-loving young woman, Tilghman recalled. When a number of young American officers and young ladies from Albany had ridden out to visit the falls of Cohoes on the Hudson (before the discovery of Niagara Falls, the scenic wonder of New York), Betsy Schuyler had impressed Tilghman with her cheerful, energetic spirit: "I fancy Miss Schuyler had been used to ramble over and climb grounds of this sort, since she disdained all assistance and made herself merry at the distress of the other ladies."[3]

If Tilghman still had any interest in Betsy Schuyler, he was quickly brushed aside by the bold Hamilton, who, by his own account, had become known for his cavalrylike advances on the latest feminine arrival in camp. As he wrote to Betsy's younger sister Margarita soon afterward,

> Phlegmatists may say I take too great a license at first setting out, and witlings may sneer and wonder how a man the least acquainted with the world should show so great facility in his confidences—to a lady.

But it appears that it was Hamilton who was now swept off his feet, or was pretending to be, by Betsy. He described her in a letter to John Laurens in Philadelphia as

> Most unmercifully handsome and so perverse that she has none of those pretty affectations, which are the prerogatives of beauty. Her good sense is destitute of that happy mixture of vanity and ostentation which would make it conspicuous to the whole tribe of fools and foplings as well as to men of understanding, so that as the matter now stands it is very little known beyond the circle of these. She has good nature, affability and vivacity unembellished with that charming frivolousness which is justly deemed one of the principal accomplishments of a *belle*.
> In short, she is so strange a creature that she possesses all the beauties, virtues and graces of her sex without any of those amiable defects ... Several of my friends, philosophers who railed at love as a weakness, men of the world who laughed at it as a fantasy, [she] has presumptuously and daringly compelled to acknowledge its power ... I am myself of the number.

Betsy had overturned "all the wise resolutions I had been framing for more than four years past," Hamilton confessed. "From a rational sort of being and a professed condemner of Cupid [she] has, in a trice, metamorphosed me into the veriest *inamorato* you perhaps ever saw." Translation: Betsy was not a *belle* yet she had attracted the flirtatious

man-about-camp Hamilton. It was as if he was surprised that someone, on the surface at least, so plain, amiable, and artless could
ensnare *him*, the playboy. That was, after all, his well-cultivated reputation. Had not Martha Washington named her prowling camp cat,
Hamilton?[14]

What may have added to Betsy's appeal was the breadth of her
accomplishments. General Schuyler had seen to it that his daughters
learned French as well as the Dutch they spoke at home and the English they spoke everywhere else. She also was an accomplished
artist. When Hamilton had known Betsy only for several weeks, he
was writing to Betsy's younger sister, alluding to her talent at portrai-
ture:

> I venture to tell you that, by some odd contrivance or other,
> your sister has found out the secret of every thing that concerns
> me and though I have not the happiness of a personal acquain-
> tance with you, I have had the good fortune to see several very
> pretty pictures of your person . . . Among others, your sister car-
> ries a beautiful copy constantly about her, elegantly drawn by
> herself, of which she has two or three times favored me with a
> sight.[15]

Meeting Betsy Schuyler drew Hamilton overnight into a social whirl
at a level that had been beyond his reach. During his Elizabethtown
schooldays, when he had first met Betsy's close friend Kitty Livingston, he had only been an outsider, a scholarship boy from the
islands. But now, when the two young women sent a note to him
shortly after their arrival at Morristown in February 1780, asking him
to take the reins for a sleigh ride, Hamilton the West Indian, aware of
his inexperience, quite wisely had to beg off. He turned the task over
to their mutual friend Tilghman. But he was still "unwilling to lose
the pleasure of the party" and joined the gay company of New York
and New Jersey sleigh-riding aristocrats.[16]

His party-going was soon cut short by another round of futile
prisoner of war negotiations at Perth Amboy that took him away

from headquarters for most of March 1780. He was only able to dash off a "hasty letter," but his friend Webb kept him posted about Betsy, her friends, and her dancing partners. On March 17, Hamilton wrote to tell Betsy of his "happiness" that, according to Webb, she had not forgotten him:

> Every moment of my stay here becomes more and more irksome but I hope two or three days will put an end to it. Colonel Webb tells me you have sent for a carriage to go to Philadelphia. If you should set out before I return, have the goodness to leave a line informing me how long you expect to be there.

Betsy had never visited Philadelphia:

> I beg, too, you will not suffer any considerations respecting me to prevent your going, for though it will be a tax upon my love to part with you so long, I wish you to see that city. It will afford you pleasure and whatever does that will always be most agreeable to me. [But] you must always remember, your best friend is where I am.

It would be a long time before Hamilton understood why, at dinners with British and American negotiators, the Schuyler sisters were "the daily toasts of our table." Captain James Beebe, an American engineer, seemed enamored of Betsy's young sister Peggy, but Hamilton didn't "think him clever enough for her." Hamilton set himself up as Betsy's adviser on family matters: "He sings well and that is all." Betsy had asked him to inquire after Captain Oliver Delancey, a wealthy New York City Loyalist who was on the British headquarters staff—and, some Loyalists gossiped, was more than a colleague to British Adjutant General John André. "I am told he is a pretty fellow," Hamilton said of Delancey. André was head of the British Secret Service in New York. Betsy had not told Hamilton why the British officers asked about her. Five years earlier, André, taken prisoner by Schuyler's forces at the fall of St. Jean-sur-

Richelieu, had spent more than a month as Schuyler's houseguest at Albany en route to a year's captivity in Pennsylvania. During that time, eighteen-year-old Betsy obviously became smitten by André, an accomplished painter, poet, and musician. He had become an intimate of the Schuyler family to the extent that, from his house arrest in Pennsylvania, he felt free to call on General Schuyler to discharge a debt for him in Albany. One family historian recently observed that "Betsy appears in particular to have cherished the memory of the handsome young British officer, despite the fact that he had become the head of British intelligence." All that Hamilton would say on the subject at this point was, "I have learnt a secret by coming down here," adding only that he had suddenly grown "tired of our British friends":

They do their best to be agreeable and are particularly civil to me but, after all, they are a compound of grimace and jargon and [outside] of a certain fashionable routine are as dull and empty as any gentlemen need to be. One of their principal excellencies consists in swallowing a large quantity of wine every day.

As he wrote this letter, another letter from Betsy arrived. Hamilton quickly responded:

I cannot tell you what ecstasy I felt in casting my eye over the sweet effusions of tenderness it contains. My Betsy's soul speaks in every line and bids me be the happiest of mortals. I am so and will be so.

The courier between these two lovers, Captain Richard Kidder Meade,

had the kindness to tell me that you received my letter with marks of joy and that you retired with eagerness to read it. 'Tis from circumstances like these we best discover the true sentiments of the heart.

But Hamilton was already half an hour late for a prisoner of war negotiation with the English. "Adieu, my charmer. Take care of yourself and love your Hamilton as well as he does you."[17]

In early April, Betsy had traveled to Philadelphia with her father, now a New York delegate to the Continental Congress. The general had met Hamilton several times at headquarters in Morristown and had already grown fond enough of Hamilton that he had lobbied Congress for Hamilton's appointment as secretary to the American mission to France when Hamilton was nominated by his friend John Laurens. But there was "one obstacle which prevents me from making up my mind," Schuyler wrote Hamilton. He would tell Hamilton "when I have the pleasure of seeing you." Schuyler was also working to help Hamilton and his fellow soldiers win some adjustment to their pay to make up for the runaway inflation that had rendered them impoverished.[18]

Schuyler took quickly to young Hamilton. Perhaps he was trying to help Hamilton receive higher pay because he could see where the relationship between his daughter and the impecunious young aide-de-camp was heading. Land rich, from a long line of Hudson River Dutch patroons, and autocratic in public life, Schuyler ruled rigidly over his household as if it were his fort. Biographer and sometime Washington aide David Humphreys, who knew Schuyler well, described him as

aristocratic in feeling and convinced of the propriety and the observance of dignities. He brought to the performance of his own duties an orderly mind and prompt execution, the same qualities he demanded of others.[19]

Two of Schuyler's four daughters had already eloped. Schuyler shared with Hamilton a devotion to Washington and deep suspicion of Congress: to Hamilton on April 8, 1780, he confided his loathing of "the pride, the folly and perhaps, too, the wickedness of some members."[20]

But it was to Betsy's mother that Hamilton must write if he wanted to "be united to your amiable daughter," as he put it in a letter on

April 14, 1780. Apparently, none of Betsy's letters to Hamilton survives. As was frequently done at the time, she must have destroyed them after his death. But whatever she wrote him to spell out her acceptance of his suit, he "took the earliest opportunity" to forward it to Betsy's mother at Albany along with his own letter, thanking Mrs. Schuyler in advance for her "acceptance" of him:

> I leave it to my conduct rather than expressions to testify the sincerity of my affection for her, the respect I have for her parents, the desire I shall always feel to justify their confidence and merit their friendship.[21]

It would take Hamilton another two months before he got around to write to his closest friend, Laurens, of his engagement to marry Betsy Schuyler, and then his tone sounded offhand, almost flippant. He may have been attempting delicacy: Matrimony was not Laurens's favorite subject. "Have you heard I am on the point of becoming a benedict," Hamilton wrote as if in afterthought at the end of a long letter of military news:

> I confess my sins. I am guilty. Next fall completes my doom. I give up my liberty to Miss Schuyler. She is a good-hearted girl who I am sure will never play the termagant. Though not a genius, she has good sense enough to be agreeable, and though not a beauty, she has fine black eyes—is rather handsome and has every other requisite of the exterior to make a lover happy. And, believe me, I am lover in earnest, though I do not speak of the perfections of my mistress in the enthusiasm of chivalry.[22]

It may have taken Hamilton so long to send Laurens such a subdued letter because of his embarrassment at being unable to arrange a prisoner exchange that would have freed Laurens from parole in Philadelphia. Hamilton was careful not to gloat over his great good fortune in marrying the daughter of one of America's wealthiest and most powerful men, facts that he did not even have to mention to his best friend.

Sometime that summer, when Hamilton learned of a ship sailing for the Caribbean, he sent off a letter to his father. He told Betsy that he knew from his involvement in planning joint operations with the French that his father would be safe. But, he reported to his fiancée, he "pressed [his father] to come to America after the peace." Another ship was about to sail with another letter in which Hamilton would tell his father about his "black-eyed daughter [-in-law]" who would be, Hamilton promised, "the blessing of his gray hairs."[23]

As the summer of his anxious, discontented waiting for war against the British, for marriage to his black-eyed fiancée, dragged on, Hamilton wrote Betsy a series of remarkable love letters that he intended her to heed carefully, that she would have done well to think more than once about. In July 1780, he wrote her tantalizingly from a militia general's house in Paterson, New Jersey:

> Here we are, my love, in a house of great hospitality—in a country of plenty—a buxom girl under the same roof—pleasing expectations of a successful campaign—and everything to make a soldier happy who is not in love and absent from his mistress. It is a maxim of my life to enjoy the present good with the highest relish and to soften the present evil by a hope of future good.

When he did not hear back from Betsy in two weeks, Hamilton chided her for "negligence":

> For god's sake My Dear Betsy try to write me oftener and give me the picture of your heart in all its varieties of light and shade. Tell me whether it feels the same for me or did when we were together, or whether what seemed to be love was nothing more than a generous sympathy. The possibility of this frequently torments me.

When letters still came too infrequently for him in August, after only a wait of one week, Hamilton began his next note, "Impatiently My Dearest." He longed "to see the workings of my Betsy's heart" in "those tender moments of pillowed retirement when her soul abstracted from every other object delivers itself up to love and to me."

Part of Hamilton's anxiety seemed to be over money:

> Do you soberly relish the pleasure of being a poor man's wife? Have you learned to think a homespun preferable to a brocade and the rumbling of a wagon wheel to the musical rattling of a coach and six? Will you be able to see with perfect composure your old acquaintances flaunting it in gay life, tripping it along in elegance and splendor, while you hold an humble station and have no other enjoyments than the sober comforts of a good wife?

Any inheritance he expected from relatives in St. Croix was dwindling but "I have not concealed my circumstances from my Betsy":

> They are far from splendid; they may possibly be even worse than I expect, for every day brings me fresh proof of the knavery of those to whom my little affairs are entrusted.

When Betsy enclosed a song she had written with a letter in late August, Hamilton eagerly responded on September 3 from Liberty Pole, New Jersey:

> The little song you sent me I have read over and over. It is very pretty and contains precisely those sentiments I would wish my Betsy to feel, and she tells me it is an exact copy of her heart.

Whatever the lyrics of this song, like all her letters to Hamilton, she destroyed it. But she saved his words to her. The twenty-five-year-old man of the world spoke of women to his sheltered country belle, with

> experience I have had of human nature, and of the softer part of it. Some of your sex possess every requisite to please delight, and inspire esteem, friendship and affection. But there are too

few of this description. We are full of vices. They are full of weaknesses.

Even though he had become Washington's confidant and chief aide, by mid-1780, the sixth year of the Revolutionary War, Hamilton was chafing for a field command or a diplomatic posting that would enhance his personal prestige and release him from the tedium of his desk job at headquarters. With Charleston and Savannah in British hands, the talk at headquarters in Tappan turned again to an assault on New York City. Hamilton eagerly seconded Lafayette's proposal for an all-out attack that would rekindle lagging French enthusiasm for the war and placate Hamilton's own rage at reports his agents kept bringing him from inside New York City. To repatriate American honor, the first assault should be on Fort Washington, which had surrendered so ingloriously in 1776, Hamilton argued. But Washington, as usual, urged caution. He refused to risk an attack until he could be supported by the French navy and army.

All of New York City, Hamilton was well aware, had been turned into a fortress. Looking through a telescope from Elizabethtown Point, on the New Jersey shore, he could no longer see any trees. The population of Manhattan, down to only five thousand when the Americans fled in 1776, five years later had reached a record thirty-three thousand. An estimated fifty thousand Loyalist refugees had crowded behind British lines in and around New York City—and that was only the civilian population. Tens of thousands of soldiers and sailors were rotated through the city, some forty thousand in the initial landings in 1776 alone. The Revolutionary War was making a seaport town into a metropolis. Soldiers, sailors, and their dependents crowded not only Manhattan but Long Island, Staten Island, and Westchester County as well. The burgeoning Loyalist population created demand for farm products from the nearby countryside and finished goods from England, but it also brought divided and shifting loyalties, a perfect setting for espionage.

James Rivington, printer of the *Gazette* who had been twice mobbed by the Sons of Liberty, became one of the most valuable

American spies, helping to obtain the code signals of the British fleet with the aid of former Loyalist businessman turned journalist Robert Townsend on Long Island. The Samuel Culper Ring at Oyster Bay on Long Island sent female spies into the city under the pretext of taking baskets of food to relatives. They signaled that they were carrying information on the movements of British troops by first hanging a black petticoat and the prescribed number of white hand-kerchiefs from a clothesline. It was dangerous work: one woman agent known only as Code Number 355 had been captured in 1779 and died aboard the prison ship *Jersey*; another helped some two hun-dred American prisoners escape before she fled with a two-hundred-pound price on her head. Spies were summarily executed by hanging. They were not entitled to death by firing squad, which was normally accorded to gentlemen. Lieutenant Nathan Hale, a twenty-one-year-old schoolteacher who was a Yale graduate, had been sent behind British lines to record troop strengths. He was hanged from a tree, in a British artillery park, now Bryant Park behind the New York Public Library. His last letter to his family was torn up by the notorious British Provost Marshal William Cunningham.

The most unlikely people seemed to be the best spies and spy catchers. Hamilton's friend and delegate to the Continental Congress, John Jay, later to become the first chief justice of the United States, was the leading spy catcher in New York State. In the relative seclu-sion of Setauket, Long Island, Major Benjamin Talmadge, Nathan Hale's classmate at Yale, used the code name John Bolton as he mas-terminded spying on Long Island. He enlisted Lieutenant Caleb Brewster to run a fleet of whaleboats to carry messages at night to Washington's outposts in Connecticut. A local woman, Anna Smith Strong, coordinated Brewster's comings and goings, using laundry on her clothesline to post signals. A black petticoat meant the whaleboat had arrived to carry information across the sound. The number of petticoats indicated which cove or inlet in Setauket Harbor would be used to take messages to Connecticut. From there, tavern owner Austin Roe carried the messages in his supply cart into the city. In emergencies, farmer Abraham Woodhull, code-named Samuel Culper, daringly rode into town with messages in his saddlebags, risking search by British pickets. Once he was accosted and searched thoroughly by four armed men who tore apart every pocket, the lining of his clothes, his shoes, and saddle—probably intending to rob him. For him to be in the city at night when he was a farmer from Long Island was already suspicious. In Culper's intelligence pipeline came the day-to-day movements of the British army and navy and their supply distribution, news of unusual boat building, a warning that the British were about to flood the city with counterfeit money printed on British ships in the harbor. And funneling much of this vital intelligence over to Hamilton at Washington's mountain stronghold was his former guardian and oldest friend, Hercules Mulligan. As a tailor he eavesdropped on British and Loyalists. He knew of urgent deadlines for orders of uniforms—and of their weight and fabric. From his brother's supply house, he knew in detail of troop movements and timetables for deliveries and destinations of provisions. From his own sources and from scores of operatives on Long Island, Manhattan, and Staten Island, details of troop and ship numbers, movements, and construction crossed at night by rowboat with Mulligan's servant, Cato, pulling on the muffled oars to the Jersey shore.

Outside British-occupied towns, life was hard for most Americans—and harder to bear as the war dragged on, especially since everyone could read in the newspapers and garner from gossip reports of the opulence and gaiety inside New York City. A frenzied social whirl included fox hunting and golf, billiards at the King's Head Tavern, horse racing on Long Island at Hempstead Plains and at Ascot Heath, only five miles from the Brooklyn ferry. There were two cricket clubs, the Brooklyn and the Greenwich, to square off on Bowling Green. There were concerts and assembly balls at City Tavern on Broadway where Captain Horatio Nelson and Prince William Henry (later King William IV) danced with Loyalists' daughters. The John Street Playhouse came back to life as the Theatre Royal, reopening in January 1777 with Perrault's *Tom Thumb*. Among 150 performances over the next six years were plays by Shakespeare and Sheridan. Up to 750 British officers and their belles crowded in to watch fellow officers, known as "Clinton's Thespians," perform before sylvan sets often designed and painted by John André and his friend Oliver Delancey. In summer, there were saltwater bathing parties; in winter, skating on Fresh Water Pond. Here, Prince William enjoyed being pushed around in a chair on skates by an orderly while he fondled the wife of Commissary General Joshua Loring. All year round, amid a terrible shortage of housing, some of the most fashionable houses around the burned-out ruins of Trinity Church brimmed over with prostitutes. Services at St. Paul's Chapel on Pearl Street at the foot of Broadway provided a favorite time to troll for trollops. As one visitor described them, these were "some of the handsomest and best-dressed ladies I have ever seen in America. I believe most of them are whores."[24]

For those Americans unfortunate enough to be in New York City against their wills, there was unimaginable suffering. Thousands of American prisoners of war were being held in and around the city. All attempts at a general prisoner exchange had come to naught. Eight hundred private soldiers were crammed in the New Gaol, renamed the Provost's Prison, in City Hall Park. Hundreds more were starving, lice-infested, in Livingston's vast Liberty Street sugar warehouse, in Van Cortlandt's warehouse at the northwest corner of Trinity churchyard, and at Rhinelanders, at the corner of Rose and Duane Streets, next door to Hercules Mulligan's swank haberdashery. In Dissenter churches such as the Middle Dutch Church on Nassau Street and North Dutch Church on William Street, half-naked, hungry American soldiers squatted on filthy straw, suffering from smallpox, cholera, and yellow fever as they fought swarms of rats and insects for scraps of food. Each morning the "dead cart" came to drag away the Revolutionaries' withered corpses; each night, Provost Marshal Cunningham strode through, cracking his bullwhip and rasping, "Kennel, ye sons of bitches!" Some two thousand inmates who for some reason earned his special attention were poisoned by arsenic placed in their flour rations or were spirited out at midnight and hanged from a portable gallows on Chambers Street in Greenwich Village as neighbors followed orders to keep their shutters, and their mouths, closed. Cunningham later confessed the mass hangings before he himself was hanged in London for forgery.

But the worst agony for an American prisoner was to be consigned to one of the prison ships across the East River in Wallabout Bay. Aboard twenty decommissioned men-of-war, some 11,500 Americans, nearly half the number killed in combat in the entire Revolution, died wretchedly, packed together in reeking holds with little or no food as they were beaten by their guards. At first, the hulks housed the prisoners from the Battle of Long Island. After they died off, the ships were used exclusively for American seamen captured by privateers and British men-of-war. One tough Nantucket sailor who somehow survived remembered "mere walking skeletons" who were "overrun with lice from head to foot." Most died of dysentery in part because only two prisoners at a time were allowed to go above decks to relieve themselves. The rest stayed below, defecating away their lives, covered with their own filth. Bodies were cast overboard each morning after the cry, "Prisoners, bring out your dead" or were dumped into mass graves ashore. For years, their bones washed up on the beaches of Wallabout Bay.[25]

HAMILTON'S MORALE, like that of most Americans, was at its lowest in 1780 as the slow-moving Revolution dragged on. In part because the value of Continental currency had plummeted, inactive fighting men became mutinous. At Morristown in May 1780, troops of the Connecticut Line who had not been paid for five months and subsisted on short rations for several weeks prepared to march home. When their commander tried to stop them, one of the men punched him. A regiment of the Pennsylvania Line called on Colonel Return Jonathan Meigs to seize the mutineers' leaders. At gunpoint, he confined the men to their huts. The next month, thirty-one men of the First New York Brigade, Hamilton's old unit, deserted from Fort Stanwix at Oriskany. They appeared to be heading for the British lines. Lieutenant Abraham Hardenburgh led Oneida Indian auxiliaries in pursuit. They shot thirteen of Hamilton's former comrades. It was the only time in the history of the United States Army that an officer employed Indians to kill white soldiers.

In June 1780, while the main British army besieged Charleston, South Carolina, its best troops siphoned off from New York City, Hessians and Loyalists again invaded New Jersey. When Hamilton and Lafayette urged a swift counterattack on thinly garrisoned New York City, Washington remained adamant that the attack on New Jersey was only a diversion. The ultimate British objective, he insisted, was to the north, the Hudson Highlands with its fifteen-mile chain of forts leading up to West Point. Washington considered West Point "the key to America." As long as the Americans held it, the army could maneuver and neutralize the British base at New York City, keeping the British in constant fear of attack, without risking American troops. The Hudson was also the link between the French army and navy, based in Newport, Rhode Island, and the main American base at Tappan. West Point was also roughly equidistant between the American winter encampment in Morristown, New Jersey, and supply bases at Albany, at Hartford, and in northwestern Pennsylvania.

At West Point, the two-hundred-foot-deep channel narrows and bends nearly ninety degrees, then immediately bends another ninety degrees, squeezing between high cliffs on the west bank and the rocky shore of Constitution Island to the east. By the late summer of 1780, the guns of ten forts bristled at West Point. British men-of-war daring to run this gauntlet against the river's strong tidal current would still have to come about twice under lethal broadsides from the forts' cannon. The guns protected a 1,097-foot-long iron chain, each twelve-by-eighteen-inch link of two-inch-thick bar iron weighing one hundred pounds, which floated on log pontoons just below the river's surface and could tear out the hull of any passing ship.

Returning victorious from South Carolina in late July 1780, the British commander Clinton called off a planned British attack on Rhode Island and withdrew his armies from eastern Long Island and New Jersey into his lines in New York City in a move that startled the Americans. Clinton was waiting for the final arrangements for American Major General Benedict Arnold to betray the Hudson River forts. They had been secretly negotiating through intermediaries for eighteen months since an embittered Arnold, repeatedly passed over for promotion, had been convicted by a court-martial of unauthorized use of army wagons while he was military governor of Philadelphia. Arnold had received only a formal reprimand from Washington, but his extreme pride could not stand the slightest public rebuke.

On the last day of July 1780, Arnold overtook Washington, Hamilton, Lafayette, and Knox on a high bluff opposite Peekskill, New York, where they were watching the last of the American soldiers being rowed across the Hudson. Off and on for weeks, unsuspecting members of Congress sympathetic to the twice-wounded Arnold had been prodding Washington to give him the command of West Point. But Washington was reluctant: he was short on battle-seasoned major generals. He needed Arnold to command half his best infantry in the field and expected Arnold to accept, gratefully. That hot afternoon, Washington later recalled, Arnold "asked me if I had thought of anything for him?" Washington was pleased to see Arnold back in the fight. Yes, yes, he answered, smiling. He was to command the army's left wing. Hamilton, sitting on his horse, close to Arnold, later testified at a court-martial that Arnold's face turned dark red. Arnold remained adamant that he was not ready, that his wounds from Saratoga, nearly three years ago, had not completely healed. Two days later, Washington relented and issued orders for Arnold to take command of West Point.[26]

Arnold soon learned by a coded message from New York City that Clinton had approved his 20,000-pound request for payment for betraying West Point and its 3,086 men. He began systematically to strip the garrison, ordering two hundred soldiers upriver to cut firewood, and two hundred downriver on outpost duty. He detached precious artillerymen to escort Loyalist prisoners on a slow march to Washington's base camp at Tappan. In all, in six weeks he reduced West Point's garrison by half, not even protesting when Washington requisitioned four companies of artillery.

At a September 6, 1780, council of war at Tappan, Washington raised questions about West Point that no one but Arnold, who was absent, could answer. Washington assigned Hamilton to draft the queries and send them off to Arnold. Arnold sent back an express rider to Washington's camp to say he would "do myself the honor to deliver [his report] in person." Arnold now had the perfect excuse to gather up-to-the-minute intelligence at Washington's headquarters. At West Point, he took an inventory of cannon and the detailed orders to be followed by the garrison "in case of an alarm." In addition, he wrote a second secret report for the British, analyzing the defects of West Point's forts. But in his covering letter to Washington, he insisted that a British attack would not be "very dangerous."[27]

On September 18, 1780, Benedict Arnold personally led his life guards to meet Washington and his entourage at King's Ferry to accompany him across the Hudson to Peekskill, where Hamilton joined them. After supper, Hamilton read over a pair of letters Arnold gave him that he had just received from a Loyalist officer requesting a meeting. Hamilton later told a friend that Arnold "asked for Washington's opinion of the propriety of [complying] with [the Loyalist's] request." According to Hamilton, Washington dissuaded Arnold from meeting the Loyalist and "advised him to reply that whatever related to his private affairs must be of a civil nature, and could only properly be addressed to the civil authority." American policy was that Loyalists were considered civilian traitors to the United States, not legitimate military personnel. Riding along with Washington's party, Arnold turned over his long, written answer on West Point's defenses to Washington. Hamilton had just received and turned over to Washington a warning from Hercules Mulligan in New York City that one of the American generals "high up" was in league with the British. Hamilton later recalled that "Arnold was very anxious to ascertain from [us] the precise day of [Washington's] return."[28]

Hamilton's recommendation that Washington refuse to write an order for a flag of truce blew Arnold's cover for an open meeting with the Loyalist Colonel Beverley Robinson and with John André, the British spymaster. Instead, after returning to West Point, Arnold decided to write a coded message to the Loyalist Robinson to be transmitted to Sir Henry Clinton: the British could capture Washington, his generals, and his entire staff when they came to West Point "to lodge here on Saturday night next [September 24]."[29] It had been essential that Arnold get the message to Robinson, who knew the lay of the land at West Point intimately. Arnold was writing the message from Robinson's own house, now serving as the quarters of West Point's commandant. If the British wanted to bag Washington, Lafayette, Knox, and Hamilton, what would become the core of the American government, as well as capture the garrison of West Point, there would be no better time. Arnold's message reached Clinton in New York City on September 19. It made Clinton so sure of the success of Arnold's treasonous coup that he requested ships to be ready to dash up the Hudson as soon as spymaster André returned from a secret meeting with Arnold. Hercules Mulligan learned of this sudden troop movement when the British ordered provisions from his brother's firm, along with the place and time of delivery. Mulligan could possibly have warned Hamilton that the British were bound for West Point. But, ignoring direct orders from Clinton, André had come up the Hudson in a British warship, the *Vulture*, and was rowed ashore. In a secret nighttime meeting, Arnold handed André the top-secret summary of the American army's strength he had gleaned at headquarters, his reports to Washington on West Point and the minutes of Washington's September 6 council of war, then rode back upriver to West Point to await the British attack.[30]

PEGGY SHIPPEN Arnold planned a breakfast reception for the commander-in-chief's arrival the morning of September 25, but Washington took a longer route back from his conference with the French command in Hartford for security reasons. Alexander Hamilton rode ahead to tell her Washington would be late and that breakfast should go ahead without him. Peggy stayed upstairs with her baby, Edward, in the master bedroom during breakfast. She was still exhausted from nine days in an open wagon as she moved her household from Philadelphia to West Point. Intimately involved in Arnold's plot, she had encoded and decoded messages and met go-betweens for fully nineteen months to shield Arnold's identity. She would later receive a handsome royal pension "for services rendered" in the conspiracy. She also was terribly fond of John André, who had frequently visited her family before and during the British occupation of Philadelphia. In fact, she may have been in love with him. When she died, she was wearing a locket of his hair around her neck. No doubt, she was anxious over the safety not only of her husband but of her old friend. She planned to go downstairs later, when Washington arrived.

Hamilton was at the table with Arnold; with a neighbor, Dr. Eustis, the fort's physician; and with Lafayette's aide, James McHenry. They had just been served when a courier clambered into the room, handing Arnold an express message. André's luck had just run out as he approached the British lines half a mile north of Tarrytown. Three young New York militiamen who were absent without leave from their unit had banded together to waylay and rob Loyalist travelers. They forced André into the woods, strip-searched him, and found only his watch and a few Continental dollars. They were on the point of letting him go when one decided to yank off his boots. Inside one, he had discovered Arnold's papers. Benedict Arnold did not take time to read the rest. Excusing himself, he vaulted upstairs to Peggy. Their plot had been discovered. The incriminating papers were on their way to Washington. Arnold instructed Peggy to burn all their other papers and stall for time. Running down to the Hudson riverbank, Arnold commandeered a boat, stepped into it, and cocked his pistols. He promised his crewmen two gallons of rum each to take him downriver.

Just after Arnold fled and before Washington arrived, Hamilton could hear Peggy Arnold shrieking as she ran down the upstairs hallway. Hamilton rushed up the stairs to find her in her dressing gown, screaming, her hair disheveled. She was struggling with two maids, who were trying to get her back into her bedroom. At a subsequent court-martial, Hamilton testified that "Mrs. Arnold's unhappy situation called us all to her assistance." Hamilton described her "hysterics and utter frenzy." She was "raving distracted." When Hamilton assured her that Arnold would soon return, she cried, "No, no, he is gone forever!" Peggy "fell to her knees at my feet with prayers and entreaties to spare her innocent babe." Hamilton helped to carry her "to her bed, raving mad." When Washington arrived, Hamilton told him of his suspicions about Arnold's treason. After a cursory glimpse at the papers found in André's boot, Washington ordered Hamilton to go after Arnold.[31]

Hamilton and McHenry spurred their horses down the shore road a dozen miles to Verplanck's Point, trying to intercept Arnold in his barge, but he had already reached the British sloop-of-war *Vulture*, where he had his life guards taken prisoners of war. Hamilton later bemoaned to his fiancée, Betsy, that they were "much too late." From Verplanck's Ferry, Hamilton sent a quick message to Washington:

> Dear Sir,
> You will see by the enclosed we are too late. Arnold went by water to the Vulture. I shall write to General Greene advising him [that], without making a bustle, to be in readiness to march and even to detach a brigade this way, for though I do not believe the project will go on, it is possible Arnold has made such dispositions with the garrison as may tempt the enemy in [West Point's] present weakness to make the stroke this night and it seems prudent to be providing against it. I shall endeavor to find [Return Jonathan] Meigs and request him to march to the garrison [at West Point] and shall make some arrangements here. I hope Your Excellency will approve these steps as there may be no time to be lost.[32]

To Greene at Orangetown, New Jersey, Hamilton dashed off another message:

> Sir,
> There has just unfolded at this place a scene of the blackest treason. Arnold has fled to the enemy. André the British adjutant general is in our possession as a spy. His capture unraveled the mystery. West Point was to have been the sacrifice, all the dispositions have been made for the purpose and 'tis possible, tho' not probable, tonight may still see the execution. The wind is fair [for a British naval attack]. I came here in pursuit of Arnold but was too late. I advise your putting the army under marching orders and detaching a brigade this way.[33]

Then, to Washington, he fired off another terse message.
Hamilton knew that Washington would remember that Meigs had

marched with Arnold to Quebec. Hamilton acted quickly, decisively, confident that the stunned Washington would not countermand his initiative. Hamilton sent off the courier toward West Point, where he knew Washington would be taking emergency measures to shore up the fort's defenses in case the British did attack. He added a brief postscript: "The *Vulture* is gone down to New York."[34]

When Peggy Arnold learned that Washington had come back from West Point, she cried out again that "there was a hot iron on her head and no one but General Washington could take it off, and [she] wanted to see the general." When Hamilton returned from his unsuccessful pursuit of Arnold, Dr. Eustis and Varick went to Washington's room and told him all they knew. Then he accompanied Washington to Peggy's bedside. Clutching her baby at her breast, Peggy said, "No, that is not General Washington; that is the man who was going to assist Colonel Varick in killing my child." Washington retreated from the room, certain that Peggy Arnold was mad but no conspirator.[35]

Hamilton wrote to Betsy Schuyler the morning after Arnold's defection that the aftermath of the treason was a "scene that shocked me more than anything I have met with." Hamilton told her he had gone "in pursuit of him but was much too late," to his utter "disappointment":

On my return, I saw an amiable woman frantic with distress for the loss of a husband she tenderly loved . . . It was the most affecting scene I ever was witness to. She for a considerable time entirely lost her senses. The General went up to see her and she upbraided him with being in a plot to murder her child. One moment she raved; another she melted into tears. Sometimes, she pressed her infant to her bosom and lamented its fate . . . in a manner that would have pierced insensibility itself.

All the sweetness of beauty, all the loveliness of innocence, all the tenderness of a wife and all the fondness of a mother showed themselves in her appearance and conduct. We have every reason to believe she was entirely unacquainted with the plan . . . She instantly fell into a convulsion and he [Washington] left her in that station.[36]

That day, September 25, Hamilton visited Peggy Arnold again:

This morning, she is more composed. I paid her a visit and endeavored to soothe her by every method in my power, though you may imagine she is not easily to be consoled.

Peggy Arnold, he added, was "very apprehensive" that her Philadelphia neighbors would take out their resentment on her if, as Hamilton had proposed to Washington, she be allowed to go home to her family:

She is very apprehensive the resentment of her country will fall upon her (who is only unfortunate) for the guilt of her husband. I have tried to persuade her, her apprehensions are illfounded, but she has too many proofs of the illiberality of the state [Pennsylvania] to which she belongs to be convinced.

Hamilton was completely taken in by the scene Peggy stage-managed, the beautiful and disheveled mother with her babe in arms:

She received us in bed with every circumstance that could interest our sympathy. Her sufferings were so eloquent that I wished myself her brother, to have a right to become her defender. As it is, I have entreated her to enable me to give her proofs of my friendship.

If Hamilton could forgive Arnold "for sacrificing his honor," he told Betsy, "I could not forgive him for acting a part that must have forfeited the esteem of so fine a woman":

At present, she almost forgets his crime in his misfortune, and her horror at the guilt of the traitor is lost in her love of the man. . . . Time will make her despise, if it cannot make her hate.[37]

Peggy Shippen could not have played a more brilliant part to a wider audience. Hamilton not only sent a letter describing the scene to his fiancée but also sent it off for publication in the *New York Packet* and *Pennsylvania Gazette.* It was soon reprinted all over North America and Europe. The next day, Peggy summoned Hamilton to her room and appealed to him to intercede with Washington for a pass for her to leave with her baby. Washington saw no reason to stop her. He, too, believed Peggy Arnold. Hamilton was able to come back almost immediately and tell her that she could go either to her father's home in Philadelphia or to her husband in New York City. She chose Philadelphia. Her deception was now complete.

In the gravest crisis of the Revolution, Washington refused to concede publicly the possibility that the Arnold-André conspiracy had included betraying him to the British, in effect carrying out a military coup. To Joseph Reed in Pennsylvania, Washington confided there had been those who had reasons for doubt, especially Hamilton. "I am far from thinking," Washington wrote, "he [Arnold] intended to hazard a defeat of this important object by combining another risk, although there were circumstances which led to a contrary belief." One of these, as Hamilton pointed out, was Arnold's precise knowledge of Washington's movements and his timetable. To Major General William Heath, Washington acknowledged that Arnold "knew of my approach and that I was visiting ["Beverly"] with the Marquis [de Lafayette]." Hamilton wrote a full report to his friend, John Laurens, still on parole in Philadelphia. He concluded that, while Arnold would have been "unwise" to try to capture Washington at the same time he surrendered West Point, "there was some color for imagining it was a part of the plan to betray the General into the hands of the enemy. Arnold was very anxious to ascertain from [Washington] the precise day of his return, and the enemy's movements seem to have corresponded to this point."[38]

To his friend, Laurens, Hamilton confided,

My feelings were never put to so severe a trial. I congratulate you, my friend, on our happy escape from the mischiefs with which this treason was big.

It would be the twentieth century before the opening of the British headquarters papers at the University of Michigan proved what Hamilton refused to believe—that a young and beautiful woman was capable of helping Benedict Arnold plot the greatest conspiracy of the American Revolution and then completely fool the veteran warriors around her. To Betsy Schuyler, Hamilton revealed the extent of his own guilelessness in the presence of a clever and manipulative woman:

> We have every reason to believe she was unacquainted with the plan and that her first knowledge of it was when Arnold went to tell her he must banish himself from his country and from her forever. She instantly fell into a convulsion and he left her in that situation.

Not only did Peggy Arnold dupe Hamilton, but Hamilton also felt great sympathy for the captured spy André. When he was asked to write and sign a letter to Clinton in New York City proposing a trade of Arnold for André, he declined it, as he explained to Betsy a week later after André's execution. But he apparently wrote over his protests a similar letter at Washington's instruction proposing just such a bargain to save André's life. He generally considered Washington's treatment of André too harsh, he told Betsy:

> It was proposed to me [by Washington] to suggest to him [André] the idea of an exchange for Arnold, but I knew I should have forfeited his [André's] esteem by doing it, and therefore declined it. A man of honor could not but reject it and I would not for the world have proposed to him a thing which must have placed me in the unenviable light of supposing him capable of meanness. I confess to you I had the weakness to value the esteem of a *dying* man because I reverenced his merit.... I wished myself possessed of André's accomplishments for your sake.

Hamilton undoubtedly had satisfied his curiosity by this time about the extent of Betsy's involvement with André during his stay at the

Schuyler mansion five years earlier, and he now intervened on André's behalf with Washington, he reported to Betsy, "to justify myself to your sentiments." Hamilton's regard for Betsy and how the news must be devastating her more than any regard for André led him to intercede with Washington to grant André's last wish. Rather than the ignominy of being hanged like a common criminal, André asked an officer's honorable execution by firing squad:

> I urged a compliance with André's request to be shot and I do not think it would have had an ill effect, but some people are only sensible to motives of policy [did he mean Washington?] and sometimes from a narrow disposition mistake it. When André's tale comes to be told and present resentment is over, the refusing him the privilege of choosing [the] manner of death will be branded with too much obduracy.[39]

In his carefully oblique criticism of Washington to the daughter of one of his top generals, Hamilton must have realized he was treading a dangerous line. Again and again, he had argued for mercy for prisoners, so much on his mind. Of all the officers and men at the execution place at Tappan, Hamilton seemed the one most capable of identifying with the condemned young artist. "Never," Hamilton wrote in admiration, to John Laurens, "did a man suffer death with more justice or deserve it less." André's graceful conduct as a condemned man deeply impressed Hamilton, filling him with "the weakness to value the esteem of a dying man because I reverenced his merit."

To Laurens, Hamilton was less sentimental, more clinical as he reported his observations of a condemned gentleman:

> There was something singularly interesting in the character and fortunes of André. To an excellent understanding well improved by education and travel, he united a peculiar elegance of mind and manners and the advantages of a pleasing person ... His sentiments were elevated and inspired esteem. They had a softness that conciliated affection. His elocution was handsome; his

address easy, polite and insinuating. By his merit he had acquired the unlimited confidence of his general..[40]

When Betsy first learned of André's capture, she immediately asked Hamilton for further details. Hamilton promised by return messenger "a particular account of André"—and he spared her no details. Yet he expressed his fear that Betsy would admire the picture he painted of the romantic prisoner so much that she would forget Hamilton, grieve more deeply for her lost love. Hamilton wished he was "possessed of André's accomplishments." Comparing himself unfavorably with André, he asked, "Why am I not handsome? Why have I not every acquirement that can embellish human nature?" He wanted to be, in his fiancée's eyes, "the first, the most amiable, the most accomplished of my sex." When Betsy did not write back to him by the third day after she learned of André's execution, he was tortured by her silence. She did not write to him often enough, he complained to her: "I ought at least to hear from you by every post, and your last letter to me is as old as the middle of September." When another week passed and still no letter came from Betsy, he reproached her again. "I tell you, my Betsy, you are negligent. You do not write me often enough. Take more care of my happiness." But Betsy's gloom only deepened as she approached the day of her wedding to the man who had helped to execute the man she had so long loved. And the picture of John André, smiling down at Hamilton from the gallows as he put the rope around his neck himself, would haunt Hamilton in the months ahead. Betsy's silence lengthened. By the middle of October, two months before their scheduled wedding day, he begged her not to wait to find out until "the day before we are married that you 'can't like the man'; but of all things I pray you don't make the discovery afterwards, for that would be worse than all." Two weeks later, he wrote uneasily, "It is still a fortnight since I have received a line from my charmer." The specter of André sleeping with his Betsy now intruded on his dreams of Betsy. He wrote to her of "a charming dream" that, when he arrived in Albany, he found Betsy sleeping "on a green near the house." Beside her he could see "in an inclined posture stood a gentleman whom I did not know." He was holding one of her hands, "fixed in silent admiration." When Hamilton challenged him, the stranger "insisted on a prior right." It was a recurring nightmare for Hamilton, André's "prior right," and he begged Betsy to reassure him: "Tell me, I pray you, who is this rival of mine? Dreams, you know, are the messengers of Jove."[41]

To Laurens, Hamilton intimated he was proud that, "in the whole progress of the affair" he had treated André "with the most scrupulous delicacy." André had "acknowledged the generosity of [my] behavior towards him in every respect." Hamilton visited André frequently in his last hours, taking personal responsibility for his treatment and winning him one major concession: pen and paper to write a farewell letter to General Clinton. André also used Hamilton's notes to him in one last venture back into the world he had wanted and had left behind for the army. On the backs of Hamilton's notes to him, André had drawn pictures of the woman who brought him his last meal from Washington's table, of the boat on the Hudson passing dark cliffs as it brought him to meet Arnold, of himself, quill poised, writing his last letter to his patron—and probably one of his lovers—General Clinton. In his long letter to Laurens, Hamilton quoted André's last words to him: "'I would not for the world leave a sting in his mind that should embitter his future days.' He could scarce finish the sentence, bursting into tears in spite of his effort to suppress them." Hamilton told Laurens that by contemplating André's fate, he had become "aware that a man of real merit is never seen in so favorable light as through the medium of adversity." The "maxims and practices of war are the satire of human nature," he added. "They countenance almost every species of seduction as well as violence."[42]

ELEVEN

"Then We Must Part"

Alexander Hamilton could think of little but his marriage—and all that it offered. His fiancée, Betsy Schuyler, wanted to elope, as her two older sisters had done, but Hamilton would not have it. Betsy could not face the prospect of marrying Hamilton at home in the very room where she had spent so many happy hours with John André. Hamilton tried in his letters to turn her mind to the day when the war would be over and he would be with his Betsy. Their separation fanned his smoldering correspondence. In early October, he wrote Betsy that she "engross[ed] my thoughts too entirely to allow me to think anything else." He wrote of his passion in words calculated to stir hers. She was in his thoughts night and day, he said. "You intrude on my sleep," he told her. "I meet you in every dream." None of the other beautiful young women who flocked to headquarters social events tempted him any longer. He was, he averred, "monopolized by a little *nut brown maid*" and he had changed "from a soldier" into "a puny lover." The months of waiting for his release from duty had become "more and more unhappy." He had grown "impatient under the hard necessity that keeps me from you."[1]

But his chances of leaving headquarters dimmed with the Arnold-André conspiracy. Stunned by the ignominious loss of one of his best generals, Washington had become even more dependent on Hamilton, who had shown such enterprise and quick thinking during the crisis. Washington could not possibly spare Hamilton to go to Betsy's side. Hamilton was also more valuable than ever as a French-speaking liaison with America's new ally. He had to keep up a steady correspondence with French officers. Not all of it was official or unpleasant. The Marquis de Fleury was in hot pursuit of Betsy's younger sister for reasons he made clear while congratulating Hamilton on his engagement to Betsy. "First of all, you will get all that family's interest," the marquis wrote, enumerating Hamilton's blessings, "and a man of your abilities wants a little influence to do good to his country. The second [is] that you will be in a very easy situation. Happiness is not to be found without a large estate."[2]

All ambition, Hamilton certainly was not oblivious to his good fortune in marrying Betsy Schuyler, and he did not let his discovery of her first love for a British spy stand in his way to her family fortune. Indeed, he seems to have exploited his unique knowledge. While he bemoaned the delay in his marriage, he used his time and privileged position at headquarters to help his new patron, his future father-in-law. When British, Loyalist, and Indian forces attacked down Lake Champlain again in October 1780, General Schuyler, in command of the Northern Department, wrote to Hamilton, seeking reinforcements from Washington. Three regiments quickly marched north, providing a safe conveyance for Hamilton's confidential letter to Schuyler. Along with the troops went another long letter to Betsy. British attacks around Albany had disrupted the mails. He had not heard from Betsy in two weeks and he sounded anxious. He would join her in a month, he promised. But when two other aides went home to Virginia to marry, Washington said he could not grant Hamilton a furlough until they returned.

And if Hamilton was yearning to be with Betsy Schuyler, at the same time he was just as certainly doing all he could to pursue laurels that would take him even farther away from her. No longer willing to be put off indefinitely, anxious that the war would end before he could distinguish himself, Hamilton tried to outflank Washington by shifting the grounds of his appeal. In 1779, he had sought a commission to go to South Carolina with his friend Laurens to raise a slave army to attack the British, but Washington had refused him. As it turned out, Hamilton would probably have been captured along with Laurens. Hamilton, in a letter that shows the formality of his relationship with Washington even after four years as his aide, again appealed to Washington on November 22, 1780. This time, he sought a joint command with Lafayette to lead an all-out attack on New York City:

> Sometime last fall when I spoke to your Excellency about going to the southward, I explained to you candidly my feelings with respect to military reputation, and how much it was my object to act a conspicuous part in some enterprise that might perhaps raise my character as a soldier above mediocrity. You were so good as to say you would be glad to furnish me with an occasion. When the expedition to Staten Island was on foot, I made an application for it through the Marquis [de Lafayette] who informed me of your refusal on two principles—one, that giving me a whole battalion might be a subject of dissatisfaction [among other officers], the other that, if an accident should happen to me in the present state of your [official] family, you would be embarrassed for the necessary assistance. The project you now have in contemplation affords another opportunity. I take this method of making the request to avoid the embarrassment of a personal explanation.[3]

Lafayette, supporting Hamilton, told him to "show me your letter before you give it." Together they had planned that Hamilton, as part of Lafayette's attack on Manhattan, would seize strategic Bayard's Hill, where, four years earlier, Hamilton had commanded an artillery company. This time, Washington did not turn him down per se: he canceled the entire expedition.

Hamilton's friends kept trying to liberate him from headquarters. Greene and Lafayette nominated him for adjutant general. Hamilton was ideally suited for the post, which involved reorganizing the army, something Hamilton had already been doing for three years. Ironically, Washington had already assigned someone Hamilton had suggested. Yet when Lafayette personally made a pitch to Washington on behalf of his friend Hamilton, Washington objected that he could not possibly have full colonels reporting to a lieutenant colonel. Didn't it occur to him to promote Hamilton, who had received no promotion in three and a half years even as he had become Washington's most trusted adviser? It apparently did not cross Washington's mind to reward Hamilton with a brigadier general's commission, even though there were younger generals with far less experience or usefulness. Perturbed, Lafayette wrote to Hamilton, "I confess I became warmer than you would perhaps have wished me to be."[4]

Hamilton's next gambit was to nominate Lafayette for a special mission to France to seek more aid. Lafayette was to take Hamilton with him. Instead, Washington dispatched Lafayette to Virginia. As he headed south, Lafayette nominated his French-speaking friend Hamilton to take his place as the new envoy to Versailles. Hamilton's friend Laurens joined Lafayette in lobbying Congress in his behalf. But it soon became apparent that Hamilton's brushes with the anti-Washington faction in Congress had seriously damaged his chances of any congressional appointment. Laurens wrote delicately to Washington that "Colonel Hamilton was not sufficiently known to Congress to unite their suffrages in his favor." The attempt to win Hamilton an appointment to Paris was a "total failure," Laurens reported to Hamilton just before he himself accepted the post on December 11, 1780. In one of his more generous gestures, Hamilton drafted a warm letter in French to introduce Laurens to the French foreign minister at Versailles. Washington then copied Hamilton's draft word for word to add the strength of his recognizable handwriting and signature.[5]

By this time, Hamilton had every reason to be magnanimous. At the end of November 1780, as the army went into winter quarters and all fighting stopped, with his friend James "Mac" McHenry, he rode north to Albany to marry Elizabeth Schuyler. It was his first leave in four and a half years in the army. It was also the first time since his mother had died twelve years earlier that he was heading toward a home and a woman who was eager to see him. And what a home! The three-story dormered brick Schuyler mansion, seven tall windows wide, stood on a handsome bluff overlooking the town of Albany with a ten-mile view of the Hudson River. The house, one of America's grandest at that time, was fully sixty feet wide with a large northwest wing and handsome horse barn. The general's sleigh fetched Hamilton and McHenry from headquarters. In the arms of Betsy amid the hospitality of her ample family, Hamilton was instantly made at home. The wedding took place December 17, 1780, in the ballroom-size second-floor hallway (now called the Hamilton Room) where John André had once spent long afternoons playing his flute and sketching Betsy. The clerk of Albany's Dutch Reformed Church recorded the marriage of "Colonel Hamilton and Elizabeth Schuyler." (He did not know the groom's first name.) Best man McHenry read verse that should have made Hamilton and his bride, if not its author, blush. Hamilton was now "embosomed" with "your Queen":

> As thus ye lay, the happiest pair,
> A rosy scent enriched the air
> While to a music softy sounding,
> Breathing, panting, slow rebounding.

But McHenry's muse imparted a warning:

> Know then, dear Ham, a truth confessed,
> Soon beauty fades, and love's a guest,
> Love has no settled place on earth;
> A very wanderer from his birth...[6]

Two days later, ensconced in the Schuyler mansion, honeymooner Hamilton took up his pen briefly and turned literary critic, using double entendre to describe both bride and bard, thanking departing "Dear Mac" for "your poetry and your confidence":

The piece is a good one... It has wit, which you know is a rare thing. I see by perseverance all ladies may be won... You know I have often told you, you write prose well but had no genius for poetry. I retract.[7]

Ten days later, when Lafayette's friend the Marquis de Chastellux visited Albany, he found Hamilton living as if he had always been part of the Schuyler family. After six weeks with Betsy, Hamilton had no choice but to return to his duties at Washington's headquarters, now down the Hudson at New Windsor, New York. On January 13, 1781, he drove with Elizabeth, wrapped in furs, in a sleigh along with a slave to set up housekeeping in rented rooms in the village near headquarters. The weeks away from headquarters had given Hamilton the time to talk at length with his new father-in-law, the frankly approving General Schuyler. Hamilton could now begin to make plans for the war's end. He would study law, living with the Schuylers in Albany until he was ready to open his practice, probably in New York City. But to help establish himself, he believed more than ever that he needed to win distinction in battle. Repeated setbacks by Congress had convinced him that all his efforts had been too anonymous, that he was perceived to be too much Washington's lackey, his own name too easily dismissed. He needed a combat command, a conspicuous assignment, a victory. He brooded that, had he stayed in the artillery, by now he would be a senior colonel, on the verge of promotion to general. As it was, his seniority had been suspended when he had joined Washington's staff. With no promotion in nearly four years, it galled Hamilton whenever Washington used Hamilton's inferior rank as an excuse to ignore his repeated requests for a combat assignment.

Yet his return to headquarters came at an unpropitious time to press Washington. During his absence, on New Year's night, 1781, some twenty-five hundred Pennsylvania troops of the Continental Line had mutinied, shot two officers who tried to stop them, and marched toward the capital at Philadelphia to demand that Congress pay them years of back pay. So bad was morale in the army in general—inflation had now reached nine hundred times the 1776 value of the dollar—that Washington did not dare march out to confront the mutineers for fear his own troops would join them. On January 3, the mutineers seized Princeton and ensconced themselves in the ruins of Nassau Hall as five hundred New Jersey troops joined them. The mutiny was finally to end fully six months later when New Jersey troops shot the two leaders of the New Jersey mutiny and "Mad Anthony" Wayne ordered four of his Pennsylvania mutineers executed. But the mutinies were making it clear that Washington had lost the initiative in the North after two years of inactivity.

Washington's headquarters staff, once numbering eleven, was now down to two, Hamilton and Tench Tilghman of Maryland. To add to Hamilton's discontent, he was constantly receiving long letters from former compatriots at headquarters, describing their successes. Robert Hanson Harrison had left to become chief justice of Maryland. Richard Kidder Meade had resigned to go home to Virginia to marry. Nathanael Greene had taken command of the Southern Army after Horatio Gates's rout at Camden, South Carolina. Each former comrade writing to Hamilton complained of desperate shortages and British successes in the South and implored him to use his influence at Washington's elbow. He was to use "great freedom" in communicating with them. Hamilton's work had kept piling up even as the driven Washington refused to take even a few days' rest to accept a sleigh ride to Albany to visit General Schuyler and his wife.[8]

The odd, isolated, high-gabled one-and-a-half-story Dutch-style house in New Windsor that Washington had chosen as his latest headquarters was, according to one understated French visitor, "not large." Surrounded by a porch, a kitchen fireplace running the width of the house, it had been chopped up into small rooms. Washington's office on the second floor had a dormer window and an adjoining bedroom where he slept with Martha. Betsy Hamilton came to headquarters daily and helped Martha pour tea for visitors, serving French officers, as one noted, "with much grace." The rest of the headquarters family was crowded several to a room, as usual.

At first, the newlyweds seemed content. Five weeks into their marriage, Hamilton felt qualified to give advice on the subject of matrimony to Betsy's younger sister Margarita. Betsy had written her, "I am the happiest of women. My dear Hamilton is fonder of me every day. Get married, I charge you." Before posting the letter, Hamilton had added his own advice on choosing a mate in a postscript:

Because your sister has the talent of growing more amiable every day, or because I am a fanatic in love, or both—or if you prefer another interpretation, because I have address enough to be a good dissembler, she fancies herself the happiest woman in the world, and would need persuade all her friends to embark with her in the matrimonial voyage. But I pray you do not let her advice have so much influence as to make you matrimony-mad. 'Tis a very good thing when their stars unite two people who are fit for each other, who have souls capable of relishing the fruits of friendship.

But it's a dog's life when two dissonant tempers meet, and 'tis ten to one but this is the case. Be cautious in the choice. Get a man of sense, not ugly enough to be pointed at—with some good nature—a few grains of feeling—a little taste—a little imagination—and above all a good deal of decision to keep you in order. If you can find one with all these qualities willing to marry you, marry him as soon as you please. I must tell you in confidence that I think I have been very fortunate.[9]

Hamilton soon heard back from Albany that the Schuylers were equally pleased with him. Crusty old General Schuyler wrote

You cannot, my dear sir, be more happy at the connection you have made with my family than I am. Until a child has made a judicious choice, the heart of a parent is continually in anxiety. But this anxiety vanished in the moment that I discovered where you and she had placed their affections.[10]

Betsy's more beautiful, more sophisticated older sister, Angelica, married to an Englishman who was growing rich by supplying the French army in America, also found her new brother-in-law Hamilton interesting. She goaded her younger sister Betsy to "embrace poor Hamilton for me. I am really so proud of his merit and abilities that even you, Eliza, might *envy my feelings.*" The comely Angelica had evidently found Hamilton charming when she met him in Morristown two years earlier and had renewed her flirting with him at the wedding in Albany. She would, she wrote Betsy, "pass with you the remainder of my days, that is if you will be so obliging as to permit my *brother* [Hamilton] to give me his society, for you know how much I love and admire him."[11]

ON FEBRUARY 16, 1781, Alexander Hamilton reported to headquarters as usual. He wrote out two sets of orders. When he finished writing, he went downstairs to deliver them to Tench Tilghman. As he went down the stairs, he met Washington on his way up. The commander-in-chief said he wanted to speak to Hamilton. "I answered that I would wait upon him immediately," Hamilton wrote two days later to his father-in-law. Then Hamilton handed the letter "containing an order of a pressing and interesting nature" to Tilghman. On his way back to Washington's office, Hamilton stopped again, this time to talk to Lafayette on "a matter of business." They talked, Hamilton wrote, for no more than a minute. Lafayette would "testify how impatient I was to get back, and that I left him in a manner which but for our intimacy would have been [considered] more than abrupt." Undoubtedly, they spoke French, which required the customary courtesies and flourishes.

As Hamilton climbed the stairs, he saw Washington pacing back and forth on the landing. Washington "accost[ed] me in a very angry tone," Hamilton explained to Schuyler. "'Colonel Hamilton,' said he, 'you have kept me waiting at the head of the stairs these ten minutes. I must tell you, sir, you treat me with disrespect.'" Hamilton was caught completely off-guard. The tedious years of frustration over Washington's refusal to allow him any field assignment, only staffwork, now welled up inside him. Something snapped. To Schuyler, he recounted, "I replied without petulance but with decision, 'I am not conscious of it, sir, but since you have thought it necessary to tell me so, we must part.'

"'Very well, sir,' said he, 'if it be your choice.' Or something to this effect. And we separated."[12]

Recoiling downstairs, Hamilton vented his outrage on Lafayette. The horrified marquis soon was writing to Washington, "From the very first moment, I exerted every means in my power to prevent a

separation which I knew was not agreeable to Your Excellency."
Hamilton later recounted to Schuyler that "less than an hour after,"
Washington's now sole aide-de-camp, Tilghman, "came to me in the
General's name, assuring me of his great confidence in my abilities,
integrity, usefulness, etc., and of his desire in a candid conversation to
heal a difference which could not have happened but in a moment of
passion." But Hamilton "requested Mr. Tilghman to tell him that I
had taken my resolution in a matter not to be revoked." Any further
"conversation would serve no other purpose than to produce explanations mutually disagreeable." Hamilton would agree to meet with
Washington if he desired "yet I should be happy if he would permit
me to decline it." Hamilton asked Tilghman to assure Washington
that he would not leave headquarters until "some other gentlemen
who were absent" returned to take his place and that he would continue to behave "as if nothing had happened." But Hamilton made it
clear to Tilghman that he had had enough of Washington. He confided
in a letter to "Mac" McHenry that "the Great Man and I have come
to an open rupture." He had rejected Washington's "proposals of
accommodation":

> I pledge my honor to you that he will find me inflexible. He
> shall for once at least repent his ill-humor. Without a shadow of
> reason and on the slightest ground, he charged me in the most
> affrontive manner with treating him with disrespect.

Washington had so offended Hamilton that he might have handed
him his commission and resigned from the army on the spot, he told
Mac. "I wait till more help arrives. At present there is besides myself
only Tilghman, who is just recovering from a fit of illness, the consequence of too close application to business." Hamilton vowed that,
except to "a very few friends," he would keep his "difference" with
Washington secret. "Therefore be silent. I shall continue to support a
popularity [Washington's] that has been essential [and] is still useful."
But he hoped that the time may "come when characters may be
known in their true light."[3]

It was to his father-in-law that Hamilton was most careful in pouring out his anger and resentment in a long, bold, and biting letter. After only two months as Schuyler's son-in-law, he must have sweated as he explained not only the rift but its background. Schuyler, after all, had long supported Washington and was the second most senior general to Washington in rank and seniority. The confrontation put Schuyler in a difficult position. Hamilton could now, more than ever, ill-afford Schuyler's disapproval:

> I always disliked the office of an aide-de-camp as having in it a kind of personal dependence. I refused to serve in this capacity with two major generals at an early period in the war. Infected, however, with the enthusiasm of the times, an idea of the General's character which experience soon taught me to be unfounded overcame my scruples. For three years past I have felt no friendship for him and have professed none.
>
> The truth is, our dispositions are the opposites of each other and the pride of my [temperament] would not suffer me to profess what I did not feel. You are too good a judge of human nature not to be sensible how this conduct in me has operated on a man to whom all the world is offering incense.

But, Hamilton promised, he would keep silent until the war was over. Washington was, he opined, "a very honest man." His rivals "have slender abilities and less integrity." His popularity was "essential to the safety of America." For that reason, "I think it is necessary he should be supported."[14]

Hamilton's weeklong wait for a reply from Schuyler was an excruciating time in the Hamilton household, even if, as is evident, Hamilton had sensed some disaffection toward Washington on Schuyler's part. Why else would he gamble so much on Schuyler's agreement with his conduct? When Schuyler's tactful letter arrived, he first assured Hamilton that he didn't think he was guilty of "any impropriety," but he worried that "your quitting your station" would produce "very material injuries to the public." He wished Hamilton would try to heal "this unhappy breach." Washington would "if you leave him have not one gentleman left" with good enough French "to convey his ideas." He urged Hamilton to reconsider: few men "pass through life without one of those unguarded moments which would [hurt] the feelings of a friend." Yet Schuyler assured the younger man he would understand if Hamilton could not return to Washington's favor without injuring his "principles of honor." These were, "if I may use the expression, the test of virtue."[15]

Schuyler's understanding letter persuaded Hamilton to stay on at Washington's side until another French-speaking aide could be found. More than two months passed and still no relief came. In late April 1781, Hamilton learned that Congress had resolved that his aide-de-camp's rank of lieutenant colonel was convertible into a similar grade in the Continental Army, with seniority dating back to his appointment four years earlier. This unexpected turn of fortune, no doubt engineered behind congressional doors by his father-in-law's friends, now opened the way for a fresh appeal. Hamilton anticipated Washington's reaction: "Unconnected as I am with any regiment, I can have no other command than in a light corps." Hamilton wrote Washington in a stiff and formal letter on April 27, 1781, "I flatter myself my pretensions to this are good." By now, Hamilton had been on active duty for more than five years. Had he remained an artillery officer, he pointed out, he would "have been more advanced in rank than I am now." Hamilton felt he deserved command of a light infantry corps that he knew was being formed to go south in the fast-approaching 1781 campaign.[16]

Washington's reply came back swiftly, the same day. While it was conciliatory in tone—"No officer can with justice dispute your merit and abilities"—once again, Washington refused. Other officers with more rank and seniority would object. Yet even as Washington worried that Hamilton might mistake his motives, Hamilton would not accept this latest rebuff without one last attempt to persuade Washington. His case was "peculiar and dissimilar" to other officers, he replied on May 2, 1781. This time he cited not only his service record, but reminded Washington of his "constant course of important and laborious services" at headquarters. And he was sure other officers would remember them.[17]

This time, he got no reply whatsoever. Even so, he kept faith with his father-in-law by accompanying Washington and Lafayette to Newport, Rhode Island, in mid-May to act as the American interpreter at a conference with the French high command to coordinate the coming campaign. But there was now only cold, formal tension between commander and aide. Hamilton actually took up quarters in a tavern away from Washington's retinue and they passed notes back and forth by courier. Finally, the strain was too much and Hamilton left without paying his hairdresser's bill. Instead of riding back to camp with Washington, he rode home to Albany, where he conferred with Betsy and her father. Washington would have to pen his own letters. Hamilton had been careful to send his father-in-law, who had gone to survey his ruined farms at Saratoga, the letters he had exchanged with Washington. On May 30, 1781, Schuyler sent him what was, in effect, the paper that manumitted him from his dependence on Washington. Schuyler wrote that he was preparing to leave for the New York state legislature. He had no doubt he could arrange for Hamilton to be elected a New York delegate to the Continental Congress. Hamilton immediately rode to Washington's headquarters and resigned his aide-de-camp's commission.

IN MARCH 1781, only a few weeks after Hamilton had resigned, Washington ordered the two-years-younger Lafayette south in command of troops—the very opportunity Hamilton had pleaded for—to reinforce a fumbling Steuben in Virginia. The Prussian was a better drillmaster than field commander. He had failed to intercept a devastating raid on Richmond led by the turncoat Benedict Arnold, who was now a brigadier general in the British Army. The long, drawn-out war, now entering its seventh year, had shifted south: in the North, Washington and the British were stalemated. Awaiting the promised congressional appointment in the isolated comfort of the Schuyler mansion, Hamilton paced, worrying that the coming campaign could be the final one and that he would not be in at the kill. He also worried that another season of war would be inconclusive.

Subsidized now by the Schuylers, Hamilton had the forced leisure to study the newspapers, forage in his father-in-law's ample library, and resume writing at length, something he had all but neglected in his four years as Washington's writing aide. In a lengthy unsolicited letter to Philadelphia financier Robert Morris, the newly appointed United States superintendent of finance, he pondered what would happen if the struggle dragged on with a toothless Congress unable to pay its debts or its troops at a time when soldiers were mutinying, deserting to Arnold's newly formed Loyalist brigade, the American Legion, or just plain going home in despair:

> We have to fear [that] the want of money may disband the army or so enfeeble our operations as to create in the people a general disgust and alarm, which may make them clamor for peace on any terms.

Ever-increasing financial and military aid from France was all that was keeping the Revolution alive, Hamilton believed. In Europe as well as America, many questioned why the Revolution was taking so long. Yet the Americans could still bring off a decisive victory this year. Only a few recent British successes—the fall of Charleston and the rout of Horatio Gates at Camden, South Carolina—had encouraged the British ministry to wring another year's war subsidy from a disenchanted Parliament. The war-weary and heavily taxed English people were losing their "expectation of success" as Hamilton phrased it, and were increasingly reluctant to continue funding a widening global conflict against the Americans, the French, and their allies. To Morris, Hamilton insisted,

> The game we play is a sure game, if we play it with skill. Many events may turn up in the course of the summer to make even the present campaign decisive.

By his own logic, Hamilton could ill afford the splendid isolation of the Schuyler mansion, especially if he intended to make one last attempt to win a share in the final glory of the Revolution. Inactivity gnawed at him. The unaccustomed domestic routine weighed heavily. Betsy was pregnant and so was her mother. Her father was seriously ill with the quinsy (acute tonsillitis) and increasingly depended on Hamilton to stay close to his family. Hamilton enjoyed long hours with Betsy and her sister Angelica, who had come home to help nurse the family. Hamilton and Angelica found each other interesting. Hamilton was coming to consider her livelier, wittier, and more cosmopolitan than his bride, the shy Betsy. By May, with Betsy three months' pregnant, Hamilton was more than ready to pull himself away and ride off to Fishkill and the American camp. Schuyler seemed far from able to resume his political activities; Hamilton's political career seemed a-glimmering, his future uncertain unless he found a way to assert himself. While Schuyler tugged at Hamilton to wait patiently at Albany, Lafayette was pulling at him, too, by letter from Virginia—come and join me, command my artillery. Hamilton decided against either course. Instead, he rented rooms in Fishkill near headquarters where he could keep abreast of developments and gather data for a series of newspaper articles.

Styling himself "The Continentalist," he penned a fifteen-thousand-word letter, which appeared as a four-part series, in about a month, putting it through the printing press of patriot Samuel Louden's *New York Packet*, relocated to Fishkill during the British occupation of New York City. Widely influential, the *Packet* was read especially by officers at headquarters and delegates to Congress. The articles, published in July and August 1781, were Hamilton's first attempt to influence public opinion since the war had begun six years earlier, when he had only been twenty. The months away from headquarters had given Hamilton the occasion to study the new nation's political problems and their deleterious effects on the war effort. America's military shortcomings, "Continentalist" declared, stemmed from a lack of power in Congress, especially from the lack of any independent sources of revenue large and reliable enough to permit the national government to function efficiently:

> Our whole system is in disorder, our currency depreciated until, in many places, it will hardly [circulate]. Public credit [is] at its lowest ebb, our army deficient in numbers and unprovided

with everything. The government in its present condition [is]
unable to command the means to pay, clothe or feed their
troops.

Hamilton, despite this pessimistic salvo, had never doubted that
America could ultimately win. The British had only fourteen thousand professional English troops on the entire continent. Half of the
thirty thousand rented Hessian mercenaries had died or deserted and
were employed mostly in garrison duty in coastal towns, rarely trusted
on the offensive by the British as the Americans tightened their
grip on the countryside. Loyalists also were dwindling, few volunteering. The number of American males of fighting age, meanwhile,
increased constantly, their Continental units, supplied by each state,
more and more made up of trained veterans who were augmented by
five thousand crack French troops. Then why was the Revolutionary
struggle taking so long? "Impolicy and mismanagement," declared
Hamilton.

The Alexander Hamilton writing in 1781 had metamorphosed since
his precocious schoolboy essay writing of 1775. He still ardently
espoused liberty and detested slavery, but he was becoming more
ambivalent about basic human nature as the war wore on. At twenty,
he had borrowed heavily from conservative Scottish philosopher
David Hume. In his 1775 pamphlet, *The Farmer Refuted*, which echoed
Hume's essay, "On the Independency of Parliament," Hamilton had
written:

In contriving any system of government and fixing the several
checks and contracts of the constitution, every man ought to be
supposed a knave and to have no other end in all his actions
but private interest. By this interest, we must govern him.

Like Hume, Hamilton believed that the people are inherently cor-
rupted by lust for power and greed for property, Government had to
be designed to control and put to work those passions "subservient
to the public good." Constitutions, congresses, and laws had to recognize that the people would act in the public interest only if their pri-

vate interests made it advantageous to them. But Hamilton had read and honored another contemporary Scot, Hume's friend Adam Smith, who contended that ambition was even more powerful a motive than greed: "That passion, when once it has got entire possession of the breast, will admit neither a rival nor a successor." Hamilton saw both passions as the powerful engines driving most human behavior.[18]

Before his break with Washington, as his every scheme failed, his natural optimism had soured into skepticism and then sharpened to pessimism. He had become, he wrote his friend John Laurens, "disgusted with every thing in this world." He saw the army, the states, and Congress in the control of "a mass of fools and knaves." But as he found time at Albany and Fishkill in the spring of 1781 to analyze the political problems frustrating the Revolution, his old self-confidence returned and he asserted himself in a brilliant critique that he now fired off to Congress's superintendent of finance, Morris. He blamed the long impasse on a weak national government. Unless Congress were given greater central authority, even if the Americans won the war, Congress would be too weak to manage the new nation. But to avert a "more general and more obstinate war, which now seemed likely," wrote Hamilton, the states and their citizens must, without delay, "enlarge the powers of Congress" and create a coherent central government. As it was, the root cause of Congress's impotence was the states' refusal to grant Congress the power to tax, leaving Congress and its armies, as Hamilton so well knew, at the mercy of requisitions that the states either could not or would not honor. For instance, Pennsylvania's Conestoga wagons were vital to supply the armies and transport its war matériel but the army had to plead each year and the state rarely met its quotas. Virginia manufactured cannon and gunpowder but its governor, Thomas Jefferson, insisted that much of its output go to support Virginia's own forces who had seized British forts in the Illinois country while providing little support for Continental armies north or south.

Its quotas unheeded at home, Congress borrowed heavily in Europe until its credit had been used up. Then it had turned to expropriation and the confiscation and forced sale of the property of

Loyalists. Congress printed enormous amounts of paper money; its so-called bills of credit were worth less each year. Paper money issued in 1777 purchased goods worth $16 million; by 1779, only two years later, $125 million yielded only about $6 million worth of supplies. It was obvious, Hamilton wrote Morris, that Congress must be granted a reliable source of revenues. The "separate exertions of the states will never suffice." All of the states' resources "must be gathered under a common authority with sufficient power to carry out the stops needed to preserve us from being a conquered people."[19]

As early as his 1779 letter to Schuyler, Hamilton had maintained that the nation's financial mess stemmed from not having a large enough supply of stable currency to pay for the war. The obvious need was creation of a national bank. At the time, there were still no banks of any kind in the country. The problem was only getting worse with the injection of large amounts of French gold and silver used to purchase supplies for French troops. Farmers and suppliers were increasingly reluctant to accept the devalued Continental currency. In his 1779 call for administrative and fiscal reform, Hamilton had argued that a national bank could be funded half by a foreign loan, half by private subscriptions to be paid off in Continental bills of credit at a depreciated value that made it profitable for merchants to accept them. Congress would use the foreign loan to pay half the national bank's stock. In turn, the bank would help finance the national government by making direct loans. The bank would facilitate taxation by increasing the supply of money in circulation, a result of financing normal business activity. Any nation at war is obliged to borrow money, both at home and abroad. The rebelling United States could not be an exception. Congress needed to borrow $5 million or $6 million annually. To secure these loans, Congress needed sure sources of revenue to pay current interest, each year setting aside the funds to retire the principal. With adequate taxes as national resources, the public debt would be wiped out in twenty years. As Hamilton scholar Forrest McDonald put it, Hamilton's earliest proposal for a national bank "was a clever one; indeed, it contained many of the principles that would later underlie Hamilton's workable plan for a national bank.

He recognized shrewdly that establishing public credit is partly a matter of creating illusions."[20]

When Hamilton wrote to Morris to refine his analysis in mid-1781, his words carried more weight than his earlier suggestions to Congress. He had to be regarded as speaking for Schuyler and other wealthy New Yorkers. In writing to Morris, he was boldly thrusting his financial thinking on the man who not only had weeks earlier been appointed to unravel Congress's tangled financial affairs, but who was one of its leading financiers and partner in the Philadelphia mercantile house of Willing and Morris, the nation's largest. At the same time, he was aligning himself with the nation's most conservative money men. Many soldiers and civilians accused Morris of "engrossing," the morally dubious practice of buying up vast amounts of wheat and other scarce supplies and speculating in them by holding on to them until prices soared. But Hamilton had decided to cast his lot with other nationalists like Morris who were taking their seats in Congress and displacing pro–states' rights members whom he believed had seriously weakened the chances of prevailing against Great Britain. In February 1781, only weeks before Hamilton fired off his missive to Morris, Congress, led by the nationalists, had voted to reorganize its departments along lines which Hamilton believed he had already suggested to New York's delegates back in 1777. Thus he felt completely entitled to reiterate and expand on his reform ideas to Morris.

"Power without revenue is a bubble," he wrote Morris. Unless the states gave Congress the means to raise revenues, they should "renounce the vain attempt of carrying on the war." Congress must "demand an instant, positive and perpetual investiture of an impost [custom duty] on trade, a land tax and a poll tax to be collected by [Congress's] own agents." When Hamilton had told his friend Laurens of his "remedies," Laurens had warned him that they "would not go down at this time." Hamilton responded, "I tell you, necessity must force them down. If they are not speedily taken, the patient will die."

Only in Hamilton's private letters to Laurens, his most trusted friend, did he reveal the depth of his disenchantment. "The birth and education of these states has fitted their inhabitants for the chair," he had written Laurens in 1779 when his friend proposed to free the slaves to fight. "The only condition they sincerely desire is that it be a golden one." As he waited for a field command a year before his wedding, he wrote Laurens, "I am a stranger in this country. I have no property here, no connections. If I have talents and integrity (as you say I have) these are justly deemed very spurious titles in these enlightened days." As Washington rejected all his efforts for a field command, Hamilton at twenty-four confided to Laurens, "I am disgusted with everything in this world but yourself and *very* few more honest fellows and I have no other wish than, as soon as possible, to make a brilliant exit."

In June 1780, he had told Laurens, "Our countrymen have all the folly of the ass and all the passiveness of the sheep . . . They are determined not to be free and they can neither be frightened, discouraged nor persuaded to change their resolution. If we are saved, France and Spain must save us." By September 1780, shortly before Benedict Arnold's defection, he wrote Laurens, "The officers are out of humor and the *worst* of evils seems to be coming upon us—*a loss of our virtue.*" To Hamilton's contemporaries, virtue meant manhood, implying sense of duty, courage and, above all, honor. "I hate Congress—I hate the army—I hate the world—I hate myself. The whole is a mass of fools and knaves." He had especial scorn for Congress: he told Laurens that "three-fourths of members of Congress were mortal enemies to talent and three-fourths of the remainder had only contempt for integrity."[21]

Hamilton's prose had become strong, self-assured. He was developing the knack of writing in maxims, many of them profound, original—and quotable. To Morris, he opined in memorable phrases:

No wise statesman will reject the good from an apprehension of the ill. The truth is, in human affairs, there is no good, pure and unmixed. Every advantage has two sides, and wisdom consists in availing ourselves of the good and guarding as much as possible against the bad . . . A national debt, if it is not excessive, will be to us a national blessing. It will be powerful cement of our union. It will also create a necessity for keeping up taxation to a degree which, without being oppressive, will be a spur to industry.

Hamilton had come to believe that many Americans were too indolent. He feared American political rhetoric would "incline us to too great parsimony and indulgence." Why had the war dragged on so long? "We labor less now than any civilized nation of Europe, and a habit of labor in the people is as essential to the health and vigor of their minds and bodies as it is conducive to the welfare of the State. We ought not to suffer our self-love to deceive us."

Hamilton's recommendations to Morris in large part were visionary but politically premature. Congress still lacked the authority to carry out his proposals. And his facts were askew because he lacked basic information, as Morris would have recognized. Congress had an immense war debt beyond its bills of credit and there would be few investors interested in subscriptions for more debt. Without accurate facts, Hamilton made inaccurate calculations in coming up with his estimates of the nation's revenues and expenses. By suggesting the use of land as capital, he mistakenly predicated Congress's ability to raise far more capital than was actually available. Yet his political principles were sound. Congress "must deal plainly with their constituents," as he contended, and "power without revenue" was, as he so succinctly put it, "a bubble." Unless the states yielded up to the national government the sources of revenue it needed to win the war and establish a sound government, it was folly to continue the war. If his proposals to tax trade and property ran counter to public opinion, it was better to bring on the collision now than allow the war to drag on to an ignominious conclusion. Hamilton's virtuoso recitation to Morris at age twenty-six prefigured his later proposals and policies and showed that, at such an early age, he basically understood the interplay of politics, finance, and war.

In his first double-barreled sortie into influencing the fiscal policy of the national government through public opinion, Hamilton exposed his financial views for public scrutiny for the first time. Pleading for greater congressional power, he proposed a national bank, a national debt, and national taxation, urging strong political medicine on the public. In private, he still believed that Americans were governed more by "passion and prejudice" than "an enlightened sense of their interests." Yet, from that time on, often in open conflict with his own private views, almost clandestinely optimistic, Hamilton threw himself, his genius, all his energy again and again against the redoubts of indifference he perceived all around him. At twenty-six, he was for the first time sure of his own source of revenue. And, from that time on, no American of the Revolutionary generation spent more of his thought, words, and time to win over the common citizen to an energetic national government.[22]

DOING ALL he could to inject himself by his writings into national politics, Hamilton maintained his resolve to win a combat command from Washington. Arriving at headquarters on July 8, 1781, he sent a letter to the commander-in-chief through an aide. No reply came. "I wrote the General a letter," he reported to Betsy, "and enclosed him my commission." This time, Washington either had to provide an opening for Hamilton or lose his services entirely for the army. Washington decided to keep Hamilton in the army. He sent Tilghman to him, urging him to stay on until he could "give me a command nearly such as I could have desired," he told Betsy. "Though I know my Betsy would be happy to hear that I had rejected this proposal" and would be coming home, "it is a pleasure my reputation would not permit me to afford her." Proudly, Hamilton announced to the Schuylers that, at last, "I consented to retain my commission and accept my command."[23]

Why, with an appointment to Congress promised and the door open to work with Robert Morris on important fiscal reforms, did Hamilton accept an unspecified military assignment? Surely one factor was his satisfaction that Washington, so recently dismissive of him, at last was acting with some consideration. At age twenty he had written in *The Farmer Refuted* that, above all qualities, he valued "natural intrepidity." To this man of so many words, action still counted more than anything he could say to prove his worth.

Awaiting assignment, Hamilton shared quarters with General Benjamin Lincoln, Washington's second-in-command. He had to move closer to headquarters or walk, after his "Old Gray Horse," wounded at Monmouth three years earlier, died. Schuyler sent him two horses, one for riding, the other a "portmanteau horse" to transport his trunks. A splendid rider, Hamilton for the first time had a suitable mount, one that, in a horse-conscious culture, signaled his new status. He also ordered a new saddle for his orderly's horse. On July 31, 1781, his long-pursued assignment appeared in general orders. Two light companies drawn from the New York First and Second Regiments and two companies of New York militia "will form a battalion under command of Lieutenant Colonel Hamilton."[24]

Once again, Hamilton was to lead New York troops. His battalion was to be attached to the advance guard as it marched south to Virginia. Later, he replaced the New York draftees with two Connecticut companies of regular troops. Major Nicholas Fish, his King's College classmate, became his second-in-command. Hamilton's best friend, Laurens, commanded another new battalion in the army's vanguard. Neither Hamilton's problems as commander nor his approach changed. His men needed shoes. Headquarters said that was the State of New York's problem, but this could take time. Hamilton went directly to Washington. He cited a precedent where "the article of shoes" was considered "indispensable" for the advance guard. The soldiers could not afford to buy their own shoes. New York was sending its best troops forward shoeless. Washington promptly ordered the shoes.[25]

On August 14, a courier arrived from French headquarters at Newport with word that a French fleet under the Comte de Grasse was sailing toward the Chesapeake with twenty-nine ships-of-the-line and three thousand troops. The French already had five thousand troops on Rhode Island. To draw off troops from the beleaguered South, Washington gave out the story that the target of the Franco-American attack was to be New York City, the original plan. A set of those earlier plans had fallen into British hands. Hamilton wrote Betsy there was "little prospect of activity." The letter may have been a ruse calculated to deceive Loyalists who frequently intercepted mails. He did not write her again until, as part of the twenty-five-hundred-man advance guard, he had been marching south for three days. From

Haverstraw, New Jersey, he sent her a letter by military courier through Schuyler's headquarters, along with his meager savings. He told her not to draw funds from her father. He would be back in October, in two months (the length of time the French fleet was available), three months at the latest, but before their baby was due. Hamilton told her he was pessimistic about their chances of trapping Lord Cornwallis's army at Yorktown. "It is ten to one that our views will be disappointed by Cornwallis retiring to South Carolina by land." But this was probably to reassure her he was in little danger. So great was the need for secrecy that Betsy knew more than Hamilton's own men, who were taking bets on their destination. They moved fast, under Washington's orders to stay "fit for action and free from every encumbrance." Women and baggage were sent off to West Point. Hamilton's spare horse carried only camp equipage that Betsy sent him and a government-issue wall tent from Albany. Hamilton and his troops woke at three every morning, were on the march by four.[26]

To maintain the element of surprise about their intended destination, the Americans did not amass boats on the Delaware River. Horses and oxen swam across. With no money to pay his men or buy supplies, Washington ordered wagons and forage commandeered on the march. By September 6, Hamilton's troops had marched through Philadelphia at night. Crowds lined the streets, cheering. In every window, war-scarce candles, often in clusters of thirteen, glimmered. Congress and French diplomats stood side-by-side to review the troops. At Head of Elk, Hamilton wrote Betsy again. He now knew that De Grasse's French fleet had safely arrived in the Chesapeake and that Robert Morris had been able to borrow $20,000 in French gold to pay the American troops, reluctant to fight unless they received some of their back pay. "Circumstances that have just come to my knowledge assure me that our operations will be expeditious, as well as our success certain," he wrote Betsy.[27]

Hamilton and his troops crowded into open boats. Bucking contrary winds that stirred up the notorious "Chesapeake chop," they took a full week in hurricane season to navigate the bay from its northern tip to Annapolis, still only halfway to Yorktown. It was an especially dangerous crossing because the French fleet under de Grasse had put out to the open Atlantic again to battle a British fleet under Admiral Graves, which had suddenly swooped down from New York in pursuit of a second French squadron carrying French troops and all the siege guns. Not until September 15 did Hamilton learn that the French had beaten back the British fleet and safely returned to the Chesapeake again to screen the American forces from attack when they were most vulnerable crossing the bay. Extremely anxious as he waited for news of the naval battle, Hamilton fired off a less-than-heartening letter to Betsy: "How checkered is human life! How easily do we often part with it for a shadow." He did not help his now-five-months-pregnant wife's gloom as he added, by way of encouragement, that "our operations will be so conducted as to economize the lives of men. Exert your fortitude and rely upon heaven." It would not have improved his mood to receive a letter from Schuyler, written about this time, that he feared Betsy would have a miscarriage. She "was so sensibly affected by your removal to the southward that I apprehended consequences," Schuyler wrote, hastily adding that "she is now at ease."[28]

With his battalion, Hamilton happily joined the advance guard as it clambered aboard larger, faster French vessels dispatched by de Grasse. But even then, Hamilton's unit stalled. The French ship ran aground in high winds at the mouth of the James River. Among the first to land on the Virginia shore, Hamilton gathered his light troops at College Landing, one mile from Williamsburg, on September 20. It took another week before the full Franco-American force completed the perilous landings. Jubilant to rejoin Lafayette at Williamsburg, Hamilton also found that John Laurens had just returned from his diplomatic mission to France and had assumed Hamilton's old job as Washington's writing aide. To his added delight, he found his Elizabethtown Academy teacher, Lieutenant Colonel Francis Barber, serving under Lafayette. He had turned "something of the color of an Indian," Hamilton wrote, from a summer under the Virginia sun.

The time for reunions was brief: at five o'clock the morning of September 27, the army began its twelve-mile march to invest the

British at Yorktown. Hamilton's men stepped off at the head of the right wing, the place of honor of the Franco-American army. Some fifty-five hundred Continental veterans in French-made blue uniforms under "Mad Anthony" Wayne of Pennsylvania, Baron Steuben, Mordechai Gist's Marylanders, James Clinton and his New Yorkers, Francis Barber and the New Jersey Brigade, all swung off in the early morning breeze, followed by the lumbering artillery of Henry Knox, to begin the slow strangulation of Cornwallis's army by siege. Another three thousand Virginia troops came ashore across the York River to prevent British escape. Strutting behind the Americans in glistening white uniforms came seventy-two hundred Frenchmen—seven regiments of infantry, eight hundred artillerists, as many cavalry. In all, Washington, the overall commander, had concentrated seventeen thousand troops, the largest army of the war, outnumbering Cornwallis's defenders inside Yorktown three to one. Hamilton's advance unit made it to within a mile of the British lines before encountering British dragoons. Taking cover in the woods, Hamilton came under artillery fire. One of the first shots sheared off one man's leg. Throwing up earthworks, Hamilton's men rested little that night, their weapons ready beside them.

The British had chosen the village of Yorktown to fortify because it was situated on a bluff thirty-five feet above the narrow York River. Shielded by scuttled merchant ships and by warships anchored offshore, the town was vulnerable from the land. Perched atop a sheer rise, it was protected somewhat by half a mile of open ground, swampy land, and two wide creeks with high steep banks. The narrow corridor between Yorktown and Wormeley's Creek made it dangerous for attackers to approach the town, the open plain all but impossible. The British had built heavily defended earthworks to sweep the open ground with cannon fire. The French and American allies pitched their camps and installed their siege guns in an arc from riverbank to riverbank a mile from the British guns. It appeared that Cornwallis planned to escape either on roughly anchored vessels or await promised reinforcements from New York. Early September 30, before an allied gun fired, the British evacuated their outer works. The astonished Allies immediately swarmed into the abandoned

British works. Hamilton's immediate superior, Colonel Alexander Scammell, was fatally shot as he examined the works.

Former artillerist Hamilton took charge, showing his men how to construct earthworks and batteries for the siege. Digging in the sandy soil was easy, but the embankments had to be reinforced with gabions (wicker baskets) and saucissons (cylinders) filled with earth to absorb enemy cannon fire, and fascines and pickets for staking down the cylinders. Off guard duty, Hamilton's men worked in the woods, fashioning their daily quota from uniform widths of wood hacked from the trees. Hamilton directed his men in keeping a constant supply on hand. Day after day, the digging and chopping went on as French engineers cut the first siege trench parallel to the British lines, in one moonless night cutting a mile-long trench seven feet wide and four feet deep across the plain. While French troops created a diversion, forty-three hundred men dug furiously only six hundred yards from British guns. On the right, Hamilton's troops, each man digging twelve feet of trench, came within eight hundred yards of the two most heavily fortified advanced British redoubts, numbers nine and ten. Within three days, the Allies had their batteries in place within the first parallel. Mortars, howitzers, cannon firing up to twenty-four-pound shot (six pounds heavier than the British could fire back) were ready before the order came to open fire at three o'clock the afternoon of October 9. Accurate French fire splintered British gun emplacements as the day-and-night bombardment commenced. Cornwallis and his staff took refuge in caves in the riverbank. From his post in a siege trench, Hamilton, excited after so many years of waiting to take the offensive again, wrote to Betsy, "Thank heaven, our affairs seem to be approaching fast a happy period." Five more days, he predicted, "and the enemy must capitulate."[29]

After five days' incessant cannonading, work began on a zigzag trench from the French left flank toward the British lines to permit digging a second parallel trench, halving the distance for cannon to bombard the enemy works. As Hamilton's parties extended the trench toward the riverbank, deadly fire came from British redoubts numbers nine and ten. Allied cannon pounded these twenty-foot-high earthen fortifications. But the redoubts were surrounded by ditches filled with sharpened logs set at an angle to impale invaders and a further barricade of felled trees, their tangled branches sharpened. Inside each, 120 British and Hessian marksmen and gunners unleashed a galling fire whenever the enemy approached. After a three-day artillery duel, French engineers decided the redoubts were weakened enough to permit an infantry attack. Hamilton, his battalion included in Lafayette's attack force, now launched his own assault: although a French officer had already been chosen to lead the charge, he wanted the honor.

This was Hamilton's last chance for glory in what he was sure was the conclusive battle of the Revolution. If the redoubts could be taken by storm, Allied cannon could fire from so close to British headquarters that Cornwallis could not possibly hold out any longer. Hamilton's long-sought moment of fame, a heroic assault on a dangerous enemy, would slip away unless he fought for it now. He promptly went to his friend Lafayette and asked him to plead for command of the American force attacking Redoubt Number Ten. Hamilton's unit had "just come from the Northward," argued Lafayette. The French officer he had assigned had fought the British all summer. Hamilton hauled out his rule book. He was senior to Gimat, the French officer. Besides, he was the duty officer of the day of the attack. Lafayette sympathized with Hamilton's demand and agreed to go to Washington. Hamilton insisted on accompanying him to plead his own case. Together, they entered Washington's high-walled, white linen marquee tent, his home since 1776. In only a few minutes, Hamilton erupted from the tent, grabbed Nicholas Fish, waiting anxiously outside, and embraced him. "We have it! We have it!" Hamilton exclaimed.

Returning to Lafayette's tent, Hamilton and the marquis planned every detail of the night assault. Redoubt Number Ten clung to the edge of the cliff and could not be climbed safely. While the French attacked Redoubt Number Nine simultaneously, Hamilton's force, divided into three columns, would clear the obstacles in the ditch with axes and charge into Number Ten. Laurens would circle the redoubt to the east with eighty men to block the enemy's retreat; Major Fish with the main force was to rush up the sloping barricade, as soon as the axmen cleared the ditch, veer off to the west and charge the redoubt at the cliff's edge. The entire force would attack silently, muskets unloaded, bayonets fixed. Until utter darkness, the men would eat their dinner of boiled beef and rest behind the lines. Shortly before dark, Washington rode over to Hamilton's battalion and made a short, earnest speech. The army expected "something grand to be done by our infantry."[30]

Soon after dark, six quick bursts by French artillery signaled the attack. Hamilton and his men sprang from their trenches and charged. A Hessian guard called a challenge, "Wer da? ("Who goes?"). When he got no answer, the redoubt's defenders opened fire. At point-blank range before he was discovered, Hamilton, not waiting for the axmen to clear a path through the barricade of pointed trees, led the charge, struggling through the jagged tangle. Leaping into the ditch under heavy fire, he led his swarming troopers up the rampart, then climbing onto the shoulders of a larger man, yelling, swinging his sword, he rode over the parapet, then jumped down. According to Colonel John Lamb, his old New York artillery commander, he was the first American to enter the British redoubt. Laurens, meanwhile, had charged in from the fort's open rear and captured the British commander. Major Fish, rushing in from the left flank, closed the ring around the enemy. For ten minutes, hand-to-hand bayonet combat raged in the dark. Four Allied officers including his former teacher, Colonel Barber, suffered bullet or bayonet wounds. A sergeant and eight privates died; twenty-five more enlisted men suffered wounds. Of the British and German defenders, eight were killed or wounded, seventeen surrendered, ninety-five escaped. A proud Hamilton had taken the key stronghold in less than half the time it took the French to capture Redoubt Number Nine. With five-to-one casualties, the Franco-American troops had taken the redoubts, enabling Allied artillery to be moved up. The British guns in the redoubts, turned against the British holdouts, hammered them at only two hundred yards now.

Writing a long field report to Lafayette the next day praising each officer by name, Hamilton then wrote Betsy:

Two nights ago, my Eliza, my duty and my honor obliged me to take a step in which your happiness was too much risked. I commanded an attack upon one of the enemy's redoubts. We carried it in an instant, and with little loss. You will see the particulars in the Philadelphia papers. There will be, certainly, nothing more of this kind. All the rest will be by [entrenching] approach, and if there should be another occasion, it will not fall to my turn to execute it.[31]

In this moment of his greatest military glory, Hamilton did not elaborate to his six-months-pregnant wife the details of his gallantry, nor did he in his report or in any other way seek praise. But here he was, hinting that his action was without possible parallel at the same time he was apologizing for it and promising not to take such a risk again. It was becoming a pattern, the bold action, then the afterthought of reassurance that he would in future refrain from yielding to his sense of "my duty and my honor." Most of all, Hamilton was keenly aware that an old wound had healed, that he had redeemed himself with his master, his master with him. He would no longer need to grovel after praise or nurse his prickly doubt of his own honor. Washington himself now praised him in his highest terms: Alexander Hamilton's "bravery" was "emulous," the commander-in-chief wrote. (Or was it an aide and Washington signed the words?) "Few cases have exhibited stronger proofs of intrepidity, coolness and firmness" than Hamilton had shown in storming redoubt number ten. And Washington singled him out for bravery in his report to Congress.

ALEXANDER HAMILTON'S last act in the American Revolution came on October 16, 1781, after six years of active duty. Three days later, the British and German regiments marched between lines of American and French troops, their flags cased and their bands playing a popular English tune, "The World Turned Upside Down." To Betsy, Hamilton wrote tersely, "Cornwallis and his army are ours." The next day, he would set out for Albany "and I hope to embrace you in three weeks." Hamilton did not stop as he raced north before winter set in along the Hudson. His father-in-law Schuyler apologized when Hamilton did not even pause to visit their close friend James Duane, who was to be Hamilton's law preceptor. "He thought of nothing but reaching his wife the soonest possible and, indeed, he tired his horses to accomplish it and was obliged to hire others."[32]

Hamilton did not even stop at Philadelphia to convey the news of victory at Yorktown to an anxiously awaiting Congress. The honor of bearing official news of the great event went to Washington's more steadfast aide, Tench Tilghman. Hamilton would hear soon enough of the embarrassing scene in the capital at Philadelphia. The American treasury was empty. Elias Boudinot reported, "When the messenger brought the news of the capitulation, it was necessary to furnish him with hard money for his expenses. There was not a sufficiency in the Treasury to do it. The Members of Congress each paid a dollar to accomplish it."[33]

IN JANUARY 1782, an exhausted Hamilton, "still alternately in and out of bed," learned that the Continental Congress, on the last day of that annus mirabilis 1781, had voted to retain Hamilton in service as the Revolution came to an end. Benjamin Lincoln, now secretary of war, who had witnessed Hamilton's bravery at Yorktown and had followed his five-year career as a staff officer, praised Hamilton's "superior abilities and knowledge." Congress voted that Hamilton was entitled to continue rank, pay, and pension, in addition to bonuses of land according to his rank. Colonel Hamilton was entitled to one thousand acres of federal land. Hamilton wrote Washington, asking to be put on the inactive list, pledging that he would be "ready to obey the call of the public in any capacity, civil or military," if the need arose. At the same time, since he saw no real prospect of a new field command, he renounced "any future involvements from my commission during the war or after it."

———— •➤• ————

TWELVE

"The Art of
Fleecing Neighbors"

From the small, shabby house along the Hudson River in Albany, New York, which he rented for his bride, Betsy, and their infant son, Alexander Hamilton sent off a letter to his old friend the Marquis de Lafayette, back in his palatial *hôtel* on the rue St. Honoré on Paris's Right Bank, on November 3, 1782. It had been a year and a few days now since the two comrades-in-arms had led the final glorious assault on Cornwallis's fortifications at York-town. Lafayette and the French army had passed the winter in Virginia, then, as the French troops sailed back to their base at Newport, Rhode Island, Lafayette had sailed for France to help move along the peace talks in Paris. Washington had marched his victorious army back north to resume the envelopment of the British in New York City. Seeing "no practice but of an inactive campaign," Hamilton explained to Lafayette, he had left the army, giving up any right to future pay and clinging only to his rank:

I have been employed for the last ten months in rocking the cradle and studying the art of fleecing my neighbors. I am now a grave counselor at law, and shall soon be a grand member of

Congress. The Legislature at their last session took it into their heads to name me pretty unanimously one of their delegates. I am going to throw away a few more months in public life and then I retire a simple citizen and good *paterfamilias*.

But the real reason behind Hamilton's newsy letter to Lafayette was that only a few days before, he had learned that, in the last land skirmish of the Revolution, in a needless, senseless little fight in the godforsaken backwater swamps of South Carolina, their dear friend John Laurens, indeed Alexander Hamilton's closest friend, had been killed. "Poor Laurens," he wrote of their old mess—and dueling—partner. "He has fallen a sacrifice to his ardor in a trifling skirmish." No one else but Lafayette could quite understand how devoted to each other Laurens and Hamilton had become during the dangerous days of Brandywine and Germantown, in the duel with Lee after Monmouth. "You know how truly I loved him." Now, at last, Laurens had distinguished himself—as the only one of Washington's aides to die in battle.[1]

In that last year of Laurens's life, Hamilton and his friend had exchanged a burst of letters after a long silence that followed Hamilton's courtship and marriage. Considering himself shamed by his capture at the fall of Charleston in 1780, Laurens had earned a reputation for desperate recklessness in battle. Wounded four times, Laurens may have survived so long only because Congress had sent him on a diplomatic mission to Paris. But he had returned to the fierce guerrilla warfare in the Carolinas. The crushing defeat of his plan to raise black troops, arm, and free them seemed to make him take even greater risks in combat. First, the legislatures of South Carolina, then Georgia, had rejected his personal appeals. Then southern officers had refused to serve under him. Yet, when Hamilton wrote to Laurens that he planned to eschew further public life, retire to a modest law practice, and enjoy the company of his wife and his firstborn son, his old friend Laurens berated him: "Your private affairs cannot require such immediate and close attention; you speak like a *paterfamilias*, surrounded by numerous progeny." When Hamilton failed to respond, Laurens wrote plaintively, presciently to him:

Adieu, my dear friend. While circumstances place so great a distance between us, I entreat you not to withdraw the consolation of your letters. You know the unalterable sentiments of your affectionate Laurens.[2]

On August 15, 1782, Hamilton finally wrote Laurens to assure him he would assume his seat in Congress. With a peace treaty at hand and British troops already beginning to embark for Europe, Hamilton wrote (from Albany) that "this state has pretty unanimously delegated me to Congress." His aim was "to make our independence a blessing." To do this "we must secure our *union* on solid foundations, a Herculean task." Hamilton already was pushing for reforms to Congress that would strengthen the new nation's government, but first "mountains of prejudice must be leveled." Hamilton urged Laurens to join him in the formidable task of nation building:

It requires all the virtue and all the abilities of the country. Quit your sword, my friend, put on the *toga*, come to Congress. We know each other's sentiments, our views are the same. We have fought side by side to make America free. Let us hand in hand struggle to make her happy.[3]

But Hamilton's belated plea did not reach Laurens in time. On Sunday evening, August 25, 1782, three hundred British soldiers raided up the Combahee River in South Carolina, landing at Arthur Middleton's plantation, where they began to round up slaves and barrels of rice. The next morning, Colonel Laurens, with only 50 men, set out to attack 150 redcoats entrenched behind felled trees and screened by dense underbrush. Refusing to await reinforcements who were only two miles away, Laurens, "who wanted to do it all himself," a subordinate wrote, "to gain a laurel for his brow before the cessation of hostilities," led the charge into deadly British volleys. Laurens collapsed, mortally wounded. His pointless death in the last engagement of a seven-year-long war stunned Americans. "Poor Laurens is fallen in a paltry little skirmish," wrote Nathanael Greene, commander of

the Southern Army. "Our country has lost its most promising character," wrote John Adams from Paris to his fellow peace commissioner,
Henry Laurens. From Albany, Alexander Hamilton poured out his
grief seven weeks later when he finally received the news. "I feel the
deepest affliction," he wrote Greene:

> How strange are human affairs [that] so many excellent qualities
> could not ensure a more happy fate. The world will feel the
> loss of a man who has left few like him behind . . . of a citizen
> whose heart realized that patriotism of which others only talk. I
> feel the loss of a friend I truly and most tenderly loved, and one
> of a very small number.[4]

Laurens's death was a doleful drumbeat at the end of the Revolution,
but for Hamilton it was not the last. A few months later, a courier
from Washington's headquarters reached Hamilton at Independence
Hall in Philadelphia, where he had taken his place behind the green
baize-covered table of the New York delegation. The courier reported
that Lieutenant Colonel Francis Barber, Hamilton's classics master at
Elizabethtown Academy and his comrade-in-arms at Yorktown, while
riding home from headquarters at New Windsor, New York, the
afternoon of February 11, 1783, to escort his wife to tea with Martha
Washington, was crushed to death by a tree felled by soldiers cutting
it down for firewood. Apparently, by this time, Hamilton was too
numb to react. No word of his survives to mourn Barber's death. But
by now, Hamilton was caught up in a new career, a new struggle,
and he rarely stopped for a minute to look back.

HAMILTON HAD returned to The Pastures, the Schuylers' Albany mansion, from the decisive victory at Yorktown in time for the birth of
his firstborn son, Philip—named for Betsy's father. The new family
lived for a while in a cottage on the grounds of the Schuyler estate,
but Hamilton wanted to be free of his father-in-law's largesse—and
the political criticism that would come with it. When the child was
seven months old, Hamilton wrote to fellow aide-de-camp Richard

Kidder Meade of Virginia that, since his homecoming, he had immersed himself in law books he borrowed from Schuyler's ample library. "I have been studying the law for some months," he wrote Meade, "and lately have been licensed as an attorney."

To his old and recently married friend living in the Shenandoah Valley, Hamilton wrote of his new life as husband and father, relishing his new voice. "I heartily felicitate on the birth of your daughter. I can well conceive your happiness," because Hamilton had just felt "a similar one." Philip Schuyler, the first of the Hamiltons' eight children, had been born on January 22nd. "The sensations of a tender father," he added, "can only be conceived by those who have experienced them." Hamilton had never experienced a happy home life before:

> You cannot imagine how entirely domestic I am growing. I lose all taste for the pursuits of ambition. I sigh for nothing but the company of my wife and baby.

Five months later, when little Philip was all of seven months old, Hamilton wrote Kidder again after Kidder reproached him for not saying "enough about our little stranger." Kidder's daughter, about the same age, "will not consult you about the choice":

> He is truly a very fine young gentleman, the most agreeable in his conversation and manners of any I know—nor less remarkable for his intelligence and sweetness of temper. It is agreed on all hands that he is handsome, his features are good, his eye is not only sprightly and expressive but full of benignity.

Hamilton doted on baby Philip's every motion in this playful letter. By "connoisseurs of sitting" he was "esteemed graceful." The infant "has a method of waving his hand that announces the future orator." The child was trying to stand up "rather awkwardly and his legs have not all the delicate slimness of his father's. It is feared he may never excel as much in dancing. If he has any fault in manners, he laughs too much."[5]

As early as his student days at King's College, Alexander Hamilton had engrossed himself in the law, surreptitiously carrying out his research for his newspaper attacks on Loyalists in the college's ample law library. On January 18, 1782, as he was recovering from arriving home seriously ill and exhausted from Virginia, the New York Assembly had passed a law suspending until the last day of April 1782 the 1778 requirement of a rigorous three-year clerkship for

> such young gentlemen who had directed their studies to the profession of the law but upon the breaking out of the present war had entered into the army in defense of their country.

As the deadline neared, Hamilton went before the State Supreme Court in the temporary capital at Poughkeepsie on April 26, 1782, and declared that he had, "previous to the war, directed his studies to law" but that his army service had made it impossible to resume his studies in time to meet the new deadline. He was telling the truth, even if he was stretching it: at King's, he had done a fair amount of reading of the law books donated by a Scottish merchant. His 1775 pamphlet, *The Farmer Refuted*, specifically cited Sir William Blackstone and Sir Edward Coke, the famous English jurists. Julius Goebel, pre-eminent authority on Hamilton's legal career, writes that Hamilton, twenty when he wrote *The Farmer Refuted*, "not only cites from law books that were standard professional fare but discloses his exposure to works on natural law—Grotius, Pufendorf, Locke and others" on which "the very babes of the Enlightenment were suckled." At most, however, as a student at King's he had devoted about two months to his studies between writing political tracts. Even here, he referred only to the opening chapters of Blackstone's 1763 four-volume *Commentaries on the Laws of England*. Yet he had also obviously consulted Beawe's scholarly *Lex Mercatoria* on mercantile law.

Alexander Hamilton's first legal filing was to seek a six-month extension for his studies. He succeeded where only one other applicant did, thus winning an advantage over many who had rushed their studies and others without the nerve to ask for more time. The other applicant who was cramming for the bar exams in the Schuyler library at The Pastures was erstwhile New York militia Colonel

Aaron Burr. A year younger than Hamilton, the son of the second president of Princeton College and grandson of evangelist Jonathan Edwards, its founder, he had graduated from the college a year before Hamilton applied, studied theology briefly, then began to study law. Serving under Charles Lee at the Battle of Monmouth and briefly a member of Washington's staff, he had left headquarters because he thought Hamilton had too much influence. He had commanded the troops at West Point briefly, establishing a reputation as a harsh disciplinarian. Once, in a rage, he had lopped off the arm of a rebellious soldier with one strike of his saber. Disgusted after Washington transferred him to command militia in Westchester County, he had resigned from the army in 1779 on grounds of ill health. He studied law in New Jersey, which had a three-year minimum. When he heard New York had waived the rule for veterans, he hurried to Albany, armed with a letter to General Schuyler, who let him share his library with Hamilton. The two had a tug-of-war for law books that ended in both of them passing the exams.[6]

Hamilton had already begun to read law in the law offices of his in-law James Duane. His bold request for a six-month extension came eleven days after his appointment as the federal tax collector for the State of New York. This, his first political appointment, evidently had less to do with the fact that he was the son-in-law of the influential Philip Schuyler than with his own audacious letters to members of Congress and "The Continentalist" newspaper articles he had published while he was still in the army. On April 15, Superintendent of Finance Robert Morris offered the twenty-seven-year-old war hero the post of Receiver of Continental Taxes for New York. The post normally provided a commission of one fourth of 1 percent of all moneys he collected. Hamilton could not have learned of his appointment, so slow were the mails, until weeks after he won from the Supreme Court his extension to study. Initially, Hamilton wrote Morris that he could not spare any time from his studies. He knew that New York had been devastated by six years of warfare and had little money to pay taxes. Five of fourteen counties, including New York City, were still occupied by the British Army, including its most lucrative port, the source in peacetime, through customs duties, of most federal revenue in the state. Hamilton calculated that the post could not pay much more than about $250 a year at present. But when he refused Morris's first blandishment, Morris counteroffered. Hamilton's commission was to be calculated not on what he collected but on what New York State owed the Continental treasury. Morris sweetened the deal by saying that Hamilton would not have to assume his duties until he completed his legal studies. Hamilton, eager to be financially independent of his in-laws, this time accepted. To Robert Morris goes the credit for spotting Alexander Hamilton's financial genius.[7]

Hamilton characteristically began to juggle his studies with his first political office. Since there were still no law schools, he persuaded his King's College roommate, Robert Troup, to come live with him and be his tutor. To make room for his star boarder, wife, baby and a serving maid, Hamilton rented a run-down little house on the Albany waterfront. He was developing a phobia against accepting any financial help from his father-in-law—even as General Schuyler's prestige and political connections distinguished Hamilton from scores of threadbare legal acolytes trying to carve out livings for themselves—and became, like so many others, a veteran without a pension at war's end. From his rented house, he could ride each day with his friend Troup over to Duane's temporary law office in Albany or out on circuit to the courthouses of surrounding counties. Duane, a specialist in land law, had an excellent private law library for the time. His shelves sagged under the leather-bound tomes of theorists of natural law, commentaries, English judicial reports—plus the standard legal reference works of the day. Hamilton's subsequent writings suggest he familiarized himself with Richardson's *Attorney's Practice*, Jacob's *New Law Dictionary*, Bacon's *New Abridgment of the Law*, Bathurst's *Introduction to the Law Relative to Trials*, and Gilbert's *History and Practice of Civil Courts*, all treatises on the laws of England that New York was to follow more closely than any other state. He now shared law books with Troup and John Lansing, another student, until they passed their bar exams in April. In all, Hamilton ranged widely over them for ten months—with Troup and Lansing answering his questions and coaching him for the examination.

Hamilton delved into two authors in particular. One was the con-servative William Blackstone, whose four volumes of published 1758 Vinerian Lectures at Oxford approached best-seller status in America, favored by lawyers such as John Adams. But his readings of Emmerich de Vattel's writings on natural law and the law of nations reshaped his thinking. He also soaked up the Dutch legal scholar Hugo Grotius's 1625 book *The Rights of War and Peace*, and the German Samuel F. Pufendorf's 1703 *Law of Nature and Nations*. He also devoured the writings of Jean Jacques Burlamaqui, a Geneva law professor whose *Principles of Natural and Political Law* drew the criticism of Hamil-ton's mentor Duane as "rather an introduction than a system." Vattel had taken Burlamaqui's undigested work and, in 1750, transformed it into his own *The Law of Nations*. Hamilton would soon marshal all these works on international law in pivotal trials in New York's courts.[8]

Of all his gleanings, Hamilton seems to have been the most impressed by Blackstone's commentary on the English parliamentary system. After years of watching a weak national government, he could only applaud Blackstone's prescription that Parliament, or an effective Congress, "can do everything that is not naturally impossi-ble." Blackstone was to influence Hamilton to part company with other American Revolutionaries such as Thomas Jefferson, who favored the natural law philosophy of John Locke. In Blackstone, he found a true conservatism, the basis for building on the law of nations and the common law of England and opposing the more radical state constitutions as well as the extremism of the French Revolution:

No human laws suppose a case which at once must destroy all law and compel men to build afresh upon a new foundation. So long as the English constitution lasts, we may venture to affirm that the power of Parliament is absolute and without control.

Hamilton had just risked his life in a long revolution against parlia-mentary power, but as the fighting sputtered out, he looked around him at confusion and ineptitude and found himself yearning for something like a powerful American parliament. In Blackstone, Hamilton found an answer to the tension he had felt between liberty and freedom. While mankind had the natural right to freedom—"one of the gifts of God to man at his creation when he endowed him with the faculty of free will"—in an orderly society the citizen had to give up "part of his natural liberty as the price of so valuable a purchase." He had to "conform to those laws which the community has thought proper to establish." Hamilton admired Blackstone's felicitous writing. He found wisdom in Blackstone's logic. "This species of legal obedience and conformity is infinitely more desirable than that wild and savage liberty which is sacrificed to obtain it." He agreed with Blackstone's conclusion that "laws, when prudently framed, are by no means subversive but rather [introduce] liberty." Even John Locke would agree with Blackstone that "where there is no law there is no freedom."

From Blackstone, Hamilton would draw his theory of federalism, but he would argue with Blackstone's indivisible sovereignty. Already, in "The Continentalist Number Two," published July 19, 1781, Hamilton had argued for a division of sovereignty. The English notion of king, lords and commons, of a king in council, must be adapted to an idea of mixed power—president, Senate and House of Representatives. Hamilton differed completely from Blackstone only on one major premise—Blackstone opposed judicial review. Hamilton would champion it.

To synthesize the vast amount of material, he found there was no manual of proper legal procedures to expedite his studies. So he wrote one, the first handbook for the use of practicing lawyers ever written in America. He summarized proper procedures and the essence of the laws in a 177-page manuscript of some forty thousand words under major headings such as Damages, Process, Joint Actions, Judgment and Execution, Pleas, Venue, and Habeas Corpus. So accurate and thorough was his research that modern legal scholars have found only eight minor errors in the lengthy work. Hamilton's *Practical Proceedings in the Supreme Court of the State of New York*, the only legal handbook available for law students struggling with the transition from British to American law, has a wry, resigned, almost sarcastic tone perfect for its audience, as in his comment on the needless complexity and jargon of judges' written decisions:

> The court lately acquired some faint idea that the end of suits of law is to investigate the merits of the case and not to entangle in the nets of technical terms.

Hamilton criticized the inconsistency of New York court pleadings as "among the absurdities with which the law abounds." One section of English common law, on trespass and ejectment, he derided as "a creature of Westminster Hall [that] subsists chiefly upon fiction." And he freely mocked his future colleagues to be for "the caviling petulance of an attorney." While he disparaged lawyers, Hamilton loved the law. Hamilton's manual was to be copied out by numerous law students, including his own, and was to be published a decade later as the standard manual for New York lawyers. Pacing back and forth and reciting aloud from it, Hamilton memorized his own book.[9]

It was Vattel's work that Hamilton most admired, for its forceful logic, thoroughness, and terse, clear style. From it he corrected and fortified his already impressive knowledge of the principles of natural law. From the Dutch master, he learned confirmation of his half-formed, intuitive ideas of the difference between natural rights and the more tough-minded natural law, of the laws of states and of nations, a realization that proved crucial in shaping his ever-stronger nationalism. Natural rights, Vattel asserted, were "nothing more than the power of doing what is morally possible," what is "proper and consistent duty." For Hamilton, this was too passive a way to build a government.

Hamilton did not need all the time he had asked to study for his bar examinations. Anxious to launch his political career, he stood for his examination and was admitted an attorney in July, three months before the extended deadline, and in October was admitted a "counselor to the bar," equivalent to an English barrister, allowing him to argue cases in court. He could afford no more time![10]

Even as he pored over the law books in the spring of 1782, he had not been able to stay out of public view. In April 1782, only a week before he applied for more time to prepare for his bars, he broke into print again in the *New York Packet* with "The Continentalist Number Five" in a direct assault on the Articles of Confederation, the new nation's frame of government. Adopted by Congress in 1777 but ratified by the states only one year before Hamilton's attack, the Articles were, Hamilton contended, deeply flawed, in great part because they left to the individual states, not Congress, control over commerce. "The power of regulatory trade ought to have been a principal object of the confederation," Hamilton began his fifth salvo against the weaknesses of the Continental Congress. He boldly took on laissez-faire capitalism:

> There are some who maintain that trade will regulate itself and is not to be benefited by the encouragements or restraints of government. Such persons imagine that there is no need of a common directing power. This is one of those wild speculative paradoxes [growing] among us, contrary to the uniform practice and sense of the most enlightened nations.

Unregulated commerce, Hamilton argued, contradicted institutions and laws everywhere "for the benefit of trade." To discontinue these laws would lead to "palpable evils." Commerce "has its fixed principles" and "it must be regulated." If they were violated, American trade would be injured. Principal among these was balance in trade:

> To preserve the balance of trade in favor of a nation ought to be a leading aim of its policy. The avarice of individuals may frequently find its account in pursuing channels of traffic prejudicial to that balance.

But the government must impose impediments to individual greed. At the same time, an enlightened national trade policy, "though accompanied with great difficulties" at first, would "amply reward the trouble and expense." He detailed how France and the Netherlands had grown into international giants of trade under strict government regulation and supervision. To inaugurate such a system in the United States would require, first of all, something else the Articles of Confederation failed to provide—a source of national revenue. "No mode can be so convenient" as moderate import duties on luxury goods, contended the newly appointed Receiver of Continental Taxes for New York.

Hamilton may have been a twenty-seven-year-old neophyte to politics, but he was not naïve. Many Americans would object to customs duties, one of the principal irritants that had helped bring on the Revolution. But circumstances had changed. His countrymen, he knew, "characteristically" were "ingenious in finding out and magnifying the minutest disadvantages" and they were equally adept at "reject[ing] measures of evident utility to avoid trivial and sometimes imaginary evils." But unless the new nation could "overcome this narrow disposition" it would "never be a great or a happy people."[11]

The surrender of Cornwallis's army in Virginia had brought about the fall of the war ministry of Lord North and the collapse of any hope for an English victory in America. British naval defeats in 1781 and early 1782 sped the progress of peace talks in Paris. A new commander-in-chief, Sir Guy Carleton, arrived in New York City in May 1782, just after Hamilton's latest critique of the American government, but it would be another year before a peace treaty won ratification by Congress and six more months before the final British evacuation of New York. Hamilton was in no hurry to hang out his lawyer's shingle until the British left Manhattan. Instead, he concentrated on solidifying his political base. With the backing of Philip Schuyler, he now set out to gain the crucial support of Robert Morris, who had emerged as leader of the nationalists in Congress.

In his new post as Continental Receiver, Hamilton lobbied the New York legislature, prodding it to vote the funds owed Congress for arrears in its proportional assessments. He also campaigned unsuccessfully for a better way to collect taxes, but everyone knew that most of New York's revenues were frozen as long as the British occupied New York City. While obviously treading water, Hamilton, with Schuyler's backing, in July 1782 persuaded the New York Assembly to pass a series of resolutions he drafted that called for a national convention to buttress the powers of the Continental Congress and amend the Articles of Confederation. Two days after these resolutions passed, the legislature elected Hamilton as one of its four-man congressional delegation. While his call for a federal reform convention fizzled, Alexander Hamilton, at twenty-seven, was appointed to the Continental Congress on July 22, 1781, and took his seat in Congress on November 25.

THE WAR was over, but the long lag in communications while draft treaties crossed the Atlantic Ocean twice in each direction led to a series of crises that awaited the first postwar Continental Congress. The first crisis had been brewing for some time: what to do about the Loyalists. Article Five of the Treaty of Paris, the most fought-over passage of the peace agreement, pledged Congress to "earnestly recommend" to the state legislatures full restitution of the rights and property of the Loyalists. In fact, no state felt bound by this recommendation while Loyalists saw British accession to this weak wording as a complete sellout of Loyalist rights. A welter of wartime anti-Loyalist laws remained on the books in each state after the peace treaty. Nine states had passed acts exiling prominent Loyalists. Those who remained had to pay double or triple taxes. Five states had disenfranchised Loyalists. Every state had barred Loyalists from public office and from the practice of law and medicine. All the states had passed laws confiscating Loyalist lands.

The fury against the Loyalists showed no sign of ending with the peace treaty. Sales of confiscated property continued, debts due to Loyalists were legally withheld. State governments shelved petitions to be allowed to return from banishment or restoration of property. Hamilton would argue in vain against these violations of the peace treaty. If the states did not restrain the violence of mobs, they became responsible for them. Worst were the continuing confiscations "going on in form of law," breaking Article Six of the treaty, which specifically promised no further injury to the Loyalists. If America repudiated parts of the treaty, so could the British. They could, he warned, refuse to give up their frontier forts, impinge access to Grand Banks fisheries, invoke their Navigation Acts, and cut off American trade with Canada and in the Caribbean.

Worse, he feared the flight of capital from the threadbare new nation. To his friend Gouverneur Morris, he wrote, "We are doing those things which we ought not to do, and leaving undone those things which we ought to do. Instead of wholesome regulations for the improvement of our polity and commerce, we are laboring to continue measures to mortify and punish Tories and to explain away treaties." Passing through New York City while Congress was in adjournment, Hamilton wrote to former New York Congressman Robert R. Livingston:

> The spirit of emigration has greatly increased of late. Some violent papers sent into the city have determined many to depart who hitherto had intended to remain. Many merchants of second class, characters of no political consequence, each of whom may carry away eight or ten thousand guineas [$350,000 to $500,000 in today's dollars] have, I am told, lately applied for shipping to convey them away. Our state will feel for twenty years at least the effects of the popular frenzy.

Hamilton's dire forecast proved accurate: on April 26, 1783, more than seven thousand Loyalists, including most of New York's lawyers, merchants, and Anglican clergy, sailed from New York harbor into exile.[12]

As the preliminary treaty sped across the Atlantic for ratification by Congress, the first shiploads of Loyalist refugees began to clear New York and Charleston harbors bound for England, Nova Scotia, and the Caribbean. A vast migration began of more than one hundred thousand Americans going into exile, more than 5 percent of the population, probably the highest refugee rate of any revolution. They left because, as a British envoy at the Paris peace talks put it, they faced the choice of fleeing or, if they remained in the United States, being "terrified into submission" by vengeful Revolutionaries, who blamed the length and severity of the war on their damned Tory brothers.

What the Loyalists could expect had been made clear by the time the British surrendered at Yorktown. All through the last two years of Revolution, the British had repeatedly left the Loyalists to Patriot reprisals as they came and went, marching and countermarching, but rarely protecting the Loyalists they left in their wake. The Loyalists had lost thousands of lives in battles with hard-riding, British-hating rebel partisans who, time after time, had cut them off from rescue by the redcoats and slaughtered them piecemeal. Of more than 1,250 military engagements in the eight-year-long struggle, the vast majority were between partisan bands. At the worst debacle, at King's Mountain in the North Carolina backcountry, more than one thousand Loyalist troops had been killed or wounded in less than an hour. Patriot mountain men had lynched eighteen Loyalist prisoners on the battlefield after they had surrendered. At Yorktown, hundreds of Loyalists rowed frantically after the crowded British sloop *Bonetta* as it sailed away crammed with British officers. The British captain allowed only fourteen Loyalists on board; the rest were overtaken and hauled back by Washington's troops. When the *Bonetta* arrived in New York City, despair swept over refugee camps in the city and on Long Island that were crowded with forty thousand Loyalist refugees from New York, Connecticut, New Jersey, and Pennsylvania.[13]

In the dying months of the Revolution, Loyalists in New York had organized a Board of Associated Loyalists that sent out partisan bands to take hostages, pillage coastal towns, and disrupt American communications. One raid, allegedly authorized by the board's president, William Franklin (the illegitimate son of Benjamin Franklin), took a New Jersey artillery officer, Captain Joshua Huddy, from a prison ship, rowed him ashore, and without the slightest pretense of a court-martial, hanged him from a gallows made of three fence rails. On Huddy's chest the Loyalist executioners pinned a placard promising to hang "man for man as long as a refugee is left existing: Up goes Huddy for Philip White!"—a Loyalist killed by Patriots.[14]

When a British court-martial acquitted the leader of the Loyalist band for lack of evidence, General Washington flew into a rage and ordered the hanging of a British officer of equal rank to the Patriot captain unless the British handed over William Franklin, the man Washington was sure had ordered the hanging. On Washington's orders, ten captains among the British officers taken at Yorktown were instructed to draw lots to see which one of them would be hanged in retaliation. When they refused, Washington ordered that lots be drawn for them. The lot fell to seventeen-year-old Captain Asgill of the Grenadier Guards, son of a member of Parliament. Washington ordered Asgill brought from Virginia to headquarters at Morristown, New Jersey, and placed in solitary confinement. When Washington ordered a gallows built in sight of the prisoner to carry out his threat, the British prisoner's mother wrote a personal letter to Queen Marie Antoinette of France, appealing to her as a mother to intercede with the king to ask Washington to relent. King Louis XVI immediately complied. The barrage of protests included an appeal from Alexander Hamilton, who wrote judiciously through General Henry Knox, now Washington's closest confidant. Hamilton knew better than to make a frontal assault on Washington.[15]

From the Schuyler mansion (making it at least appear that his father-in-law agreed with him), Hamilton wrote Knox a stinging letter, intended for Washington's eyes, that Asgill's "execution by way of retaliation" appeared "clearly to be an ill-timed proceeding" that would be "derogatory to the national character" and "entirely repugnant to the genius of the age we live in." It was "without example in modern history" and in Europe would be considered "wanton and unnecessary":

> So solemn and deliberate a sacrifice of the innocent for the guilty must be condemned, and encourage an opinion that we are in a certain degree in a state of barbarism. It would argue meanness in us. The death of André could not have been dispensed with, but it must still be viewed at a distance as an act of *rigid justice*. If we wreak our resentment on an innocent person, it will be suspected that we are too fond of executions.

Hamilton argued that Washington's reputation as "the first and most respectable character among us" would be irreparably damaged. Hamilton made it clear to Knox that he opposed capital punishment as "extreme severity" and trusted Knox's "liberality and influence" with Washington. Such behavior was "out of season." The "time for it, if there ever was one, is past."[16]

Hamilton's letter coincided with the plea passed through diplomatic channels from the French monarchs who instructed the French minister in Philadelphia to intercede with Congress. Their letter was "enough to move the heart of a savage." By now, Washington was only looking for a way out. He bowed to the wishes of Congress and the king of France. Elias Boudinot, now the president of Congress, added that he never saw so much ill blood in Congress as during the three-day debate it sparked. A chastened Washington reluctantly released Asgill, who now seemed, after six months under sentence of death, much older than his seventeen years.[17]

FOR THE next six years, Alexander Hamilton was essentially a New York politician in and out of Congress. Preparing himself for a prominent role in the first postwar Congress, Alexander Hamilton drew on his seven years of private and public contacts with New York's Revolutionary leadership and wrote a confidential report to Superintendent of Finance Morris, the man with whom he was most eager to work on framing a stronger national government. Promising a "full view of the situation and temper" of New York, drawing on sources "not disposed to exaggerate its distresses as an excuse for inactivity," he led off with the shocking statement that the war had cost New York "at least two thirds" of its revenues. Of the nine counties still in American hands, three had revolted against paying any taxes, two had been desolated by "the ravages of the enemy and of our own troops," and the remaining four were only slightly less badly injured. Much of the manpower had been siphoned off by British and American recruiting; many others had immigrated to the relative safety of neutral Vermont. "The fact is, labor is much dearer than before the war." The state had become impoverished and fatigued. What trade survived, with New York City still an enemy camp, was lucrative smuggling of luxury goods to the British and Loyalists. It was forbidden by "a severe law," but, Hamilton said, "what will laws avail against the ingenuity and intrepidity of avarice?" While tea was the hated symbol of the English before the Revolution, New Yorkers spent more to smuggle in this luxury than any other commodity. The state's only successful—and legal—industry was selling supplies to the American and French armies, a $5.5 million trade, in modern terms.

The political landscape, Hamilton reported, suffered from "the general disease which infects all our constitution, an excess of popularity." There "is no *order*." Politicians only cared "what will *please*, not what will *benefit* the people." The only possible result, Hamilton believed, was "temporary expedient, fickleness and folly." Yet he reserved his severest criticism for a system of taxation based on "*circumstances and abilities collectively considered*" out of a "desire for equality." This attempt "at perfect equality has resulted in total inequality." It had only succeeded in discriminating against the Loyalists, who formed a majority in many counties and was overburdening them. What a man looked like, "the decency or meanness of his manner of living, [his] personal friendships or the dislikes of the assessor" had more to do with what he paid than his "proportion of property."

But the "temper" of the state, of its rulers and its people, drew Hamilton's most acute assessment. Its "zealous" leaders were "jealous of their own power" yet they were willing to part with power "to the Federal Government"—and here he seemed to be using the words for the first time. Many who had served the common cause were disenchanted because they were so little appreciated. They were now determined only to maintain their own state government. The governor, George Clinton, had declined in popularity, partly because, Hamilton felt, he was poorly qualified to rule, partly because he ruled too well, insisting on strict adherence to law and to discipline in the militia. "He is, I believe, a man of integrity," Hamilton told Morris, adding acidly, "He passes with his particular friends for a statesman."

Surprisingly, Hamilton reported that his father-in-law, General Schuyler, had great influence in the assembly but not enough to keep his pet projects from "frequently miscarry[ing]." But Hamilton made it clear that Schuyler supported Morris and the nationalists. Hamilton dealt harshly with his fellow delegate to Congress, John Morin Scott: "Nature gave him genius, but habit has impaired it. He never had judgment; he now scarcely has plausibility." He only embarrassed New York by his "violent professions of popular principles. His views as a statesman are warped." His principles were "not the purest." Rating every state senator and judge in this scathing white paper, Hamilton called Senator Abraham Yates, a Clinton lieutenant, "a man whose ignorance and perverseness are only surpassed by his pertinacity and conceit." He had done so much damage to American credibility that he "deserves to be pensioned by the British Ministry." Another Clintonian was "pretty remarkable for *blunder*." Pointing out what must have become obvious to Robert Morris by now, that "I have neither flattered the state nor encouraged high expectations," Hamilton closed his confidential critique of his adopted home state: "I thought it my duty to exhibit things as they are, not as they ought to be."[18]

ALEXANDER HAMILTON's first brief brush with congressional politics, from November 1782 to July 1783, came when Congress was at its weakest, challenged by the states at every turn. Hamilton was not very enthusiastic about the ability of Congress to govern the nation. "God grant the union may last," he wrote soon after he took his seat. "But it is too frail now to be relied on, and we ought to be prepared for the worst." But here, during one of the most fertile periods of his intellectual life, Hamilton made friends and built alliances with the brilliant handful of founders left over from the glorious days of 1776. Few of them stayed long amid the disarray of the Confederation Congress, but Hamilton won the respect in that short time of James Madison of Virginia, Robert Morris and James Wilson of Pennsylvania, John Rutledge of South Carolina, and Oliver Ellsworth of Connecticut. During his entire stay in Philadelphia, Elias Boudinot, his old mentor, presided over Congress. Together, these men worked hard if futilely to buttress the sagging reputation of the Confederation and its feeble Congress.[19]

As soon as he arrived at the imposing redbrick Independence Hall at Fifth and Chestnut Streets in Philadelphia on December 2, 1782, Hamilton encountered once again, as he had so often in the army, the obstructionism of the individual states. The delegates from Rhode Island brought assembly resolutions in their saddlebags to block the 5 percent general customs duty, approved by Congress early in 1781, the only hope for the solvency of the federal government to pay an increasingly impatient army, which refused to disband without at least part of its back pay and assurances of arrears and pensions. The money also was to pay the interest on foreign loans. The states had voted a $6 million Confederation budget for 1783, with $2 million to come from assessments on the states, and the balance expected to come from foreign loans. President Boudinot immediately appointed Hamilton, Madison, and Thomas Fitz-Simons of Pennsylvania to the congressional committee to report to the full Congress on Rhode Island's objections. Rhode Island was contending that a national customs duty fell hardest on commercial states and would set up a federal bureaucracy unaccountable to the states, its officials not elected by each state's citizens.

In his first report to Congress, a form he was to master and make the bedrock of his political career, Hamilton, writing for the committee from its inception, wrote on December 16 that the Revolutionary Congress was trying to preserve "a just measure to the abilities of individuals," a progressive system of taxation that "promotes frugality and taxes extravagance." Import duties fell on "the rich and luxurious in proportion to their riches and luxury, the poor and parsimonious in proportion to their poverty and [thrift]." State taxes had not worked. Many states had failed to pay their share of federal expenses, chiefly because they relied on borrowing. Only a central financing authority—"a central will"—could assure the credit of the new nation. If each state constantly revised Congress's collective will, the United States could not hope for a good reputation among nations, and reputation and credit were inseparable. Already, the actions of individual states "inspired distrust." Here, he was referring to many states printing their own devalued currency and paying debts with it. Hamilton warned Congress that the British were still "an enemy vigilant, intriguing, [and] well acquainted with our defects and embarrassments."

At this point, Hamilton seized the opportunity to unveil his ingenious plan for a national debt to pay off the war loans of the confederated states and Congress. Unless interest was paid every year, the default "would stamp the national character with indelible disgrace." To rely on annual votes of states in their legislatures and by delegations in Congress "will be too precarious." To fund the national debt and then sell negotiable bonds based on this "active stock of the nation," as he described such a debt, would increase this stock "by the whole amount of the domestic debt." He insisted that, with a national debt funded by customs duties and the sale of government bonds instead of individual state debts, "the national credit would revive and stand hereafter on a secure basis."

Hamilton's proposal, supported by Madison—it was their first collaboration—came down hard on backsliding Rhode Islanders. For years, Congress had undertaken "the most full and solemn deliberation":

> Under a collective view of all the public difficulties, they recommend a measure which appears to them the cornerstone of the public safety. They see this measure suspended for nearly two years—partially complied with by some of the states, rejected by one of them. The public embarrassments [are] every day increasing, the dissatisfaction of the army growing more serious.

In a long catalogue of vices, Hamilton warned that "the hopes of our enemies" were being rekindled, "encouraged to protract the war" by the states' pulling apart on basic policy. Not only was the "national character suffering" but the "national safety" was now at the mercy of each state's self-interests.

Congress reacted to Hamilton's report by voting to send a delegation to Rhode Island to urge compliance with the customs duty, but Rhode Island's delegate, David Howell, moved for repeal. The

December 17 motion was voted back into Hamilton's committee, where it stagnated. Frustrated, nearly out of cash himself, Hamilton fired off letters to Poughkeepsie asking Governor Clinton to speed along his pay, preferably in notes drawn on Robert Morris's Bank of North America. He had little confidence in Continental currency! And he pleaded with his wife to come to Philadelphia. It had been more than a month since he had left her at The Pastures with her family. The trip around enemy-occupied New York City over badly rutted roads in winter had a month earlier dissuaded him from bringing Betsy and their nine-month-old son with him to Philadelphia, only to stay in a boardinghouse. But now he had prepared lodgings. Betsy destroyed all her letters to Hamilton after he died in the course of the fifty years she outlived him, obliterating her intimacies, but a letter from Betsy unleashed all his loneliness: "I thank you, my love, for your precious letter," so "full of that tender love which I hope will characterize us both to our latest hour." Yet he felt compelled to reassure her of his constancy: "There never was a husband who could vie with yours in fidelity and affection." He was beginning to be "insupportably anxious to see you again. I hope this pleasure may not be long delayed." Winter snows made travel easier—by horse-drawn sleigh. "I wish you to take advantage of the first good snow that promises to carry you through," the West Indian urged the upstate New Yorker. Betsy and their baby were to stop over at Parsippany, New Jersey, at the home of one of the Van Cortlandts, relatives of her mother. She was to seek the advice of her friends about the best route, which would depend on how solidly frozen the Hudson River was when she sledded across with her servant and the baby. He did not want her to "make so long a journey alone." When she reached New Jersey, "write me of your arrival and I will come for you." Come to think of it, she was to write first when she set out. If his letter did not already terrify her, he did not help matters with his "for God's sake take care of my child on the journey, I am very apprehensive on his account."[20]

BORN IN debt, the United States had not even a rudimentary tax system during the Revolution, raising money by confiscation of Loyalist property, fines of pacifists, forced loans of its citizens, just under $11 million ($140 million in today's dollars) in foreign loans: $4.4 million from the French, $1.8 million from the Dutch government, $3.6 million in loans from Dutch bankers, and $175,000 from the Spanish treasury. The greatest source of United States cash was its own printing presses. By the end of the war, this fiat money amounted, at face value, to more than $200 million, about $2.5 billion in today's money. By the time Hamilton took his seat in Congress, it had been forced to revalue earlier issues of Continental dollars at only 2.5 percent of face value—a devaluation of forty to one—thus coining the phrase "not worth a Continental."

In theory, the financing of the Revolution was simple, the states supplying the funds and the Continental Congress distributing them. In practice, both the states and Congress spent large sums on their own initiatives. The states spent over $100 million ($1.3 billion in today's money) for the common defense. Each state believed it had spent more than its share and was not receiving fair credit according to congressional accounting methods. New Englanders insisted on receipts for everything and believed Southerners used lax accounting methods to justify fraudulent claims. Southerners relied on slave labor and believed in pay-as-you-go while Northerners believed in investing in debt by discounting government vouchers and notes. Without congressional approval, Virginia, under Governor Thomas Jefferson, had backed George Rogers Clark's expedition to seize the Ohio Country, and Virginia had been holding it for three years with a costly garrison of one thousand men, while Massachusetts carried out its own operations against the Loyalist stronghold of Penobscot, Maine. Both states insisted that the Union should reimburse them for their costs.

In addition, each state and the Continental Army used what were, in effect, forced loans, requisitioning food and supplies from citizens and promising to pay for the goods with IOUs that quickly depreciated as they passed from hand to hand. While these expedients had, with the help of France, its armies and navies, produced victory, by the time the Treaty of Paris, on September 3rd, 1783, acknowledged American independence from the British Empire, the United States was free, but in complete fiscal chaos. Congress was no longer paying interest on its bonds held by its own citizens, was months in arrears in paying its army, and had defaulted on its foreign debts. The cost of servicing the foreign debt approached $1 million a year, multiplied by a factor of seventeen into $17 million in hard money, or by a factor of forty, or $680 million, if any banker would accept depreciated Continental paper, which no one would.

WHILE CONGRESS quaked at the threat of tiny Rhode Island's refusal to pay its fair share of the Continental expenses, another marginal New England entity—although no one knew what to call it yet—sprang onto the stage at Independence Hall. Vermont, as settlers between Lake Champlain and the Connecticut River called it, or the New Hampshire grants, as other New Englanders knew it, or the four easternmost counties of New York, as New Yorkers insisted on describing it, demanded to be admitted to the Continental union after five years as a self-proclaimed republic. In 1760, during the French and Indian Wars, the French had blown up their forts in the Champlain Valley and retreated into Canada, which they ceded to the English by the Treaty of Paris of 1763. That started a land rush into the vacuum they left. Two English colonies, New York and New Hampshire, claimed the unnamed territory. In one hour on one day, June 7, 1763, New Hampshire's corpulent royal governor, Benning Wentworth, signed the papers chartering half a dozen townships with one hand as he pocketed gold coins, his fees for granting lands to investors he never saw, with the other. Between 1749 and 1764, Wentworth issued 135 township grants. Some twenty-five thousand settlers, the overflow population of Connecticut, the most crowded colony by the eve of the Revolution, flowed up the Connecticut River, filling forest clearings on the eastern slopes of the Green Mountains. On the western slopes, settlement was much slower, spreading north from Wentworth's namesake, Bennington. The reason few settlers put down stakes along the Lake Champlain shore was that New York took issue with New Hampshire grants, arguing that the 1664 royal grant to the Duke of York included "all the lands from the west side of the Connecticut River to the east side of the Delaware Bay."

Agreeing to turn the dispute over to the King's Privy Council in London for arbitration, the New Yorkers sent agents to the hearings—who lied by testifying that all the settlers already on the contested ground were amenable to New York government and wouldn't mind applying for—and paying fees for—second, or confirmatory grants. The 1764 royal ruling was that New York, indeed, extended to the "western bank of the Connecticut River." At first, the settlers on the grants were not worried. They believed the ruling applied only to future grants. But not so New York's officials, who declared all the New Hampshire grants null and void. They also annexed the disputed territory to New York's existing counties, in each of four new counties creating New York courts and appointing sheriffs to enforce New York's rights. Lord Dunmore, New York's governor, began to issue new grants and pocket fees for them.

Organizing the settlers already on the land, Ethan Allen and his brothers, who had paid good money for the land, appealed to the New York courts, which ignored them. The Allens wrote pamphlets defending the settlers' rights while the settlers raised the money to send agents to London to plead their case. As a result the British Crown in 1767 ordered New York to stop making grants to the disputed lands, but New York's governors ignored the royal order from faraway London and sent sheriffs and posses to evict the settlers. On the eve of the Revolution, the Allens organized the Green Mountain Boys, the largest organized armed force in the colonies at the time, to resist New York's actions. Unless they ousted the New Yorkers, they believed their lands would be worthless. Declared outlaws by New York, the Green Mountain Boys defended their settlements and evicted the New York sheriffs' eviction parties. Acting as a provisional government based in a tavern in Bennington, they issued decrees and enforced them, in 1772 holding a convention and ordering that "no person should take grants" from New York. Up to two hundred Boys raided and destroyed settlements the New Yorkers attempted to plant. In 1774, the New York Assembly countered by passing a law "preventing tumultuous and riotous assemblies," aimed at the Boys. Anyone assaulting a civil New York official or burning or destroying grain or hay would "suffer death." A 50-pound reward was offered for

Ethan Allen or other "ringleaders." The Boys responded by seizing the Westminster courthouse. Two Boys were killed in the attack.

When the Revolutionary War broke out, the Boys joined the fray within days of Lexington and Concord, seizing Fort Ticonderoga and Crown Point. When Ethan Allen led an unauthorized attack on Montreal in an attempt to annex French Canada, he was taken prisoner and shipped to England in chains. As a commissioner for prisoner exchanges, Alexander Hamilton helped arrange his release after three years of harsh treatment. The British counterattack of 1776 had all but emptied Vermont, but diehard settlers had organized their own government and sent delegates to the Continental Congress. There, New York objected to admitting Vermont to the Union. Congress had shelved Vermont's petition, effectively upholding New York's claim to control over the territory. Undeterred, Vermonters formed a republic in 1777 and sent troops to support the Continental Army in key battles, but they asserted their independence by negotiating with both the British in Canada and the Americans, managing to stay neutral through much of the war. Vermont again petitioned to join the union in 1777; again New York's Convention countered by claiming Vermont was trying to "dismember" New York.[21]

In 1779, a British officer in full regalia appeared one day in Manchester and handed Ethan Allen an envelope. Within minutes, Allen turned it over to Governor Thomas Chittenden and his council. Under the guise of prisoner of war negotiations, Vermont's leaders secretly brought about a ceasefire with the British in Canada that included New York's frontier forts. At every step, Chittenden kept Philip Schuyler and through him General Washington, informed, even as Governor Clinton and his ruling New York faction worked hard to turn Congress against Vermont's appeals for statehood. The controversy deepened when nineteen New Hampshire towns in the Connecticut Valley asked to be annexed by Vermont. When Vermont accepted, New Hampshire threatened to invade unless Vermont handed the towns back. Washington warned that when the territorial integrity of one state—New Hampshire—was violated, all of the United States would be obligated to respond militarily against Vermont.

As if to call Washington's bluff, Vermont's governor issued a proclamation declaring that Vermont's southeastern boundary was the Hudson River. At a stroke of his quill, he added twenty miles of New York State to Vermont, including the Lake George region and a sizable chunk of Philip Schuyler's lands. Now Ethan Allen and the Green Mountain Boys were driving out New Yorkers living in Vermont, banishing them, telling them that if they returned they would be put to death and their properties confiscated and sold by Vermont. As Congress took up the Vermont crisis again, couriers raced between Vermont and American headquarters at New Windsor, New York. Secretly, Washington provided Chittenden with Congress's resolutions. Only weeks after his victory at Yorktown, Washington warned Vermont that its "late extension of claim [has] rather diminished than increased the number of your friends [in Congress]. If such extension should be persisted in, it will be made a common cause." Vermont's annexations were "too serious to escape the ire of many Americans." Washington predicted "a calamity": he knew that, as the commander of New York's militia, Governor Clinton was chomping at the bit to attack Vermont. This was "more to be dreaded than a necessity of coercion" by Congress and the Continental forces under Washington. The commander-in-chief wrote privately to Philip Schuyler, who had swung his support to Vermont's independence, a letter Schuyler assuredly shared with Hamilton. Washington said he had shown his "private and confidential" letter to Chittenden "to a number of my friends, members of Congress." He bluntly warned Governor Clinton that the majority of New Englanders, especially among his officers, supported Vermont statehood. Vermont then decided to return to its former boundaries and sent four agents to Congress to negotiate admission to the Union.[22]

Few members of Congress could have a more intimate knowledge of the Vermont controversy than Hamilton. His law preceptor, James Duane, was a major speculator in Vermont land; Hamilton's father-in-law had launched the American attack on Canada in 1775 from Vermont's shores and had long commanded the Northern Department, which included Vermont. As New York's delegate to Congress, Hamilton would not be expected to take Vermont's side, but he naturally arranged, with the support of President of Congress Boudinot, to serve on the key committee that would be considering Vermont's and New York's claims.

So "dangerous to the Confederacy" had the Vermont question become that, right after studying how to pay the army, Congress took up the New York Assembly's demand for "the immediate and decided interposition of Congress." In a motion Hamilton seconded, and in a report he prepared, Congress resolved that Vermont must give back any lands confiscated from New Yorkers and pay damages to four evicted landlords. At the same time, without mentioning the word Vermont, Congress asserted its authority over "the said district claiming to be independent," and ordered both New York and Vermont to back away from the brink of an armed clash. Hamilton made Congress's threat clear, however. "The United States will take effectual measures to enforce" its resolution, but Congress overruled the committee and struck out this menacing language.[23] Cautious not to acknowledge the legitimacy of Vermont's governor—and thus declare Vermont as a de facto legal entity—Hamilton sent a copy of the toothless resolution to "Thomas Chittenden Esquire of Bennington." Privately, Hamilton wrote to his friend John Laurence, a New York legislator returning to Albany from a business trip to Philadelphia, to urge New York's governor and assembly to "be moderate by all means."[24]

HAMILTON'S FRUSTRATION over the weakness of the Confederation Congress grew as he realized that what he had once considered blundering and corruption by individual members was actually structural. Even the smallest state, Rhode Island, could refuse to pay its fair share of the army's pay and the interest on foreign loans without fear of repercussions. When Congress did manage to pass a resolution calling for a visit to the Rhode Island Assembly by a congressional delegation to bring pressure on the recalcitrants, it later aborted even that weak maneuver when Virginia's delegates also demurred from paying the largest state's requisition for the second consecutive year. Determined to push for some small step toward reform, on December 20, Hamilton made a fresh motion to revise the requisitions on the states. According to the notes of an equally disgusted fellow com-

mitteeman, James Madison, that motion, too, met "with little patronage." Hamilton withdrew it, and it never was entered in the congressional journal. As a result, the veto of the Rhode Island Assembly
was enough, in Madison's word, to "blast" the import duty so vital to
funding the Confederation. "They absolutely refuse the only fund
which could be satisfactory to lenders," wrote Madison. His "indigna-
tion against this perverse sister is increased by her shameful delin-
quency in requisitions."[25]

Only heavy winter snows in the Hudson Valley slowed the next
round of rebuffs by New York in the Vermont controversy. Hamilton,
earlier than most other New Yorkers, had come to favor a peaceful
settlement. Governor Clinton was anything but mollified by Hamilton's call for moderation. He was not convinced that Congress, after
seven years of postponing any action, could be relied on to use appropriate force to stop the annexations. "If force is necessary," Clinton
told Hamilton, "the longer it is delayed, the more force it will
require." To the contrary, Clinton believed some members of Congress
were encouraging Vermonters by "secret assurances that Congress will
not direct any coercive measures against them." Hamilton, aware that
the New York Assembly was about to reconvene, hastily fired back a
letter to Clinton that it was "of great importance" that New York give
up any pretensions to winning its ancient claims to all of Vermont.
He, too, had heard the rumors that many New England officers in the
Continental Army had taken land grants in Vermont as rewards for
their Revolutionary services. But now that Vermont had annexed
lands in Massachusetts and New Hampshire, those states, too, would
insist on a compromise, an idea Hamilton now urged on Clinton. He
recommended that each state send peace commissioners. Once again,
he was urging compromise to solve a stubborn problem. One month
later, he wrote Clinton again that, in Congress, the Vermont question
was "a business in which nobody cares to act with decision." And the
army—that meant Washington—was "much opposed to any experiment of force" where private interests, such as those of New York
land speculators versus Vermont settlers, were at stake. "A peace may
soon take place!" He urged that the affair should be speedily settled.[26]

So engrossed had Hamilton become by Congress's "immediate con-

cerns," he wrote to his wife, that he had forgotten to tell her a "disagreeable piece of intelligence" he had received from Nathanael
Greene when that general informed him of his friend Laurens's death.
The shock of that news, now two months old, had distracted Hamilton from telling his wife that his half brother, Peter Levine, had died
in North Carolina. He felt little grief, he told Betsy. "You know the
circumstances that abate my distress." Levine "dies rich but has disposed of the bulk of his fortune to strangers." Hamilton had not
inquired how much Levine had left him, but "I am told he has left
me a legacy." Even after fifteen years, the bitterness of his penniless,
orphaned childhood still came through.[27]

AND STILL Betsy did not come. It had been six weeks since Hamilton
had left Albany, and his yearning for her mixed with his anxiety that
something had befallen his wife and child along the treacherous
roads. Adding to his worry was his knowledge that Loyalist raiders
had disrupted the mails, "which deprives me of the pleasure of hearing from you." Hamilton was "inexpressibly anxious":

> I write this for fear of the worst, but I should be miserable if I
> thought it would find you in Albany. Lose not a moment in com-
> ing to me. I have borne your absence with patience until about
> a week since. But the period we fixed for our reunion being
> come, I can no longer reconcile myself to it. Every hour in the
> day I feel a severe pang. Half my nights are sleepless. Come, my
> charmer, and relieve me. Bring my darling boy to my bosom.[28]

The longest-smoldering fuse, as the War for Independence sputtered to an end, was army back pay, always a problem after such a
long and costly struggle but especially acute in America, where
exports to Europe were blockaded by British warships, the only trade
was in war matériel, and the only money was worthless. In early
January 1783 a delegation of high-ranking army officers from the camp
at Newburgh, New York, arrived in Congress with a petition for back
pay. They were all, it turned out, Hamilton's old friends, including
Hamilton's former mentor, Major General Alexander McDougall; Col-

onel Mathias Ogden, the brother-in-law of Hamilton's teacher, Francis Barber; and Colonel John Brooks, who had supported Hamilton when a pernicious preacher libeled him and nearly touched off a duel. President Boudinot understandably appointed Colonel Hamilton to chair the committee, meet with the officers, and prepare recommendations for the full Congress. The army petition, signed by General Knox, among others, was clear, eloquent, and allowed for no more delays:

> Shadows have been offered to us while the substance has been gleaned by others. We have borne all that men can bear. Our property is expended. Our private resources are at an end. The uneasiness of the soldiers, for want of pay, is dangerous. Any further experiments on their patience may have fatal effects.

The solemn words of the soldiers at last forced Congress to face squarely its fiscal impotence. It took a soldier sitting in Congress to see how clear and present the danger really was: unless the army was given some of its back pay and reliable documentation that promised back pay someday, it would not lay down its arms, disband, and go home. Hamilton recommended that Superintendent of Finance Morris give the men their present pay. Each state was to pay its line regiments up through August 1780, when they had gone on the national charge. Congress must draw on the states to fund "the whole debt of the United States"—here he was bringing up a national debt again— and the soldiers were to be paid like any other creditor. All officers should have the choice of remaining on half pay for life or accepting a single lump sum buyout. He left the number of years blank, but he had studied the calculations of radical English economist Dr. William Price and he penciled in six years' pay. Congress should decide how to compensate widows and orphans. On January 25, Congress swiftly adopted Hamilton's recommendations, although no one had the slightest clue where the money would come from.[29]

Congress's willingness to accept his proposal for paying the army fired Hamilton's confidence and touched off three days of debates that gave Hamilton a pulpit for his first bold plan for paying off the debts of the United States by creating a national debt. Rising at New York's table on January 27, he gave his colleagues a lecture on how the debt could be apportioned between the nation and each state. A national debt was simpler because it avoided the thorny business of fixing state quotas. Here, everyone could remember the Rhode Island debacle. The current method of collecting state revenues, by confiscations and fines, Hamilton called "a vicious system" that was "more subservient to the [tax collectors'] popularity than to the public revenue."[30] When Oliver Ellsworth of Connecticut objected that the states should raise permanent debts that the federal government could then draw on, Hamilton counterattacked on January 28. Hamilton, according to Madison's notes of the all-day debates, "dwelt long on the inefficacy of state funds." Tax collectors should be appointed by Congress. Since the federal government, he argued, obviously lacked the "energy" needed for "uniting the states," it would take professional tax officers dependent on Congress for their pay—and thus interested in supporting its power. Madison considered Hamilton's comment on Congress's lack of energy "imprudent and injudicious to the cause it was meant to serve." The creation of a federal government with its own tax agents and the power to appropriate revenues was the "very source," Madison wrote, "of jealousy" by the states:

All the members of Congress who concurred in any degree with the states in this jealousy smiled at [Hamilton's] disclosure. [They] took notice in private conversation that Mr. Hamilton had let out the secret.[31]

What Hamilton had revealed was what Virginia's most influential states' rights delegates had suspected, that Hamilton spoke for Robert Morris and the Northern financial interests. Hamilton had joined Morris's inner circle of nationalists who were quietly working behind the scenes. His inadvertent revelation touched off a decade-long struggle in Congress over how better to pay off the nation's staggering wartime debt, which had grown to twenty times the money in circulation.

By February 12, Hamilton, after more than two months of prodding and behind-the-scenes maneuvering, had been able to wrench from Congress only its "opinion," in the form of a motion, advocating the establishment of some sort of permanent fund. In his first draft, he wrote, "to be collected under the authority of the U.S. in Congress assembled." After yet another debate, Congress ordered even these words deleted. When Madison's proposal that taxes be collected by Congress was also defeated in committee, neither version went before the full Congress. It was obvious to both men their plans would only be rejected.[32]

The very next day, Hamilton wrote to his old commander, George Washington:

> The state of our finances was never more critical. There has scarcely been a period of the revolution which called for more wisdom and decision in Congress. Unfortunately for us we are a body not governed by reason [or] foresight but by circumstances. It is probable we will not take the proper measures.

Hamilton forecast "an embarrassing scene" whether the war continued or there was peace.[33]

On March 4, 1783, a grateful Washington, stunned by the dire note in Hamilton's letter, wrote back in a new and confiding tone, no longer general to subordinate, high priest to acolyte. He had always been candid with Congress, he said, and he was shocked that Congress had not shared his "free communication of sentiments":

> The public interest might be benefited if the Commander in Chief of the Army was let more into the political and pecuniary state of our affairs than he is. Where there is a want of information, there must be chance medley, and a man may be upon the brink of a precipice before he is aware of his danger—when a little foreknowledge might enable him to avoid it.

All the information Washington had received "of the danger that stares us in the face on account of our funds" he had deduced from newspapers or from Hamilton's warning. Washington had been given the impression by Congress that "we should be able to rub along" with another loan from Dutch bankers, "so far was I from conceiving that our finances were in so deplorable a state."

Separated now by distance as they rarely had been, Hamilton and Washington grew closer by letter. "To you, who have seen the danger," Washington wrote appreciatively to his former aide, "to which the Army has been exposed," there could be a "political dissolution for want of subsistence." Just short of victory the army could collapse, the Union dissolve, so "fatal" was the tendency of Congress's "unhappy spirit of licentiousness." Unless Congress quickly took prudent measures, "I shall give it as my opinion" that there could be "riots that end in blood! God forbid." Washington's "predicament," he told Hamilton, was "critical and delicate":

> The sufferings of a complaining army on one hand and the inability of Congress and tardiness of the states on the other, are the forebodings of evil.

The threat of renewed mutinies in the army over back pay worried Washington, too. "The old leaven," and here he meant Horatio Gates, "is again beginning to work under the mask of the most perfect dissimulation and apparent cordiality." Once again, Gates was plotting behind the scenes—"I have no proof of it"—to oust Washington, who now said he was sure that the "sensible and discerning part of the army" still supported him.

Washington confided to Hamilton that he, in turn, supported Hamilton in his position that there had to be a stronger, firmer federal government:

> For it is clearly my opinion [that] unless Congress have powers competent to all general purposes, that the distresses we have encountered, the expenses we have incurred and the blood we have spilled in the course of an eight years' war will avail us nothing.[34]

Hamilton responded quickly that he "sincerely wish[ed] *ingratitude* was not so natural to the human heart as it is." Yet, he told Washington, some of the distrust swirling around army and Congress, as the war ended, had "too much foundation."

> Republican jealousy has in it a principle of hostility to an army whatever be their merits, whatever be their claims to the gratitude of the community. It acknowledges their services with unwillingness and rewards them with reluctance.[35]

ONE WEEK later, on March 12, 1783, the American merchant ship *Washington* arrived in Philadelphia with the news from France that on November 30, 1782, a provisional peace treaty had been signed in Paris granting American independence. It had taken three and a half months for the treaty to cross the Atlantic. Congress had accomplished little during the year-long peace talks. It had handed out contracts to its more influential friends to feed the army. It had appointed Robert Morris as superintendent of finance but thwarted his policies, and he had resigned in disgust. It elected Washington's second-in-command, General Benjamin Lincoln, as the first secretary of war but made no provision for Washington. In his first foreign policy speech, Hamilton urged coolness and circumspection by Congress when it took up ratification of the treaty. Hamilton rose and delivered a detailed critique. His friend Madison took careful notes. Hamilton "disapproved highly" of the three American negotiators, Benjamin Franklin, John Adams, and John Jay, for "submitting" to the wishes of France. He felt they had procrastinated until French fleets had won back territory and naval battles to gain concessions from the English. Yet he opposed repealing the treaty and he opposed recalling or "reprehending" the American ministers for fear that "they would be disgusted and head and foment [political] parties in this country." He especially targeted John Jay, his erstwhile ally, characterizing him before the entire Congress as "a man of profound sagacity and pure integrity" but "of a suspicious temper" that "might explain [his] extraordinary jealousies."[36] Finally, Hamilton agreed to commend the peace commissioners and accept the treaty.

His influence in Congress growing, his rapport with his old commander restored, Hamilton had the satisfaction to write Washington frequently now of his progress in the great hall and committee rooms in Philadelphia where Washington had sat so long ago. On March 24, he fired off a salute of his own to Washington:

I congratulate your Excellency on this happy conclusion of your labors. It now only remains to make solid establishments within, to perpetuate our union to prevent our being a ball in the hands of European powers bandied against each other at their pleasure.

Washington borrowed this felicitous phrase from the letter of his erstwhile writing aide when he wrote his last "Circular to the States" warning against "the ill-fated moment for relaxing the powers of the Union," advising the states to "give such a tone to our Federal government" that it could carry out its "ends"—a "destiny" that would be "a blessing" to "unborn millions"—he cautioned against "annihilating the cement of the Confederation" and becoming "the sport of European politics which may play one state against the other." Circulated in newspapers all over America and Europe, Hamilton's thoughts and words in Washington's dress uniform became known as "Washington's Legacy."[37]

THE "EMBARRASSMENT" that Hamilton had predicted came soon enough. The resentment of officers long underpaid and overpromised by Congress boiled over at headquarters at Newburgh, New York. Washington got wind that someone high up on his staff had anonymously circulated a memo among his officers calling a secret meeting on March 12. He moved quickly. Denouncing "such disorderly proceedings" and postponing the meeting for three days, he marched to the large new officers' barracks on March 15, his arrival a surprise. He strode to the lectern and pulled a paper from his pocket. For five minutes, obviously agitated, he lectured his officers, urging them not to take any steps which, "taken in the calm light of reason," would "lessen [their] dignity and sully the glory" they had earned: "Let me request you to rely on the plighted faith of your country and place a full confidence in the purity of intentions of Congress."[38]

The so-called Newburgh conspiracy collapsed but, on June 17, far from Washington's commanding presence, eighty armed Pennsylvania troops under "Mad Anthony" Wayne in Lancaster broke away from their officers and marched to Philadelphia to rendezvous with sergeants and new recruits demonstrating outside Independence Hall against accepting their discharges from the army without getting paid. Inside, the Pennsylvania Executive Council, responsible for keeping order, convened across the hallway from Congress. Council President John Dickinson, a famous Quaker lawyer, a man in a gray satin suit who had signed the Declaration of Independence, transmitted to Congress letters from the mutineers' commanding officer in Lancaster that said they intended to rob the treasury. Congress's President Boudinot appointed Hamilton to head a committee to work with the Pennsylvania government. Hamilton urged a firm show of force. Pennsylvania should send out militia to intercept the mutineers before they could reach the city. But the Pennsylvania Council turned down Hamilton's plea. Unless the mutinous soldiers actually committed some physical violence to congressmen, no force would be threatened or used.

Asserting his newfound congressional authority, Hamilton dispatched the assistant secretary of war, Major William Jackson, to meet the marchers and assure them fair treatment if they returned peacefully to their barracks in Lancaster. The mutineers brushed Jackson aside and kept marching toward Philadelphia. When they reached the city on Friday, June 20, more than seven hundred veterans from the city's two barracks joined their ranks as Boudinot adjourned Congress for the weekend. Hamilton hurriedly arranged for Robert Morris to pay the men with his own personal notes. General Arthur St. Clair, commander of the Pennsylvania Line, prepared his troops at the Charleston barracks to arrest the mutineers. But on Saturday, the rest of St. Clair's veterans joined the mutiny amid rumors they were about to break into Morris's Bank of North America to pay themselves. What members of Congress may or may not have known was that Hamilton had more than one way to influence

Morris. The Bank of North America, which had opened its doors only in January 1782 as a private bank under Congress's auspices, was managed by a twelve-man board of directors who annually selected one of its number as president. Morris was president at the moment, but the second-largest stockholder was John B. Church, who had married Angelica Schuyler, Betsy's older sister. Church, who had fled England, thinking he had killed a nobleman in a duel, had grown rich selling supplies to the American and French armies. Church had just sailed for France and had turned his legal business over to Hamilton, enabling him to put pressure on Robert Morris.

Posting armed guards at the doors of Independence Hall, Boudinot summoned Congress into an emergency session at one o'clock Saturday afternoon. Delegates had to shoulder their way inside past some three hundred mutineers milling on Chestnut Street. Armed with weapons they had looted from the city's arsenals, the mutineers, some of them drunk and shouting obscenities, crowded up against the windows of the council chamber, trying to hear the proceedings above the din from the street. Some even poked bayonets through the windows of Independence Hall. A terrified President Dickinson rushed into the congressional chamber with the mutineers' demand that they be allowed to choose their own officers to negotiate their grievances. Boudinot ordered St. Clair to try again to restore discipline among his troops. When he failed, after three tense hours, congressmen quietly filed out of the building. Only catcalls assaulted them.

After one more fruitless meeting with Pennsylvania authorities, Hamilton and his committee recommended that Congress adjourn and leave the city, to meet at Princeton, New Jersey, the following Thursday, June 26. Boudinot, meanwhile, dispatched an express rider to Washington to bring back troops. Congressmen rode out of the city, shielded by five hundred hastily mustered militia. From Princeton on June 29, Hamilton reported to Governor Clinton on the meeting. He called the Pennsylvania Council's conduct "to the last degree weak and disgusting." Their "feebleness" had determined Congress's decision to flee "a place where they could receive no support."[39] Hamilton was stung, he wrote Madison, that he was being accused of being too precipitous in recommending that Congress flee the capital.

As the ringleaders of the mutiny fled and the troops returned to their barracks, Hamilton turned his thoughts toward home and Betsy, who had never budged from her father's house. Had Hamilton now some second thoughts about her safety? Winter roads with an infant were one thing, drunken mutineers quite another. On July 22, 1783, more than six months since he had last seen her, Hamilton wrote that the definitive peace treaty had just reached New York, and under the treaty the city was to be immediately evacuated. He wanted to rush north, gather his family and his law books, and move into Manhattan, but so few members of Congress remained at Princeton that he had to stay on to assure a quorum to ratify the peace treaty. "I will not be long from my Betsy. In a very short time I hope we shall be happily settled in New York."[40]

One month later, Alexander Hamilton, still only twenty-eight but now one of America's most controversial and conspicuous leaders, returned to The Pastures for a brief summer vacation in Albany after his first nine-month term in Congress. As he ended that term, Hamilton sagely wrote to John Jay:

> We have now happily concluded the great work of independence, but much remains to be done to reach the fruits of it. Our prospects are not flattering. Every day proves the inefficacy of the present confederation. The common danger being removed, we are receding instead of advancing in disposition to mend its defects.
>
> The road to popularity in each state is to inspire jealousies of the power of Congress, though nothing can be more apparent than that they have no power . . . We, at this moment, experience all the mischiefs of a bankrupt and ruined credit. It is to be hoped that, when prejudice and folly have run themselves out of breath, we may return to reason and correct our errors.[41]

He left amid charges by Pennsylvania's Dickinson that he urged Congress to abandon the capital without cause. Madison came to his defense, writing that Hamilton only agreed to the evacuation after every other committee member insisted. James McHenry, Hamilton's best man and now a congressman from Maryland, soothed him: "No one but believes you are a man of honor and republican principles. Were you ten years older and £20,000 richer, there is no doubt but that you might obtain the [votes] of Congress for the highest office in their gift."[42]

AT NOON on November 25, 1783, under a cold bright sky, Colonel Alexander Hamilton, resplendent in his dark blue, gold braided Continental Army uniform, joined General George Washington's honor guard of handpicked officers that led one thousand shivering soldiers from Harlem south into Manhattan to take the last major post in America from her former British rulers. The peace treaty affirming American independence had been signed more than a year ago but the British commander, Sir Guy Carleton, had refused to leave until he had positive written orders from London. As a result, Washington had refused to disband his army as long as a redcoat remained. For four months since New York had called him home, Hamilton had waited impatiently but not idly in Albany, rehearsing his plans with his father-in-law. He wrote a "Vindication of Congress," addressed to John Dickinson, but then thought better of mailing it; he started a long "Defense of Congress" to send to the Philadelphia newspapers, but then filed it away. Only the arrival of a brevet promotion to full colonel from Washington in mid-November banished his gloom, and he proudly rode south to join his old commander for the triumphal march into New York City.

At Bull's Head Tavern in the Bowery, the victory parade ran headlong into a crowd on horseback. The wartime refugees who had fled their homes in 1776 returned now from their long exile in the countryside, sprigs of laurel stuck in their hats. They mingled with old army friends like Hamilton, who wore the black-and-white cockade of the Franco-American union on their chests. A cheering crowd lined Broadway as the victory column swelled and slowed. Not everyone was cheering. One woman wept and went home to write:

We had been accustomed for a long time to military display in all the finish and finery of [British] garrison life. The troops just leaving us were as if equipped for a show, and with their scarlet uniforms and burnished arms made a brilliant display. The troops that marched in, on the contrary, were ill-clad and weather-beaten and made a forlorn appearance. But then, they were our troops and as I looked at them and thought upon all they had done and suffered for us, my heart and my eyes were full.[43]

The city would long celebrate Evacuation Day and remember the spectacle as the ragged Revolutionaries marched in and the last red-coats paraded down the Bowery to the East River wharves to be rowed out to the fleet. Thirteen guns on the parapets of Fort George saluted as an American soldier scampered up the flagstaff, yanked down the Union Jack, and nailed up the Stars and Stripes.

THIRTEEN

"Acquisition of Power and Profit"

T he morning after the triumphal American reentry into New York City, George Washington rode with Alexander Hamilton, according to tradition in both families, to the William Street home of Hercules Mulligan, Hamilton's onetime guardian and a key intelligence operative inside the city through most of the Revolution. All the day before, Hamilton had ridden through streets thronged with cheering Patriots, but just behind them he could not overlook the devastation of seven years of war. No tree or fence remained standing, all sacrificed to the need for firewood and barricade. In the burned-out district between the charred shell of Trinity Church and King's College, block after block was choked with rubble. Hamilton's friend William Duer recalled that the spectral walls of gutted buildings "cast their grim shadows upon the pavement, imparting an unearthly aspect" to the streets. Much of the remaining housing was unfit for human habitation. On Evacuation Day, Hamilton's mentor James Duane found two of his houses looking "as if they had been inhabited by savages or wild beasts." Commandeered by the British as stables, hospitals, or barracks, every church and public building was filthy and dilapidated. Where once there had hovered majestic rows of shade trees, trenches and redoubts now lingered, garbage and trash forming windrows of refuse between them. Along the waterfront, empty wharves and warehouses bore witness to the hasty departure of the merchant ships, the debris left behind by thousands of fleeing Loyalists bearing witness to the haste and disorder of their panicky flight.

But today was to be Hercules Mulligan's day, and Hamilton chatted happily with him and with his former commanding general as they rode through the devastation to the spy's house. Expert at passing along information on the movements of British ships and troops, Mulligan had done such a good job disguising his activities that, like every other American who had remained in the city during the British occupation, he was now considered a Loyalist and detested as a collaborator with the British. In the last weeks of the British slow-march evacuation, vengeful Sons of Liberty had rampaged through the streets, hunting down suspected Loyalists, sacking their houses and stores and, in some cases, tarring and feathering them, hastening the departure of thousands more on crammed merchant ships.

Hercules Mulligan had lost everything in the clandestine service of the Americans. Because Washington had paid his secret service operatives through intermediaries, in gold out of his own purse, he had kept no records that could compromise an agent—or clear him. For fully four years, Mulligan had fed Hamilton information he had gathered, sending it by boat at night across the East River, his black servant, Cato, rowing to New Jersey as if to fish or buy food. From the time Mulligan was captured in the Battle of Long Island after delivering Hamilton's plan for an escape route to Washington, he had been under suspicion as a spy. Paroled by the British on his honor not to leave New York City, Mulligan had been a conduit for information flowing from Long Island and Manhattan through the British lines to the American headquarters in the western hills of New Jersey. Benedict Arnold himself suspected that it was Mulligan who had tipped off American intelligence officers in late summer of 1780 that a high-ranking American general was about to defect. Mulligan knew from informants working in his brother's waterfront export-import warehouse that the British had drawn enough supplies for a quick thrust up the Hudson to support Arnold's attempted surrender of West Point to the British. When the Arnold-André treason plot came unraveled and Arnold fled to New York, he turned over to British authorities a list of fifty American operatives he had worked with. At the top of the list was Hercules Mulligan, who was promptly arrested, jailed in the notorious Provost's Prison, beaten, and tortured. But big, burly Hercules Mulligan had never cracked, and his influential relatives— he was married to a Livingston and his brother and his partners were key British contractors—had helped to arrange his release. But the British never trusted him, and the Loyalists on at least one occasion chased him through the streets in a failed attempt to tar and feather him. Customers for red British dress uniforms and the latest London finery shunned Mulligan's haberdashery, and it had folded. At war's end, he became a real estate agent, flogging at low rents the deserted town houses and storefronts of departing Loyalists.

Arriving days before Washington's formal entry into the town, Hamilton found his old mentor terrified because he was perceived by the Patriots to be a leading Loyalist and could expect to have his home and business either mobbed or confiscated. Hamilton, who owed Mulligan so much, prevailed on Washington to demonstrate his close friendship—and protection—for Mulligan by favoring his family with a visit. Nothing could have been more symbolic or more intimate than having his first breakfast in the weeklong victory celebrations at his former spy's house. Rumor took care of the rest.

When he had passed through the city in August on his way home from Congress, Hamilton had seen the turmoil being caused by Patriot reprisals on suspected Loyalists in retaliation for the city's wartime devastation. In two great fires, one probably ordered by Washington after the American evacuation of 1776, more than eight hundred houses had been destroyed. Hamilton had slipped into the stripped and battered city on the eve of British evacuation because he knew good housing and office space would be in short supply. Patriots whose homes and goods had been confiscated by the British now exacted their revenge.

From all over America came reports of similar violent retribution. In Elizabethtown, New Jersey, where Loyalists had targeted for destruction by fire the Presbyterian church and academy Hamilton had attended only ten years before, a Loyalist tried to visit his old neighbors to collect bills they owed him. A crowd immediately surrounded him, yelling, "Hang him up! Hang him up!" until a justice of the peace persuaded them to escort him to the New York ferry landing. Word came from the South, where the Patriot-Loyalist guerrilla warfare had been recent and most savage, of the fate of Loyalist men, women, and children who tried to stay behind and hold on to their homes and businesses when the British sailed away. "No sooner had the evacuation taken place at Charleston," wrote the Loyalist historian Thomas Jones,

> than the rebels, like so many furies, entered the town. The Loyalists were seized, shoved into dungeons, tied and whipped, tarred and feathered, dragged to horse ponds and drenched till near death, carried about the town in carts with labels upon their breasts and backs with TORY in capitals. All the Loyalists were turned out of their houses and obliged to sleep in the streets and fields. A universal plunder took place. A gallows was erected and twenty-four reputable Loyalists hanged in sight of the British fleet with the army and thirty-five thousand Loyalists looking on.[1]

In New York State, more than one fourth the prewar population was driven out. Hamilton's reunion with his old friend Hercules Mulligan bore fruit for both men. Mulligan helped Hamilton rent an office at 56 Wall Street and the house next door at No. 57. There, Hamilton was able to settle his small family while he set to work building up his law practice. While some historians have doubted the extent of his friendship with Hamilton, at least in part because a spy's life defies documentation, Hamilton and Mulligan pitched into many postwar civic causes, including helping to found, a little more than a year later on January 25, 1785, the Society for Promoting the Manumission of Slaves in New York.

Honoring the memory of his dear friend John Laurens, and never forgetting the slave markets of his St. Croix childhood, Hamilton became a prime mover in the early abolitionist group. He pressured the state legislature and helped to raise money to buy and free slaves. The society's founders, meeting at the Merchants Coffee House, elected Hamilton chairman to draw up recommendations for "a line of conduct" for any "members who still possessed slaves." He also established a registry for manumitted slaves, listing their names and ages, "to detect attempts to deprive such manumitted persons of their liberty." Hamilton, his college roommate, Robert Troup, and Hercules Mulligan were among the large number of New Yorkers who signed the petition, probably drafted by Hamilton and sent to the New York Assembly in March 1786. He called attention to the fundamental contradiction between the state lawmakers' Revolutionary principle of personal liberty and their religious beliefs on the one hand, and the continuance of slavery in New York: "Although free by the laws of God, they are held in slavery in New York." New York's slaves—"those unhappy people"—remained, amid freedom, in "miseries" that had begun with "the practice of exporting them like cattle." Hamilton, in writing the petition, alluded especially to the African trade with "the West Indies and the Southern states" and called on the New York Assembly to ban further importation of slaves from Africa and thus end "a commerce so repugnant to humanity and so inconsistent" with the ideals of freedom and justice "which should distinguish a free and enlightened people."[2]

Within months of the claim in the Declaration of Independence that "all men are created equal," Gouverneur Morris and John Jay had tried, in 1777, to insert a clause into the New York state constitution "recommending" the abolition of slavery. But they had run into a solid wall of resistance. Jay himself owned five slaves, Governor Clinton, eight. In 1781, in response to an offer of freedom by the British commander-in-chief, Sir Henry Clinton, for any slaves who remained loyal to the Crown, the New York legislature grudgingly agreed to manumit any slaves who had taken up arms against the British. When the Quakers freed all the slaves they owned in New York, few imitated them. It was not until after Hamilton, Mulligan, and their friends organized the Manumission Society that the state legislature brought in a bill late in 1785 providing for the gradual abolition of slavery. But the bill passed only over the fierce opposition of assemblymen from agricultural Kings, Richmond, and Ulster counties, whose predominantly Dutch constituents still depended on slave labor. After all that, the states' Council of Revision vetoed the bill because it did not include the right to vote or to hold public office for freed blacks.

Only after a bitter fight in the legislature did it enact a watereddown bill, a voluntary emancipation law that allowed masters to free slaves between ages twenty-one and fifty without obligation for their subsequent care, and then only after the local overseers for the poor first certified, in writing, that the slaves would be able to provide for themselves. Owners of slaves over age fifty had to post a bond of 200 pounds, a considerable amount, guaranteeing that the freed slave wouldn't become a burden on the public charge. The "poor certificate" was to become the hardest hurdle to overcome: in the next fifteen years, few New Yorkers followed the lead of Hamilton and his friends. Hamilton himself never owned a slave, but he could never convince his wife to free her one slave, her body servant.

During that time, the Manumission Society was able to concentrate only on keeping up to date its registry of freedmen to prevent their reenslavement, and the society publicized cases of abuse by masters, even though the law provided no punishments. In 1786, the society pushed a bill through the legislature freeing all slaves from confiscated Tory estates that still remained state property. The society that year also founded a one-room African Free School on Cliff Street where, besides learning to read and write, boys were supposed to study the Puritan ethics of how to keep themselves from "running into practices of immorality or sinking into habits of idleness." By 1792, girls also were admitted. To be admitted, the freed black child had to pledge to stay sober, stay away from slaves, and not incite them, and live clean lives, that is, to avoid "fiddling, dancing or any noisy entertainments in their houses."

A strong reaction to the work of this antislavery group came swiftly. Many New Yorkers, anticipating further reforms, sold their slaves to the agents of Southern plantation owners. In 1788, the society pressured the state legislature to ban the further sale of slaves to another state and to prohibit importation of any more slaves into New York, yet it failed to persuade the state or New York City to close the port to ships involved in the slave trade, as other Northern states did. The 1790 census revealed why emancipation seemed to become more distant by the year. Only seven years after independence, the percentage of slaves in New York City had fallen by half to 10 percent of the population, and roughly one third of the city's blacks were now free. That first federal census showed why, in absolute terms, slavery was spreading in the southern six counties, where three of every four blacks were still enslaved. The 9,447 men, women, and children who were still slaves had a market value of $1.5 million, about $20 million in today's money, and represented one of the state's leading forms of investment. Slavery was reestablished in New York State and the legislature had just adopted a new slave code that guaranteed the institution's survival. Indeed, one in five households in New York City, including all but the very poorest, owned at least one slave. Fully two thirds of all merchants kept slaves as domestic servants who worked as cooks, butlers, gardeners, and stable hands. One in eight artisans, numerically the largest group of slave owners, depended on slave labor in their workshops, breweries, ropewalks, shipyards, and sail lofts. In the ten-mile radius, the ring of rural counties feeding the fast-growing city, 40 percent of white households, a higher percentage than in any Southern state, owned slaves. In some parts of Kings County, two out of every three white households owned slaves.[3]

HAMILTON'S LIFELONG friendship with Hercules Mulligan extended to his taking Mulligan's son without fee as his law clerk for three years, a service for which he usually charged a $150 fee, about $2,000 in today's money. Young law students flocked to study with the dashing, eloquent Hamilton, whose law practice was flourishing. Hamilton became an overnight success because he wasn't afraid to take on unpopular causes. Even before the British had evacuated the city, wealthy Loyalist exiles hired him because of his moderate views. When, in March 1783, New York passed a Trespass Act that allowed lawsuits for damages against the property of Patriots seized or used by the British or Loyalists, Hamilton alone spoke up to warn about the danger. On his way home from Congress in August 1783, he wrote in alarm to James Duane, his fellow New York delegate to Congress and soon-to-be mayor of New York City, that indictments under the state's Confiscation Act "have given great alarm here: many who have all along talked of staying now talk of going. We have already lost too large a number of valuable citizens." In all, thirty-five thousand Loyalists sailed out of New York harbor in 1783, roughly equal to the seaport's wartime population.[4]

Governor Clinton had unleashed the anti-Tory campaign when the assembly convened in New York City Hall for the first time since independence. In the opening session, he attacked "cruelty and rapine" by the Loyalists amid "the ruins of this once-flourishing city." A series of Sons of Liberty mass meetings led to a huge demonstration on the common by the end of March 1784. Particularly obnoxious Tories were tarred and feathered or hamstrung. Hamilton feared that the persecution of the Loyalists and their resultant flight would seriously weaken not only the state's but also the new nation's economy. Other worried statesmen gathered around his banner as he made the difficult and dangerous decision to challenge New York's anti-Loyalist frenzy. Robert R. Livingston, chancellor of the New York bar, agreed with Hamilton that the "violent spirit of persecution" was motivated not only by a "blind spirit of revenge" but "the most sordid interest." The persecution was "unmixed with pure or patriotic measures":

> One wishes to possess the house of some wretched Tory, another fears him as a rival in his trade, a fourth wishes to get rid of his debts by shaking off his creditors or reduce the cost of living by depopulating the town.[5]

While many of the city's more conservative lawyers and businessmen privately agreed with Hamilton, he alone had the courage to go public with his indictment of the majority in the state legislature and in the streets of New York City who were violating Articles Five and Six of the peace treaty not only by refusing to restore confiscated Loyalist property but by ignoring the ban on further confiscations or prosecutions. Prompted by vituperative articles in the Patriot press that insisted all Loyalists make a "voluntary departure" or face exile, Hamilton penned a pair of essays he signed "Phocion." He chose as his nom de plume an Athenian general who had proven his patriotism in battle but won lenient terms from the conqueror and gained the confidence of both sides. In his *Lives*, Plutarch wrote that Phocion had "espoused the cause of those who differed most from him when they needed his patronage," advocating the "forgiveness of those who had been banished."

In two small pamphlets, Hamilton accused state legislators and the New York City newspapers of fanning the anti-Loyalist hatred. "Such inflammatory and pernicious" behavior was threatening "all private security and genuine liberty" and was violating "the most solemn obligations" of the peace treaty. Hamilton wrote he had "too deep a share in the common exertions in this revolution to be willing to see its fruits blasted by the violence of rash or unprincipled men without at least protesting." In the recent New York City elections for representatives to the state legislature, the Loyalists had been the major issue and their denunciation particularly vehement. As Hamilton's first "Phocion" pamphlet came off the press, the first signs of political parties were appearing in New York along the fault line of the treatment of Loyalists. Some New York Patriots formed a Whig Society to put pressure on the city's aldermen to prosecute, penalize, or drive out the Tories, a name Loyalists never called themselves.

Arguing that these were not true Whigs unless they would cherish legal liberty, hold individual rights sacred, and condemn and punish no man without trial, Hamilton castigated these Whig pretenders for wanting to expel "a large number of their fellow citizens, untried" or disenfranchise them "without the judgment of their peers." The New York State constitution guaranteed no one could be disenfranchised without due process of law, Hamilton reminded his readers. He warned that the state government risked being regarded as a tyranny if it punished a "whole class of citizens" by any general description. The result would be a restricted electorate, "a small number of partisans" who would "establish an aristocracy or an oligarchy." Without a hearing or a trial, "no man can be safe." If "a few designing men" overleaped the barriers of the state constitution, they would violate "the solemn engagements of the United States" and become "the scorn of nations." Ending with a plea for moderation, Hamilton contended that truly great victors such as Caesar Augustus and Queen Elizabeth I had forsworn vengeance against their enemies. "Their moderation gave a stability to their government which nothing else could have affected. This was the secret of uniting all parties."[6]

This was Hamilton's first postwar political salvo, and it shocked many of his neighbors. Why would the heroic leader of New York's soldiers in the climactic charge of the last battle of the Revolution risk the ruin of his political future? A bit of anonymous doggerel in the *New York Journal* appeared shortly after "Phocion's" blast, obviously addressed to Hamilton:

> To Lysander
> Wilt thou, Lysander, on this well-earned height,
> Forget thy merits and thy taste for same,
> Descend to learn of law, her arts and slight,
> And, for a job, to damn your honored name?[7]

It was hard for Hamilton to refute the accusation that he was cynically arguing from self-interest, especially after so many Loyalists, including scores who had already fled, paid his 6-pound (about $250) retainer. Between 1784 and 1791, Hamilton defended some forty-four Loyalists prosecuted under the Trespass Act and twenty under the Confiscation Act. Yet, these sixty-four cases aside, he seems to have been sincere in his larger concern that the crowned heads of Europe, shocked by a successful revolution, would rub their hands with glee if Americans dishonored the peace treaty and fell to preying on now defenseless refugees from the war.

Hamilton's most important civil case pitted the fragile young American democracy against international law. Under the Trespass Act of 1783, defendants were prohibited from pleading that they had acted under orders of the occupying British. Contradicting international law and established legal tradition, the act also denied defendants the right to appeal to a higher court. Passed while Hamilton was in Philadelphia, serving in Congress, by New York legislators who were seeking to obstruct ratification of the peace treaty, the Trespass Act openly violated the law of nations by contravening the very peace treaty that granted American independence. It ignored, as well, the mandate of Congress to the several states. Hamilton decided to make the suit of Mrs. Elizabeth Rutgers against Loyalists Joshua Waddington and Evelyn Pierrepont the test case. Mrs. Rutgers, a seventy-something widow and the aunt of New York State's attorney general, fled the city when the British conquered it in 1776, abandoning substantial property, including a large brewery and alehouse on Maiden Lane. Waddington and Pierrepont refurbished the gutted buildings in 1778 and made, as one historian put it, "a whopping profit throughout the war," escaping to England with their profits at war's end. The brewery had burned mysteriously, possibly torched by an anti-Tory mob, and lay in ruins when Mrs. Rutgers returned to the city. She sued under the Trespass Act for 8,000 pounds, about $325,000 in today's money.

Hamilton saw that the case was far from clear cut. The two Loyalist brewmasters had spent 700 pounds to fix up the brewery and had themselves lost 4,000 pounds in goods in the fire. Yet the central point of the case was the fact that the Loyalist brewmasters had taken over the brewery under British Army authority. As Hamilton knew from reading his Vattel, an occupying army had the right to use all conquered property in any enemy territory it held. Mrs. Rutgers, under the general amnesty extended by the peace treaty, had no right to any compensation. The case hinged on the precise dates of military authorizations: from 1778 to 1780, Waddington and Pierrepont had used the buildings without paying any rent. After a 1780 order from General Clinton, they had to begin paying 150 pounds annual rent to the Trinity Church Vestry for the Poor.[8]

Cleverly, Hamilton had prepared the ground for his defense by publishing his two "Phocion" pamphlets, which led opposing counsel, including his college roommate, Robert Troup, to believe that he would, as usual, follow his printed arguments point by point in court. Because he was sure Mrs. Rutgers's lawyers would prepare just such a point-by-point rebuttal, Hamilton also mapped out an alternate legal strategy. In the crowded courtroom of City Hall on June 29, 1784, the handsome, flamboyant Hamilton rose to argue before the Mayor's Court of New York, made up of Mayor James Duane, his erstwhile law preceptor, five aldermen, and city recorder Richard Varick, also a former aide to Washington. Duane and Varick sympathized with Hamilton. New York Attorney General Egbert Benson pressed his aunt's case.

According to legal historian Julius Goebel, Hamilton was introducing a new legal technique in his New York cases: he carefully prepared in writing the arguing points for each case, even if, in court, he set them aside to adjust for contingencies. His argument in the Rutgers case followed three major points. First, New York's Trespass Act violated the laws of war. New York's own constitution embraced English common law, incorporating it as part of New York's laws. Common law included the law of nations. The law of nations included the laws of war. In Hamilton's second argument, he pointed out to the court that, under the Articles of Confederation, only Congress had the power to enter into peace treaties. The law of nations demanded a general amnesty. Congress, by ratifying the treaty, accepted the general amnesty. Article Six of the treaty expressly forbade further confiscations or prosecutions for the role anyone on either side had played during the war. Third, Hamilton argued, the New York City Mayor's Court had to decide whether the state Trespass Act conflicted with any higher law. The state law violated the law of nations, the peace treaty, and the mandate of Congress. Therefore, the city court must declare the state statute null and void.

Mayor Duane, in his written opinion, stopped short of establishing a precedent of judicial review, "for this were to set the judicial above the legislature." Nevertheless, he conceded Hamilton's entire line of reasoning and ruled in favor of Waddington. The city court decided that Mrs. Rutgers was entitled to only 800 pounds damages, not 8,000 pounds, and that as rent for the first two years. Hamilton had won his case by arguing, for the first time, the principle of judicial review that would eventually grow only a few years later into the establishment of the United States federal judiciary, including the Supreme Court. His thinking on the subject would evolve over the next three years, maturing into Federalist Numbers 22 and 78. But, for the moment, he had made it quite clear that one of the principal defects in the Articles of Confederation was the lack of any judiciary. He had also argued successfully that international treaties must be considered the law of the United States. Only a supreme international tribunal, and not any state law, could invalidate them, and none existed.[9]

HAMILTON'S CONSPICUOUS success as the leading lawyer in New York City by 1786 (when he was thirty-one and when there were only thirty-five attorneys in the city) was bound to create jealousy, and it took the channel of his defense of the Loyalists. While some of his colleagues good-naturedly shrugged, assuming he took such cases only because of the fees, Governor Clinton and his supporters were furious at Hamilton. Clinton would not accept Hamilton's warning that, if New York dishonored any provision of the peace treaty, the British, who still occupied their forts on New York's northern and western frontiers, would feel justified in dragging their feet in evacuating the forts, jeopardizing the state's flourishing fur trade with the Indians. Clinton already had a reputation for harshness in his dealings with the Indians. As commanding general of New York militia, he had unleashed his troops on their 1779 campaign of destruction through the Six Nations homeland, devastating their villages and driving them back onto British protection at Fort Niagara. The influence of the British still radiated from their Great Lakes forts at Niagara and at Detroit, Sandusky, and Michilimackinac. Yet Indian raids and retaliation by frontiersmen were continuing, long after Yorktown and the commencement of peace talks. Frontiersmen, Hamilton insisted, jeopardized the peace treaty as they remained bent on killing Indians and seizing their lands.

The cycle of revenge and reprisal raged from the Delaware River to the Ohio Valley. The death of pro-Revolutionary Delaware chief White Eyes and the succession of a pro-British chief, Captain Pipe, gave Pennsylvanians a pretext to attack Christian Indians at the Moravian mission of Gnadenheutten, near Bethlehem. Ninety-six unarmed, hymn-singing Delawares died in an unprovoked massacre. Their killings touched off the torture and burning at the stake of Colonel William Crawford, a Continental officer, captured in a skirmish on the Upper Sandusky River in Ohio. Erroneously held accountable for the Gnadenheutten massacre, Crawford was captured by Loyalist Rangers and Delaware Indians. The Indians scalped him alive and then, according to a Loyalist eyewitness, "laid hot ashes upon his head after which they roasted him by a slow fire."

Reports of continuing frontier atrocities thoroughly alarmed Hamilton. From his seat in Congress, Hamilton had lectured Governor Clinton on the "intemperate proceedings" of his administration in passing the Trespass Act and other anti-Loyalist measures. Then, early in 1783, many towns in New York State adopted resolutions forbidding Loyalists to settle within their limits. Statewide, Loyalists were also barred from practicing the legal and medical professions, from voting, from holding public office, and from serving on juries. New Yorkers, Hamilton maintained, "ought to take care that nothing is done to furnish a pretext on the other side even for delaying, much less for refusing, execution of the treaty." Hamilton was especially opposed to "violations going on in form of law." Further confiscations, especially in New York City, were "a palpable infraction" of Article Six of the peace treaty.[10]

Clinton merely snorted. He exclaimed that he would "rather roast in hell to all eternity than be dependent on Great Britain or show mercy to a damned Tory." Clinton's political allies attacked Hamilton for criticizing their party. Clinton accused Hamilton of exhibiting "that great disqualification for a statesman, an uncontrollable warmth of temper." In a very rare apology, Hamilton, in his second "Phocion" pamphlet, apologized for his "injudicious appearance of warmth," but he assured Clinton it was aimed at only "a *very small* number of men who are manifestly aiming at nothing but the acquisition of power and profit."[11]

While the public sensed that Hamilton had won an important victory in *Rutgers v. Waddington*, the state legislature took it as a direct challenge to its authority, adopting a resolution that attacked Duane's decision as "subversive of all law and good order." If a court could "dispense with and act in direct violation of a plain and known law in the state," it would "end all our dear-bought rights and privileges and legislatures [would] become useless." Accusing the New York Mayor's Court of usurping its authority, an assembly committee said Duane and his panel of jurists had "assumed and exercised the power to set aside an act of the state." The city court's decision was "inconsistent with the nature and genius of our government." A motion to impeach Duane lost, thirty-one to nine, in the assembly.

But a new fault line had opened up. Now not only were state governments at odds with Congress, but local and state authorities were clashing over whom, and how, to govern. Hamilton had emerged as the champion of the disenfranchised Loyalists. By 1787, after a three-year personal crusade, he successfully won, mostly in the courts and finally in the legislature, repeal of the Trespass, Citation, and Confiscation Acts on the grounds he first spelled out as "Phocion" and then argued in the Rutgers case. New York became, at Hamilton's insistence, the first state to restore the full civil rights of the Loyalists.

At the same time, Hamilton was becoming the advocate of New York's commercial interests. But his conspicuous pro-business stance, his consistent defense of the Loyalists, and his liberal antislavery views increasingly put him at odds with Governor Clinton and his adherents, especially after the Rutgers case. Tensions were bound to run high, now that the New York Assembly and the Congress of the United States crowded into City Hall along with the seaport's Common Council, its municipal government. Only Hamilton's status as war hero saved him from the anger of the Sons of Liberty as it continued its attacks on suspected British sympathizers.

Alexander Hamilton did little to avoid the censure of his critics, especially Governor Clinton. To Robert Morris, he wrote that Clinton "has declined in popularity." In fact, Clinton's popularity among farmers, artisans, and workers—the majority outside and inside New York City—remained relatively constant over the next twenty-five years as he became the leader of the Anti-Federalists, and then as a leading follower of Thomas Jefferson, two-term president of the United States. Yet, writing privately to Robert Morris, Hamilton opined that Governor Clinton suffered from "a defect of qualifications" to be governor. "His passions are much warmer than his judgment is enlightened." Privately and publicly, Hamilton accused Clinton of profiting personally from his policies of confiscation, intimidation, and hostility to Indians and Loyalists.

In fact, it was his detestation of profiteering from the wartime, and now postwar, confiscations that drove Hamilton to publicly break with many of New York's wealthy Patriots. In particular, he decried the behavior of former New York delegate to Congress Robert R. Livingston, a Hudson Valley manor lord and leading Revolutionary who, in 1783, resigned as the U.S. secretary for foreign affairs to become chancellor of New York. Livingston's job change paralleled a radical shift in his declared view of the Loyalist problem. In 1779, he had written to John Jay, "Never was there a greater compound of folly, avarice and injustice than our [New York's] confiscation bill." In 1783, he had echoed Hamilton's view: "I seriously lament with you the violent spirit of persecution." It was, he had written, "unmixed with pure or patriotic motives." Yet, only a few months later, on January 25, 1784, Livingston wrote to Jay in Paris to arrange credit for him in Europe of 6,000 to 8,000 pounds to help him buy up confiscated Loyalist lands in New York. The state was selling the lands in large blocs at public auction at a time when only the wealthiest had any cash. Even depreciated state securities were being accepted for payment at par. To Hamilton, this was "the most sordid interest." To many New York landowners, Livingston could justify his speculations by pointing out that his vast landholdings had been damaged by Loyalist and British troops during the war, that his tenants were now behind on their rents, and that he had not been paid his salaries either as a state official or as a member of Congress.[12]

Ironically, Livingston's scheme fizzled because many European bankers were cool to the idea of being repaid with New York's depreciated currency. Dutch bankers twice turned down Jay's requests on Livingston's behalf. In New York, the Chancellor, as he was known, could borrow only about $12,500, of which $2,000 was a personal loan from Governor Clinton himself. Livingston was able to buy several brick town houses in New York City with this money.

Livingston's land-engrossing scheme involved many other New York Revolutionary leaders and precipitated a race to form the first

bank in the city's history. Livingston and his friends in state government, unable to come up with foreign capital, next tried to get the
state government to finance their speculations in government property.
His next scheme was to persuade the legislature, where he had enormous influence, to establish a land bank, no ordinary bank. Private
stockholders were to pony up a total of $250,000 in hard money col-
lectively. The state would then match it, two for one, with paper
money. This, in turn, was to be issued to the stockholders against the
security of the mortgages on their real estate. This state land bank
supposedly would create millions of dollars in new currency. Relying
on their influence with Clinton and on cash payoffs or shares of
stock distributed among upstate legislators, Livingston and friends, on
February 17, 1784, presented their formal petition to the New York
Assembly.

To his brother-in-law John Church, Hamilton wrote snidely, "The
Chancellor [Livingston] had taken so much pains with the country
members [of the legislature] that they all began to be persuaded that
the land bank was the true Philosopher's Stone that was to turn all
their rocks and trees into gold. I thought it necessary," Hamilton told
Church, the largest stockholder in Morris's Bank of North America,
"for the sake of the commercial interests of the state to start an opposition to this scheme." He pointed out the "absurdity" of the land
bank to "the most intelligent merchants." The city's merchants
induced Hamilton to launch a "money-bank."[13]

In March 1784, Hamilton drew up the outline for a charter for the
Bank of New York, America's second bank, with an original capital of
$125,000 (about $2 million today). Taking a leading role in setting up
the bank and becoming one of its original directors, Hamilton, bon-
ing up on how banking worked, steered many of his wealthy in-laws
and Loyalist clients to BONY, in the process pulling the plug on Livingston's land bank scheme. But Livingston and Hamilton backers in
the legislature deadlocked. Neither scheme received a charter. Boldly,
Hamilton persuaded his codirectors to open the bank anyway in July
1784, and Robert Livingston, chancellor of the New York bar, became
a political ally of Governor Clinton—and an enemy of Hamilton.

The banking controversy in New York ran parallel to a crisis in

Pennsylvania, the wealthiest state in post-Revolutionary America. To compete with Morris's Bank of North America, a coalition of speculators, Loyalists, and radical politicians in the fall of 1784 won control of the Pennsylvania legislature, revoked Morris's bank charter, and pushed through a bill that set up a state-owned bank. Pennsylvania took over servicing its own war debts but also its share of the national debt owed in the state. Of the $400,000 in paper capital, two thirds of the newly minted money went toward paying back interest on the national debt. The rest backed loans written against real estate mortgages three times the value of the loans. A speculator could borrow 100 pounds from the state against the collateral of land he already owned, then with it buy public securities on the open market at a third of face value, then turn these securities over to the state at par in exchange for public lands, sell the land, and repay his loan, reaping a windfall profit. For Philadelphia speculators, there were windfall profits, but Hamilton saw only more commercial capital being drained away. Yet he was intrigued by the possibility of adapting the Pennsylvania plan for a national scheme. For the moment, however, Pennsylvania broke ranks with the other states. If others followed suit, it could prove fatal to the already nearly bankrupt national government. Among the speculators seeking huge profits at the expense of the Confederation was one of its founders, Declaration of Independence signer James Wilson, attorney for the Bank of North America. He had received nearly $100,000 in loans on doubtful security. Stockholders of Morris's Bank of North America, watching with alarm as the value of their stock slid from $500 a share to $370 after Pennsylvania annulled its charter, consulted Hamilton for legal advice. He recommended instituting a lawsuit in the Pennsylvania courts to test whether the bank's corporate existence, originally chartered by Congress, still survived.

Hamilton's deepening involvement in banking only soured him on the financial speculators who were further weakening the national government. Building a lucrative law practice in New York City by representing its businessmen, he could see that the actions of the individual states were only undercutting the reputation of the Confederation in Europe and playing into the hands of the British. The

New York merchants watched helplessly as the British reimposed the Navigation Act of 1756, allowing only English ships to transport goods to English ports in Canada and the Caribbean, an obvious attempt to destroy the American merchant marine. As American trade withered, the Spanish and Portuguese joined their treaty allies the British, and closed their Caribbean ports to the American carrying trade.

Watching as the vital New York–Caribbean trading networks of his youth shriveled and died, Hamilton groped for an answer. He had spurned nomination to the New York Assembly, yet he could not be content to sit on the sidelines or merely reap the rewards of his burgeoning law practice. As he always did in times of crisis, he sought solutions in books. In the quiet of his study in the house he had bought on Wall Street—Aaron Burr had handled the real estate settlement for the seller—Hamilton, able to sight-read French, devoured the three-volume memoirs of Jacques Necker, France's reformist minister of finance. Hamilton found in Necker's autobiography detailed, practical fiscal management. More than this, Hamilton imbibed from the Swiss banker-turned-politician the great influence on national affairs an active finance minister could have. Hamilton, looking into Necker's works, saw himself in a mirror. Necker's closing lines riveted Hamilton:

> There are men whose zeal ought not to be cooled: such are those who, being conscious that they are qualified for great things, have a noble thirst for glory; who, being impelled by the force of their genius, feel themselves too confined within the narrow limits of common occupations; and those, more especially who, being struck with the idea of the public good, meditate on it and make it the most important business of their lives. Proceed, you who, after silencing self-love, find your resemblance in this picture.[14]

The editors of the Hamilton papers cite numerous instances in Hamilton's reports and letters where he praises Necker or was directly influenced by his thinking. It may have been Hamilton's friend the Marquis de Lafayette who, reading Necker's visionary phrases, thought they suited Hamilton and brought them to him when he returned to America late in 1784, visiting Washington first at Mount Vernon and then touring the new nation with an entourage of young French aides and liveried servants. He refused Washington's invitation to accompany him on a voyage into the Ohio Valley where the retired general was having trouble collecting rents on his thousands of acres of lands. Described by Thomas Jefferson, the new American envoy to France, as possessing "a canine appetite for fame," Lafayette was eager to see as much as possible of the young nation he had fought for, and he headed south for a six-week tour while Washington rode west. Because of the popularity of his American wartime adventures, Lafayette had risen rapidly in French politics since he had last visited Alexander Hamilton. Two years younger than Hamilton, Lafayette had been promoted by Louis XVI over the heads of many older generals to the rank of *marechal de champ*, making him a general officer in the French army before he reached twenty-five, the French age of majority. He had been scornfully dubbed *le Vassington français* by rivals at court when he bought a splendid Paris town house in the rue de Bourbon and then insisted on following the American style of family life, which meant spending his days and evenings with his wife and children instead of gambling and taking a mistress.

Lafayette thrilled as he pranced through peacetime America in his splendid white uniform on his tall white horse, amazed at the warmth of his reception as he paraded south, then north, with two young French noblemen and their servants. Throngs of Revolutionary War veterans turned out in the first opportunity since war's end to celebrate anything. For the veterans, politicians, women, and children, it was an occasion to celebrate, to burnish the memories of the sufferings the French had endured beside the Americans, a respite from the depression that had engulfed the cashless, divided, devastated country. Lafayette's emotional reunion with Hamilton came as a badly needed tonic. Lafayette arrived in New York City with Congressman Madison, who was on his way to the new session of Congress. Hamilton could not travel on with his two friends, however, when they rode north to an Indian conference at Fort Schuyler on the Mohawk River. Hamilton had decided to stay close to Betsy. By the time Lafayette arrived in Albany, Philip Schuyler already knew of the birth of Angelica Hamilton, the couple's first daughter, named after Betsy's sister. "With all the warmth of my long and tender friendship," Lafayette wrote, "I congratulate you upon the birth of your daughter." Lafayette had come to the Indian conference at a propitious moment. Many northern Indians, facing eviction from the new states, remembered the more fatherly treatment by the French and thronged to meet Lafayette:

> It has been found that my influence with the Indians, both friendly and hostile tribes, was much greater than the commissioners and even myself had conceived—so that I was requested, even by every one of those [tribes] to speak to those nations.[15]

Lafayette's appearance when he arrived also must have intrigued the Indians. Madison wrote Jefferson in Paris that Lafayette wore a gummed taffeta raincoat that had been covered in Paris newspapers that had stuck to it in his trunk at sea. As they rode the narrow Indian trail single file, Madison could read the French news on Lafayette's back. Lafayette still had to visit Hartford, Boston, and Newport before he rendezvoused with Washington again at Mount Vernon, but he promised to return to New York to pay a courtesy visit to Congress before he said his adieu to Hamilton and sailed home to France. When the adulation of Bostonians delayed him again, Lafayette wrote Hamilton on October 22 that he still planned for them "to spend some days together. My stay in your city has been too short—far inadequate to the feelings of my gratitude." But Hamilton had little time to grieve over the delay. Baron Steuben, the impecunious drillmaster of Valley Forge, was in town, and Hamilton wrote out in English his speech accepting "the freedom of the city," honorary citizenship. Steuben was busily lobbying Congress for compensation for his services to America.

Carrying the pollen of revolutionary ideas not of his making, Lafayette brought with him news from Virginia of a plan, the joint thinking of Washington, Jefferson, and Madison, to organize a company to develop an inland waterway. The Potomac Company would link the Potomac, by a series of canals, roads, and interior rivers, with the Ohio River to open up the Old Northwest and make it possible to bring the harvests of the American interior down the Potomac to Alexandria en route to the Atlantic.

Lafayette and Hamilton had other business. Both were founding members of the Society of the Cincinnati, named for a Roman, Lucius Quintus Cincinnatus, who twice left his farm to defend the republic and then returned to his plow. When the Continental Army was disbanded, Henry Knox won Washington's support for a society of officers. Steuben had presided at the first meeting in May 1783. The second paragraph of its constitution read that its purpose was "to perpetuate" the "remembrance of this vast event [the Revolution]" as well as "the mutual friendships formed." What triggered angry attacks by three noncombatants—Benjamin Franklin, John Adams, and Samuel Adams—was the society's hereditary nature, passing down from officers through "their eldest male posterity." While the society turned out to be only an innocent veterans' lodge, angry Rhode Islanders disenfranchised members in their state, and patriotic clubs such as the Tammany Club in New York City formed to resist its influence. Lafayette was instrumental to its founding in France, where its zealous members used it as a vehicle to bring pressure to bear on Congress for back pay. George Washington was the society's first president-general; Hamilton, founder of the Society's New York State branch, was its second national president.

In its early days, the society served a less pretentious function: helping threadbare officers survive. Writing back and forth to Washington about the society's affairs, Hamilton urged Washington to use his influence to help fellow member Steuben. "The Poor Baron is still soliciting Congress and has every prospect of indigence." Hamilton's cash book shows that, over the next four years, until Steuben finally received a government pension, Hamilton paid a whopping 200-pound note Steuben owed and advanced him another 461 pounds in cash, in all about $27,000 in today's dollars—and there is no record Steuben ever was able to repay him.[16]

* * *

IN A rare moment of interstate cooperation at the birth of the nation, Virginia in 1776 had granted Maryland jurisdiction over the Potomac River. On June 2, 1784, James Madison, who recently had arranged to have himself appointed chairman of the commerce committee of the Virginia House of Delegates, sponsored a resolution to pave the way for joint Virginia-Maryland jurisdiction over the Potomac. Madison had himself appointed to the waterway commission that also included George Mason and Edmund Randolph. The commissioners were to negotiate with Maryland. All through the summer, Tidewater taverns and drawing rooms buzzed with rumors about the waterway. Everybody knew George Washington was behind it and that Virginia's commissioners would be negotiating with their good friends in Maryland. That fall, workers built huts on both sides of the Seneca Falls of the Potomac.

On November 15, 1784, when Virginia's House of Delegates convened in Richmond, Washington appeared with a "numerous and respectable" group of Virginians and Marylanders who told anyone who would listen that the canal project was "one of the grandest chains for preserving the Federal Union." Washington had already grown impatient with the "limping behavior" of the two state legislatures to fund the project and had decided the project "had better be placed in the hands of a corporate company." The company was to be capitalized at $1 million (about $13 million today) and shares would be sold to stockholders. The proposal now sailed through both legislatures in a single day: on January 25, 1785, both states adopted identical bills. A triumphant Madison relayed the good news to Jefferson in Paris. So confident were the lawmakers on both sides of the Potomac that each state subscribed to fifty of the needed two hundred shares to begin construction. Washington bought five shares and armtwisted Robert Morris to build a large tobacco warehouse at Alexandria. One German visitor to Mount Vernon reported that salesman Washington bored him for two days with facts and figures.

The negotiations between the two states' commissioners were scheduled for March 1785 in Alexandria. They heard that more than double the number of shares, some five hundred, had already been sold to Americans. But the canal hit an unexpected snag at this eight-day Alexandria meeting: Maryland's delegates refused to discuss anything until Virginia agreed to forgo collection of tolls at the entrance to Chesapeake Bay. Toll collections for the waterway would be allowed only at the sites of the waterfalls removed from the river and along a toll road. Virginia's delegates had instructions not to yield on tolls but, fearing the talks would collapse, huddled with Washington, supposedly a spectator, then decided to ignore their instructions. The commissioners further agreed to allow joint commercial and fishing rights. Then Maryland delegate Thomas Stone introduced a resolution that called for a joint application to Congress to request permission to organize a small independent navy in case the federal government, which had no navy, failed to protect the waterway. Stone then urged that the joint commission apply to Congress for joint Maryland-Virginia regulation of state currencies and import duties and hold annual meetings to review commercial regulations. Stone proposed that delegates be invited from Pennsylvania and Delaware to their next meeting, scheduled for Annapolis in May 1786. The delegates agreed unanimously.

The depression in trade in America in the mid-1780s caused growing political discontent as well as economic hardship. With the public credit destroyed, currency in free fall, the loss of British and French gold, widespread unemployment as the army disbanded, uncontrolled land speculation, and the loss of the West Indian trade and the fur trade to Canada, the Confederation teetered on the brink of collapse. Every state attempted to save itself by some means of counteracting the general business distress, and all of them failed. In New York, Governor Clinton and his constituency, mostly farmers north of Westchester County, distrusted and resisted the calls for stronger national solutions to interstate problems coming from New York City merchants, most of whom they put down as too pro-British. Clinton, sixteen years Hamilton's senior, wielded growing power as a populist. He stoutly refused the call of Congress for a special session to consider customs duties to support the Confederation.

Just such spite between state and nation had grown even sharper between New York and New Jersey. New York demanded a customs duty on every boatload of firewood from New Jersey vital to fueling and heating New York City: "every wood-boat and shallop from New Jersey of more than 12 tons shall be regularly entered and cleared out at the customs house as if they had arrived from any other foreign port." Pinched New Jersey boatmen put pressure on their legislature to tax New York for the lighthouse and plot around it on Sandy Hook that belonged to New York City. New Jersey resented its popular conception, spawned by Benjamin Franklin, that it was "a barrel tapped at both ends." In a letter to Jefferson, Madison characterized North Carolina, trapped between Virginia and South Carolina, as "a patient bleeding from both arms." Connecticut exacted heavier customs duties on imports from Massachusetts than from Great Britain.

In 1784, Congress had asked the states to grant it control over commerce by allowing it to prohibit the entry of ships and goods from countries that did not have commercial treaties with the United States. Eleven states eventually agreed. New York, with its vital port, balked; by 1786, even Rhode Island had approved the customs duties Hamilton had sought during his first stint in Congress. But again, New York refused to cooperate, and under the rule of unanimity of the Confederation, one state could block any measure. By the summer of 1786, the postwar depression had reached a critical stage and no sector of the American economy was immune. International trade had all but stopped. Farmers could not pay their taxes or their loans and faced widespread foreclosures. Scottish merchants who operated hundreds of country stores had cut off credit, even refusing to supply seed for farmers, and were suing to collect the debts on their books. Most import-export trade once again moved between England and the United States. Imports had dropped from 2.3 million pounds in 1785 to 1.6 million pounds in 1786, nearly a thirty percent decline. Farm wages had dropped more than 20 percent in five years. Several states had passed "stay" laws, stopping collections of debts to meet demands for relief from the vicious combination of a money shortage, high taxes, and insistent creditors. Seven states were running their printing presses, producing ever-less-valuable currency. Only Rhode Island had barred paying creditors with state fiat money.

To RESCUE the nation from the petty jealousies of its member states, Alexander Hamilton decided to join with a handful of like-minded statesmen, including Washington and Madison. First, he reentered state politics in the annual legislative elections in April 1786, throwing his hat into the ring as a candidate for one of the eight assembly seats from the City and County of New York. Garnering 332 votes, he ran fourth among sixteen candidates. When Governor Clinton refused to summon the legislature to consider Congress's call for an emergency session, he managed to put off any assembly meeting until January 1787. But, meanwhile, the old assembly had agreed to send delegates to the Annapolis commercial convention at the invitation of the Virginia legislature that summer. Lining up the support of his friends Troup and Duer in the assembly and his father-in-law in the senate, Hamilton won election of his entire nationalist slate of delegates to Annapolis.

While Alexander Hamilton's legal career flourished, more and more he led a lonely existence as his wife and small children continued to live more with Betsy's parents at The Pastures than in the crowded, dirty city. Betsy seemed always to be ill, pregnant, or both. She was not the social creature her older sister Angelica was, and she did not relish New York City's vibrant society as Hamilton did. After living in rented quarters on Wall Street from November 1783 to March 1785, Hamilton felt strong enough financially to buy the twin houses at 56–57 Wall Street, although he found it necessary to ask Betsy to pledge her family's collateral to make the 2,100-pound (about $85,000 today) purchase. "Colonel Burr just tells me," he wrote to her on March 17, 1785, "that the house we live in is offered for sale." Burr, already Hamilton's chief rival at the New York bar, would not accede to Hamilton's offer of a ninety-day note for the house unless the Schuylers posted security for him. As much as he disliked depending on Schuyler money, Hamilton wanted Betsy to feel the house was hers in every sense. Maybe that would induce her to spend more time with him in the city. But his loneliness and her sickly, shy, receding nature come across repeatedly in his surviving letters to her.[17]

One of Hamilton's earliest clients, and eventually his most important, was his brother-in-law John Church. At war's end, learning that, contrary to what he believed, he had *not* killed a nobleman in a prewar duel, Church joined the flood of Loyalists returning to England and there eventually won a seat in Parliament. He made Hamilton his lawyer and then his New York business agent. For long periods, he left behind in America his wife, the beautiful Angelica, while he pursued his fortunes abroad. Over the years, Hamilton grew increasingly fond of her high-spirited, flirtatious way, even comparing her company adversely with that of his taciturn, shy wife.

When Angelica went back to England after a short visit in 1785, a dalliance, at first merely literary, began to bloom. As early as January 27, 1784, Angelica pulled herself away from the endless round of parties and balls in Paris to write to her sister Betsy, complaining that she had not received a separate letter from Hamilton:

> I should like Paris if it was nearer to America, for I have a very agreeable set of circumstances. Mrs. Jay lives in a small house about half a mile from Paris. The Americans have the pleasure to drink tea with her once a week. Mr. Franklin has the gravel [kidney stones] and desires to return to America. They talk of Papa or Col. Hamilton as his successor. How would you like to cross the Atlantic? Is your lord a Knight of the Cincinnati?

She asked Betsy to send her the newspapers "but the papers must be those that contain your husband's writings." In Paris, she read "Phocion," eagerly awaiting the next installment:

> Adieu, my dear, embrace your *master* for me, and tell him that I envy you the fame of so clever a husband, one who writes so well. God bless him, and may he long continue to be the friend and brother of your affectionate Angelica.

As if that were not enticing enough, Angelica added in a breathless
postscript, "P.S. Tell Colonel Hamilton, if he does not write to me, I
shall be very angry." To Hamilton, she would soon enough write
directly, telling him her husband's "head is full of politics" so much
so that by him, "I am now no longer heard."[18]

Over time, they worked out a subtle code between them, scarcely
if at all noticeable to Betsy, who had fifty years to edit Hamilton's
papers after his death. In August 1785, again alone in New York City
while Betsy and the babies visited the Schuylers in cooler Albany,
Hamilton, thirty now—and no longer considering himself youthful—
shoved aside the law books and spread out a fresh sheet of his best,
heavy, cream-colored paper, then dipped his freshly sharpened quill
to start a long letter to Angelica. "You have been much better to me
My Dear friend since you left America"—he capitalized "My Dear"—
"than I have deserved, for you have written to me oftener than I
have written to you." Her letter had come to Hamilton by a trusted
courier, returning with Loyalist Peter Van Schaack, without passing
through Betsy's hands. After the initial formalities, Hamilton grew
bolder:

> You have, I fear, taken a final leave of America and those that
> love you here. I saw you depart from Philadelphia with pecu-
> liar uneasiness, as if foreboding you were not to return . . .
> Judge the bitterness it gives to those who love you with the
> *love of nature* and to me who feel an attachment to you not less
> lively.

Hamilton's affection for Angelica, he said here, was not less than the
"love of nature" of her family. Could that not only imply it was
greater? "My affection for Church and yourself made me anticipate
much pleasure." It was the convention in letters between lovers to
include by way of protection the name of the spouse. "I confess for
my own part I see one great source of happiness snatched away." As
matters stood, "an ocean is now to separate us." But the soil of Europe,
she would find, was "less propitious" than that of America for her.
"Go where you will[,] you will find no *such* friends as those you have

left behind." And then he closed the letter with a careful grammatical error that was to become a hallmark of their letters over the years. "I remain as ever you affectionate friend & Brother A Hamilton." By leaving out the "r" at the end of "you," he made it, "you affectionate friend." And he made her heart race faster.[19]

———— ◆ ————

FOURTEEN

"What May This Lead To?"

Alexander Hamilton left New York City for the Annapolis trade talks on September 1, 1786, traveling with the "profane bachelor" Egbert Benson, state attorney general and a henchman of Governor Clinton. Betsy Hamilton was already tired of her husband's political friends, and, at her request, Hamilton ducked a farewell dinner invitation from his good friend Richard Varick. He sent a note to his former comrade-in-arms, explaining that "Mrs. Hamilton insists on my dining with her today, as this is the day of departure." The state of Virginia had chosen the small-town Maryland capital as the convention site instead of holding it in any of the large commercial towns, Madison wrote Jefferson, "to avoid charges of undue influence by local merchants." Hamilton had been ill as he often was from the pollution generated by thousands of cook fires. He always revived when he rode out into the countryside, this time for a canter of some two hundred miles at harvest time, averaging a brisk thirty-five miles a day in the saddle. "My health has been improved by traveling," he wrote Betsy when he arrived in Annapolis after a week on the road. He promised Betsy he would only be detained at the conference "for eight or ten days perhaps a fortnight."[1]

He almost left even before the convention began. Delegates from only five states had arrived—New York, Pennsylvania, Maryland, Delaware, and Virginia. Representatives of four other states had promised to attend but would arrive too late, after the conference broke up. Here, in Annapolis, as Hamilton was well aware, nearly three years earlier Washington had foreseen the danger of congressional weakness. When the commander-in-chief had ridden south from New York City in December 1783, after a tearful farewell to his officers—how could Hamilton forget the moment and their embrace— he had come here, to the State House at Annapolis, to tender his resignation to the Congress that had appointed him. The Revolution was now complete. Washington was there to give up his military power to affirm Congress as the sole source of power. And yet they had kept him waiting for three days because not enough congressmen were in town to make up a quorum. When at last Washington had been ushered into the vast redbrick capitol building and, under its overpowering dome, had breathed life into America's civilian government, he had issued a challenge, which now, nearly three years later, remained unfulfilled. In a toast hardly anyone understood at the time, Washington had uttered: "Competent powers to Congress for general purposes."[2]

When the Annapolis Convention opened on September 11, 1786, John Dickinson, Hamilton's nemesis from his days in Congress, became chairman. Because only twelve delegates from a handful of states appeared, Hamilton could see it would be useless to undertake any systematic study of the interstate commercial crisis or to try and work out, on the spot, an interstate agreement. Instead, he offered a resolution declaring the task impossible in such few hands, in so little time. After only three days, when the other delegates still had not arrived, Hamilton grabbed the initiative. He wrote a brief report that seized on the broader powers given New Jersey's delegates to delve into not only trade but "other important matters [that] might be necessary to the common interest and permanent harmony of the several states." Hamilton had examined the written instructions of delegates from Virginia and Pennsylvania. They were, he found, similar to the far-reaching New York Assembly authorization, which he himself had drafted. This allowed him "to take into consideration the trade and commerce of the United States [and] to consider how far a uniform system in their commercial intercourse and regulations might be necessary to their common interest and perfect harmony."[3]

Hamilton, noting that delegates from only five of thirteen states had arrived, now pushed hard for the Annapolis Convention to call for a wider conference, then adjourn before the other delegates could arrive. Supported by Madison and, to his surprise, Dickinson, in his written declaration Hamilton underscored what should have been obvious, "that there are important defects in the system of the Federal government." Foreign and domestic "embarrassments" demanded a "deliberate and candid" discussion by representatives of all the states. In a second draft of his report, he called for a convention in Philadelphia the following May "to devise such further provisions as shall appear to them necessary to render the Constitution of the Federal Government adequate to the exigencies of the Union." His first draft, now lost, had irked Virginia's governor, Edmund Randolph, who considered it "too strong." Madison warned Hamilton, "You had better yield to this man, for otherwise all Virginia will be against you." Already learning political compromise, Hamilton rewrote the convention's report to Congress and the states, "toning it down to suit tender stomachs." Three years later, Hamilton remembered that all the delegates at Annapolis, frustrated in their stated purpose, demanded some more radical reform and unanimously recommended the Constitutional Convention in Philadelphia to overhaul or thoroughly change the Confederation form of government. When Congress, in session in New York City Hall, received Hamilton's "Address of the Annapolis Convention" on October 11, 1786, it referred it to committee, where it remained bottled up for four months.[4]

As THE months ticked by and the crisis deepened, Alexander Hamilton saw all around him evidence that, unless the Confederation government underwent a drastic overhaul, the thirteen states would degenerate into a helpless collection of squabbling debtors ripe for foreign exploitation or even reconquest. Hamilton knew many New Yorkers were suffering from the refusal of the British to evacuate their

Great Lakes forts. As further proof of American impotence, Spain had been able to flout the 1783 Treaty of Paris by closing off the Mississippi River to Americans. No longer could barges or canoes from the Ohio and Tennessee Valleys transport furs or other commodities downriver to the French port at New Orleans. After a year of fruitless negotiations between John Jay, the emissary for Congress, and Don Diego de Gardoqui, Spanish minister to the United States, in August 1786, just as state commissioners converged on Annapolis, Congress, after a bitter debate, split seven states to five in favor of giving up rights to the Mississippi in exchange for a trade treaty with Spain. Federal feebleness had now closed off trade on the western border of the United States.

And it was on the frontier that the revolt Hamilton had so long dreaded finally broke out. Only two weeks after the Annapolis Convention ended so abruptly and inconclusively, debt-ridden farmers in the Berkshire hills of western Massachusetts rebelled. Because many of the region's farmers—a considerable number of them veterans of the Revolutionary War—could not pay their debts to storekeepers or tax collectors, they faced imprisonment or eviction with their families from their farms. The rebels, as Massachusetts politicians quickly denominated them, were especially bitter because the Massachusetts legislature had adjourned on July 8 without heeding their petitions for issuance of paper money or passage of "stay" laws that would halt foreclosures on farms and homes. At a town meeting at Worcester on August 15, discontent boiled over into angry calls for action that led to a Hampshire county convention of some fifty towns at Hatfield only a week later.

In a tense gathering that lasted longer than the Annapolis Convention, town delegates condemned the Massachusetts Senate, lawyers, the high costs of obtaining justice, the entire tax system, and the lack of paper money. While the conventioneers advised against the use of force, armed violence broke out. One week after the Hatfield convention, an angry crowd of armed men on August 31 prevented the sitting of the court at Northampton; another week and a mob closed the September session of courts at Worcester. Mobs barred judges and lawyers from entering the courthouses at Concord and Great

Barrington, chasing away the sheriffs and stopping the sheriffs' sales. Near panic, Governor James Bowdoin dispatched six hundred militiamen to guard the state Supreme Court in Springfield.

There, Daniel Shays, a destitute farmer who had attained the rank of captain in the Revolutionary army and had since held town offices in Pelham, had gathered about six hundred armed men who had taken down their flintlocks and were ready to fight. On September 26, they confronted an inferior force of state militia, obliging it to back away. The Supreme Court adjourned. In panic, Secretary of War Henry Knox reported with wild exaggeration to Congress that Shays commanded ten to fifteen thousand men and they were besieging the federal arsenal at Springfield. Civil war appeared imminent. Thoroughly alarmed at reports that the armed rebels were about to seize cannon from the Springfield arsenal, Congress did the one thing it had clear-cut authority to do under the Confederation. On October 20, it voted to raise an army, even if it did it on tiptoes. Congress authorized the gargantuan secretary of war himself, three-hundred-pound Henry Knox, to raise 1,340 men, ostensibly to serve against the Indians. But the federal forces gathered so slowly that they never saw combat. The insurrection suffered a severe setback with the capture of one of its organizers, Job Shattuck, on November 30.

As snow blanketed the Berkshires, Captain Shays gathered his own army of about twelve hundred men in November and December. The day after Christmas, 1786, he led a march to Springfield on the Connecticut River to join forces with other insurgents under the command of Luke Day. They aimed to intimidate the small militia force already guarding the federal arsenal. Their march thoroughly alarmed Governor Bowdoin, who now called up forty-four hundred men and put them under the command of the veteran General Benjamin Lincoln. Authorized for one month, it was the largest armed force mustered in the United States since the Revolution. But Shays and Day made the classic mistake of keeping their forces divided by the Connecticut River as they rushed toward Springfield and attempted to scatter the arsenal's guard before Lincoln could reinforce it. When Shays proposed a joint attack, Day's reply that he could not attack for another two more days was intercepted. Shays pressed on, attacking the arsenal in West Springfield, confident that Day would strike simultaneously. The Shaysites marched up within one hundred yards before the arsenal's gunners unleashed a volley of cannon fire. Four rebels dropped dead; the rest broke and fled. When Lincoln arrived with his army, he pursued Day, splitting off his force. Day fled to the hills of New Hampshire. Hard-marching all night, Lincoln and his army surprised Shays at dawn of February 4 and captured 150 insurgents. The rest fled, Shays and two of his aides disappearing across the Vermont border to seek refuge in Bennington.

THE SHAYS Rebellion thoroughly alarmed many Americans who were worried that the fragile Union was on the verge of collapse. Shays's escape into Vermont threatened to ignite another tinderbox of rebellion. Alexander Hamilton had steeped himself in land law and had followed Vermont's claims for independence from New York both as a lawyer with clients in the Green Mountains and as a vigilant member of the New York Assembly. He had once been one of the Continental officers supporting Vermont's request to join the Continental Congress. Increasingly, he had opposed Governor Clinton's belligerent insistence that New York militia should be mobilized to crush resistance in Vermont and force it back to its claimed status as part of New York.

The arrival of Shaysites leaders in Vermont alarmed Hamilton, who feared that the rebellion now would spread because it followed four months of turmoil in the Green Mountains. In the half-dozen years since Yorktown, the population of the little republic, scarcely a hundred miles wide and only its southern third inhabited, had been filling up with New England veterans, eager to cut down the hardwood trees, build houses and barns, and plant the rich soil with wheat for export to New York, Massachusetts, and Canada. By the 1791 Vermont census, the mountainous republic would have the highest per acre wheat yield in the United States. One reason its land was so coveted, as a Boston newspaper printed shortly after Shays's arrival noted, that "more families have moved into [Vermont] for six months past than has done in the same space of time since the first settlement of that country." More than any other place in America, they came to stay: 95 percent who arrived before the Revolution remained in the Green Mountains for the Vermont census of 1791. Still, those two thirds of Vermonters who had migrated, mostly from Massachusetts, since the Revolution had run up more debts than the original settlers and were being sued as a consequence. And that attracted lawyers. One unpopular Princeton-educated lawyer, Isaac Tichenor, who came to Bennington to hang out his shingle, had earned the nickname "Jersey Slick." As Vermont's courts filled with debt cases and still more attorneys rushed in, dozens of petitioners besieged the assembly, complaining of outrageous legal fees and court costs. Tensions boiled over in 1786 as settlers demanded expulsion of all lawyers and cancellation of all debts. Angry crowds milled outside courthouses. In October, only a sheriff's posse had persuaded debtors in Windsor in the Connecticut Valley not to close the courthouse. Nine towns petitioned the assembly that month for relief from taxes and lawyers—called "pickpockets" and "banditti" in court papers— and begged to have court costs lowered. The hard-pressed assembly passed a series of temporary laws requiring creditors to accept payment in kind and providing that creditors from any state where Vermonters could not bring suit (specifically New York) were barred from suing Vermonters. Ethan Allen offered partial restitution for one debt with cattle. But still the crowds cordoned off the courthouses. In Rutland in late November, as Shaysites gathered armed forces just across the border in the Berkshires, one hundred Vermont veterans seized the county courthouse, dispersing only at the approach of hundreds of state militia, who arrested forty-seven of them.[5]

What added urgency to Hamilton's sense of foreboding was still another smoldering brushfire of revolt in the Wyoming Valley of northwestern Pennsylvania. Before the Revolution, hundreds of settlers overflowing Connecticut's crowded hills had bought land from the Susquehannah Company in the Pocono Mountains. After the war, in yet another example of the feebleness of diplomacy between states under the Confederation, Pennsylvania laid claim to the region and insisted the Wyoming Valley settlers did not hold clear title to the lands unless they repurchased them—exactly as New York had done in Vermont before the Revolution. Irate settlers appealed their plight to Congress. On December 30, 1782, a five-man congressional tribunal ruled unanimously that the disputed lands belonged to Pennsylvania because its territory was contiguous. Without waiting to settle individual claims, the Pennsylvania Assembly approved plans to evict the Connecticut settlers. Only the denunciation of the assembly's plans prevented military action against the settlers.

In desperation, some of the Wyoming Valley settlers turned to that legendary defender of local autonomy, Ethan Allen of Vermont. Allen had resigned his command of Vermont troops during the Revolution to take part in secret negotiations with the British in Canada that dangled the possibility that the Republic of Vermont, if not granted statehood by the United States, would become a separate province of Canada loyal to the British. By 1786, the time of Shays's Rebellion, he had left Bennington and retired to a thirty-five-hundred-acre farm in Burlington, in northern Vermont. The Wyoming Valley settlers became convinced that Allen and his rough-riding Green Mountain Boys would be "particularly serviceable" in their cause by striking terror into the hearts of lawyers and lawmakers in Philadelphia. Allen's presence in the Poconos with some of his Boys would coerce Pennsylvania into negotiations. To lure Allen, they offered him the two commodities he loved the most, land and command. He declared that the Wyoming Valley cause—"our cause"—was "just." Writing from Vermont, Allen promised to fight to the death the "avaricious men [who] make interest their God." On his advice, the Wyoming Valley settlers procured guns and ammunition and recruited more Connecticut settlers, as many as they could crowd in. By late December 1785, Wyoming Valley's armed forces amounted to four hundred men waiting for the arrival of the "head doctor from the North with his glister pipe" (a device for giving an enema) to lead their little army. But first Allen warned a Connecticut delegate to Congress that he intended to "speedily repair to Wyoming with a small detachment of Green Mountain Boys to vindicate" their claims. Confident that Congress could hardly respond quickly enough, Allen rode into Pennsylvania on April 27, 1786, boasting to a crowd "that he had formed one new state" and now would do it again "in defiance of

Pennsylvania." One anxious official reported to Philadelphia that "since [his] arrival every idea of submission to the laws of Pennsylvania has vanished."

When Alexander Hamilton passed through Pennsylvania on horseback to attend the Annapolis Convention, Philadelphians were reading a broadside reminiscent of Allen's rhetoric before he led his Boys to seize Fort Ticonderoga a decade earlier. He scorned Congress's "tribunal of land monopolizers." Addressing "the court of conscience, of the people at large," he declared that the Wyoming settlers—and he now counted himself one of them—"will not tamely surrender our farms, orchards, tenements, neighbors and right to soil to a junta of land thieves." He threatened to "smoke it out at the muzzle of the firelock." Did Philadelphia's "pious legalists" believe that the farmers had fought the Revolution in vain, only for Pennsylvania and Congress to "cram their laws down our throats"? As panicky rumors of the approach of an army of Green Mountain Boys flew through the streets of Philadelphia, the state legislature hastily convened inside Independence Hall. Terrified lawmakers reported that "bandittis [are] rising up against law and good order in all quarters of our country," declaring Ethan Allen and Daniel Shays part of the same lawlessness that threatened to destroy the Union.[6]

NEW YORK'S legislature finally reconvened in Manhattan in January 1787 after Governor Clinton had ignored for five months the emergency call by Congress to hold a special session to consider a national customs duty that supposedly rescued the national government from insolvency. In a pair of indignant speeches to a packed gallery in New York City Hall on January 19, Alexander Hamilton hammered hard at Clinton's refusal on the grounds it violated the state's constitution:

What kind of emergency must exist? Is the preservation of our national faith a matter of such trivial moment? Is the fulfillment of [our] public engagements [debts], domestic and foreign, of no consequence? Must we wait for the fleets of the Netherlands or France to enforce them?[7]

As Shays and his followers melted into the hills of New England and Ethan Allen menaced the Pennsylvania legislature, at the New York Assembly session of 1787, Governor Clinton's supporters still balked at even considering Congress's call for funding the national government. Hamilton, who attended Congress daily now, lashed out in frustration:

> Sir, are we not to respect federal decisions? Are we, on the contrary, to take every opportunity of holding up their resolutions and requests in a contemptible and insignificant light? And tell the world their calls, their requests are nothing to us? That we are bound by none of their measures? Do not let us add to their embarrassment, for it is but a slender tie that at present holds us [together].
>
> You see, alas, what contempt we are falling into since the peace. You see to what our commerce is exposed on every side. You see us the laughing stock, the sport of foreign nations. And what may this lead to? I dread, sir, to think.[8]

In his two brief visits to the Wyoming Valley, Ethan Allen eventually managed to jolt Pennsylvania's legislature into confirming the settlers' claims to their lands and forming their settlements into a separate county. But, in the short term, Allen's threats and Shays's attacks electrified discontented frontiersmen all up and down the Appalachian backcountry. At Mount Vernon, George Washington became convinced that the rebellion could spread into a full-scale resumption of the Revolution. His fears of congressional helplessness confirmed, he decided to join Virginia's delegation to the Philadelphia Constitutional Convention. He feared that the "levelers" were seeking agrarian reforms that would reapportion wealth. Washington had good reason to fear. His estate had dwindled by 50 percent due to currency depreciation and the curtailment of trade, and he had recently failed to collect rents during a personal inspection of his western Pennsylvania lands. His western partner was so heavily in debt that he could pay Washington only 5 percent of what he owed.

When Washington tried to auction off a mill in which he had invested 1,200 pounds (about $50,000 today), no one could afford to bid on it. Before he rode home to Virginia, Washington stopped off at the courthouse of Fayette county and instituted eviction proceedings against squatters on his lands, many of them his former troops. When he arrived home at Mount Vernon, he wrote to Madison, "We are fast verging to anarchy and confusion."[9]

After General Benjamin Lincoln scattered the Shaysites in western Massachusetts in early February 1787, Governor Bowdoin decided to hunt down and punish the rebels. He called on the governors of neighboring states to arrest the "malcontents." The governors of Connecticut and New Hampshire promised aid; New York's Governor Clinton marched with three regiments of militia to reinforce Lincoln. Twice, Lincoln called for Vermont's Governor Chittenden, whose state was closest to the rebellion, to help. Chittenden promised to see what he could do. Vermont's white-haired legislators dreaded being dragged into the war with their neighboring states even as they sought their neighbors' support for their petition for statehood. More radical Vermonters, including Ethan Allan and Governor Chittenden, thought that promises to intervene in Massachusetts would actually increase Vermont's leverage in Congress. A scant majority of the Vermont legislature voted to disavow the Shays Rebellion, and at the end of February, after Shays fled to Vermont, Chittenden, his tongue planted firmly in his cheek, issued a proclamation warning citizens not to "harbor, entertain or conceal" Shays and the three other rebel leaders—who were staying on the farm next door to Chittenden's.

But Vermont's waffling only led worried leaders in New York and Massachusetts to believe that Vermonters were planning, once again, to annex the rebellious border regions of both states. In Boston, Governor Bowdoin heard that hundreds of Shaysites were massing near Ethan Allen's homestead. Allen openly sympathized with the rebels. Fresh from his triumph in Pennsylvania, he tongue-lashed Bowdoin, Lincoln, and the Adamses. Those who "held the reins of government in Massachusetts [are] a pack of damned rascals and there is no virtue among them," he bellowed. In February, Shays sent two fellow insurgents, Luke Day and Eli Parsons, to Allen to offer him command of a "revolutionary army."[10]

By February 1787, as civil war loomed along the Vermont–Massachusetts–New York borders, Assemblyman Alexander Hamilton rose at his desk in City Hall in New York City to propose one of his most important compromises. Hamilton had already drawn hisses from Clinton's camp whenever he championed the rights of women. Hamilton acquiesced, temporarily at least, in a divorce bill rejected by the state's Council of Revision. Under a bill passed by the assembly, a marriage partner convicted of adultery would not be allowed to remarry. Unless such "offenders" were to be confined in a "cloister," it was foolish to expect them to live celibate. Under the Danish law of St. Croix, Hamilton's mother had been unable to remain legally married to his father, as she no doubt would have done, because she had been unable to contest Levine's charge of adultery. As it was in the New York Assembly climate of 1787, Hamilton let the punishment stand without a fight, perhaps unwilling to call further attention at the time to his illegitimate status. He decided to wait to introduce a better law in a higher-toned legislative gathering. An illegitimate son—and all the assembly knew it—Hamilton objected to forcing a woman "to publish her shame to the world." In his own notes, he wrote that he "expatiated feelingly on the delicate situation" until the assembly voted to remove the draconian punishment.[11]

Gathering support in the assembly, he pushed hard, in a one-hundred-minute speech, for New York's support for federal customs duties. In a brilliant compromise, he proposed New York would appoint tax collectors to collect duties, and then turn the money over to Congress. Overcoming Clinton's objection that a federal customs service in New York intruded on its independence, Hamilton succeeded. Emboldened, he pressed for the appointment of five New York delegates to the August 1787 convention in Philadelphia "for the sole and express purpose of revising the Articles of Confederation." Here, Hamilton suffered a setback. Despite Schuyler's support, the Senate voted for a three-man delegation, not the five Hamilton had hoped for. Outvoted two-to-one in the House, Hamilton had to content himself with his appointment as one of three, knowing full well that Clinton would send two supporters who would neutralize his votes at the convention. It was no surprise when Clinton chose two devout Clintonians, John Lansing and Robert Yates.

In the months before the Constitutional Convention, Hamilton distinguished himself in the New York Assembly in a series of debates and resolutions. He led a crusade to end the twenty-year-old confrontation with Vermonters, introducing a bill directing the states' congressional delegates to support independence for Vermont. "Vermont is in fact *independent*," he contended, "but she is not confederated." He understood Vermont's shrewd efforts to exploit the Shays Rebellion. "Is it not natural for a free people, irritated by neglect, to provide for their own safety by seeking connections?" Vermont had turned first to the British, now to Shays. New York must finally settle the controversy. "They are useless to us now," he said of Vermont, "and if they continue as they are, they will be formidable to us hereafter." The New York Assembly agreed, but the Senate refused.[12]

Hamilton's support in New York struck Ethan Allen like a lightning bolt, coming just when Shays was offering him command of a revolution. Allen had to choose between the independence for Vermont he had pursued for more than twenty years or a brief, glorious command that might end on the gallows. He chose statehood. He "contemptuously refused" Shays's offer of command and ordered him and his lieutenants to leave Vermont. Alexander Hamilton had long ago helped prisoner of war Ethan Allen to escape from British confinement in a New York provost jail by arranging his exchange. Now, Allen gave Hamilton the political victory he needed. Allen would not live to see it, but Hamilton, four years later, would usher Vermont into the Union as the fourteenth state, a free state, an antislavery state, just before Kentucky, the stepchild of Virginia, a slave state, could be admitted by its slave-owning stepfather, Secretary of State Thomas Jefferson.[13]

Accustomed now to giving shocking speeches, being voted down by lawmakers, and then appealing over their heads to the electorate through persuasive essays in New York's newspapers, Hamilton next set out to devise a system of taxation that would eliminate inequalities and the favoritism of tax assessors. Once again, he was rejected by the Clinton party. But they could not deprive him of the experience, for the first time, of crafting a complicated financial system.

ARRIVING IN Philadelphia in the blistering first burst of a Philadelphia summer on May 18, 1787, Alexander Hamilton checked into the Indian Queen Tavern on Third Street between Market and Chestnut, a short walk to Independence Hall. At thirty, he was half the age of most delegates, many of whom were famous leaders of the Revolution. Inside Independence Hall, as the old Pennsylvania State House was renamed, he took his place at the green baize-covered table designated for New York beside one of the state house fireplaces. Before the debates began in earnest, he had time to visit the airy, high-ceilinged wing on the south side of the building, where he had always been able to find virtually any law book he needed for his arguments on constitutional law. Probably the largest library in America, it contained glass-covered bookcases with hundreds of gold-stamped, calfskin-bound volumes on colonial, British, and international law. Here, the real work of the convention would be performed by committees meeting before and after each day's plenary session, and here Hamilton probably drew up the detailed notes of each of his speeches and comments, as he always prepared for court cases.

Alexander Hamilton's principal contributions to the drafting of the Constitution of the United States came before, during, and after the Philadelphia convention. He was the first to recognize the defects in the Articles of Confederation and, after the Constitution was drafted, he proclaimed those weaknesses to the public in the *Federalist Papers* to bring about popular ratification of the new Constitution. For the first four weeks in Philadelphia, he said little, observing and then deferring to the more famous delegates. Then, gradually, he began to point out the flaws in their proposals. Appointed to the key rules committee, he agreed to set aside his belief that public discussions should be held in public. In his first stint in Congress in 1783, he had written the nation's first "sunshine" law. All through the Revolution, when there had been the danger of spying, Congress had kept the doors and windows closed and its debates secret. Now, Hamilton considered the health of the nation once again in just such critical condition. Many delegates would fear that their ideas, if aired prematurely, would provoke controversy—and probably wouldn't be adopted anyway: time enough for public scrutiny after the document was drafted and presented to the individual states.

The convention achieved a quorum of seven states by May 25. The delegates ranged in age from twenty-six-year-old Jonathan Dayton of New Jersey to the venerable statesman and inventor Benjamin Franklin of Pennsylvania, so feeble at eighty-one from gout and kidney stones that he had to be carried in a sedan chair by prisoners and seemed always to be asleep, partially because he had to be dosed with laudanum (a mixture of opium and honey) to mute his pain. Most of the delegates were already outstanding public figures. Washington presided from a raised dais; his next-door neighbor on the Potomac, legal scholar George Mason, graced Virginia's table along with thirty-six-year-old James Madison. As a member of Congress, Madison, like Hamilton, was a proponent of customs duties on imports to raise federal revenues. An accomplished compromiser, as Governor Thomas Jefferson's floor manager in the Virginia House of Delegates, Madison had worked out Virginia's cession of the western lands it had claimed for nearly two centuries to the federal government, setting the example for other states to turn over their conflicting claims to form a vast federal territory called the Old Northwest. Madison had maneuvered for ten years to win adoption of a statute on religious freedom that had been written by Jefferson before he had gone to France as a diplomat. That act ended state subsidies for the support of clergy and established the doctrine of separation of church and state. Hamilton's friend Gouverneur Morris and famed Scottish legal expert James Wilson joined Franklin at Pennsylvania's table. Of the fifty delegates, twenty-nine were college-educated.

Robert Morris nominated Washington as president. As president, he could not speak, only direct the debate and exert influence by his mere presence. Wilson nominated William Temple Franklin, grandson of Dr. Franklin and illegitimate son of exiled Loyalist leader William Franklin, as the convention secretary. Young Franklin had served as secretary of the American delegation at the Paris peace talks and was better qualified than the man Hamilton nominated, former assistant secretary of war William Jackson. Jackson had assisted Hamilton during the mutiny of Pennsylvania troops in 1783, and Hamilton was repaying the favor. The convention accepted Hamilton's recommendation but it turned out to be a poor choice. Jackson kept erratic and incomplete notes of the Constitutional Convention. Five delegates took notes: Hamilton's fellow New Yorkers Yates and Lansing, and Rufus King of Massachusetts took down what could embarrass Hamilton and provided the notes to Clinton. No one's notes came close to Madison's for care and comprehension.

The convention came to life on May 25 when Edmund Randolph introduced the Virginia Plan of Union. A series of fifteen resolutions, it went far beyond the convention's revisionary mission, as authorized by Congress, and proposed a totally new national government. It featured a two-house national legislature, representing the states proportionately, with the lower house elected by the people and the upper house elected by the lower house from nominees proposed by the state legislatures. The national legislature was to choose a chief executive. There was to be a federal judiciary, including a supreme court and inferior federal courts. Bills enacted by the national legislature were to be subject to review by a council of revision made up of the chief executive and several judges, with veto power over the legislature's acts. On May 30, the convention resolved itself into a committee of the whole and for two solid weeks debated the Virginia Plan.

At the outset of this heated debate, Alexander Hamilton made a motion to revise one feature of the Virginia Plan. Whereas Randolph wanted voting rights to be proportionate to the tax contributions of the states or to the number of their free inhabitants, Hamilton could see that deciding the vote according to a state's tax payments would be totally unacceptable to the smaller states. He moved that Randolph's plan be altered to provide the vote strictly on the basis of the number of freemen in each state. Despite a second by a Southerner from North Carolina, the convention postponed consideration of Hamilton's resolution.

After more than two weeks of speeches on the Virginia Plan—

which had become known as the large-state plan—William Paterson introduced the New Jersey Plan on June 16. Robert Lansing of New York, a Clintonian, seconded it. Paterson, a revolutionary lawyer and jurist, led the opposition to the Virginia Plan, which centered chiefly on the provision for proportional representation, as Hamilton had predicted. The New Jersey, or small-state plan, called for equal representation of the states in both houses. Paterson's nine resolutions stressed retaining the Confederation but granting Congress the powers to tax and regulate foreign and interstate commerce. The New Jersey Plan also called for naming a plural executive, not a single chief executive, but without veto power, and a supreme court appointed by Congress. As Hamilton had so long demanded, U.S. treaties and acts of Congress were to be the supreme law in the states. The lines were now drawn for a battle between delegates willing to content themselves with amendments to the Articles of Confederation and advocates like Hamilton of scrapping the Confederation and drawing up the framework of an entirely new national government.

Two days into an intense three-day debate on the New Jersey Plan, Hamilton asked President Washington if he could have the floor. It was early in the session of June 18 when the tall, thin, angular-faced New Yorker in elegant black and white stood and began a six-hour speech. Carefully prepared notes lay beside him, but he did not have to consult them. Madison, deeply impressed, recorded the scene:

> Mr. Hamilton [said that he] had been hitherto silent on the business before the Convention, partly from respect to others whose superior abilities, age and experience rendered him unwilling to bring forward ideas dissimilar to theirs and partly from his delicate situation with respect to his own state.

Madison was wrong about Hamilton's silence. He had already made two key motions. But, as it would later turn out, Madison was dead right about Hamilton's delicate situation in the New York delegation, where he was sure to be outvoted—and in bloc voting that meant nullified—by the pro-Clinton delegates. But that also meant he had nothing to lose. While Hamilton declared that he could not possibly accede to the views of his fellow New Yorkers, he said that the crisis "which now marked our affairs was too serious to permit any scruples whatever to prevail over the duty imposed on every man to contribute his efforts for the public safety and happiness."

Hamilton felt he was "obliged therefore to declare himself unfriendly" to both the Virginia and New Jersey plans. He was "particularly opposed" to Paterson's small-state plan. No amendment of the Confederation that left the states sovereign "could possibly answer." Yet he was "much discouraged" by the "amazing" number of delegates who expected the "desired blessings" by merely substituting a federal national government for a loose-knit confederation of sovereign states. He agreed with Randolph of Virginia that "we owe it to our country to do in this emergency whatever we should deem essential to its happiness." To do anything less, just because it was "not clearly within our powers, would be to sacrifice the means to the end."

To Hamilton, all the defects lay with the states. Massachusetts was feeling the lack of a "certain portion of military force that is absolutely necessary":

All the passions we see, of avarice, ambition, interest, which govern most individuals and all public bodies, fall into the current of the states and do not flow into the stream of the general [national] government ... How then are all these evils to be avoided? Only by such a complete sovereignty in the general government as will turn all the strong principles and passions [to] its side.

Hamilton argued that Paterson's plan provided no remedy. Small states like New Jersey and North Carolina, "not being commercial states and [only] contributing to the wealth of the commercial ones," could never meet proportional tax quotas as Randolph of Virginia had proposed. "They will and must fail in their duty, their example will be followed, and the Union itself will be dissolved." What, then, was to be done? The expense of a national government over so great an extent of land would be "formidable" unless the cost of state government diminished. He did not mean to shock public opinion but he favored "extinguishing" the state governments: "they are not necessary for any of the great purposes of commerce, revenue or agriculture." What would work better would be "district tribunals: corporations for local purposes." The "only difficulty of a serious nature" which he foresaw was in drawing public officials from the edges to the center of the national community. "Moderate wages" would only "be a bait to little demagogues." Hamilton's views "almost led him to despair," Madison noted, "that a republican government could be established over so great an extent." In his private opinion, Madison wrote of Hamilton, "he had no scruple in declaring, supported as he was by so many of the wise and good, that the British government was the best in the world." He dared to say this because, he said, he had seen a profound shift in public opinion as the members of Congress who were the most tenacious republicans were as loud as anyone in declaiming against "the vices of democracy." He agreed with Necker, the French finance minister, who viewed the British Parliament as "the only government in the world 'which unites public strength with individual security.'"

Many in his audience reeling at such heresy in a Revolutionary council, Hamilton raced on:

> In every community where industry is encouraged, there will be a division of it into the few and the many. Hence, separate interests will arise. There will be debtors and creditors. Give all power to the many, they will oppress the few. Give all power to the few, they will oppress the many. Both, therefore, ought to have power, that each may defend itself against the other.

Hamilton submitted "a sketch of his plan" to the Committee of the Whole, warning that "the people" outside the convention's walls would not adopt either the Virginia or New Jersey plans. Hamilton said he saw the Union dissolving. "He sees evils in the states which must soon cure the people of their fondness for democracies," reported Madison.

Hamilton then read aloud his own plan of government. He proposed a two-house Supreme Legislative Power "in two distinct bodies of men": an elected assembly, elected by free men, serving three-year terms, and a lifetime senate, like the English House of Lords but not hereditary, serving "during good behavior." The senators would be chosen by electors chosen by the people, would form "a permanent barrier against every pernicious innovation." Judges also would be elected by the people and serve during good behavior. The supreme executive would be a governor chosen in the same fashion, for life, but only during good behavior: could there be "a good government without a good executive"? This "governor"—Hamilton did not use the word "president"—would be able to veto "all laws about to be passed" and would be in charge of executing the laws. He would be "the commander in chief of the land and naval forces and of the militia." He would have "with the advice and approbation of the Senate" the power of making all treaties. He would appoint the heads of the departments of finance, war, and foreign affairs. He would nominate all ambassadors subject to Senate approval, and he would "have the power of pardoning all offenses but treason," which would require the assent of Congress.[14]

In one brilliant, six-hour, standup oration that left the convention stunned, Alexander Hamilton, with only the exception of term limits and the rules and qualifications for voters, laid out what would become the basic framework of the United States government. Off and on for the next few days, he rose to defend portions of his plan. Hamilton's plan coincided with the Virginia Plan on the major premise that there should be three branches of a national government, legislative, executive, and judiciary. On June 19, when the revised Virginia Plan came out of committee, he rose to elaborate on where his plan differed. His suggestion that the states should be abolished had drawn sharp criticism overnight. By "abolish," he meant their authority must be lessened. It should be "indefinite," but they should be left as "subordinate jurisdictions," as Persia within the Roman Empire. That same day, he rose again to contest a part of the Virginia Plan written by Luther Martin of Maryland that said the thirteen states were "in a state of nature," the old argument of philosopher John Locke. But Hamilton found James Wilson of Pennsylvania's resolution more palatable: the states had won their independence from Great Britain not individually but collectively. He did not fear combinations of states. The large states, Virginia and Massachusetts, were separated by too great distance.

Once again, on June 21, he rose to challenge Charles Cotesworth Pinckney of South Carolina, who wanted Congress to be elected by the state legislatures. Without direct election by the people, Congress would be "engrafted" to state governments that could dwindle and die. The same day, he remained adamant on the term of representatives to the lower house. Three years in office was better than a shorter term because too frequent elections made the "people listless to them." He argued against letting state governments pay national salaries: "Those who pay are the masters of those who are paid." And he argued vigorously against the holding of more than one public office:

> Take mankind in general, they are vicious—their passions may be operated upon. Take mankind as they are, and what are they governed by? Their passions. There may be in every government a few choice spirits, who may act from more worthy motives [but] one great error is that we suppose mankind more honest than they are. Our prevailing passions are ambition and interest. Wise government should avail itself of those passions, to make them subservient to the public good.[15]

And then, sure that no one at the convention would follow his advice, he went home.

BEFORE HE left Philadelphia, Hamilton went for a "long afternoon's walk" with James Madison. Five years later, Hamilton still remembered how the two men discussed the vexing problem of the state debts and agreed perfectly that all outstanding state debts must be assumed by a stronger national government when and if it was formed. They also agreed that this problem should be kept out of the Constitution because it would multiply the obstacles to its reception. Madison came away more deeply impressed by Hamilton than were most other of his convention colleagues. Major William Pierce of Georgia called Hamilton "rather a convincing speaker than a blazing orator" who "requires time to think—he enquires into every part of his subject with the searchings of philosophy." But Southern officer Pierce found Hamilton's manners "tinctured with stiffness and sometimes with a degree of vanity that is highly disagreeable." William Samuel Johnson of Connecticut put it more laconically. Hamilton was "praised by everybody but supported by none."[16]

Pleading urgent legal business, Hamilton rode back to New York City, expecting to return to the convention in ten days or so. Curiously, he was delayed because Major Pierce, despite his sharp-penned description of Hamilton, his friend, had apparently been cut by remarks made by one of Hamilton's clients. Pierce asked Hamilton to be the second in a duel between two acquaintances, both merchants and public figures, which he spent several days trying to avert. In a note to his opposite second, Hamilton spelled out his reluctance to be a second in a duel until he had failed as a mediator. He then enunciated his justification for any duel. The only excuse was a "necessary sacrifice to the prejudices of public opinion."

As he had ridden home, Hamilton had stopped to sound out many people. On July 3, he fired off a letter to George Washington that he intended as encouragement. His own faith that reforms could emerge from Independence Hall that summer had faltered as he listened to the endless motions and resolutions, but a summer's canter through the countryside and a chance to talk to people outside the process made him more confident the convention would develop some useful plan. To Washington, he spoke bluntly. He was "more and more convinced" that this was the "critical opportunity" to establish "the prosperity of this country on a solid foundation." Hamilton had talked to many New Yorkers and had found

an astonishing revolution for the better in the minds of the people. The prevailing apprehension among thinking men is that the Convention, from a fear of shocking the popular opinion, will not go far enough.

While Clinton and his cronies were "taking all possible pains" to slight the reformers, "the current seems to be running the other way." Hamilton clung to no illusion, he told Washington, that the public was ready "for such a plan as I advocate" but were sympathetic to one "equally energetic."

Retreating from ebullience to formality, Hamilton acknowledged he "cannot judge how far our sentiments agree" but his own "anxiety," his distress at the convention when he left, made him "fear that we shall let slip the golden opportunity of preserving the American empire from disunion, anarchy and misery." No "feeble measure" would succeed or win public support. "Decision is true wisdom."¹⁷

Washington shot back a letter that, while assuring Hamilton he was grateful for his candor, filled Hamilton with even greater apprehension. "The state of the councils" was "if possible, in a worse train than ever." Washington gloomily reported "little ground" for "the hope of a good establishment." Hamilton's alarm grew as he read on: "I *almost* despair of seeing a favorable issue" and "do therefore repent" having anything to do with the convention. The opponents of "a strong and energetic government" were, to Washington, "narrow minded politicians." But Hamilton should not be discouraged to the point of abandoning the fight. "I am sorry you went away, I wish you were back," Washington wrote simply. "The crisis is equally important and alarming."

Before returning to Philadelphia, however, Hamilton published in the *New York Daily Advertiser* an angry rebuke to Governor Clinton for his public attack on the Constitutional Convention. Once, during the Revolution, they had been friends, Clinton providing medical care for the young officer when he fell desperately ill; Hamilton, in return, recommending Clinton for promotion. But since Clinton had obstructed Hamilton's efforts to raise revenue for Congress, he and Hamilton had become bitter rivals. Now Hamilton castigated Clinton for "greater attachment to his own power than to the public good":

If there be any man among us who acts so unworthy a part, it becomes a free and enlightened people to observe him with a jealous eye and [to] examine whether they have not more to apprehend from *himself*.[18]

As soon as he returned to the convention, Hamilton found himself again on the defensive. Elbridge Gerry of Massachusetts tried to restrict eligibility for a seat in the proposed Congress to "natives," a provision that would have excluded Hamilton. He knew he could not vote for New York at the convention—his two fellow delegates had walked out, hoping to wreck the convention—but he decided to speak out. As the nitpicking continued in Philadelphia, he dashed home again in August to attend to business but, when the two Clinton delegates refused to return to the convention, Hamilton arranged with Rufus King to send him a courier "to let me know when your *conclusion* is at hand." New York would not be shut out. "I choose to be present," he wrote, "to sign the new Constitution."

Still opposed to either the Virginia or New Jersey plan, Hamilton was only slightly less cool to the compromise put forward by Roger Sherman of Connecticut. Using a compromise concocted by Madison that each state's representation in the lower house should be based on the total of its white population and three-fifths of its black population, the so-called Connecticut Compromise also provided that each state should be equally represented in the Senate. Hamilton returned right in the middle of the "great debate" in time for Washington to appoint him to a five-man Committee on Style and Arrangement, which also included his allies, Madison, King, and Gouverneur Morris.

Hamilton rose on September 6 and said he had restrained himself from entering the discussions by his "dislike of the scheme of government in general" but he intended to support it "as better than nothing." He objected to the "Monster" powers to be given the president and feared he "would be tempted to make use of corrupt influence"—and here he meant bribes and political appointments—"to be continued in office." What was the remedy? The greatest number of votes possible.[19]

In the last day's debate, he espoused enlarging the House of Representatives to affect the combined interests of the president and the

Senate. He also called for a dual mode of amending the Constitution, with amendments emanating either from the states or from Congress. On both these major points he prevailed, supporting Madison's motions. With Washington's tacit support and with Madison at his side, Hamilton succeeded in arranging for adoption of the Constitution once two thirds, or nine of the thirteen states, ratified it in specially called conventions.

On the last day of the four-month-long constitutional convention, three of the forty-two members present remained so bitterly opposed to it that they refused to sign. Irked, Hamilton sprang to Washington's desk, where the document lay, and wrote the names of each state in a column to the left, allowing room for each signature. Still, Elbridge Gerry of Massachusetts, and Edmund Randolph and George Mason of Virginia, refused. Madison recorded Hamilton's agitation. "Mr. Hamilton expressed his anxiety that every member should sign. A few characters of consequence, by opposing or even refusing to sign, might do infinite mischief." Hamilton said that he himself was signing despite the fact that "no man's ideas were more remote from the plan than his were known to be. But is it possible to deliberate between anarchy and convulsion on one side and the chance of good?"

And then Hamilton scratched his name, the only New Yorker to sign the Constitution of the United States.[20]

As HE returned to New York, his home and his law firm, over the last two weeks in September, Hamilton assessed the chances for ratification. The "very great weight" of the framers headed the list, particularly "the universal popularity of General Washington." The good will of the "commercial interest," of "most men of property," the "hopes of the creditors," he listed before "a strong belief in the people at large" that the Confederation form of government was "insufficient" to "preserve the Union." Against all of this he worried about "the dissent of two or three important men" who "think their characters pledged" to defeat the new government. Hamilton predicted a fight. "The causes operating against its adoption are powerful." He would not be astonished at its defeat but, if the framers succeeded,

Washington probably would become the president, assuring "a wise choice of men to administer the government and a good administration." Hamilton was already imagining himself in that administration. Savoring the "promise" of "so great a country" by "triumph altogether over the state governments," he set to work to "reduce them to an entire subordination." He expected the fight would take "eight or nine months," and he set to work to marshal a war of words in the nation's newspapers and state conventions.[21]

HAMILTON WAS not prepared for the ferocity of the fight over the Constitution. He returned to New York to find himself personally attacked by "Inspector" in the *New York Journal*. Stung, he wrote to Washington in October, enclosing a copy of the diatribe. Hamilton told Washington the opposition was doing anything it could "to diminish whatever credit or influence I may possess." His opponents "stick at nothing." It may have been "Inspector's" attack that made Hamilton decide to devote most of the next seven months to his own newspaper crusade, not only against Clinton's party but against anyone who stood in the way of state-by-state ratification. According to "Inspector," an "upstart attorney" had "palmed himself upon a great and good man [as a] youth of extraordinary genius and, under the shadow of such a patronage, make himself at once known and respected. But, being sifted and bolted to the bran, he was at length found to be a superficial, self-conceited coxcomb and was of course, turned off and disregarded by his patron." Washington wrote back immediately: "I do therefore explicitly declare that both charges are entirely unfounded." But he was distressed that, "when the situation of this country calls for unanimity and vigor, "such talented gentlemen should disagree." Washington was sure, however, that there would be "violent opposition" in Virginia "by some characters of weight." Hamilton set out at once to recruit his allies, James Madison and John Jay, to write a series of newspaper articles that were to become famous as the *Federalist Papers*.[22]

As HAMILTON mounted his most important political campaign, he received a letter from London from Angelica Church. His heart must have raced as he read that she was writing to him alone, not to either of her sisters or her father, and had spirited the letter off to the New York packet boat while her husband, once again, was out of town. "Church's head is full of politics. He is so desirous of making once in the British House of Commons, and where I should delight to see him if he possessed your eloquence." Again, she used the pinprick of a comma, or, in this case, the absence of one, to communicate her strong emotions: "Indeed my dear, Sir, if my path was strewed with as many roses." She could not bear to write to her family. "It is too melancholy an employment today." Her husband "is not here." He had gone off campaigning to Newmarket. In a postscript, anxious that Hamilton, her brother-in-law, her sister's husband, might still be enamored of his first love, she asked, "Is Kitty Livingston married?" In the Churches' town house, The Albany, on Sackville Street in fashionable Piccadilly, Angelica pulled the silk cord to summon her footman and sent him off to meet the weekly mail.[23]

GOVERNOR CLINTON's decision to attack the Federalists—as the party favoring ratification of the new Constitution was being called—made Hamilton certain he must organize a newspaper campaign to win over the public before the New York State ratifying convention. Clinton had decided to split off New York from states farther south where Federalist support was strong. Taking the penname of the Roman censor "Cato," he attacked the Constitution. Combined with the vicious ad hominem attack of "Inspector" against Hamilton, Clinton's "Cato" letter prompted Hamilton to gather a group of Federalists for what he projected as twenty-five newspaper articles, but the bitter controversy led to far more essays than Hamilton envisaged while fewer leading Federalist writers volunteered or stayed the course. Initially Hamilton, who conceived the idea of the *Federalist Papers*, thought there would be five writers dividing the work equally. Gouverneur Morris declined; financier William Duer decided to write his own occasional pieces. That left Hamilton, Madison, and John Jay, the former congressional secretary of foreign affairs.

Each author was to write to his own strength. Jay was to write on foreign affairs, but after writing four pieces, he was stricken by a severe bout of rheumatism and contributed only one more essay. So, in all, Jay wrote five pieces. Madison, in New York and busy as a Virginia delegate to Congress, became the historian of the team, writing on the failures of ancient and modern confederacies. His most famous contribution, Federalist Number 10, attacked the popular myth that confederations could thrive only in small geographical areas such as Switzerland. To Hamilton, who had his law practice and his growing family but who had studied the laws and constitutions of every state by now, fell the awesome task of writing on the military and fiscal affairs of a national government. At Hamilton's suggestion, the Federalist authors intended to publish their articles once or twice a week in New York City newspapers, each going over the others' drafts before publication. According to Hamilton's plan for the project, after the essays appeared in newspapers Hamilton would write a preface and put them through the press in book form, with a fancy binding for a few luminaries such as Washington but a cheaper version binding that sold for six shillings so that they could quickly distribute them in Virginia or any other state where strong opposition materialized, and where they could be reprinted in local newspapers. He outlined broad topics to cover: "The Utility of the Union," "Insufficiency of the Present Confederation," "The Need for an Energetic Constitution," "The Constitution's Conformity to True Principles of Republican Government." Under this last heading, they laid out the "general form of the government and its powers," and "the government's structure and its distribution of powers in general." Under that heading, he listed the House of Representatives, Senate, executive, and judiciary branches of the proposed government.

As a nom de plume for the Federalists, it was probably Hamilton who chose "Publius." He had used this sobriquet in attacking Samuel Chase of Maryland in 1778. Publius Valerius had been instrumental in overthrowing the last Roman king and establishing the Roman Republic. His name was familiar to the readers of Plutarch's *Lives* as one who had "resolved to render the government as well as himself familiar and pleasant to the people."

The work expanded as the number of writers dwindled. When Jay bowed out, Madison and Hamilton stuck to their original charges but gave up any hope of editing each other's drafts or collaborating. Addressing their newspaper articles "To the People of the State of New York," they accepted Clinton's Anti-Federalist challenge and, deciding to eschew personal attacks, settled on a calm, patient, expository tone. Hamilton led off, writing Federalist Number 1 on a sloop returning him to New York City from arguing a case before the state Supreme Court at Albany in late October 1787. It appeared in the October 27 issue of the *New York Independent Journal*, taking up a full column on page two—the only page without advertising—and then jumping to a third-of-a-column runover on page three. (This turned out to be the usual layout.)

As Hamilton set to work writing his introduction to the *Federalist Papers*, a letter from his friend Lafayette in Paris, on growing turmoil in Europe, was crossing the Atlantic. The flame of revolution appeared to be igniting all of Europe. In February, a debt-ridden Louis XVI had summoned the Assembly of Notables at Versailles. Lafayette sat in his marquis's robes as he heard the king's finance minister, Calonne, outline his bold plans for fiscal reforms. "Great reforms are taking place at Court," Lafayette wrote Hamilton. Calonne, calling for regional assemblies and an end to the tax-exempt status of the nobles and the Church, was quickly dismissed, but the kings and queens of Europe would not long be able "to extinguish a fire that is catching at every [assembly] of Europe." When the king's new finance minister, de Brienne, tried to have new taxes registered by the Parliament of Paris, it refused, and its members were sent into exile by the king. Howls of protest came from *parlements* all over France, and mobs began to riot in Paris. In the Netherlands, the *stadtholder*, William V, had to call in Prussian troops to restore order, the English fleet standing by to assure the revolt did not spread while the Prussians routed the rebels. Lafayette predicted renewed war between England and France and urged Hamilton to maintain "a friendly, helping neutrality."

The October 17 *Independent Journal* on page one gave its own spin to the news from France. A dangerous mob had assembled at the Tuileries Palace when the king exiled the Parliament. At home, on the Georgia frontier, Indians had shot a girl "in three places" and scalped her "notwithstanding which it is expected she will recover." The Federalists' first essay was surrounded by pages of advertisements for imports ranging from Swedish bar iron to Madeira wine, calicoes, mohair shags, breeches, and gloves from London made "in a far superior manner to any yet manufactured in this country." For the men, there also was Kitefoot "smoaking" tobacco and a "new invented vegetable waistcoat in patterns vastly elegant"; for madame, "muffs of marten throat and real ermine."

But the big news was Federalist Number 1, and the gossip on the street was that its author was Alexander Hamilton. New Yorkers recognized his familiar style. They had followed his political argument for thirteen years now. His rich vocabulary combined with a colloquial directness, drawing them in on the first line:

> After a full experience of the insufficiency of the existing federal government, you are invited to deliberate upon a new Constitution for the United States of America. The subject speaks its own importance, comprehending in its consequences nothing less than the existence of the UNION, the safety and welfare of the parts of which it is composed, the fate of an empire in many respects the most interesting in the world.

Using a broad brush and speaking directly to his fellow citizens, Hamilton appealed to their historical sense of duty, confiding in them that they shared with him a bold destiny. It was up to "the people of this country to decide by their conduct and example the important question whether societies of men are really capable or not of establishing good government from reflection and choice" or whether they would forever depend "on accident and force." If they made the "wrong election" at this point, it would be "the general misfortune of mankind."[24]

What man on the street could miss the urgency of Hamilton's impatient, dead-level appeal? Who could duck the responsibility it carried? He attacked the state bureaucracy and the upstate politicians at the outset, not opponents by name, but warned that it was in "the

obvious interest of a certain class of men in every state" to resist anything that diminished "the power, emoluments and consequences of
the offices they hold under the States." He had decided to attack
publicly state governments, but he also went after profiteers and land
speculators, the "perverted ambition of another class of men aggran-
dizing themselves amid the confusions." And he warned that the
"great national discussion" would unleash "a torrent of angry and
malignant passions." Was not "jealousy the usual concomitant of violent love"? The "noble enthusiasm of liberty" carried with it "a spirit
of narrow and illiberal distrust." Knowing he was gambling not only
the dissolution of the Union but his own political future, Hamilton
anticipated the question: "My motives must remain in the depository
of my own breast." But Publius's "arguments will be open to all and
may be judged by all."[25]

As Federalists and Anti-Federalists waged a wintertime war of
words for minds and votes in the upcoming New York Assembly
elections that would, in turn, decide the assembly's vote on the Constitution, news came from other states where there was less opposition. In Philadelphia, where the Constitution had been argued all
summer, Federalists from the city and other commercial towns had to
defeat a series of Anti-Federalist amendments and delays in the Pennsylvania convention until they finally won on December 12 by a forty-
six to twenty-three vote. Less than a week later, on December 18,
New Jersey, a Federalist stronghold, needed only a one-week convention to ratify. But to Delaware went the honor of being the first state
to ratify the Constitution by a unanimous vote, on December 7, 1787.

After John Jay wrote four essays on foreign affairs and, unable to
write rapidly, withdrew from the grind of preparing and proofing
articles that appeared once or twice a week, Hamilton jumped into
the gap. He produced seven essays in six weeks while Madison wrote
one, his Federalist Number 10. But there seemed no jealousy between
them. Hamilton sensed how important it was for Madison to dispel
Montesquieu's widely believed dictum, and a popular Anti-Federalist
argument, that a federal government could not work in such a large
and expanding country, in anything but a small republic. In numbers

15 through 22, first Hamilton, then Madison pointed out the inadequacy of confederacies throughout history. Hamilton called the Confederation government's record over the past four years since the Treaty of Paris "the last stage of national humiliation." His pen dripping sarcasm, he said the "imbecility" of the American government made embassies abroad "mere pageants of mimic sovereignty." Enumerating the weaknesses of the Confederation, he ticked off the government's inability to make laws for individuals, its complete lack of sanctions against the excesses or insults of member states, its good-faith dependence on state quotas for revenues, its inability to regulate commerce, and its lack of authority to adjudicate interstate disputes. Moving on in essays numbers 23 to 36, Hamilton single-handedly laid out "the necessity of a Constitution" which would be at least as energetic as the one devised in Philadelphia.[26]

By late winter, Madison began to withdraw from the writing and prepared to return to Virginia to run for a seat at that embattled state's ratifying convention. Hamilton wrote, in numbers 59 through 61, regulations for elections, then Madison and Jay, writing their last Federalist essays in February 1788, each wrote one on the Senate (Madison had already analyzed the House of Representatives). But from that point on, it was all Hamilton's thought, sweat, effort as he produced the final twenty-one essays himself in three months, putting down his quill and pushing the last galley proof across the stone to the printer in time for the May 28, 1788 edition. In Federalist Numbers 65 and 66, he wrote about impeachments. In the final essay, Federalist Number 85, he defended the overall effect of the Constitution. "I am persuaded that it is the best which our political situation, habits and opinions will admit." The new system, which he had come to like better as he wrote about it, "may not be perfect in every part [but it] is, upon the whole, a good one."[27] In all, Hamilton had written fifty-one of the eighty-five *Federalist Papers*, produced them in book form, and sent them off all over America by courier in seven months. It was his greatest political achievement. Receiving his copy at Mount Vernon, Washington wrote, "When the transient circumstances and fugitive performances [of] this crisis have disappeared, that work will merit the notice of posterity because in it are candidly and ably discussed the principles of freedom and the topics of government, which will be always interesting to mankind." But the Constitution was still in peril in New York, and Hamilton was still the unappreciated prophet in his adopted land as each state jostled to be last, and most decisive, in the battle over ratification.[28]

On January 2, Georgia had become the fourth ratifier and the third to do so unanimously. Two days later, Connecticut convened its delegates, and voted a lopsided 128–40 for ratification on January 9. That same day, Massachusetts met. Anti-Federalists counted 192 votes against 144 for ratification when the convention opened, but by January 30, when Federalists promised a list of amendments would immediately follow ratification, Sam Adams dropped his opposition, and the Constitution passed February 6, along with nine recommended amendments. The first state to reject the Constitution outright did so despite the fact it never sent a delegate either to Annapolis or to Philadelphia. Refusing to have a convention, Rhode Island put the question by referendum on March 24. The count was 2,945 against ratification, only 237 in favor. Three states still were needed to make up the two-thirds majority for ratification. Maryland said yes on April 28; South Carolina, by a wide 149–73 margin, on May 23. When New Hampshire's delegates met, they decided to adjourn until late June, throwing the decision to the two largest and most divided states, New York and Virginia.

THE ELECTIONS for delegates to New York's ratifying convention sharply divided the state into greater New York City and everywhere else. Federalists Hamilton, Jay, and Robert R. Livingston carried Manhattan, Richmond, West Chester, and Kings County, but split the rest of Long Island with Clinton's Anti-Federalists. The Anti-Federalists swept the rest of the state, going into the convention with a forty-six to nineteen margin, nearly three to one against ratifying the Constitution. Clinton's majority party in the assembly had shrewdly relaxed the usual property qualification for voters, for the first time allowing every free male citizen above the age of twenty-one to vote. In a rural state where many farmers had land but little cash and resented the moneyed voters of New York City and its suburbs, the Anti-Federalists promised to be unsympathetic to Hamilton and his allies, many of them bankers, lawyers, and merchants. The city dwellers, on the other hand, desperately sought an end to the commercial crisis and were whispering threats of seceding from New York State and forming a new state that would affirm the Constitution rather than face isolation from the rest of the United States.

When two of the city's delegates—Hamilton and Jay, still the supposedly anonymous authors of the *Federalist Papers*—sailed upriver to attend the convention, a thirteen-gun salute from the Battery saw them off. When they arrived at the booming Hudson River port of Poughkeepsie, they confronted a less enthusiastic reception. Capital of the state since the British had burned Kingston in 1777, Poughkeepsie was the seat of Dutchess County, with a population of thirty-two thousand, the state's second most populous county and Clinton's power base. A thriving supply depot during the Revolution, it had armed all New York and even outfitted expeditions against Canada and a naval battle on Lake Champlain. Here, there would be little horse trading. The farmers and country lawyers who packed the handsome, two-story, one-year-old courthouse (on the west side of Market Street between Main and Union) were not easily swayed by the city-slick Federalists. Added to their natural reticence, they were in an ugly mood because of their sixth bad harvest in a row, and their perception that the city traders and lawyers were also partly traitors grew worse with every wheat-destroying Hessian fly they found ravaging their fields. The voracious insects laying their larvae among the stubble of each year's harvest had been spreading north since they had arrived on Staten Island in the holds of British supply ships, ravaging more of the state's wheat and rye crops every year. Although it would be another three years before two Virginia farmers, Jefferson and Madison, unraveled the mysterious pattern of the hated Hessian fly, farmers watching a hundred of the insects on every blade of wheat were finding it hard to think of the benefits of treaties and renewed trade with the wartime enemy that had left this winged plague behind. Had Hamilton and his colleagues ridden north and talked to the farmers as he had en route south to Annapolis the year before, he might have been less shocked at the intransigence of Clinton's backers at the convention.

Hamilton and his eight fellow urban dwellers in the assembly would have to grow a majority, and in arguments over the next six steamy weeks in the packed courtroom—some two hundred spectators plus sixty-five lawmakers jammed the small chamber—Hamilton employed every trick he knew and some that were new to obtain unconditional ratification. Realizing it would probably not be possible for New York to become the ninth ratifier, he arranged for express riders from New Hampshire and Virginia to rush him news if either state approved the Constitution. And he wrote out the first New York Assembly motion to assure that the Constitution did not come to a hasty up-or-down vote. Until it had been thoroughly debated, the Constitution would be considered by a Committee of the Whole. Confidently, Clinton agreed to Hamilton's motion.

A young attorney in Poughkeepsie, James Kent, who attended every debate and became New York's chancellor, would write out for Hamilton's widow a detailed account of Hamilton's role. It corroborates the shorthand notes of journalist Francis Childs, editor of the *New York Daily Advertiser*, which had published many of the *Federalist Papers*. Hamilton and his Federalists faced Clinton's best Anti-Federalist minds. They included John Lansing, who had studied law beside Hamilton in Albany only six years earlier and was anything but awed by him, and who had, with Robert Yates, now at his elbow, made up the two-thirds majority of the state's delegation to the Constitutional Convention that had all but neutered Hamilton's efforts. Both pro-Clinton lawyers knew firsthand the holes in Hamilton's arguments. Other Clintonian lawyers not known for compromising included Melancthon Smith of Dutchess County and Samuel Jones of Queens.

For the Federalists, Chancellor Livingston led off by pointing out the dangers of isolation, but among the Federalists, it was Hamilton who was on his feet most often, some twenty-six times. His opponents rose to fight back even more often, Smith forty-five times, often to offer crippling amendments, and Lansing thirty times over six weeks. As the drama unfolded, it became clear that the Anti-Federalists hoped to block ratification by making a long list of amendments that could be approved only by another national convention before New York would ratify. Hamilton did not speak until the second day, and then his comments were terse and impatient. He had hardly been able to endure the slurs against the Constitution. "I will not agree with gentlemen who trifle with the weaknesses of our country," he declared. "No, I believe these weaknesses to be real, and pregnant with destruction." He considered it absolutely necessary "to dwell upon the imbecility of our Union and to consider whether we, as a state, could stand alone." Now he had tightened the agenda to two key issues, at the same time raising the tone above the personal attacks of the Anti-Federalists.[29]

Shrewdly appealing to the memories of New Yorkers whom he knew had shouldered far more of their share of the burden of the war than many other states, Hamilton won over Clinton by having the secretary of the convention read Clinton's own complaints about the weakness of Congress and its inability to enforce quotas in speeches to the assembly in 1780, 1781, and 1782. But so stubborn was the Anti-Federalist resistance that, even when news came by express rider on June 24 that New Hampshire had ratified on June 21 by fifty-seven to forty-seven, the debate in Poughkeepsie raged on. Shortly after noon on July 2, Governor Clinton was making one of his rare comments on the Constitution when the respectful silence was broken by "such a buzz through the House that little of His Excellency's speech was heard." Colonel William S. Livingston had ridden eighty-two miles of rough road from New York City in ten hours (changing horses only twice). He jumped down from his foam-flecked bay horse with dispatches for Hamilton. Madison had mailed the news to Congress. Virginia, over the powerful objections of Patrick Henry, had ratified. As the doorkeeper handed a beaming Hamilton Madison's letter and convention president Edmund Pendleton's certification, a Federalist crowd cheered and, following the ragtag music of a fife and drum, marched around the courthouse.[30]

But the fight inside was still not over. As both sides menaced each other with New York's isolation from the Union, for two days Hamilton and Lansing attacked each other bitterly. Lansing reminded Hamilton that he had proposed the annihilation of the states at the Philadelphia convention. Hamilton interrupted him, denying he was inconsistent. "I am not one of those indifferent mortals who either never form opinions or never make them known." But a "warm personal altercation" filled up two already searing summer days before Clinton stepped in and played the peacemaker. After a series of resolutions in favor of amending the Constitution made it clear that a Bill of Rights would have to be appended, the Constitution passed by a thirty to twenty-seven vote. Clinton saw that its opponents probably never would be satisfied but he pledged to "keep up peace and good order."[31]

Two days later, Hamilton returned to New York City and personally carried the ratified document to Congress. He arrived too late to witness his moment of public triumph. Ten days before, a huge crowd could be restrained no longer from paying its homage. The victory parade was led by a mock frigate, the name "Hamilton" emblazoned across its capstan. Firing a thirteen-gun salute from real cannon, the federal ship led the procession [which] "made a very pompous appearance." The "Hamilton's" sailmakers followed with a float pulled by four matched horses and bearing "in the center, Colonel Hamilton, the new constitution on his right hand and the [Articles of] Confederation in his left." Everywhere, there were nationalist symbols. Eagles and stars plastered tavern signs and would soon decorate furniture, clocks, and doorknockers. Thirteen thirteen-year-old coopers' apprentices led other apprentices sporting green oak branches in their hats. Workmen on the coopers' float showed how impossible it was to repair a broken barrel of thirteen staves and made a new cask for the roaring crowd. Between marching bands, tailors wore fig-leaf aprons and flanked naked effigies of Adam and Eve while Rhode Island wore mourning clothes. Furriers had a would-be Indian delivering pelts while a brewer's wagon carrying a three-hundred-gallon cask of ale topped by a live Bacchus bore a banner reading, "Ale, proper drink for Americans." Five years earlier, through the wreckage of the Revolution, Alexander Hamilton had ridden down this same route to City Hall in a crowd of horsemen accompanying George Washington. Now the crowd cheered for Hamilton.[32]

FIFTEEN

"The Compass of National Authority"

On a clear April day in 1789, young girls and their mothers from Trenton, New Jersey, wearing long white gowns, gathered under garlands of laurel at the bridge over Assunpink Creek where British grenadiers with fixed bayonets had tried to dislodge Alexander Hamilton's artillery a dozen years before. Today, the women, led by Annis Boudinot Stockton, sister of Hamilton's old friend and former president of Congress, strewed flower petals at the feet of George Washington's horse as Philadelphia's First City Troop of Cavalry escorted him toward his inauguration in New York City. Washington hated the adulation of people who wanted to treat him like a king. He had not wanted to be president, preferring to remain, retired and beloved, on his farm at Mount Vernon. But Alexander Hamilton would not leave him alone. If Washington didn't accept the presidential nomination, Hamilton feared that an Anti-Federalist—George Clinton or, even worse, John Adams, the man Washington and Hamilton had despised and distrusted ever since the Conway cabal—would carry the electoral college and become the president, and the Union would not survive.

In mid-August 1788, only a few weeks after his victory in the battle for ratification, Hamilton had sent Washington a handsomely bound set of the *Federalist Papers*. He was sure Washington "understood that the writers of these papers are chiefly Mr. Madison and myself with some aid from Mr. Jay." As if offhandedly, Hamilton said he took it "for granted, Sir," that Washington would "comply with the general call of your country." Hamilton had learned of Washington's reluctance but "it was indispensable you should lend yourself to its first operations." George III had said that if Washington could give up power, he would be the greatest man of the eighteenth century. So enormous was Washington's reputation that his mere presence at the Annapolis Convention in 1786 and the Constitutional Convention in 1787 had assured serious consideration for the bloodless revolution that had, in turn, overthrown the first United States government and replaced it with a far more conservative institution. But the new federal government faced apparently insurmountable financial, diplomatic, and political obstacles. If it foundered with Washington at its helm, his reputation would be dashed. In a confident, uncompromising tone, the former aide-de-camp now lectured his general: "It is to little purpose to have introduced a system if the weightiest influence is not given to its firm establishment at the outset."[1]

Writing back to praise "the triumvirate" of the *Federalist Papers*, Washington told Hamilton, "It is my great and sole desire to live and die on my farm." Washington's letter astonished Hamilton. He shot back that he was "deeply pained" but not surprised. He urged Washington to defer a final decision. But he was certain that Washington would have to acquiesce to "the unanimous wish of your country even if the absolute retreat which you meditated at the close of the late war was natural and proper." But, after Confederation had not worked smoothly, by coming "again into the public view" to review the structure of government, Hamilton was "clear in the opinion that you are, by that act, *pledged* to take part in the execution of the government":

In a matter so essential to the well-being of society, as the prosperity of a newly instituted government, a citizen of so much consequence as yourself to its success has no option but to lend his services if called for.

If the new government should miscarry because Washington did not follow through on the pledge implied by his signature to the new Constitution, there would be "a greater hazard to your fame" by not offering "indispensable" aid.[2]

Far from being taken aback by Hamilton's bold new tone, Washington replied by the next mail, thanking Hamilton for his "frankness" and for his "manly tone of intercourse." He was "particularly glad" that Hamilton had spoken "freely and like a friend." Washington had otherwise foregone the "counsel of my best friends" and maintained a "guarded silence" because any "premature display of anxiety" about his nomination "might be construed into a vainglorious desire of pushing myself into notice as a candidate." But Washington hastened to add his fervent wish that the electoral college would vote for someone else and "save me from the dreaded dilemma of being forced to accept or refuse." He told Hamilton of "a kind of gloom" about the decision, which was giving him "more diffidence and reluctance than ever I experienced before in my life." He would only consent to accepting the office if, "at an early period," he would once again be "permitted" to retire, "to pass an unclouded evening after the stormy day of life." Yet Washington was equally worried by the possibility that many Anti-Federalists, concerned that he would strengthen the new government, would run for seats in the electoral college just to block him. He believed the Anti-Federalists planned "systematic" opposition. What Washington was not saying was that he believed George Clinton had organized secret support for his own candidacy for president. One reason Washington hesitated to show any public interest in the presidency was that he feared that Anti-Federalists in Virginia and in other states would punish him for his support of the new Constitution by voting against him.[3]

Next, Hamilton shared with Madison his analysis of comparative Federal and Anti-Federalist strength. "If pains are taken, the danger of an Anti-Federal vice president might itself be rendered the instrument of Union." They discussed three vice presidential candidates bluntly. John Adams would be a strong candidate in New England, New York, and New Jersey, but not from Pennsylvania south. Hamilton did not think Clinton would exchange the governorship of New York for the office "or risk his popularity by holding both." Henry Knox simply couldn't afford the office: "A salary must of necessity be a primary object with him." Hamilton had decided to support Adams "though I am not without apprehension." Adams, wrote Hamilton, would put off passing necessary constitutional amendments. A Bill of Rights had been promised in several major states as a condition of constitutional ratification. And, Hamilton thought, an Easterner was needed to balance the ticket with the Southerner Washington. Unless Adams received the vice presidential nomination, Hamilton predicted, he would "become a malcontent." Adams could "possibly espouse, and give equal weight, to the opposition." Hamilton had obviously told Madison how strongly he and Washington disliked Adams for his open support in Congress of Horatio Gates's attempt to fire Washington as commander-in-chief in the Conway cabal. If Adams and Clinton joined forces, Clinton could deprive Washington of a substantial margin of victory. It was better, Hamilton counseled Madison, to give Adams the vice presidency under Washington.

There was another dreadful possibility, Hamilton reminded Madison: a flaw in the Constitution "rendering it doubtful who is appointed President." The candidate they intended for vice president, if he garnered more electoral votes than the presidential candidate, could win the presidency. Either Clinton or Adams could declare that he was a candidate for the second-highest office, but if more electors voted for one of them and fewer for Washington, or if there were a tie vote, "the Constitution has not provided the means of distinguishing." Before the Twelfth Amendment was adopted in 1803, electors did not cast one vote for a two-man ticket but two votes for two candidates. The candidate with the most votes became president; the runner-up, vice president. The likelihood was slim, but, Hamilton said, "It would be disagreeable even to have a man treading close upon the heels of the person we wish as President." Could not the "malignity" of the opposition lead the Anti-Federalists against Washington?

Hamilton and Madison would have to wait until they knew who

the electors were and then "we must in our different circles take our measures accordingly." The last Congress under the Articles of Confederation had chosen New York as the temporary capital and set the date for appointment of presidential electors as January 7, 1789, and for their balloting, February 4. The first Congress under the new Constitution would meet on March 4 and the first president would be sworn in on April 30. In the meantime, Hamilton said he was chagrined to hear that Madison did not want a cabinet office. Without Madison, the new government would "severely" suffer from not enough men with the skills and the zeal to parry "the machinations of its enemies."[4]

Just what measure Hamilton would take while he waited for the election became clear when he launched a brutal series of newspaper attacks on Clinton. Hamilton clearly intended eight letters signed "H.G." to the *New York Daily Advertiser* to discredit Clinton both as a vice presidential candidate and for reelection as governor of New York. Governor Clinton, and Hamilton maligned him by name, was "artful," he was "CUNNING" (he capitalized the entire word), he was a "source of the greatest mischief." Hamilton attacked Clinton's Revolutionary War record. Clinton, he averred, had been in "actual combat" only once, had been defeated after a "feeble" defense, and had beaten a hasty retreat while his troops fell captive. And he had failed to prevent the burning of the Revolutionary capital at Kingston. Hamilton flailed Clinton for stirring up mobs against the Loyalists at war's end, but his most serious charges were that Clinton "prejudged and condemned" the new Constitution and now opposed New York City as the nation's capital. Hamilton's hard-hitting campaign journalism once again succeeded in the short run, but it made him even more personal enemies in New York.[5]

To constitutional law expert James Wilson, whom Hamilton would keep from high office, Hamilton nevertheless intimated his anxiety over

That defect in the constitution that renders it possible that the man intended for Vice President may in fact turn up President. Everybody sees that unanimity [for] Adams as Vice President and a few votes insidiously withheld from Washington might substitute the former to the latter.

Hamilton worried to Wilson that "personal caprice or hostility to the new system" would lead half a dozen electors to withhold their votes from Washington while Adams won what was supposedly the vice presidential slot unanimously. Hamilton suggested that Wilson urge Pennsylvanians to throw away their votes—"say 7 or 8"—rather than vote for Adams, giving them "to persons otherwise not thought of." He told Wilson he had urged Federalists in Connecticut and New Jersey likewise to throw away two electoral votes each. He suggested that Wilson "prudently" arrange for Pennsylvania to throw away three or four. "For God's sake, let not our zeal for a secondary object defeat or endanger a first." He feared Adams would become "a formidable head to the Antifederalists." He urged Wilson to pass along his suggestion to Federalists in Maryland "to *qualify* matters there."[6]

In the first presidential election, held in New York on February 4, 1789, George Washington swept the electoral college with all sixty-nine votes cast by electors from ten of the eleven states that had ratified the Constitution. Only New York State, Clinton's anti-Federalist stronghold, failed to send electors to cast their ballots at New York City Hall. John Adams, running second with thirty-four ballots, became vice president. Hamilton and Madison's successful campaign to win ratification of the Constitution followed by their behind-the-scenes maneuvering to help Washington win election unanimously in the electoral college probably made it inevitable that Washington would defer to their judgment on setting up his government. Adams may have won the vice presidency but, from the outset, he was not consulted on the makeup of the cabinet. For almost every post, it was Hamilton or Madison, with the concurrence of Henry Knox, Washington's oldest friend, and to a lesser extent, John Jay, who made up Washington's inner circle, but John Adams never successfully influenced Washington's choices. Working behind the scenes, Hamilton more than any of the others arranged for his own candidates to fill the key posts of government and excluded the enemies of his friends.

In several cases, this meant antagonizing some of his own allies. Robert R. Livingston had helped Hamilton win the battle for ratification in New York and, as chief justice of such an important state, expected to become the first chief justice of the United States, but Hamilton remembered Livingston's land-grabbing in New York at the end of the Revolution at the expense of Loyalist businessmen. Hamilton, with Madison's aid, kept Livingston out of office. To save Livingston's face, they arranged for him, as New York's chief justice, to administer the oath of office to Washington at his inauguration. That cost nothing politically, especially since no federal judicial appointments had yet been made and there was no United States chief justice.

In several cases, Hamilton and Madison manipulated Washington to put together the team they thought would best serve him. Washington wanted John Jay, secretary of foreign affairs under the Confederation government, as his secretary of state, but Jay told Hamilton he preferred to be chief justice and he got that post. So a Livingston in-law garnered the top judicial job at the expense of a Livingston, in part appeasing the large Livingston clan, Hamilton's father-in-law's principal political allies. As a consequence, Washington appointed Madison's closest friend and political ally, Thomas Jefferson, as secretary of state without consulting him. Jefferson would not discover the appointment until he came home on leave from his post as minister plenipotentiary to France. If he had refused it, Jefferson would probably have been replaced in Paris by Hamilton's old friend Gouverneur Morris, who soon afterward became the top American diplomat in Europe.

Two expectant Founding Fathers received no appointment at all. James Wilson of Pennsylvania, a signer of the Declaration of Independence, had been a member of Congress through most of the Revolution and Confederation years but had opposed Benjamin Franklin's Pennsylvania Constitution as too democratic and had aligned himself with Robert L. Livingston and John Dickinson, both anathema to Hamilton. The fact that, as chief legal adviser to Robert Morris's Bank of North America, he had received, while the bank's attorney, almost $100,000 in loans on questionable security, made him odious to

Hamilton who had learned of the deal as proxy for the bank's largest shareholder, his brother-in-law John Church. One other shareholder Hamilton blocked from office was Congressman Arthur Lee of Virginia, not only a well-known enemy of Madison but a borderline paranoiac who bought Bank of North America stock just so he could spy on Robert Morris. Lee coveted a federal district judgeship. He didn't get it. Lee also was the longtime enemy of Benjamin Franklin, onetime British postmaster general for America, who had been publicly humiliated and fired after he opened sensitive mails between royal officials. Under the new Constitution, Franklin became the first postmaster general of the United States.

FOR THE key post of secretary of the treasury, Washington's first choice was Robert Morris, superintendent of finance under the Confederation, the nation's leading financier and founder of its first bank, the Bank of North America. When Washington inquired delicately who Morris thought should have the top treasury job, Morris recommended Hamilton. Hamilton was "damned sharp," Morris told the president-elect. According to a persistent legend, Washington had broached the subject of the public debts and what to do about them, expecting Morris, as in the past, to offer his services. To Washington's surprise, Morris replied, "There is but one man in the United States who can tell you. That is Alexander Hamilton." Washington had all the confirmation he needed of his own judgment after working with Hamilton for five years of war.[7]

But while Washington wanted Hamilton, Hamilton, too, remembered the years as aide-de-camp. He evidently took his time making up his mind. He was already trying to repair the damage of three years of relative neglect to his law practice from his political crusading. He was seriously considering concentrating his talents on making money. He had just taken on Charles Adams, the vice president's second son, as a law clerk, something that required Hamilton's physical presence in his office and in New York courtrooms. His cashbook shows that John Adams had paid a deposit on Hamilton's fee.

Hamilton's wallet was flat and his family growing. Philip, his firstborn, was seven years old by now; Angelica, nearly three. While

Hamilton had been away serving in Congress in 1786, a second son, Alexander Hamilton, Jr., was born. A third son, James Alexander, came while Hamilton was churning out the *Federalist Papers*. Betsy had some modest income from rents on farms on fifteen hundred acres of Schuyler lands at Saratoga, which provided the collateral Aaron Burr had demanded when the Hamiltons bought their Manhattan house and office, but for most of their expenses they depended on Hamilton's earnings as New York City's leading marine lawyer. When the new Congress got around to creating the executive departments of the federal government, the secretary of the treasury's salary was fixed at a niggardly $3,500, only one seventh of the president's salary. A further check to Hamilton's best-laid plan for an alliance with Madison in the Senate came when he learned that a vengeful Patrick Henry, former governor of Virginia and the principal opponent of ratification in the South, had used his influence to punish Madison for his successful constitutional crusade by blocking Madison's election to the Senate by the Virginia legislature. Madison had already turned down a cabinet office. He entered the new government as a lowly freshman congressman. Publius had lost his left hand.

ON APRIL 22, 1789, George Washington arrived at Elias Boudinot's house in Elizabethtown, New Jersey, and met with a joint delegation from the new House of Representatives, the Senate, and his putative cabinet. The visit to the Boudinots held added significance for Hamilton, who, fifteen years earlier, had begun his American odyssey in these rooms. Washington had exchanged worry for gloominess. He learned it would take another six weeks to gather a congressional quorum that could create executive departments so he could, in turn, appoint his cabinet. Congressman Hamilton, still undecided on a Treasury post, could only add to Washington's concern: unless the new legislative body established the Treasury Department under the new Constitution before the spring fleets from Europe arrived in America, he pointed out, upward of $300,000 in customs duties, the bulk of the federal budget he projected for the year, would be lost. Washington set the date of his inauguration for only one week later. Meanwhile, Adams and the Congress had to be sworn in so that government business, at a standstill since the old Confederation Congress had adjourned sine die more than six months earlier, could resume.

While Washington traveled the last fifteen miles to Manhattan through a parade of ships in a thirteen-oared barge, painters and carpenters were rushing last-minute renovations to City Hall, renamed Federal Hall, at the intersection of Broad and Wall Streets. The city council, eager to keep the capital in Manhattan, had hired the French architect Major Pierre L'Enfant to carry out $65,000 of alterations so that the building could accommodate the House on the first floor and the Senate on the second, creating space for committee rooms, a library, and a "machinery room" to display and promote inventions. The Supreme Court would meet in a separate building on nearby Broad Street, above a sheep market.

At noon on April 30, Hamilton and Washington's other advisers arrived in carriages and took their places behind Washington's cream-colored, garland-festooned state carriage as it set off between troops and marching bands and a long line of the carriages of congressmen and foreign ambassadors. Hamilton and three other former aides-de-camp escorted Washington into Federal Hall and up the stairs to the Senate chamber. Washington bowed to Adams, then to Congress, then stepped out onto a small balcony. Chancellor Livingston administered the oath of office. Washington's left hand rested on a Bible held by his old aide, Colonel Samuel Blachley Webb. He added the words, "So help me God" to the oath Livingston dictated, bowed twice to the huge crowd roaring "God bless our Washington! Long live our beloved President!," then stepped back inside and, hand trembling, read a twelve-hundred-word inaugural speech, the shortest on record. He recommended swift passage of a Bill of Rights and then walked out.

Leading the House and Senate on a seven-hundred-yard march past houses and storefronts illuminated by hundreds of candles to St. Paul's Chapel of Trinity Church at the foot of Broadway, he sat on a high-backed gold brocade chair set off to the left of pews packed with dignitaries for a thanksgiving service and "Te Deum."[8]

After a private dinner that night, Washington took aside Hamilton and Adams and asked their advice. The day's rituals, the adulation of the crowd vexed him. He was already so anxious that many Americans wanted him to behave like a king while others objected to the creation of the hereditary Society of the Cincinnati, causing his decision to boycott that organization's first national convention. He asked Hamilton and Adams to make recommendations on presidential protocol. His query led to the first presidential crisis. What should the president be called? How formal should be his conduct? Should he go out for drives, for visits or dinners at the homes of congressmen, ambassadors, private citizens?

A chasm instantly opened between Hamilton and Adams. On May 5, Hamilton wrote Washington "on the etiquette proper to be observed by the President." It was essential that "the dignity of the office" be put above "momentary dissatisfaction." Americans were "prepared for a pretty high tone" in presidential demeanor but there were already too many "notions of equality." But Washington should avoid creating too much distance between the president and "other branches of the government." The president should hold a levee "once a week for receiving visits." Invited visitors should assemble first. The president should "remain half an hour," conversing on "indifferent subjects," then "disappear." No visits were to be returned. The president was to accept no invitations but give "formal entertainments two to four times a year on the anniversaries of important events in the Revolution: if twice, on the Fourth of July and the anniversary of his inauguration; if four times, add the anniversaries of the Treaty of Alliance with France and the peace treaty with England. Congressional and government leaders, ambassadors and "distinguished strangers" were to attend these state dinners. Hamilton's prescriptions were precise, minute. "There may be separate tables in separate rooms." On levee days, there should be smaller dinners for six or eight congressmen or other officials. But the president should never "remain long at table." On the question of "the door of access" for official business, cabinet officers and foreign ministers alone should "have this privilege." Senators had a stronger claim than mere congressmen because the Constitution made senators "his counselors" on "certain executive functions, treaties and appointments."[9]

Hamilton was nervous about his "frankness," but the same day he received Washington's "unfeigned thanks." The president's note was short. He liked Hamilton's written answer. "It is my wish to act right." Hamilton had become the first presidential adviser. From experience, he knew what Washington wanted: thoughtful, timely advice, the exact opposite of what he was getting from Federal Hall. It would take two weeks of debate before the Senate could decide what to call the president. In the meantime, Adams wrote Washington that he was opposed to state dinners and thought the president should be free to call on and entertain anyone he wanted. But his recommendations on what to call the president, especially since he always assumed he would succeed Washington, made him, as president of the Senate, slow down crucial government business for two weeks. First, Vice President Adams, presiding over the Senate, thought there had to be a Senate committee to ponder the great question: Should the president be called "the Honorable," "His Elective Highness," or "Majesty," "His Exalted High-Mightiness?" Adams first favored "His Majesty the President," then "His Highness the President of the United States and Protector of the Rights of Same," which the committee recommended to the full Senate. In the safety of his diary, Senator William Maclay, a rough-cut lawyer from Harrisburg, Pennsylvania, called Adams "silly." Rising to read from the Constitution, Maclay repeatedly reminded his colleagues, "No title of nobility shall be granted by the United States." To his diary, Maclay confided that whenever he looked up at Adams, "I cannot help thinking of a monkey just put into breeches."

Finally, on May 14, the Senate voted to follow exactly what the House had recommended. Washington's only title would be "the President of the United States." Washington himself simplified what he should be called in person: "Mr. President." He took Hamilton's advice on protocol almost to the letter. He would receive "visits of compliment" two afternoons each week, each an hour. He would not go out of the President's House to be a dinner guest at any private residence. He would hold a public levee for suitably dressed men, but not women, for an hour every Tuesday afternoon. The first lady would preside over a public tea for ladies and gentlemen every Friday night and host a small dinner by invitation every Tuesday, where the president would join her. The first couple followed this tradition for the next eight years. For most of that time, Washington sought and followed Alexander Hamilton's advice over that of any other adviser.

IN THE interregnum between the death of the Confederation and the creation of new federal departments, Hamilton set about repairing his own finances, quickly becoming one of America's highest-paid lawyers. His principal client was his brother-in-law John Church, who had decided to stay in England, pursue parliamentary politics, and sell off his American holdings with Hamilton acting as his agent. Hamilton's account books show him advertising Broadway real estate, trying to sell Church's 140 shares of Bank of North America stock to Robert Morris—and handling the increasingly private affairs of Angelica Schuyler Church, who arrived from Europe with the spring fleet early in March 1789. She arrived without her husband, her children, or any money. For the first two months of her eight-month sojourn, she stayed with the Hamiltons but, by mid-May, her further stay had become uncomfortable and Hamilton rented her a town house apartment nearby. Hamilton drew heavily on his savings. On May 15 he advanced Angelica a whopping 500 pounds (about $20,000 today); Betsy contributed 100 pounds (about $4,000) from her savings. He rented Angelica a coach and matched pair of horses, and paid the coachman for driving and boarding and for the bran that fed them. He hired her a *valet de chamber*, converting his accounts from dollars to pounds sterling so that he could reimburse himself later from Church's earnings. At first, Hamilton was careful to extract advances from a Church business associate as well, keeping up the appearance of propriety, of a businesslike transaction. Angelica went shopping; Hamilton paid her tailor's bills. He paid for goods she ordered and imported from Europe.

But then, in mid-August, the precise bookkeeping became mysteriously vague. It was the time of summer when Betsy took the children to her parents' Saratoga farm. Hamilton remained in the city and hired a different (and unrecognizable) carriage, paid off the first landlady through October 7, tipping her handsomely, and then paid 23 pounds, nine shillings, three pence (about $900 today) for damages done by Hamilton's servants when they hastily transferred Angelica's belongings to a second apartment. This time, no landlord is mentioned in Hamilton's cashbook, no address listed. But now, Hamilton was no longer billing Angelica's husband for her expenses. The money was coming from his own bank account. By the time he paid 40 pounds (about $800) for a mysterious "Music Master" (could this be for the rental of a harpsichord?), and paid for Angelica's and her servant's ship passage back to England and gave her 200 pounds (about $8,000) of the 377 pounds, 66 shillings he still had left in his private account, his wallet was nearly flat. But from the tone of his letters, he had enjoyed some of the happiest and most productive months of his life.[10]

ALEXANDER HAMILTON'S affection for his wife's older, more sophisticated sister had been growing since the first day he met her. More beautiful, worldlier, Angelica was impressed by the dashing young Hamilton and, because of her travels in the haut monde of London and Paris, she was able to appreciate the high pitch of his charm and intelligence. Angelica was, by now, thoroughly bored with her rich and neglectful husband, as bored as Hamilton was with his shy, plain country wife. Angelica loved music and literature, was widely read in the classics, knowledgeable about politics. She loved the city and the salon, wrote passionate letters—and, in the exile imposed by her husband, yearned for the company of the man she accurately called, until that summer of 1789, her "brother," as was then the custom. She loved to talk about her travels and the people she met while Hamilton soaked up every detail. Betsy refused to travel farther from Albany than New York City or, under the duress of her husband's political appointments, at farthest Philadelphia.

Angelica knew Hamilton's friends probably better than Betsy, who detested political entertainment. Angelica could tell Hamilton the latest gossip from New Yorkers who had gone to Europe, from Lafayette in Paris. She had lived in Paris for two years near the Opéra, a short carriage ride from the Hôtel de Langeac, at the head of the Champs Elysées, where Thomas Jefferson, who had replaced Franklin as minister, lived, and where her friend and Hamilton's, artist John Trumbull, was painting portraits of French officers Hamilton knew for his *Surrender of Lord Cornwallis*. She sent her daughter to the Panthemont School with widower Jefferson's daughters; she visited Jefferson inside his walled garden, where she no doubt met Jefferson's paramour, and Angelica's "dearest sister," Maria Cosway. Angelica conveyed political gossip that Hamilton wanted to hear, enough to last through the summer and into the autumn of 1789, as news arrived from turmoil-wracked France on the eve of revolution.

Hamilton liked his father-in-law, the old Dutch patroon, better than his wife. Betsy, often pregnant, gave birth to eight children in eighteen years, not counting the miscarriages. Nervous, probably depressive, she was bedridden for long periods. She loved to do needlepoint, embroidering whole sofas and chairs, while her husband and her sister played the harpsichord and sang Revolutionary War songs together. Betsy hated the filth and noise of New York City, where pigs roamed the unpaved streets harvesting the garbage that the rains didn't wash away. She was never happier than when she took her children to the hearthside provincial circle of her upstate New York home, more and more without her Hamilton.

WHILE HAMILTON waited for Congress to create the Treasury office, he dabbled again in New York politics, working to have his father-in-law, Schuyler, and his friend Rufus King appointed as New York's first U.S. senators by its legislature. Schuyler won unanimously; King also won, running second, defeating James Duane, Hamilton's former law preceptor and a Livingston in-law. When Hamilton tried to assure that Duane, who was mayor of New York City, would not be succeeded by "some very unfit" Clintonian, he locked horns with state attorney general Aaron Burr. There had been a special assembly caucus that chose the senators. The Federalists in the legislature had taken care of everything, Burr wrote, warning Hamilton to stay away from the city elections.

FILLING HIS workdays with lucrative legal business, his evenings and weekends with the women who loved him, Hamilton atypically wrote few letters that summer. He still had not answered the question that could not yet be officially asked when, on July 21, Vice President Adams asked him if he did not "become a minister of state or some other thing better, or worse" in the new government, would he tutor his Harvard-educated second son, Charles. Was Adams trying to draw out Hamilton about his plans? The feisty Adams said his son would live at home outside the city. "He may go into town and come out with me every day." Adams dictated his son's hours to Hamilton from ten to eleven in the morning, from three to four in the afternoon. Rather than tip his hand, Hamilton signed up Adams's son and pocketed the customary fee for precepting. He was soon happy to return it. On September 11, 1789, President Washington submitted the name of "Alexander Hamilton of New York" as secretary of the treasury to the Senate, John Adams presiding.[11]

The nomination was approved the same day. The Senate approved four other Treasury officials that day, all former Revolutionary officers, as were virtually all the one thousand men Washington personally hired. Hamilton immediately set to work administering the largest government department, with five hundred federal employees, most of them customs collectors. And within forty-eight hours, he set to work to liquidate the United States' original sin, its enormous war debt. President Washington's first command to his thirty-four-year-old treasury minister was to design a new federal financial system and submit it, in writing, to Congress, in only 110 days.

Congress left to Hamilton the hiring of an assistant secretary of the treasury. He chose his friend William Duer, perhaps the clearest exhibit of Hamilton's fatal flaw in his judgment of people. A vain man, Alexander Hamilton repeatedly chose as friends and colleagues people who responded strongly to him, his ideas, and his appearance, and people he perceived to have things in common with him. Like Hamilton, Duer was an outsider. Born in England, educated at Eton, he had served briefly as an aide to Lord Clive in India before finding his way to the West Indies, where his family owned slave-labor sugar plantations on Antigua and Dominica. He first came to New York in 1768 to buy lumber and met Philip Schuyler. On his advice, Duer bought up land east of the Hudson opposite Saratoga, made it his home, and over the next six years, until the Revolution, made a fortune from timbering, supplying masts for Royal Navy ships. He also became a leading speculator in New York lands. In 1776, he became the main supplier of Continental forces in New York State, profiting handsomely from selling thousands of dollars a month in provisions and war matériel. He married Kitty Alexander, the daughter of General William Alexander, self-styled Lord Stirling, who had first offered Hamilton a staff job. Duer paid off his huge prewar debts with depreciated Continental currency.

Selling to both combatants, he used flags of truce to sell flour, cattle, and other supplies to the British inside occupied New York City, making 500 percent profits. Conniving with his father-in-law, a leading New Jersey ironmaster, he sold iron shot manufactured at Lord Stirling's foundry to the British when the American Congress balked at his father-in-law's high prices. He helped himself to $200,000 in Continental appropriations funds meant to buy food for American troops, passed the money through his personal accounts, and bought Continental Loan Office certificates, lending the supply money back to the government at a sizable profit. Just how much Hamilton knew, or cared, about Duer's reputation when he appointed him to the number two treasury post is uncertain, but he surely must have been aware that Duer was considered by some members of Congress and army officers, as historians Burrows and Wallace call him, "the kingpin of corruption among military suppliers." At the time, the appointment seemed logical enough: Duer, secretary of the treasury board since 1786, supposedly knew more about the nation's muddled affairs than anyone else.[12]

IF HAMILTON had any sense of foreboding, it was less about American finances and his role in their future than about the news he was hearing from Paris. He had listened to Angelica's descriptions of riots in the provinces as politicians jostled to become delegates to the first meeting of the French Estates-General since 1648. He had talked to Brissot de Warville, assigned to a diplomatic post in Philadelphia during the Revolution and recently returned to New York to speculate in its financial market. He had talked at length with the Comte de Moustier, the departing French ambassador to the United States. Hamilton knew from official correspondence that Jefferson, before leaving his Paris post for a home leave, had attended the Estates General at Versailles every day, writing in dispatches to John Jay, "Abundance are affrighted and think all is lost." By the time Hamilton wrote Lafayette on October 6, 1789, that he had been appointed secretary of the treasury, Lafayette, as head of the Patriot Party, had failed to unite the different factions clamoring for reform. Hamilton, like Jefferson, supported the call of Necker, once again the king's minister of finance, to create a two-house parliament like England's. Secretly, Lafayette and Jefferson had worked together to frame the French Declaration of Rights of Man and Citizens at the American mission. But there was a three-month lag for a message to sail from Paris to New York and back, and Hamilton did not know that Lafayette and Necker were at odds now.

In July, the American mission in Paris had been robbed three times and Jefferson was seeking police protection. On July 12, the Customs House at the head of the Champs Elysees, right outside Jefferson's front window, a hated symbol of taxation, was burned by rioters after the king again dismissed the popular Necker. That same day, Jefferson was driving his distinctively tall black phaeton through the present-day Place de la Concorde when he encountered a crowd gathered at the entrance to the Tuileries Gardens menacing the royal cavalry guarding the king and queen. The crowd had picked up paving stones and were hurling them at the horsemen. The crowd parted to let Jefferson pass "but the moment after I passed, the people attacked the cavalry."[13]

George Washington's acolytes only a dozen years earlier, Hamilton and Lafayette now addressed each other in letters from their new eminences with "a mixture of pleasure and apprehension," as Hamilton put it, drawing on his own recent experiences:

You will ask why this foreboding of ill when all the appearances have been so much in your favor. I will tell you: I dread disagreements among those who are now united ... about the nature of your constitution. I dread the vehement character of your people, whom I fear you may find it easier to bring [out] than to keep within proper bounds after you have put them in motion. I dread the interested refractoriness of your nobles, who cannot be gratified and who may be unwilling to submit to the requisite sacrifices.

Hamilton's letter could not have been more prophetic.

Hamilton was sure that, by now, Lafayette knew Hamilton had been "appointed to the head of finances of this country." In a rare confession, he told his oldest friend, "in undertaking the task, I hazard much." But if Congress supported him, "the public may be satisfied."

Hamilton was really writing to ask for help of a kind he felt only Lafayette could provide by ameliorating the American debt to France. On his second day in office, Hamilton had met unofficially with Ambassador Moustier. As yet, there was no American secretary of state, but still the talk had to be unofficial, and Hamilton was taking his first step across the line between executive branch departments. The United States was far in arrears in payments of both interest and principal on the loans France had advanced during the Revolution. Hamilton was seeking a breather before strapping further the limited revenues of his treasury. He could not publicly seek a deferral of loan payments without undermining public confidence. Even news of such an official request would depress American credit, especially in Amsterdam where the United States owed more than half of its war debt and where interest rates were set. At first in private conversation with Moustier, then in his letter to Lafayette, he was seeking an "unsolicited" offer, "as a fresh mark of goodwill," to forgo temporarily France's claims for principal if the arrears of interest were paid. Historian Forrest McDonald notes, "There is no surviving evidence as to whether Hamilton made these moves known to Washington."[14]

FIRING OFF volleys of letters seeking knowledge about counterfeiters, smugglers, ships and shipping lighthouses, packet boats, the French national debt, the duties on tea and brandy, Hamilton designed inquiries to his customs officials, in the process inventing the socioeconomic questionnaire to gather up-to-the-minute data, informing his correspondents, to make his Treasury Department work. He needed timely information. He was developing his own administrative style. To run the largest federal department, he worked long hours. John Marshall wrote, years later, that Hamilton had "a patient industry, not always the companion of genius." The Prince de Talleyrand, recommended to Hamilton's hospitality and protection during the Reign of Terror by his friend Angelica, strolled past Hamilton's offices on Wall Street late one evening and was astonished to see the secretary of the treasury hunched at his desk, working by candlelight. "I have just come from viewing a man who made the fortune of his country but now is working all night in order to support his family."[5]

Hamilton broadly patterned himself, as America's first lord of the Treasury, on the principles of the French reformer Necker, and based the financial system he devised on English institutions created in the preceding century. From Necker's works he studied the qualities of a great minister of state: regularity, prudence, firmness, and encyclopedic knowledge. Necker had written in his three-volume memoirs, which Hamilton read and reread, that the genius of administration was to have the capacity to grasp, simultaneously, an entire system and the relationships of its parts to one another and to the whole, then to be able to notice a change in any part. To encourage regularity, a minister not only had to apportion his time and his tasks but also discipline the habits of his thinking. For a finance minister, prudence, knowing when to act and when to stop acting, was paramount: he "must not commit any errors" but must carry out his reforms slowly, methodically, to avoid alarm. By firmness, Necker meant to be inflexible: worse than a dishonest finance minister was a weak one. Finally, a finance minister had to know the nation microscopically while following events and innovations in the rest of the world. Necker nowhere mentioned humility in his rules for a finance minister: "If men are made in the image of God," he wrote, "then the minister of finance, next to the king, must be the man who most closely approximates that image." Hamilton was to follow Necker's principles with one great exception: prudence. He was innovative and adaptive and he knew he had to act quickly. Event and circumstance would not wait. For prudence, he substituted a combination of prodigious effort, originality, and secretiveness.

An apostle of the revolutionary eighteenth-century idea of national credit, Hamilton set to work taking an inventory of the extent of America's financial problems. The public debt was in three categories, foreign, national, and state. The United States had borrowed slightly more than $10 million during the war, roughly $4.4 million from the French royal treasury, $1.8 million from Dutch bankers in loans guaranteed by the French, $3.6 million in direct loans from Dutch bankers, and $1.75 million from the Spanish royal treasury. By the time Hamilton became treasury secretary, the United States was $1.6 million in arrears on the interest payments and $1.4 million in arrears on scheduled principal payments. The cost of servicing the foreign debt was $1 million a year. The cost of current and overdue debt service alone would eat up all the revenues from the 1789 customs duties, still the national government's only tax. Nothing would be left to pay domestic debts, let alone the expenses of the new national government. Considering that British taxation had led to the American Revolution, to raise taxes adequately to pay off debts was not a sane possibility. If the French would be satisfied with interest payments alone, Hamilton believed the annual interest of roughly $500,000 could be met. That would make possible a new Dutch loan that could repay all existing foreign debts. What Hamilton had in mind was debt consolidation. In his report to Congress, he budgeted $542,599 for foreign debt.

To pin down the domestic debt, Hamilton found, was trickier. The Continental Congress had raised wartime revenues in three ways. To pay and supply the army, Congress had issued unsecured paper money—"not worth a Continental"—bonds called loan office certificates yielding 6 percent interest, and promissory notes. Some $200 million in paper money—at least that was its face value—had depreciated so badly that it had been devalued at a rate of forty to one. It was replaced by new paper, which was virtually worthless.

About $11 million in loan office certificates was outstanding, held by speculators such as William Duer. Instead of paying interest, Congress issued certificates of interest, paying them with a portion of its requisitions on the states. The states, in turn, had levied taxes paid in part by indents: as a result, about $1.5 million had been returned to the national treasury and canceled. Several states accepted as taxes the army requisitions handed out when the quartermasters or commissaries helped themselves to necessities for the troops: about $10 million had been paid into the Continental treasury and thus canceled, but $16 million in requisitions were outstanding. Adding up the $13 million in arrears of interest due, Hamilton calculated that the national debt was roughly $40 million. Several states complicated matters further by speculating in Continental securities. As a consequence, state governments owned about one third of the national debt.

On top of this whopping national war debt, the individual states had spent about $100 million on the war. Some states, like Massachusetts and South Carolina, paid as they went as honestly as they could but were hopelessly behind; others, like Rhode Island, Virginia, and North Carolina, paid bills with worthless depreciated currency. Hamilton estimated that the combined outstanding state debt was somewhere between $21 million and $25 million. The state debts usually carried 6 percent interest. In all, the combined American war debts amounted to $76 million. The interest bill now due was $4.5 million, about three times what Hamilton thought could be raised by taxation and tariff duties.[16]

Congress had given Hamilton the power not only to appoint his staff but to superintend the collection of revenues, create the forms of accounts he would need, and prepare and report budget estimates to either branch of Congress. His most important mandate, in fact indispensable, was "to digest and prepare plans for the improvement and management of the revenue and for the support of public credit."

Since he had been a boy in a St. Croix countinghouse, Hamilton had practiced order and system, keeping careful books. He set out to bring to the U.S. Customs Service standardized procedures of collection, calculation, and reporting that all offices had to follow. Yet he fought overrigid bureaucracy. He allowed collectors in major ports some discretion to allow for local practice. He required weekly reports on collections and payments, the volume of shipping of exports and imports on every port, but he also asked for the ideas of Treasury employees on what worked and he wanted to hear the complaints of the merchants. The forms that he required to be filled out also provided room for essays. The results poured in, making him undoubtedly the best-informed federal official, or American citizen, for that matter.

If Hamilton analyzed the federal debt in per capita terms, it was staggering. Out of a population of nearly four million Americans, only 160,000 white males over age twenty-one had property enough to qualify to vote in the constitutional ratification elections. With a combined war debt of $76 million, it meant that the average voter owed $475 in 1789 currency which, factored out, in today's money would mean a debt of $6,175 per voter, more than the vast majority made in a year in a country short on cash.

Once Hamilton knew the depth of the hole the United States was in, he had to think hard about the least unpopular way to fill it. While the new Constitution spelled out the taxing power of the federal government, Hamilton knew he was limited in carrying out his task by political and economic reality. His success depended in large part on how well he knew and gauged national and international economic conditions and financial institutions and how well he played them off to the advantage of the United States. His first careful step to raise sufficient revenue was to decide which forms of taxes to recommend to Congress.

Hamilton basically had only three categories of taxes to choose from. The most unpopular would be direct taxes on people or their property: here his hands were tied by the constitutional requirement that such taxes be apportioned among the states according to population rather than property holdings. It was for this reason that Hamilton eschewed direct taxes, preferring to let the states collect them. Hamilton liked customs duties, a form of tax exclusively reserved to the federal government, as they were the easiest to collect and fell on those who could best afford to pay them. Both federal and state governments could collect excise taxes on particular goods, but, as

Hamilton would soon learn, excise taxes were the least popular. While some congressmen, including Madison, thought the states could levy them, Hamilton believed that taxes sought by two different governments could be evaded more easily than if both were collected by two agencies of the same government, the Federal government. It was this kind of double Federal scrutiny, without the possibility of state interference or profiteering, that Hamilton wanted. The federal government would then be forced to assume full responsibility for the states' debts, exactly what Hamilton wanted. He could expect the states that benefited most to espouse his principle of "assumption": Massachusetts, Connecticut, and South Carolina owed almost half of all state debt. New York, Pennsylvania, and Maryland would have to support any effort to raise revenues because the federal government owed them so much money. Only two states, Virginia and North Carolina, had nothing to gain from assumption of their debts because they had paid them, albeit largely with depreciated currency. And these two states held nearly one in four seats in the House as well as some of the most outspoken spokesmen for states' rights.

How to raise revenue was only slightly less thorny than who would pay. Excise taxes fell on liquor, and there were two basic kinds distilled in America: rum in New York and New England, whiskey in the backcountry. The rum distillers, mostly wealthy, were already creditors of the federal government through speculation, but whiskey came down from countless small stills in the hills from Pennsylvania south, and they were run by Scots-Irish frontiersmen with little interest in supporting the remote federal treasury's needs. Far easier to police would be imports of wine from Spain and Portugal, manufactured goods from England, and sugar and its products from the West Indies. Most of the imports would come through six ports: Charleston and Norfolk from Europe, Boston and Baltimore from the West Indies, and New York and Philadelphia in general. Where Hamilton could expect opposition was in the North, where manufacturers wanted protective tariffs that undercut foreign imports. Eager to appease this powerful voting bloc, Hamilton planned to promise adjustments to the tariff schedule after letting in all the imports he could to pay off the national debt. Again, he faced Madison, the spokesman for Southern tobacco planters, who blamed Robert Morris for monopolizing the tobacco trade with France. In fact, while planters expected to be able to grow rich exporting their crops directly to Europe, England remained the main importer of American tobacco. Hamilton's old collaborator was to be his greatest obstacle as he went about forming an anti-British coalition in Congress that included Southern planters, New England shippers, whalers and fishermen, and Northern manufacturers.

By far the busiest congressional lobbyists were the least popular men in America, the speculators. Generally regarded as unscrupulous, they were not considered investors. Among the bulls were the original holders of public paper paid for service in the army or for supplies. Somewhere between 25 and 40 percent of them still held their securities by 1789. But far more soldiers, their families, or suppliers had sold their paper at deep discounts to one of several hundred merchants who paid as little as 10 cents on the dollar to the hard-pressed original holders. These same speculators, mostly importers, had customers for warehouses crammed with imported goods and, as British creditors cracked down, faced ruin unless the public securities they had bought up were made whole by the new government. One dilemma Hamilton faced was the vexing question whether original holders of public securities or current holders, if they were speculators, should be treated equally. To some Americans, it was a moral as well as an economic question. Hamilton, no doubt with some relish, wrote to John Witherspoon, the president of Princeton who had rejected his plan to go through college on the fast track, to ask him to give some advice to his would-be former pupil. Witherspoon, signer of the Declaration of Independence as a congressman in 1776, had reentered politics as a New Jersey assemblyman. He also had long been the leader of Presbyterians in America. Did Hamilton know (and he possibly had heard from his friend Elias Boudinot, a long-time Princeton trustee) that Witherspoon was speculating in Vermont real estate? In his research, Hamilton may have learned that Witherspoon had taken part in banking systems in the 1750s in Scotland and had, as Witherspoon now wrote Hamilton, "read much and wrote some" on banking theory. Witherspoon agreed to meet Hamilton in

New York City, but in the meantime unburdened himself on the "proper provision for public debt." He reared back and told the young treasury secretary, "The evil that has pervaded our whole affairs in America has been the want of a just sense of the sacredness of public credit." He did not approve of distinguishing between debtors. He pointed to the 25 percent discounts paid in England for "sailors tickets and Navy debentures," and continued:

> Now if any minister in Parliament or any person in the pay office should say to one bringing a number of them, "Where did you get these? You are a speculator. You never drew a rigging rope on a ship. You did not pay the full value of them and we will not pay you the full value of them." Such a thing reported and believed on the Exchange of London would bring the whole national debt to the ground in two hours.[17]

Behind this speculative binge was the American belief in land. If only the speculators could make a killing in discounted securities, they could reinvest it in far safer landholdings to the West. Benjamin Franklin had tried to corner millions of acres in the Midwest before the Revolution and now owned thousands of acres in Pennsylvania. Washington had bought up nearly five hundred thousand acres of frontier land; Henry Knox was on his way to going bust on speculations in Maine. Some speculators, such as William Duer, were actually gambling that the value of government securities would stay depressed so that, if they could buy impoverished Continental soldiers' pay certificates for 10 cents on the dollar and then buy unclaimed government land at a dollar an acre, they could parlay an investment of $100,000 into one million acres of western lands to sell to future settlers as fast as the government cleared out the Indians.

But Hamilton was facing east and hoping to establish a more stable financial climate. He knew that, in Amsterdam, the financial capital of the world in 1789, the Dutch had been dumping their British investments and investing in American and French loans since 1780, when the British provoked a four-year war with them. With France sliding into revolution, the Dutch had lent more money each year that kept the United States from defaulting on its loans to France, and by 1789, the Dutch had also bought $1 million in Continental securities on the New York open market. To achieve the sort of stability the United States needed to attract more foreign investment that would, in turn, pay off the American debt, Hamilton turned to the English model. While Necker had sought to build up France's credit by cutting royal waste and streamlining its tax system, England for a century had been encouraging a national debt.

During the past century since the founding of the Bank of England in 1694 by the Dutchman King William III, while British tax revenues sextupled, the national debt rose fifteen fold. Up to 40 percent of the national debt was covered by loans, and military spending devoured as much as 14 percent of national income. Yet, as the national debt grew, Britain rose from a marginal, civil war–torn state to an empire with colonies on three continents and the financial resources to subsidize the world's largest navy and—except for the aberration of losing the American Revolution—most successful armies. A series of brilliant finance ministers from Horace Walpole to William Pitt the Younger had turned its national debt into a great asset. The Bank of England was able to raise money, once extracted from land taxes as high as 20 percent in wartime, by issuing long-term bonds that could be traded on the open market. The British government was able to raise money at relatively low rates of interest whenever it needed it, thus making war possible at virtually all times without bringing on revolution by unhappy taxpayers.

As he studied the English financial system in 1789, Hamilton also struck on the latest British expedient, the sinking fund. Earmarking a portion of tax revenues each year to pay off the national debt, the sinking fund was the brainchild of the current treasury lord and first minister, William Pitt the Younger (the term "prime minister" did not exist yet). Introduced in 1787, the 1-million-pound annual sinking fund had restored investor confidence even as the Dutch dumped British investments. In November 1789, Hamilton heard back from William Bingham, the richest merchant in Philadelphia, in answer to a query marked "private" asking for "any thoughts" Bingham might have on American "finances and debts." Bingham wrote a long and detailed analysis of the British system that Hamilton no doubt leaned on heavily as he set about writing his own report to Congress at the end of November 1789. But these words jumped out of Bingham's letter: since Pitt had introduced the sinking fund, putting 1 million pounds a year out of reach of the government, "This stroke of finance [has] operated like a charm." Hamilton needed little more persuasion. As long ago as 1778, his friend Gouverneur Morris had advocated a sinking fund using the profits of the post office to reduce national debt. Bingham, probably America's most respected businessman, strongly encouraged Hamilton to pursue his own plans:

> Much dependence is placed on your exertions, and I am happy to find that there is a general disposition to give you credit by anticipation for the soundness of your systems and the honesty of your views.[18]

Hamilton's reputation for honesty went beyond his opinions; he demanded a higher standard for himself than his friends or employees. Yet it was impossible to order the affairs of his family. While he developed the nation's financial plans, he represented his brother-in-law John Church in selling 140 shares of Bank of North America stock to Robert Morris, even though he himself owned no bank stock. When his friend and mentor Robert Morris tried to put up public securities for collateral for the shares, Hamilton insisted on more conventional collateral in the form of real estate mortgages. His father-in-law, General Schuyler, owned or would soon acquire $67,000 in public securities (roughly $1 million today).

And when his old army friend Henry "Light-Horse Harry" Lee, in November 1789, wrote him to ask if it would be proper for Hamilton to advise him on investing in public securities, Hamilton responded, "You remember the saying with regard to Caesar's wife. The spirit of it [applies] to every man concerned in the administration of the finances of a country. Suspicion is ever eagle-eyed. And the most innocent things are apt to be misinterpreted."[19]

* * *

THE TIME to prepare his plan for rescuing the American economy quickly eroding, Alexander Hamilton faced a crisis in his personal life that almost wrecked his marriage. All through the summer and autumn, he had slipped away from the frenetic activity of organizing the treasury and studying the data he had gathered from all over the new nation to participate in the tense drama of Angelica Schuyler's return to England. For all that Betsy knew, Angelica would be leaving America forever. With revolution in France, and England once again menacing her ancient enemy, Atlantic voyages were becoming too dangerous. Betsy's depression deepened as she anticipated her sister's departure. Bedridden for weeks, she demanded constant attention until, finally, it was decided that she should remain in Albany at the end of her usual summer visit, where her parents could care for her. That left Hamilton and Angelica alone together in New York City.

In a town of thirty-five thousand people, their long strolls through the streets and evening promenades on the Battery, his frequent arrival at her rented house, and her comings and goings in a now-familiar carriage were bound to lead to gossip. The dashing Hamilton had become a local celebrity, Angelica his elegant constant companion. The couple—and, according to the persistent gossip, they had become a couple sometime that fall—took to clandestine meetings. To all but the most discerning, once Congress adjourned, Hamilton had left town with his family. Hamilton's personal papers, later heavily edited by Betsy, and his cash book fail to reveal exactly where he and Angelica made their love nest, but Hamilton's records of unreimbursed expenses hint that he was trying hard to avoid scrutiny.

But by November, Angelica would either have to leave on the last ship for England before winter—or stay, which would have been a very serious step. To remain with Hamilton, or even with her family, would represent a serious break with her husband, who had no intention of returning from England. Even if they had wanted one, divorce was out of the question either for Dutch Reformed like Angelica or an Anglican like John Church. The scandal of Hamilton and Angelica remaining together and apart from their spouses could wreck three political careers—of Senator Schuyler, member of Parliament John Church, and the new secretary of the treasury. By November, the situation had become so awkward that both Philip Schuyler and his wife were writing letters to Angelica. Schuyler, offended and outraged that Betsy and the children had arrived in Albany while Angelica remained with Hamilton, bluntly told Angelica she must break it off, leave, return to her husband. Betsy, returning from Albany, became inconsolable, poured out her grief at her older sister's departure. In a letter full of yearning that Hamilton wrote to Angelica on November 8, 1789, he recounted how he, his seven-year-old son Philip, and their star boarder Baron Steuben had watched from the Battery as Angelica's ship sailed past the tip of Manhattan, out of sight toward the Narrows. Hamilton, his boy, his baron, all wept:

> After taking leave of you on board the packet, I hastened home to soothe and console your sister. I found her in bitter distress, though much recovered from the bitter agony in which she had been. After composing her by a flattering picture of your prospects for the voyage and a *strong infusion* of hope that she had not taken a last farewell of you, the Baron, little Philip and myself, with her consent, walked down to the Battery where, with aching hearts and anxious eyes, we saw your vessel, in full sail, swiftly bearing our loved friend from our embraces! Imagine what we felt. We gazed, we sighed, we *wept*; and casting "many a lingering longing look behind," returned home to give scope to our sorrows and mingle without restraint our tears and our regrets . . .

In quoting from Virgil, their favorite poet, Hamilton evoked their memories of reading, in Latin, about Aeneas's fated parting from his lover, Dido, as he left Carthage behind to found Rome. Hamilton could not restrain his pen. In a letter he would send on the next ship with a trusted friend, Hamilton asked, "Why should I alloy the happiness that covets you?" But he would not make their loneliness worse: "However difficult or little natural it is to me to suppress what the fullness of my heart would utter, the sacrifice shall be made to your ease and satisfaction." He reassured Angelica that he had smoothed things over with her father, still irate that his daughter had taken an apartment away from her family. "I have no doubt the arguments I used with him will go far towards reconciling his mind to the unexpected step you took." And he enclosed two letters from her mother and father that he had undoubtedly intercepted from Schuyler but not let her see before she sailed. "They arrived the day after you set sail," he added blandly. Sealing the envelope with wax, Hamilton returned to the pile of papers that he now, in two months, must transform into an outline for an economic miracle. In addition to gathering information from all over America, that same day the former spymaster devised a scheme for entrapping counterfeiters in Connecticut. More and more, he worked in secret now, confiding in no one until he was ready. Sometimes, that was too late.[20]

SIXTEEN

"A Host unto Himself"

By the first British mail packet to sail for London in the year 1790, Alexander Hamilton wrote to tell Angelica that "tomorrow," January 8, three days before his thirty-fifth birthday, "I open the budget." Actually it would be January 9, 1790, when Hamilton presented his twenty-thousand-word "Report on the National Credit," his first and most important plan to rescue the anemic American economy, to Congress. He was, as Angelica could imagine, "very busy and not a little anxious." Hamilton had every reason to be apprehensive. When he had notified Congress a few days earlier that his first report as secretary of the treasury was ready and that he would present it in person, he had triggered an angry debate. He had not expected any objection, but in the first test of the doctrine of separation of powers, of the checks and balances among the branches of the new federal government, Elbridge Gerry of Massachusetts had led strenuous resistance to the notion of a cabinet officer making a speech to the House of Representatives that might unduly influence Congress's deliberations. Too many Anti-Federalists in the House of Representatives remembered the impact of Hamilton's passionate speeches at each stage of the battle for a new form of government.

Hamilton had to content himself with a plug for his budget report by President Washington who, in his speech opening the second session of the First Congress, urged swift action on the nation's dire fiscal problems. Signing his hasty note to Angelica, "Adieu Love"—with no punctuation between the words before he added "to Mr. Church"—Hamilton returned to dotting the last "i's" on his master plan to rescue the floundering fathers of the new republic from their own chaotic financial practices.[1]

Personally delivering his report to Elias Boudinot, Speaker of the House and ever his friend and patron, a red-faced Hamilton had to pick his way to a seat in the packed visitors' gallery of Congress Hall as congressmen began to take apart his plan. When Boudinot opened the debate, there was complete, tense silence. Where should they begin? Boudinot asked. If no one else knew, then he suggested they debate each provision. The silence did not last long. Soon the arguing, which went on for fully two weeks, became so loud that, upstairs in the Senate chamber, Vice President Adams ordered the windows shut. In the halls of Congress that day, five of the first seven presidents of the United States heard one of the most important and acrimonious debates in the nation's history begin. Washington was there, and Adams and James Madison and James Monroe and a visiting prosecutor from Nashville (still part of North Carolina), Andrew Jackson.

Many of the congressmen who took turns in the long battle over Hamilton's financial strategy in the next year were veterans of the Revolution, many of them veterans of the divisive political tug-of-war over ratification. Few were awed by young Hamilton. Some, like Madison, always underestimated Hamilton's intellectual powers because Hamilton did his most brilliant work so quickly, with such panache that, together with his eloquence, his handsome physical appearance and flamboyant gestures persuaded the dour Madison that Hamilton's intellect was merely facile. Too, old friend Boudinot, it would turn out, was regarded by Southern and rural members as emblematic of speculators who would most profit from Hamilton's proposal. There were many able, confident men in that first federal Congress even if not one of them was a financial genius or necessarily capable of recognizing one in Hamilton. Always secretive, Hamilton, even as he seemed open because he appealed so often to the public print, was and would remain in some ways naïve. He gave the impression he had scorn for Congress even as he petitioned it. He had not yet bothered to build a solid base of support. True, there were still no political parties. The Constitution not only failed to provide for them but most of the Revolutionary generation considered political parties anathema, historically evil and corrosive. Most agreed with one of their favorite contemporary philosophers, David Hume, that parties—"faction" is the word he used—were dangerous. On the eve of the Revolution, when Hume had learned that his old friend Benjamin Franklin was a secret leader of the Revolutionaries, he had written of his shock that Dr. Franklin was a man of faction and said that, in his opinion, faction, above all, was a dangerous thing.

The Founding Fathers, including Hamilton, did not believe that, besides providing creative dissent, political parties could provide support, especially in presenting innovations. Parties were seen as destructive forces. Hamilton's principal support was to come increasingly from bankers and businessmen, and business was still spurned by the English aristocracy, whose power was based on land and hereditary wealth, not industry and trade, which they considered beneath them. Businessmen still were not integrated into American politics. In fact, they were hated and distrusted by many of the Founding Fathers. Hamilton, over the next year, would come to be regarded as their spokesmen by men who still saw the world in seventeenth-century terms of a corrupt royal court kept honest only by the country ideals of Horace and Virgil. The Stuart kings, brought to grief in the English revolutions of 1649 and 1688, had been supported by newly wealthy merchants, the first venture capitalists, men with a global outlook who had founded Virginia and New England. But the country, or Whig Party, had won the English and the American revolutions. Hamilton and America's businessmen would need many more years to shake their image as somehow corrupt and evil.

For the moment, Alexander Hamilton did not even have enough clout to insist on reading his most important speech to Congress. He had to lay it on the House table until copies could be made and con-

gressmen given a week to read it. Boudinot's contention that it would
be better to have Hamilton himself answer knotty fiscal questions in
person only aroused suspicion. The secretary of the treasury was rel-
egated to the grandstands and to pacing the corridors outside the
congressional chambers, lobbying for his program. But once the congressmen began to read, it became evident that Hamilton's 265-page
rescue plan was so clear, straightforward, and high-toned that it
spoke directly to its readers, answering their questions if not their
objections. Each member, picking it up for the first time, had to
admit he shared at least some of Hamilton's sentiments. Hamilton
began by confessing that he "felt in no small degree the anxieties
which naturally flow from a just estimate of the difficulty of the
task." The task was humbling indeed. This rare flash of Hamiltonian
humility disarmed many members, coupled as it was with Hamilton's
reminder that it was Congress, not the president, that had commissioned him to make "an adequate provision" for public credit, "a matter of high importance to the honor and prosperity of the United
States." Having cleared his throat, Hamilton went on swiftly, bluntly
laying the groundwork for national solvency. "Emergencies are to be
expected," he emphasized. "There will be a necessity for borrowing."
Even in the wealthiest of nations, "loans in times of public danger,
especially from foreign war" are an "indispensable resource." In a
country like the United States of 1790, "possessed of little active
wealth," little "monied capital," as he put it, borrowing was "propor-
tionally urgent." To be able to borrow "upon *good terms*, it is essential
that the credit of a nation should be well established":

> For when the credit of a country is in any degree questionable,
> it never fails to [pay] an extravagant premium, in one shape or
> another, upon all the loans it has occasion to make. Nor does
> the evil end here. The same disadvantage must be sustained on
> whatever [is] bought on terms of future payment.

So far, Hamilton's report had been an appeal to "the wisdom of the
House," but it also hit home with the New Yorkers, many of them
businessmen, packing the galleries overhead. If a nation's credit was so

important, how was it to be maintained? "By good faith," Hamilton answered himself, "by a punctual performance of contracts":

> States, like individuals, who observe their engagements are respected and trusted, while the reverse is the fate of those who pursue an opposite conduct. Every breach of the public engagements, whether from choice or necessity, is, in different degrees, hurtful to the public credit.

Hamilton spoke out boldly for the nation's creditors. "Those who are most commonly creditors of a nation are, generally speaking, enlightened men," he contended. To his listeners, Hamilton knew, the enlightened man believed in order and system. At the root of good credit was good faith, based not only on political "expediency" but also, by a "still greater Authority," on "immutable principles of moral obligation." Hamilton insisted on "the order of Providence, on [the] intimate connection between public virtue and public happiness."

When one congressman finally insisted that the clerk of the House, John Beckley, read Hamilton's report aloud, it took an hour and a half. Hamilton, using charts and exact numbers, dollars and precise pennies to undergird his theories, spoon-fed his remedies to the new nation's financial ills. He laid out a five-point program. First, the combined national and state war debts must be "funded," not abandoned or paid off with depreciated money or securities, or, for that matter, paid off all at once. A permanent appropriation, taking the highest priority and placed in trust by Congress, would pay the interest and the annual cost of government, including loan office certificates, army pay certificates, and all other state and national securities. To do this, there must be a new series of interest-bearing United States securities. The principal of all outstanding debts was to be retired by payments from a $1 million per year sinking fund, which was to be financed by the net proceeds of the nation's post offices. In effect, the sinking fund would convert the debt payments into an annuity.

Hamilton reported to the penny the embarrassing particulars of the debts inherited from the Confederation. By 1790, the foreign debt was $11,710,378; the domestic debt, including arrears of interest and unliquidated claims and Continental and state currency, stood at $44,414,085; state debts, $25 million. Hamilton recommended funding the national debt at par, enabling creditors, both original holders and speculators, to exchange depreciated securities for new interest-bearing bonds at face value. He also urged "assumption": that the federal government assume, to the extent of $21.5 million, the debts incurred by the states during the Revolution. Hamilton's proposals had a twofold purpose: to establish and maintain the public credit, thereby reviving confidence in the government at home and abroad, and to strengthen and stabilize the national government by creating the consciousness of a national solidarity of interest among the business and commercial groups, which held the majority of the domestic debt.

The House, by an almost unanimous vote, approved Hamilton's proposal to fund the national debt, authorizing him to borrow $12 million to pay arrears of interest on the debt and current interest and another $2 million for the sinking fund appropriation and the roughly $600,000 he estimated the federal government would cost for the year. But congressmen representing the debtor and agrarian interests, many of whom had been forced to sell their government securities at deep discounts (up to 85 percent), bitterly opposed funding the state debts at par. Madison vehemently argued that the government should discriminate between original holders and subsequent purchasers.

Hamilton spelled out his opposition to discrimination between classes of creditors clearly enough in his report:

> How should it be known whether, if the purchaser had employed his money in some other way, he would not be in a better situation though he should now receive the full amount? Questions of this sort, on a close inspection, multiply themselves without end and demonstrate the injustice of a discrimination, even after the most subtle calculations of equity [if they are] abstracted from the obligations of contract.

He suggested a schedule for paying off the national debt by the sinking fund and the state portion of the debt by tariffs on a list of imported goods including tea, coffee, and liquor. He hinted that he hoped to tax consumption of "pernicious" luxuries out of existence. "The consumption of ardent spirits," he wrote, "is carried to an extreme which is truly to be regretted, as well in regard to the health and morals as to the economy of the community."

The first signs of a North-South split began to appear over opposition to funding the state debts at 100 cents on the dollar. The New England states, especially Massachusetts, with the largest unpaid war debts, generally favored assumption. The only alternative they saw was for heavy long-term taxation, exactly what had triggered Shays's Rebellion only three years earlier. But the Southern states, most of which had either paid their war debts or made other arrangements to pay them, remained vociferously hostile to what they saw as a gigantic increase in the national debt for which their citizens would again be taxed. Moreover, Southerners, who believed deeply in their individual states' rights, feared that assumption would aggrandize federal power at the expense of the states. When the question of discrimination between holders of securities came to a vote on February 22nd, Hamilton's allies won by almost three to one.

Madison's antiassumption faction received more reinforcements from the newly arrived delegation from North Carolina, which had ratified the Constitution on November 21, 1789. Attempting to block assumption, Alexander White of Virginia insisted that Hamilton submit estimates of the costs of assuming each state's debt. Hamilton supplied this latest report the very next day. He knew that the stumbling block was taxation of houses, lands, livestock, and farm produce. Instead, he proposed to increase import duties by 10 percent and lay additional duties on sugar, molasses, spices, salt, spirits, and manufactured (that is, foreign) tobacco. These taxes would yield $1,040,000, declared Hamilton, some $40,000 a year more than the sinking fund appropriation he was seeking. But Hamilton still could not win when the House voted on federal assumption of all state war debts. Madison's forces defeated assumption by a narrow thirty-one to twenty-nine margin. Madison thus reversed his long-standing position on both issues.

But Hamilton was struggling to replace all wartime debts with a new kind of currency, a national debt, "a national blessing," as he called it:

> It is a well-known fact that, in countries in which the national debt is properly funded, and an object of established confidence, it answers most of the purposes of money.[2]

Government paper, more than the commercial paper then in use, was as good as gold "in the principal transactions of business [passing] current as specie." As recently as their long, late afternoon walks during the Constitutional Convention of 1787, Madison had agreed with Hamilton that state debts incurred in the common cause of winning independence should be assumed by the national government. What accounted for Madison's sudden and dramatic change of mind, his willingness to abandon his successful alliance with Hamilton? The answer, which eluded Hamilton, may lie in the spurt of inside trading that resulted from his report and from the presumption that the government would adopt the recommendations of its own secretary of the treasury. In the House, in the Senate, all over New York City and as far south as Charleston, the streets and hills were alive with speculation. Hamilton did not learn for years that a corrupt clerk in the Treasury office had sold Hamilton's assistant, William Duer, a ledger listing the names, locations, and amounts of back pay in the Continental Lines from Virginia, Madison's home state, and North Carolina. Duer, joining forces with leading Philadelphia merchant William Bingham, had raised large amounts of cash and sent agents south to buy up the cash-strapped soldiers' pay certificates in the backcountry. Senator Maclay of Pennsylvania, himself a frontiersman and a veteran, recorded in his diary that a senator arriving from North Carolina had passed on the road "two expresses with very large sums of money." Hamilton's plan, in Maclay's eyes, would "damn [his] character forever." A bombastic Georgia frontiersman, Senator James Jackson, railed at the "spirit of havoc, speculation and ruin," adding loudly, "My soul rises indignant at the avaricious and immoral turpitude which so vile a conduct displays." Upstairs, in the Senate, the windows slammed again "to keep out the din." There was so much tension in the Senate during one day's debate, Senator Maclay recorded, that Philip Schuyler's "hair stood on end, as if the Indians had fired at him." It was at this point that, as Madison led Southern opposition to Hamilton's assumption scheme, the two original Federalists split.[3]

ALEXANDER HAMILTON's first official efforts to replace the American economy of debt with a cash economy stalled in the spring of 1790. Few of his auditors understood that, by creating a national debt that paid off all existing state and federal debts, he would give the United States a high credit rating, keep taxes low, encourage foreign loans, and, therefore, stimulate foreign investment. His secretly speculating assistant Duer resigned in April. Hamilton, meanwhile, had won congressional approval to arrange the Dutch bank loans that bailed out the arrears of interest on the Confederation's debt and paid the $600,000 needed for the first federal government's expenses for one year. Overnight, Hamilton had repaired American credit abroad. But it would take a dramatic compromise to break the stalemate over the thornier question of whether the federal government should assume state debts. That spring of 1790, Madison received powerful reinforcement in the person of Thomas Jefferson, returning after five years as American minister plenipotentiary in Paris. Neither Jefferson nor Madison understood money. Both were virtually always heavily in debt, typical of much of their Southern planter class. Both had accepted payment of debts owed to them in depreciated currency but still had huge debts in England, where creditors had refused Continental money and demanded pounds sterling. Both shared a view, prevalent in America and especially in Congress at the time, that America's riches lay in its vast untouched reserves of western lands— even if, as Washington had found, they were usually not liquid and were, among other troublesome details, still inhabited by Indians. In fact, only by using an Indian war to illustrate why Congress could not wait for customs duties to come in but would have to borrow in advance to fight to defend itself did Hamilton prevail on Congress to fund the Confederation's debts.

Hamilton had, by his impressive research, his willingness to work all night, and his self-confidence, cut some of the ground from under his more astute opponents, especially when he posited import duties on luxuries versus high taxes. The debate got sidetracked, however, when petitions of Pennsylvania Quakers seeking a ban on further imports of slaves from Africa infuriated Southerners at the very moment that the choice of a site for a new national capital came up for debate. Most Southerners, irked by the trouble and expense of traveling all the way to New York City twice a year, insisted on a site along the Potomac, at the moment still a swamp and mutually inconvenient to North and South. The Southerners, alarmed at the possible concentration of money and power in the North, especially in the commercial center of New York City, were willing to move to Philadelphia, the old capital, temporarily while a new capital city was built on the Potomac.

According to Thomas Jefferson, the deadlock over assumption explains why, when he and Hamilton literally bumped into each other one day late in June 1790 outside the President's House at Sixth and Market Streets, Hamilton's "look was somber, haggard and dejected beyond description, even his dress uncouth and neglected." (Jefferson, a widower and slave to Parisian fashion, probably overlooked the possibility that Hamilton's wife and children had gone north again to the Schuyler mansion and that Hamilton was batching it, virtually living at the Treasury offices.) "He asked to speak with me," Jefferson recorded. "We stood in the street, near the door. He opened [the conversation with] the assumption of the state debts, the necessity of it in the general fiscal arrangement, and its indispensable necessity toward a preservation of the union." If Hamilton did not have enough influence to carry assumption through Congress, he "was determined to resign." Hamilton took Jefferson by the elbow and said that, as cabinet colleagues, they should cooperate. Jefferson wrote that he "thought the first step would be to bring Mister Madison and Colonel Hamilton to a friendly discussion of the subject." Jefferson invited both of them to have dinner with him the next day.[4]

Inviting congressmen from Maryland and Pennsylvania as well, Jefferson worked out a compromise that could lead to congressional passage of Hamilton's entire assumption package and location of the new national capital in a federal district between Maryland and Virginia. Jefferson suggested that night "that as the pill [assumption] would be a bitter one to the Southern states, something should be done to soothe them. The removal of the seat of government to the Potomac was a just one." While Madison still held out momentarily for discrimination between classes of debt holders, he finally acquiesced. When Hamilton's supporters brought assumption up for another vote in Congress a few weeks later, Madison would "leave it to its fate." A few pro-Madison votes would shift to the Hamilton column and assumption would pass. In exchange, when the site of the permanent capital came to a vote, Hamilton's growing Federalist Party, which had taken shape over the past year of angry debates over the national debt, would vote to leave New York.

The secret "dinner table bargain" of June 20, 1790, led on July 10, to relocating the nation's capital in a federal district ten miles square along the Potomac, the precise location to be selected by the president. The government would temporarily move to Philadelphia, where the Second Congress would convene on December 6. The Quaker City would remain the capital until 1800. Two weeks after Hamilton marshaled the votes needed for the capital shift, Madison and Jefferson's adherents allowed passage of Hamilton's assumption plan by a healthy thirty-four to twenty-eight vote. The funding of America's debts by the new federal government, the birthday of our national debt, was August 4, 1790. Hamilton could now turn his energies to the second stage of his master plan, creation of a national bank. That autumn, the Hamiltons moved to Philadelphia into a rented brick mansion at Third and Walnut Streets, the former home of Israel Pemberton, "King of the Quakers" and a leading Loyalist in the Revolution. The moving of the capital out of New York City shocked and angered many New Yorkers, who had paid thousands of their precious dollars to renovate buildings and were prepared to do even more to make Manhattan the political as well as the financial capital of the United States. Hamilton's desertion of his adopted home made him many new enemies, but he was content to have saved the Union by rescuing its economy.

THE PHILADELPHIA of 1790 was the nation's largest town, with a population of thirty-five thousand, and America's wealthiest, "a London in wealth," as Congressman Fisher Ames put it, "and more than a London in arrogance." Contrasted to New York City, it was clean. Many of its streets were paved, the garbage picked up each day by street sweepers, not free-ranging pigs, as in Manhattan. Philadelphia was pricey; Betsy Hamilton had to budget her purchases at the open-air covered sheds on Market Street. Hamilton had turned over his law practice to his old college roommate, Robert Troup, and the nation's treasury secretary was trying to live with four children on his $3,500-a-year salary. But Betsy Hamilton had never seen such abundance and variety. At one dinner given by the president and first lady, there was no hint of remaining Quaker simplicity. A guest listed "an elegant variety of roast beef, veal, turkey, ducks, fowl, ham, puddings, jellies, oranges, apples, nuts, almonds, figs, raisins, wines and punch." Philadelphia now had its own Anglican bishop; its style was no longer Quaker but High Episcopalian, the city's sophistication adorned by the profits of trade with Europe and the Caribbean. By contrast, a visitor noted that, in Hamilton's office, the files sat on planks, supported by sawhorses, Hamilton himself laboring at a plain pine desk covered with a piece of green cloth.[5]

And there, late into the night, Hamilton worked to devise his grand plan to make America financially independent. His second report to Congress called for a national bank, the Bank of the United States. Here, Hamilton could draw directly on the collateral of his own experience as cofounder, six years earlier, of the Bank of New York, of which he was still a director and stockholder. His blueprint for a national bank, submitted to Congress in December 1796, had been inspired by successful institutions in the Netherlands, England, and Spain. It called for capitalization of $10 million, five times the capital of all existing banks in the United States at the time. In enumerating the benefits of a national bank, Hamilton explained to Congress that, by making loans, the bank could multiply its hard-money cash reserves. "Credit keeps circulating," he wrote, "performing in every stage the office of money." In time of emergencies, such as war, the national bank could lend money to the government. To objections that the interest paid to foreign depositors could suck the capital out of the United States, Hamilton countered that, on the contrary, interest "arises from the employment of [their] capital by our own citizens." To the fear that banks only profited speculators, Hamilton argued that banks "more frequently enable honest and industrious men," many of them "of small, or, perhaps of no capital, to undertake and prosecute business." It's hard to imagine a time when Americans had to be told such basics, but no member of Congress had any banking experience in 1790. Such help by banks for businessmen had certainly been the case with the shopkeepers and farmers' economy of England but Hamilton stressed that he wasn't parroting Bank of England policies. Among his innovations, the Bank of the United States would be operated by private citizens. He feared that government control would "corrode the vitals" of the bank's credit. The self-interest of private bankers would be "keen, steady" and "magnetic"; it would provide "the only security that can always be relied upon for a careful and prudent administration." The bank, not the Federal government, would have the power to issue paper money in the form of bank notes. Hamilton was vehemently opposed to the government's running of the printing presses to produce money. "The wisdom of the government will be shown in never trusting itself with the use of so seducing and dangerous an expedient." To capitalize the national bank, Hamilton set forth a federal appropriation of $2 million drawn from import duties and excise taxes and $8 million, the remaining four fifths, by private subscriptions of shares of stock. The bank was to be chartered by Congress for twenty years; the government would pay its managers.

Hamilton's "Report on the Bank" takes up eighty-six printed pages in the latest edition of his personal papers and is introduced by twenty pages of fine print to explain its origins and meaning. It drew on his studies and proposals to Robert Morris over a fifteen-year period. It included consideration of the wisdom of Adam Smith, Necker, Robert Morris, and John Witherspoon, president of Princeton. He probably showed drafts to William Bingham, a leading Philadelphia merchant and major stockholder and director of Morris's Bank of North America, as well as to Samuel Osgood, a member of the Board of Treasury under the old Confederation and cashier of the Bank of Massachusetts. The report showed little change in nearly ten years from Hamilton's first proposal to Robert Morris of 1781, when Hamilton had been only twenty-six years old. Overnight, at word of his plans, securities in New York rose by 50 percent and Dutch bankers wrote Hamilton he could have $1 million and "as much credit as any nation in Europe."[6]

In all his brilliant calculations and exposition, Hamilton had failed to address one point, and James Madison, who, like many Southern plantation owners and farmers and workingmen and women nation-wide, was suspicious of this mysterious, devious, seemingly invisible and immoral new fiscal entity where speculators would make money without appearing to work for it, pounced on it. Was a national bank constitutional? Madison asked. The Constitution included no provision for the federal government to charter a bank, or any other corporation, for that matter, Madison pointed out on the floor of the House. Hamilton quickly countered by enunciating for the first time the doctrine of implied powers. Chartering a national banking corporation fell within the rubric of the last article of the Constitution, which allowed Congress "to make all laws which shall be necessary and proper" to carry out all the powers that were enumerated in the document. This brilliant rejoinder legalized the creation of the first modern for-profit corporation. Until then, only hospitals, orphanages, and such charitable, nonprofit institutions in England and America had received government charters. Hamilton's answer also was a slap at Madison, who, in *The Federalist*, had upheld the federal government's implied powers: "Wherever the end is required, the means are authorized." Privately, Madison lobbied Marylanders and Virginians, Congress, and even Washington (who was already at work laying out a capital city on the Potomac) that to create a national bank with a twenty-year charter in Philadelphia would build support for keeping the capital there permanently. Washington turned to his cabinet members, allowing them ten days to rebut or reinforce Madison's argument on constitutionality. On February 15, Jefferson opined that the bill was unconstitutional. He coined the doctrine of "strict construction," taking as his ground the Tenth Amendment to the Constitution (not yet adopted), which declared that all powers not specifically enumerated in the Constitution were reserved to the states. Incorporation of a bank, Jefferson contended, was not among the powers specifically delegated to Congress. In appealing for a "loose constructionist" view, Hamilton argued:

> If the *end* be clearly comprehended within any of the specified powers, and if the measure have an obvious relation to that *end*, and is not forbidden by any particular provision of the Constitution, it may safely be deemed to come within the compass of the national authority.

In this flourish, Hamilton not only breathed life and vigor into the American economy but kept the Constitution from becoming rigid, ossified, and before long a dead letter.

On February 21, Hamilton paced up and down in a neighbor's walled garden all afternoon, muttering to himself, marshaling his arguments. All that night, he hunched over his desk, in the guttering candlelight writing out his opinion of the constitutionality of a national bank—or any corporation. His rebuttal cut first to the heart of a government's nature. "*Inherent* in the very *definition* of a government," he emphasized the words, was "that every power vested in a government is in its nature *sovereign* and includes, by the *force* of the *term*, a right to employ all the *means* requisite." To Hamilton, "the only question" is "whether the means to be employed, or, in this instance, the corporation to be erected, has a natural relation to any of the acknowledged objects or lawful ends of government."

At every step, Hamilton had to educate his audience—Congress, the president—about money, banking, and business. The financial vocabulary we use today in our daily lives was utterly unknown except to a handful of Americans. Most Americans were sole proprietors of farms, ships, and buildings. Some few had formed partnerships for trade, but the corporation, with the anonymity and limited liability of its shareholders and its directors protected from individual lawsuit and the sale of shares of stock to raise capital, was entirely new language. Nine foreign currencies, such as English pounds sterling, French livres, and Spanish dollars, were accepted, but the United States had no viable currency of its own. Most transactions were by bills of credit based on the reputation of individual businessmen like Robert Morris. Hamilton not only had to invent a national bank that would be incorporated—literally brought to life—by Congress, but he also had to build a mint and coin U.S. money.

Hamilton pointed out that Congress could not form a corporation to supervise the police force of Philadelphia (if one existed, which it did not for another fifty years) because Congress was "not authorized to regulate the police of that city." But Congress could erect any corporation related to tax collection or to trade "because it is the province of the Federal government to regulate those objects." Regulating them meant "employing all the means" that exist "to the best and greatest advantage."

To drive home his point, Hamilton turned to the Indian war that President Washington said had become necessary on the Miami River in present-day Indiana. Indians had repelled with heavy casualties an army Washington sent to the Miami in 1789. Congress had authorized Washington to prepare for war but where was the money to come from? Hamilton used this example to prove that establishing a national bank was the best and most advantageous means to carry out the government's powers:

> A nation is threatened with war [and] large sums are wanted on a sudden to make the requisite preparations. Taxes are [assessed] for the purpose, but it requires time to obtain the benefit of them. If there be a bank, the supply can at once be had. If there be none, loans from individuals must be sought [but] the progress of these is often too slow.

As matters stood, without a bank "the only fund out of which the money [for a war] can arise," Hamilton demonstrated, "is a tax which only begins to be collected in July next. The preparations, however, are instantly to be made. The money must, therefore, be borrowed—and of whom could it be borrowed if there are no public banks?" For future loans for larger wars a national bank was indispensable.[7]

It would be another twenty-eight years and Hamilton would be long dead before the test of his vision in empowering the corporation came when Chief Justice John Marshall upheld, by majority opinion, the constitutionality of the second Bank of the United States in *McCulloch v. Maryland*. And the sanctity of the corporate veil that Hamilton was pulling down now over the liability of individual stockholders, which was at the heart of Hamilton's defense of the American-style corporation, would be upheld in 1819 when the Supreme Court protected the trustees of Dartmouth College from being sued individually. But Hamilton would not have to wait to have his national bank. On February 25, 1791, this time after a ten-week struggle, President Washington signed the bill chartering the Bank of the United States. He was not fully convinced by either Jefferson or Hamilton's argument but he chose to uphold Hamilton's view because he believed that, when his cabinet was divided, the president must support the cabinet officer whose department is directly involved, or call for his resignation. Hamilton had succeeded, with Washington's backing, to draw up a blueprint for a relationship between government and money, to delineate the public sector and the private sector.

By now, the battle over Hamilton's master plan had raged for more than a year, splitting Washington's cabinet in the process. Madison had pulled away from Hamilton, especially alarmed when, at a dinner given by the Washingtons, they heard Hamilton expatiating on the virtues of the British government. Jefferson was already angry that Hamilton had ignored diplomatic channels by having supposedly "off the record" conversations with unofficial British envoy George Beckwith even while the British officially refused to exchange diplomats with the United States. The infighting was about to become public. Jefferson opposed as too pro-British Hamilton's trade policies and decried a series of essays by Vice President Adams, published under the nom de plume "Davila" in the pro-Hamilton *National Gazette,* advocating stronger diplomatic ties with Great Britain. When Jefferson received a copy of Thomas Paine's latest anti-British blast, *The Rights of Man,* published in London, he wrote a note recommending publication in the United States and sent it off to a printer, intending, he later insisted, for his comments to remain private. He was, after all, a member of Washington's cabinet along with Hamilton and Adams. The printer published Jefferson's signed letter as the introduction to the American edition. Jefferson went on record as opposed to Hamilton and Adams as the authors of "the political heresies that have sprung up among us." Scores of newspapers reprinted Jefferson's letter. "I am sincerely mortified," Jefferson wrote apologetically to Washington, "to be thus brought forward on the public stage."

But, secretly, Jefferson and his newfound ally Madison set to work to launch their own newspaper to oppose the Hamilton-backed *National Gazette.* In a letter to his son-in-law, Jefferson described its editorial policy as "pure Toryism, disseminating [Hamilton's] doctrine of monarchy, aristocracy and the exclusion of the people. We have been trying to get another weekly or half-weekly [newspaper] excluding advertisements set up, so that it could go free through the states in the mails and furnish [our own] vehicle of intelligence."

That summer, on a visit to New York City, Jefferson and Madison recruited Philip Freneau, who had worked for Francis Childs's *New York Advertiser* as a journalist and was known for his biting political sarcasm, to come to Philadelphia to establish the pro-Jefferson *Gazette of the United States* with a subsidy to Freneau as a no-show translator for the State Department. Thrice-weekly salvos from the opposing newspapers were the first step toward the formation of separate political parties, still anathema in the America of 1791.[8]

With his pass key, Freneau entered Jefferson's office at night, copied out reports left in plain sight for him, then ran them in his newspaper, sometimes before President Washington ever saw them.

WHILE THE president and first lady rattled over seventeen hundred miles of southern roads in the cream-colored carriage painted with woodland scenes, and Jefferson and Madison visited northeastern towns and poured punch for Anti-Federalist politicians and former Shaysite rebels, Alexander Hamilton stayed in Philadelphia, the only cabinet officer still at his desk. Adams and Knox had fled the oppressive humidity and endemic yellow fever to their cooler homes Down East. Hamilton had sent Betsy and the children north to the Schuylers' summer retreat at Saratoga. She was happy to leave the new capital, its high prices, its crowds, and the incessant clatter of wagons and carriages outside the windows at Third and Walnut Streets. The family budget was strained not only by the inflated prices of everything since the government had moved to Philadelphia but, unknown to his wife, Hamilton had spent nearly 800 pounds, roughly $30,000 today, on Angelica's elaborate establishment during her stay in New York City. Just before Betsy drove north for the summer with her Schuyler relatives, James McHenry, Hamilton's best man, wrote to chide Hamilton that Betsy was a better financial manager than the secretary of the treasury.

Following up on his "Report on the Bank," in January 1791, Hamilton recommended the founding of a U.S. mint. He was supported, for once, not only by bankers Robert and Gouverneur Morris but by Jefferson, a disciple and personal friend of Condorcet, the French philosopher of money. It was Jefferson who contributed the idea of a decimal system. Briefly collaborators, the two cabinet secretaries exchanged ideas on monetary relationships at home and abroad. Hamilton's "Report on the Mint" stood on the shoulders of Jefferson's "Report on Weights and Measures," which recommended the use of the dollar as America's unit of currency. They fell out over coinage. Jefferson's silver dollar in virtually universal use in America was heavier than the Spanish dollar. That summer, Hamilton wrote to foreign governments to learn the official weights of their coins. He hit on a ratio of fifteen to one pure silver over alloy in the dollar, deliberately overvaluing it to encourage foreign trade. The silver dollar would remain the most common American specie until the California Gold Rush of 1849, when abundant gold led to the brief banishment of silver. It was not until the Union introduced the "greenback" paper dollar during the Civil War that Americans were again willing to rely on paper money after the fiasco of the Continental dollar dur-

ing the Revolutionary War. Hamilton was also busy writing regulations for customs collectors and captains of revenue cutters—in the
process, he created the Coast Guard—and in designing lighthouses,
making all the arrangements and purchases right down to the whale
oil for their lamps. But he focused most of his energy that summer
on researching and preparing his fourth report to Congress, his
famous "Report on Manufactures." He assigned U.S. marshals and
customs collectors to gather exact information for him on the character and extent of all existing American industry. In this report,
Hamilton proposed a system of tariffs to protect America's fledgling
industries from foreign, chiefly British, competition. He established
the doctrine of protectionism. Where Americans could provide their
own finished goods, import duties should be prohibitively high. He
also recommended federal bounties to stimulate agriculture plus a
network of federally sponsored internal improvements.[9]

Hamilton was nowhere more visionary, nor more at odds with
most Americans of his time, than in his glimpse into the future of
American industry. Where Jefferson and Madison understood the
eighteenth century, Hamilton could foresee a far different landscape
and he tried to prepare Americans for the Industrial Revolution,
which he knew was stirring in England. Already, under the existing
American system, there were too few free laborers for the nation's
farms to spare many for manufacturing. His answer was not, like the
South's, to import or breed more slaves. The wives, daughters, and
children of farmers would provide the growth in the labor supply.
Factory workers "would probably flock from Europe to the United
States," Hamilton prophesied, if they could employ their skills in
America. Power-driven machinery, discreetly smuggled out of Europe,
could be copied and constructed by immigrant mechanics. Foreign
investors were eager to bankroll American industry.

As a companion piece to this report, Hamilton was helping to
launch the Society for Establishing Useful Manufactures, or SUM, a
New Jersey corporation chartered that November, the first sizable
industrial undertaking in the United States. That August, the society's
organizers asked Hamilton to find "artists" (artisans) to direct workers

in the spinning and weaving of cotton and printing of cloth in a new industrial town in North Jersey. Pouring more time into the corporation than its directors, he would report to a directors' meeting in October that he had rounded up superintendents for the cotton mill and printing departments, a recruiter to go to England to find skilled workers, an inventor to devise looms.

Hamilton proposed that the mills be located at the falls of the Passaic, the highest falls east of Niagara. His father-in-law traveled from Albany to advise the directors on waterpower, something he knew about. Water would be taken from above the falls over a short aqueduct that spanned a ravine and then would travel into a canal passing the mills. Hamilton named the town after Governor William Paterson, five years earlier his antagonist during the Constitutional Convention. The society would also build homes for the mill workers.

As the plan came to life, there were to be a carding mill, a plant for spinning and weaving, a printworks, and a sawmill to provide lumber for the first fifty homes for workers. Loans would be provided for supervising mechanics to build their own homes. The funded debt of the United States would serve as collateral for a bank loan to cover construction costs. The society's directors, cheered on by the society's flamboyant governor (and Hamilton's former assistant at the Treasury) William Duer, accepted all Hamilton's utopian recommendations.

In the midst of all the meetings and memos, Hamilton received a visit one day in July from a beautiful twenty-three-year-old woman who introduced herself as Maria Reynolds. "Sometime in the summer of the year 1791 a woman called at my house," Hamilton recounted the episode, "and asked to speak with me in private. She was shown into the parlor where I went to her." With "a seeming air of distress," she told Hamilton

that her husband had lately left her for another woman and [that she was] so destitute that, though desirous of returning to her friends, she had not the means—that knowing I was a citizen of the same state of New York she had taken the liberty to address herself to my humanity for relief.[10]

She told Hamilton that her husband, James, had deserted her and her small daughter. She said she was the sister-in-law of one of the New York Livingstons. Could Hamilton help her?

Hamilton may have known her husband, a former commissary in the Revolution and one of the men who had illegally attained the lists of Revolutionary War veterans of the Virginia and North Carolina Continental Lines and had defrauded them or their widows and children of their back pay. Reynolds and an accomplice, Jacob Clingman, had sailed south in the summer of 1790 with about $30,000 in silver and gold coins furnished by speculators and with a second set of lists they had forged. These showed far lower amounts of back pay owed to officers. A captain who was really owed 24 pounds in back pay saw only 6 pounds written down beside his name. Reynolds offered him two shillings or about 3 percent, in hard money. Impoverished veterans who had little hard money and had long ago lost faith in ever being paid, accepted it.

"A pretty woman in distress," as Hamilton later described her in a publicly circulated confession six years later, the comely Mrs. Reynolds cast a spell over Hamilton with her "odd" tale of abandonment by a scoundrel "who had for a long time treated her very cruelly." Hamilton said he was sorry he was short on cash at the moment, but he could bring her money that night at her boardinghouse. Few nonpartisan accounts of what followed survive, but according to Richard Folwell, the publisher-son of Maria's landlady, Maria had an "innocent countenance." "The variety of shapes that she could assume was endless," he reported. Hamilton would later claim that he was struck by Maria's "simplicity and modesty." If her appeal was to his "humanity," it was a loaded word when he used it to characterize his reaction to a lovely, seemingly helpless, married woman on a lonely day when his wife was far away. That evening, Hamilton called at Maria's lodgings with a $30 bank bill (about $400 today). Maria opened the door to her apartment at the head of the stairs. She ushered him into her bedroom, "where it was quickly apparent that other than pecuniary consolation would be acceptable." Over the next thirteen or more months, Hamilton returned frequently to the house on Arch Street. Always entering by the back door, he carried on a passionate affair that his wife did not learn about until she read it in the *Philadelphia Aurora* six years later.

Little is known about Maria Reynolds except that she was probably the daughter of Thomas Lewis of Farmington, Connecticut, who had dealings with David Reynolds, her future father-in-law, in supplying cattle to Continental troops during the Revolution. One historian has described her as "a bold, florid, handsome woman." A young Philadelphia merchant, who met her years later after she had married two more times, described her as intelligent, sensitive, and gentle. Hamilton wrote that she was highly emotional and given to weeping. Whatever combination is true, Hamilton could not seem to pull away from her. He kept putting off his wife's return to Philadelphia. At the end of July, he wrote Betsy, professing his worry about her being in the capital during yellow fever season. He wanted her away from "the hot city of Philadelphia"—he knew she hated the heat and humidity. He was "in good health," he assured her, "and you may depend, I shall take all the care in my power to continue so. Will you, my Angel, do the same? Consider how much our happiness depends on it." And he said he had gone to see their new quieter, safer, if somewhat smaller and less fashionable house, farther from the Treasury but nearer to Maria. "I have been to see your new house and like it better than I expected to do. It will soon be ready and I shall obey your orders about papering, etc."

Betsy returned to Philadelphia that autumn, but Hamilton continued his visits to Maria, who had given up all talk of returning to New York. Sometime that winter, James Reynolds reappeared. Maria told Hamilton that her husband wanted to return to her. Hamilton encouraged their reconciliation. She also told him, Hamilton said, that he could make public evidence of illicit speculations in the Treasury office. When Hamilton sent for Reynolds, he was told that William Duer had furnished Reynolds with the lists of veterans' claims. Reynolds wanted a job in the Treasury office. He left with the impression that Hamilton was considering hiring him. As eager as Hamilton was to buy Reynolds's silence, he decided not to employ him. In mid-December, Maria told Hamilton that Reynolds had learned of their affair. By now, Hamilton had begun to suspect collusion, but when he confronted Maria, her "agonizing distress" dissuaded him.

When Reynolds continued to write him long letters threatening exposure, it became clear that Reynolds intended to blackmail him. On Sunday, December 18, 1791, Hamilton dashed off a note to his trusted friend Oliver Wolcott, comptroller of the treasury. "I am this moment going to a rendezvous which I suspect may involve a most serious plot against me. As any disastrous event might [injure] my fame, I drop you this line." Hamilton never mailed the letter but left it where it could be found if something happened to him. At the meeting, Reynolds, learning he could not have a job, demanded $1,000 in cash in exchange for leaving the state with his daughter—and leaving Maria to Hamilton. Hamilton paid up. He borrowed $500 from his friend and law partner Robert Troup.

For two weeks he stayed away from Maria, but still he could not, he must have told himself, abandon her to her criminal husband. Meanwhile, Maria besieged Hamilton with notes. She seemed to be threatening suicide. Maria wrote that she had

> Ben Sick all moast Ever since I saw you . . . I solicit a favor . . . for the Last time. Yes Sir Rest assured I will never ask you to call on me again. I have kept my Bed those tow dayes and now rise from my pilliow wich your Neglect has filled with the shorpest thorns . . . I only do it to Ease a heart wich is ready Burst with Greef. I can neither Eat or sleep. I have Been on the point of doing the most horrid acts . . . I feel as If I should not Contennue long and all the wish I have Is to se you once more . . . for God sake be not so voed of all humanity as to deni me this Last request but if you will not Call some time this night I no its late but any tim between this and twelve A Clock I shall be up. Le me Intreate you If you wont Come to send me a Line oh my head I can rite no more. Do something to Ease My heart . . . Commit this to the care of my maid be not offended I beg.[11]

When Hamilton still did not come, Maria, "whos greatest fault is loveing him," implored Hamilton to come, even if, this time, he could not stay. "P.S. If you cannot come this Evening to stay just come only for one moment as I shal be Lone Mr. Is going to sup with a friend." After two weeks, as her husband hit him up for "loans," first $100, then another $100, Hamilton resumed his clandestine backstairs visits, refusing to come in the front door, careful he was not observed, through August 1792. Betsy had gone home again for the summer to Saratoga to have their fifth child. Ten days after his second son, John Church Hamilton (named for Angelica's husband) was born, Hamilton ended the Reynolds affair. Later, he would blame himself for his "vanity." But was that all there was to it? He had already demonstrated that he could be completely fooled by an actress feigning desperation over her abandonment by a rogue husband: Peggy Shippen Arnold had completely gulled him at West Point. Was he not reminded of another woman, his own mother, tied by law to a man she hated and feared? And could he become his father, deserting her, without money, with a small child? Hamilton was always confused about the relationship of women and money. He had first become sexually aware of women in the Livingston society whirl of pre-Revolutionary New Jersey, but he was a poor scholarship boy and Kitty Livingston, the governor's daughter, was unattainable. Angelica still chided him in her letters. Was Kitty still available? she worried. He had, quite simply, married Betsy for the Schuyler money and name, not for her looks or charm or wit. Once he had his own money from his lucrative law practice, his vanity and pride had compounded his lust for Betsy's more beautiful, more sophisticated sister. He set aside any pangs of conscience, any rules of polite society, as his vanity, his lust, his psychological baggage propelled him back into Maria Reynolds's bed. He could make the rules in the new order of American wealth and power he was fashioning, but he could not change the rules of the society in which he lived. Soon he was being called "the double adulterer" by his enemies.

IF 1791 WAS Hamilton's annus mirabilis, the wonderful year in which his financial genius for planning, organization, and administration had, at last, been recognized and carved in the stone of the still-surviving system he created, then the year 1792 became his annus horribilis. On March 19, his friend and law partner Robert Troup wrote him a letter informing him of terrible financial "convulsions" in New York City being blamed on "our friend Duer's failure." William Duer, for nine months Hamilton's top aide at the Treasury and the son-in-law of Lord Stirling, had gone broke. "The truth is that [his] unpaid notes amount to about half a million dollars [about $7 million today] and Duer has not a farthing of money or a particle of stock to pay them with." Duer's "total bankruptcy" triggered the nation's first financial panic. It also pulled down the Society for the Establishment of Useful Manufactures: Duer, as its governor, had siphoned off $20,000 of its treasury (about $260,000 today), much of its fund for building houses for workmen. Another SUM director, John Dewhurst, had gone under, losing $50,000 of SUM's money, which he held for the purchase of machinery abroad. As one New York City businessman put it, "In this city, many who were worth handsome fortunes three or four months ago are now probably not worth a groat." Duer had only survived an angry mob because he was arrested and locked in the New Prison's debtors' wing where there were guards.

When Duer wrote Hamilton, "my ruin is complete," he pleaded with Hamilton to stop Wolcott's suit to recover the Treasury's money. As Duer literally fled his creditors, he was pursued by shopkeepers, widows, orphans, even the noted bawd Mrs. Macarty. Hamilton would not help him. The Duer affair had caused him "infinite pain," and he was outraged at the scandal caused by the man he had counted on to help him establish the nation's credit. "These extravagant sallies of speculation," Hamilton railed, "do injury to the government and to the whole system of public credit by disgusting all sober citizens and giving a wild air to everything."[12]

Quickly stepping in to avert the spread of panic, Hamilton authorized the Treasury to buy up stocks for its sinking fund. It was the first time the federal government came to the aid of a particular region. Hamilton's fast action contained the collapse to the New York market, keeping it from spreading to Philadelphia. He would later be accused of commingling government and private funds, but at the time, when he authorized William Seton of the Bank of New York by express rider to buy up $150,000 worth of securities if it would avert "a pretty extensive explosion," it would have taken days to transfer that much from the Treasury in Philadelphia to New York or to buy up individual notes. Records of Seton's return of purchases for the sinking fund for eleven days in early April 1792 show he bought up securities from ninety-five individuals and firms, usually in amounts greater than $1,000 each; the transfers kept sixteen clerks scribbling fast, day and night. By acting so fact, Hamilton actually helped the federal budget and cushioned the crash, keeping it from spreading and ruining major taxpayers. By mid-May, after two tense months, business was back to normal. Quietly, Hamilton sold his last one and a half shares in the Bank of New York and used the money to pay off the debts of his old friend Baron Steuben, keeping him out of jail. By acting alone, without waiting for Congress, he left himself open to a later investigation and attempted impeachment. The collapse of the New York market only compounded the interest of Hamilton's growing number of political enemies in his affairs, public and private.[13]

THE NEAR-COLLAPSE of the nation's new financial system gave Jefferson and Madison the opportunity they wanted to try to discredit Hamilton and bring about his firing from the cabinet by President Washington. On March 8, in the midst of the crisis, Madison attempted to strip Hamilton of his treasury post. Hamilton was accountable to Congress, Madison argued, because his job and his achievements all flowed from the Act of Congress of 1789 that had coined the Treasury Department and that required Hamilton to report to Congress. Madison attempted to use Hamilton's brilliant reports as a weapon against him. Hamilton wrote afterward that his "overthrow was anticipated as certain and Mr. Madison, laying aside his wonted caution, boldly led his troops, as he imagined, to a certain victory." Hamilton's supporters rallied and thwarted Madison's forces, but only by a four-vote margin.

Four days after Duer went to jail, Madison tried again. Madison and Jefferson had learned that Duer had the army supply contracts for the failed 1792 expedition against the Indians: they demanded that Hamilton and Secretary of War Knox be investigated. House hearings only showed that Knox had failed to heed Hamilton's advice, and Hamilton survived this House vote of confidence by a wider margin. After many House members went home, Madison introduced another motion to tighten controls on sinking fund purchases, a measure that would have hampered Hamilton's quick success in stemming the Panic of 1792. This time, Madison won by a single vote. As the Second Congress ended, it was obvious to Hamilton that Madison and Jefferson had formed a political party. It was obviously opposed to Washington, whose term as president was running out. Hamilton implored Washington to seek a second term.[14]

Until Madison's attempts to have him fired, Hamilton had refused to believe his old friend had turned against him. But that spring, he learned also that Jefferson had written privately to Washington blaming him for the financial panic, blaming it on a "corrupt squadron" of speculators in Congress protecting Hamilton. Washington had invited Hamilton to respond. In a fourteen-thousand-word memo, Hamilton successfully defended himself. When the congressional investigation was over, Congressman William Heth of Virginia wrote, "The more you probe, examine and investigate Hamilton's conduct, rely upon it, the greater he will appear." But the widening rift between his two closest advisers and the Reign of Terror in France persuaded the sixty-year-old Washington to stay on. By that time, too, all the news from Europe was bad. That spring, Louis XVI and Marie Antoinette were guillotined. Lafayette's moderate Constitutionalists had been brushed aside by the radicals of the Gironde. An attempt by royalists and the armies of European monarchs to crush the revolution by force of arms had been defeated by a revolutionary army at Valmy, hastening the royal executions and the flight of the royalists, many to America. No longer a monarchy, France was now a republic appealing to the American republic for payment of its debts from the American Revolution. Ever more bitterly, Hamilton and Jefferson clashed in cabinet meetings. Hamilton maintained that the United States had made its treaties with the king of France and therefore owed neither alliance nor recompense to the French republic. Jefferson argued that the treaties and loans were made with the French nation and, for once, Washington backed him up. But so great was the gulf between factions in his cabinet that Washington acquiesced to Hamilton's argument that, if Washington did not remain in the presidency, the Union might come apart. By this time, cabinet and Congress had already split into Federalist (more or less today's Republicans) and Democratic-Republican (today's Democrats).

IN MID-NOVEMBER 1792, Treasury Comptroller Oliver Wolcott discovered that James Reynolds and his partner-in-crime, Jacob Clingman, had attempted to defraud the government by making themselves executors of a claimant against the Treasury who happened to be very much alive and turned up at Third and Chestnut Street for his money. Wolcott had Reynolds and Clingman arrested. Reynolds asked Hamilton to help have the charge quashed: Hamilton refused. Then Clingman appealed to his former boss, Congressman Frederick Muhlenberg, a Pennsylvania Federalist famous for appearing in his pulpit at the onset of the Revolution and, at the end of his sermon, tearing off his clerical robes to reveal a Continental Army uniform. This extremely ethical man, now a merchant, was Speaker of the House of Representatives. Clingman hinted to Muhlenberg "that Reynolds had it in his power very materially to injure the Secretary of the Treasury and that Reynolds knew several very improper transactions of his."[5]

Deeply worried, especially in the wake of Duer's arrest and the by now well-known swindling of some of his own former soldiers, Muhlenberg confided Clingman's insinuations to Senator James Monroe and Congressman Abraham Venable, both Virginia Democratic-Republicans close to Jefferson and Madison. The three visited Reynolds in jail; he repeated Clingman's charges and went further, alleging that Hamilton was deeply involved in speculations with Treasury funds. The three congressmen then went to question Maria Reynolds for corroboration of her husband's story. They left with several incriminating scraps of paper Hamilton supposedly had written Maria in a disguised handwriting and which she had omitted to burn as he had requested. The threesome decided to call on Hamilton before turning over their suspicions to Washington. They called on Hamilton at his office the morning of December 15; this time Senator Aaron Burr, identifying himself as Reynolds's lawyer, accompanied them. When Muhlenberg informed Hamilton of the charges against him, Hamilton said he would prove beyond any doubt that his relationship with Reynolds had nothing to do with the Treasury or had compromised its integrity if they would come to his house that evening.

That night, with Wolcott as his witness, Hamilton laid out the whole story of his affair with Maria Reynolds, providing what letters and receipts he had saved. He had barely begun to blurt out his confession when Muhlenberg and Venable, embarrassed by the personal nature of Maria's letters, asked Hamilton to say no more. They were completely satisfied that this affair was not the concern of Congress. But Monroe, a former Continental Army intelligence officer and close lieutenant of Jefferson's, was noncommittal. When Hamilton insisted on going on in an attempt to clear his name, all three listened, and before they left, all agreed they were satisfied. This was a private matter of honor and they would respect Hamilton's privacy. Hamilton thanked them for their "fairness and liberality" and they left, Monroe taking the letters Hamilton had shown them. But Monroe did not believe the gentleman's code superseded national politics, and he quickly briefed Jefferson and his chief party operative, Clerk of the House John Beckley, who copied out the documents and turned the originals over to Jefferson.[16]

The matter might have rested there except that, late in November 1792, Hamilton had submitted a plan to Congress to retire the national debt without increasing taxes. That gave Madison and the Jeffersonians a fresh excuse to call Hamilton to account for how he had used all previous foreign loans. His report appeared with alacrity, but it showed that Hamilton had mixed funds from two separate loans, without reauthorization from Congress but with the approval of the president. The result was a well-orchestrated uproar. Jeffersonian Representative William B. Giles of Virginia, famous for demanding investigations, sponsored five resolutions demanding a detailed accounting of all foreign loans, all transactions between the government and the Bank of the United States, and all sinking fund transactions, and an audit of all government moneys, accusing Hamilton of hiding shortages in his accounts, unlawfully favoring the bank, and drawing funds illegally from Europe to benefit speculators. Even Hamilton's friends could not allow the charges to stand past congressional adjournment on March 3 and into the presidential elections. Reluctantly, they passed the Giles resolutions on January 23, 1792.

By February 19, in only three weeks, Hamilton buried Congress under seven reports totaling sixty thousand words he had written longhand, together with a mountain of figures that represented the financial history of the United States. At the same time, a fifteen-member committee headed by Giles could turn up no dirt in its own probe of the Treasury. Giles was forced to withdraw his strongest charges. In what amounted to the first impeachment, the remaining nine charges were debated by the House on February 28, 1793 and late into the night of March 1. Every charge against Hamilton was defeated by a wide margin. James Madison was one of only five members who voted against Hamilton on every charge.

Hamilton took little part in the 1792 presidential election except to write privately to friends in New York not to support Aaron Burr, who was challenging Clinton, who in turn opposed Adams, for the vice presidency. When the presidential electors cast their ballots, Washington received 132 votes and was reelected. John Adams, with seventy-seven electoral votes, defeated George Clinton, whose fifty electoral votes encouraged the Republicans, as many of the former Anti-Federalists now called themselves, to attack Hamilton even more ferociously in Washington's second term. For the most part, Hamilton was preoccupied by fiscal problems created by the spreading war between England and revolutionary France. He gradually brought Washington around to his view that, if the United States paid off its loans to French rebels and England won, the English could claim that money paid to an illegal government had not been paid at all and was still owed when a legitimate government was restored. Hamilton counseled a policy of strict neutrality. But the war was making the lines between Federalists and Republicans clearer.

Once Hamilton realized that his old friend Madison was now his implacable foe, he unleashed a series of venomous articles against the

Republicans in Fenno's *National Gazette*. After one salvo, Jefferson responded by writing to Madison, "For God's sake, my dear sir, take up your pen, select the most striking heresies, and cut him to pieces." As Jefferson so accurately put it, the war in Europe "kindled and brought forward the two parties with an ardor which our own interests merely could never incite." The old epistolary combat broke out in the Philadelphia press in 1793. Hamilton, as "Pacificus," argued in defense of neutrality exactly as he did in the increasingly acrimonious Tuesday afternoon cabinet meetings. Madison counterattacked his former *Federalist Papers* coauthor as "Helvidius," in five articles attacking executive power.[17]

The cabinet crisis came to a head when a new French minister to the United States, Citizen Genêt, defied American neutrality and commissioned four privateers to prey on British vessels in American waters. In the cabinet, Hamilton, who had learned that Jefferson was privately corresponding with Genêt, demanded that France recall Genêt and, in a forty-five-minute speech, that Jefferson be made to turn over their letters. The cabinet voted instead to send the letters to France to force Genêt's recall. Outvoted again and again, Jefferson resigned as Secretary of State on September 15. He told Washington he was tired of moving "exactly in the circle which I know to bear me peculiar hatred, that is to say the wealthy aristocrats, the merchants connected closely with England, the new created paper fortunes." Washington persuaded Jefferson to stay on until the end of 1793.

By now, Hamilton had also told the president he would resign at year's end. By then, too, Hamilton had fled the worst yellow fever epidemic in Philadelphia's history. Some four thousand people died, at least in part because of the ancient medical practice of bleeding and purging. Many doctors, including the notorious Dr. Benjamin Rush, removed as much as 110 ounces of blood from swooning patients who, weakened, often succumbed to the cure. When both Hamilton and his wife contracted the dread fever, they were fortunate to be treated by Hamilton's boyhood friend, the Edinburgh-trained Dr. Edward Stevens, who eschewed bloodletting in favor of rest, a full diet with old Madeira wine, cold baths followed by brandy burned with cinnamon, and at night, a gentle dose of opiate with a few grains of salts and a "grateful aromatic." Dr. Stevens also administered a little quinine each day, an infusion of camomile to reduce vomiting, small doses of a mixture of oil of peppermint and spirits of lavender. Recovered but weak, the Hamiltons left for Albany; their five children had been sent ahead when the parents became ill.

Alexander Hamilton might have stayed in New York and returned soon to his law practice and the repair of his own diminished finances after five poorly paid years at the Treasury if it had not been for an armed revolt against one of his pet tax policies. In the backwoods of the Monongahela Valley of Pennsylvania, the Whiskey Rebellion broke out in the summer of 1794. Since the passage in 1791 of the revenue-raising excise tax on whiskey that Hamilton recommended in his "Report on Credit," frontiersmen in western Pennsylvania had resisted collection of the tax. The French Revolution, Citizen Genêt, and the proximity, in Pittsburgh, of the most militant, pro-Jefferson, Democratic-Republican societies all fanned the spirit of resistance. When violence erupted, Hamilton believed that the rule of law was seriously threatened. He recommended an immediate and massive display of armed force by the federal government to restore law and order. He urged first that frontiersmen drink less to save on taxes and that Washington call out thirteen thousand militia from four states to crush the rebellion by an armed mob. The government should "exert the full force of the law." Colonel Hamilton rode alongside "Light-Horse Harry" Lee, a feared Revolutionary War cavalry leader—and the father of Robert E. Lee. Hamilton loved nothing more than to be in his dashing officer's uniform, prancing off to enforce laws of his own making. Actually, that year, the excise tax laws had been eased: moonshiners could appear in a state court if no federal court were nearby. Hamilton's army relieved the siege of the federal excise inspector who, cornered in his house, had engaged in a two-day gun battle. After robbing the mails, the Whiskey Rebels, seven thousand strong, gathered in a field and threatened to burn

Pittsburgh—then march on the capital at Philadelphia. When Hamilton's army appeared, no resistance materialized. While the most dedicated rebels melted into Ohio, the militia rounded up 150 prisoners and marched them back to Philadelphia. Two leaders were convicted of treason, were pardoned by the president, and went home. And so did Hamilton, retiring from public office at the age of forty, unaware that he would never be elected to any office again.[18]

As THE end of the first president's second term loomed, the new political parties squared off. Adams had always assumed he would advance automatically to the highest office, but many Federalists considered him a placeholder who had contributed nothing to the republic as vice president. Over the years, Hamilton had emerged as the leader and spokesman of the Federalists, and he had every right to assume he would be rewarded someday with higher office. But when Noah Webster, editor of the pro-Federalist *Minerva*, started a boom for Hamilton as president, a sinister warning began to circulate, undoubtedly emanating from the Jefferson-Madison camp: if Hamilton or his friends persisted, unpleasant truths about his affairs would appear in the nation's newspapers. The scurrilous journalist James Thompson Callendar printed the threat in the pro-Jefferson *Philadelphia Aurora* after he saw the Reynolds correspondence taken away from Hamilton's home that night in December, 1792, copied out by John Beckley, and sent off to Jefferson at Monticello against the day it would be useful to the Jeffersonian camp. The threat succeeded. Hamilton evidently asked Webster to refrain from any further hints of his candidacy. Hamilton contented himself with dipping his pen in vitriol and, with his friend Rufus King, wrote thirty-eight articles entitled "The Defense," overwhelming their opponents. He was defending the unpopular Jay Treaty of 1795, which reopened the Caribbean to American ships but forced Americans like Jefferson to pay, finally, debts of twenty years and more to British merchants. While Jay burned in effigy, Hamilton received praise even from Jefferson. From atop Monticello Jefferson wrote, "Hamilton is really a colossus to the anti-Republican party. Without numbers, he is a host unto himself." But Hamilton could not be content to remain at his desk. He took to the streets on Saturday, July 18, when New York Democratic-Republicans led by Aaron Burr called for a mass protest against Washington signing the treaty. Some seven thousand people showed up, the crowd packing the wide Broad Street from Wall Street to Trinity Church. Hamilton, King, and a group of Federalists stood on the steps of a house on Broad Street to add their boos and hisses to the speeches as several Livingstons damned the treaty (written by a Livingston brother-in-law). When Hamilton spoke up, moving that the assemblage show "full confidence in the wisdom and virtue of the President," the crowd began throwing stones at the Federalists: one stone hit Hamilton in the head, drawing blood. Once, he had been part of the New York crowd protesting government policies: now they were attacking him, policies he had created, friends of his. Shortly afterward, Hamilton had his friend Troup draw up his will.[19]

On January 31, 1795, Alexander Hamilton, just turned forty, left behind his post as the first secretary of the treasury, secure that he had left the government solvent and able to continue functioning, its creditworthiness establishing it as first- or second-best national credit risk in the world (depending on whether England paid or defaulted on a loan that day). Both Hamilton and Jefferson had stayed on long after their threatened resignations, each unwilling to yield power to his rival. While Hamilton moved back to New York City and devoted himself primarily to his law practice, he nevertheless remained President Washington's favorite adviser, a sort of unpaid prime minister in absentia, counseling cabinet officers as well as giving advice on fiscal matters. Advertising in the newspapers for the return of scores of law books he had lent out, he distinguished himself among the nation's top half-dozen attorneys, transforming New York law, the new nation's standard, by articulating the law of contracts, basing it on market considerations. He pioneered, by developing case law as opposed to politically vulnerable statute law, the privileges and obligations of corporations, and he rewrote the rules of marine law, making them case-driven as well. Ironically, despite all his recent wrangling with Congress, in *Hylton v. United States* (1796) he won the first ruling by the United State Supreme Court on the constitutionality of an act of Congress.

As one of the nation's most productive writers, he repeatedly
acceded when President Washington asked him to write his speeches.
He composed Washington's seventh annual message to Congress, his
"State of the Union." When Washington decided he could no longer
endure the weekly abuse he increasingly received from the press, the
president asked Hamilton to write his Farewell Address. Madison
had written the valedictory for Washington at the end of his first
term; now Washington asked Hamilton to take his old Federalist collaborator's draft and transform it. It would not be until 1859, after his
wife died and his papers were opened, that it was discovered that
Hamilton, not Washington, wrote the famous speech. One last time,
as if they were both back at headquarters at Valley Forge, Hamilton
was the mind and writing hand of Washington. But, in public,
Hamilton still had to defend his actions as secretary of the treasury.
The radical Democratic-Republican press hectored Hamilton, publicly
charging him with having paid blackmail to James Reynolds to cover
up irregularities in the treasury.

In the summer of 1797, Hamilton, fearing that, if the public
believed the charges of speculation at the Treasury, his entire financial
system and the public credit would be seriously damaged, decided to
publish the entire story of his involvement with James and Maria
Reynolds. Choosing between great pain to his wife and friends and
defending his public reputation and creations, he printed an excruci-
atingly detailed account of his affair. And then he insisted that Monroe, Venable, and Muhlenberg write him sworn statements that they
had dropped their investigation five years earlier because they
believed Hamilton was innocent of any financial wrongdoing. When
Monroe refused, Hamilton threatened him with a duel. Monroe
chose Aaron Burr as his go-between in lengthy negotiations in which
Monroe finally backed away from settling the issue with pistols. But
Burr, ignoring Monroe's wishes, averted the duel to neither man's satisfaction. Monroe still would not absolve Hamilton in writing, and
Hamilton came away hating both Monroe and Burr, and he apparently
did not realize how much he had damaged himself by his public
confession of his adultery. Henry Knox wrote:

Myself and most of his other friends conceive this confession humiliating in the extreme, and such a text as will serve his enemies for a commentary while he lives and his name is mentioned as a public man.

Episcopal Bishop William White, a leading Federalist, refused in public to drink a toast to Hamilton, citing the disclosures in Hamilton's pamphlet. Most leaders in both parties maintained embarrassed silence, but Madison, writing to Jefferson, came close to gloating. The publication

is a curious specimen of the ingenious folly of its author. Next to the error of publishing at all, is that of forgetting that simplicity and candor are the only dress which prudence would put on innocence.

Senator Maclay of Pennsylvania put it more simply. The more serious charge of peculation remained: "nobody can prove these things, but everybody knows them."[20]

Hamilton's reputation partially recovered the next year as the Napoleonic Wars lapped America's shores. In the Quasi War of 1798–1800, the United States built up its military forces for an undeclared war with its old ally, France. Pro-war Federalists wanted an outright war after years of French privateering against American shipping in the Caribbean. A more prudent President Adams favored an unofficial military buildup. When he asked Washington, in blissful retirement at Mount Vernon, if he would accept appointment as commander-in-chief, Washington acceded on condition that Hamilton be his second-in-command—and do most of the work. Adams agreed and Hamilton achieved one of his greatest goals, a major general's stars and epaulets. As inspector general, Hamilton was frustrated, however, by foot dragging in the War Department and in Congress. His one permanent accomplishment was to create the United States Navy on May 3, 1798. In the undeclared war, American navy ships distinguished themselves against superior French forces.

But peace with France brought renewed political warfare at home, especially after the death of Washington on December 14, 1799. Hamilton's protector, the one man who always seemed to understand him, was gone. Hamilton wrote, "He was an aegis very essential to me. If virtue can secure happiness in another world, he is happy." In utter grief, Hamilton became an unrestrained spoiler more than the kingmaker he fancied himself. He worked secretly to oppose the reelection of Adams, who had called him the "base-born brat of a Scots peddler"—a bastard. This was a serious slur, a revelation for most people that further damaged Hamilton among New England Congregationalists and Middle States Presbyterians, who refused communion to the illegitimate. In a circular letter he intended for private consumption by two hundred leading Federalists, he enumerated Adams's "defects of character": the second president was "eccentric," had no "sound judgment" or "steady perseverance" but his "extreme egotism" worsened his "unfitness for the station contemplated." Hamilton urged fellow Federalists to support Charles Cotesworth Pinckney of South Carolina over Adams since the primary objective was to keep Jefferson and his running mate, Aaron Burr, out of office. Burr got a copy of the letter and saw that it was published in newspapers all over America.

Hamilton not only cost Adams reelection but, in so doing, destroyed the Federalist Party he had done so much to create. Jefferson and Burr tied, with seventy-three electoral votes each. Hamilton's long-ago fears of the flaw in the Constitution in the case of a tie vote now became a public nightmare. Burr refused to acknowledge that Jefferson had asked him to run as his vice presidential candidate. Congress would have to resolve the dilemma in a runoff election in its nearly completed chambers in the new District of Columbia. Hamilton worked incessantly behind the scenes to persuade Federalists to throw away their votes rather than give them to the hated Burr. Finally, after thirty-five ballots, on the thirty-sixth, William Bayard of Delaware, the only state with a single vote, cast a blank ballot, as did Federalists from Vermont and Kentucky. Jefferson became President, Burr became Vice President. Hamilton's party, and his own political career, were destroyed. The Federalists never won another presidential election; Hamilton would never be elected to public office again.

To give himself a base to continue his political attacks, Hamilton founded the *New York Post* and used it to hurl invectives at the Jefferson-Burr administration. But, for the most part, he confined his energies to litigating, taking on important constitutional cases, especially buttressing the freedom of the press. In February 1804, he traveled to Albany to try an appeal before the New York Court of Errors. In *People v. Croswell*, he sought a new trial for a New York Federalist publisher convicted of libel. Virtually all the New York Assembly packed the courtroom as Hamilton made his last great speech. Tyranny, Hamilton argued, "can never be introduced in this country by arms." It could "be subverted only by a pretense of adhering to all the forms of law" while "breaking down the substance of our liberties." Hamilton, now forty-nine, seemed to rear back and hurl the words at the judge, jury, makers of law. Any truth could stave off tyranny in America. Truth, if not used "wantonly," must be reckoned by all reasonable men as a defense. Without the freedom of the press to utter the truth,

> You must forever remain ignorant of what your rulers do. I never did think the truth was a crime, for my soul has ever abhorred the thought that a free man dared not speak the truth.

Hamilton lost the requested appeal for his client, but his words had such a profound effect on the legislators who heard them that day that, in the next year's session of the New York Assembly, they enacted into law the principle of truth as a defense.[21]

But, by then, Alexander Hamilton was dead. In the New York gubernatorial election of 1804, Hamilton fiercely opposed Aaron Burr's bid to replace Governor Clinton. Hamilton and Clinton, after twenty-five years as political enemies, renewed their old friendship and defeated Burr. A few weeks later, Burr sent an emissary to Hamilton, accusing him of slandering Burr in a dinner table conversation. Burr demanded a written apology or satisfaction in a duel. Hamilton refused to apologize. He was bereft over the death of his firstborn son in a duel after a political argument three years earlier. His daughter Angelica had become deranged with grief after Philip's death. Hamilton had become obsessed with Burr, who, with Jefferson, he believed, would destroy the Union.

Alexander Hamilton refused to back down. Writing a last note to Betsy but not telling her where he was going, he told her she would not have been proud of him if he did not maintain his honor. As usual, he did not ask Betsy what she thought. He borrowed a pair of English Wogdon dueling pistols from his old friend John Church, long-suffering husband of Angelica. Why he did not use his own is unfathomable. The Churches had come back from England and they were very close to the Hamiltons, Angelica living in town near Hamilton while John traveled on business and Betsy stayed in the country at the Hamiltons' new manor house, The Grange, eight miles from Hamilton's downtown Manhattan office, where he spent most of his time. Church's pistols were the same weapons that Hamilton's son had been offered for his fatal duel. They had specially designed hair triggers that, if set, would fire fast and accurately at the slightest squeeze, jerking little; if not, it would take a determined, slower squeeze to fire the oversize, .554-calibre ball.[22]

Early the morning of July 11, 1804, Hamilton climbed into a rowboat with his second and a doctor. Shortly after dawn, on the same strip of cliff at Weehawken where his son had died, he faced Aaron Burr. The sunlight was in Hamilton's eyes. He had told his second that he intended to fire into the air to end the affair with honor but without bloodshed. Burr made no such promise. Hamilton did not set the hair trigger on his pistol; Burr did. Two shots rang out almost simultaneously. Burr's struck Hamilton in the right side, tearing through his liver. Hamilton's shot, according to his second, went off a split second later, snapping a twig overhead. Thirty-six hours later, a grieving crowd gathered at Hamilton's door. As Burr prepared to flee New York City, Alexander Hamilton, age forty-nine, died. Betsy lived another fifty years, editing his papers, burnishing his image, finding the perfect biographer, their son. And when by-then former president James Monroe came one day to call, she refused to let him sit down—after what he had done to her poor Hamilton.

ABBREVIATIONS USED IN THE NOTES AND BIBLIOGRAPHY

AH = Alexander Hamilton
AHM = *American Heritage Magazine*
AMH = Allan Maclane Hamilton, *Intimate Life of AH*
ASC = Angelica Schuyler Church
BA = Benedict Arnold
BF = Benjamin Franklin
ESH = Elizabeth Schuyler Hamilton
FTMB = *Fort Ticonderoga Museum Bulletin*
GC = George Clinton
GM = Gouverneur Morris
GW = George Washington
HG = Horatio Gates
HGP = HG Papers, NYHS.
HK = Henry Knox
HL = Henry Laurens
JCC = *Journals of the Continental Congress*
JCH = J.C. Hamilton, *Works of AH.*
JH = John Hancock
JJ = John Jay

JL = John Laurens
JM = James Madison
LDC = U.S. Continental Congress, *Letters of Delegates to Congress*
LOC = Library of Congress
MHM = *Military History Magazine*
ML = Marquis de Lafayette
N-YHS = New-York Historical Society
NYPL = New York Public Library
PAH = Syrett et al., *Papers of AH*
PBF = Labaree, *Papers of BF*
PGW = Twohig, *Papers of GW*
PMHB = *Pennsylvania Magazine of History and Biography*
PH = *Pennsylvania History*
PS = Philip Schuyler
PNJHS = *Proceedings of the New Jersey Historical Society*
PTJ = *Papers of TJ*
QN-YHS = *Quarterly of the N-YHS*
RM = Robert Morris
TJ = Thomas Jefferson
UVA = University of Virginia
WLCL = William L. Clements Library, University of Michigan
WMQ = *William & Mary Quarterly*
WW = Fitzpatrick, *Writings of Washington*

NOTES

———◆———

Preceding the numbered notes in each chapter are background subjects, each with sources that I found especially valuable and pertinent. Full particulars of each work together with other readings carefully considered are listed in the bibliography.

ONE: "THE WISH OF MY HEART"

Fatal Duel and Death: PAH, 26:235–349; Syrett, *Interview in Weehawken*; Mitchell, *AH*, 1:533–37; Fleming, *Duel*, 321–45; McDonald, *AH*, 355–63; Hendrickson, *Hamilton*, 2:624–47.

1. Dr. David Hosack to William Coleman, Aug. 17, 1804, *PAH*, 26:344–47.

2. Bishop Benjamin Moore to William Coleman, Aug. 12, 1804, *PAH*, 26:314–16.

TWO: "A SHORT TIME TO LIVE"

AH Orphaned: PAH, 1:1–3; Mitchell, *AH, Youth to Maturity* (hereafter *Youth*), 1–18; Hendrickson, *Hamilton*, 1:1–19.

1. Mitchell, *AH, Youth*, 1:16.

2. *PAH*, 1:2–3.

3. AH to William Hamilton, May 2, 1797, *PAH*, 21:77.

THREE: "TWICE GUILTY OF ADULTERY"

Caribbean Origins: PAH, vol. 1; Mitchell, *AH, Youth,* 1–14; Hendrickson, *Hamilton,* 1:1–19; Flexner, *Young Hamilton,* 8–33; Lodge, *Works of AH,* vol. 6; L. Gipson, *British Empire,* 2:181–290; Edwards, *The History, Civil and Commercial, in the West Indies, of the British Colonies,* 1; Pares, *West-India Fortune.*

1. AH to William Jackson, Aug. 26, 1800, *PAH,* 25:80.
2. Quoted in Gipson, *British Empire,* 2:222–23.
3. Ibid., 223.
4. Mitchell, *AH, Youth,* 3.
5. Quoted in Hendrickson, *Hamilton,* 1:19.
6. AH to ESH, [1781], *PAH,* 3:235.
7. Mitchell, *AH, Youth,* 6.
8. "Historic Keeps and Castles and Stately Homes of Ayrshire," *Kilmarnock Standard,* April 5, 1924.
9. AH to William Hamilton, May 2, 1797, *PAH,* 21:503–05.
10. Mitchell, *AH, Youth,* 11.
11. J.C. Hamilton, *Life of AH,* 1: 3.
12. Ibid., 7.
13. Quoted in Lodge, 6:243.
14. *Royal Danish-American Gazette,* Jan. 23, 1771.
15. AH to James Hamilton, June 22, 1785, mss., NYPL.

FOUR: "I WISH THERE WAS A WAR"

Apprenticeship: PAH 1:39; Mitchell, *AH, Youth,* 15–34; McDonald, *AH,* 1–10; PNJHS, 69 (1951) 88–114; Flexner, *Young Hamilton,* 34–52; Hendrickson, *Hamilton,* 1:20–36; Mulligan and Troup, "Narrative;" *Princetonians,* 1:101–05.

1. Quoted in Mitchell, *AH, Youth,* 23, 27
2. AH to Edward Stevens, Nov. 11, 1769, *PAH,* 1: 4.
3. *Royal Danish-American Gazette,* April 6, 1771.
4. Mitchell, *AH, Youth,* 28.
5. AH to Tileman Cruger, Nov. 16, 1771, *PAH,* 1:12–13.
6. AH to William Newton, Nov. 16, 1771, *PAH,* 1:14.
7. Ibid., Nov. 27, 1771, *PAH,* 1:17–18.
8. AH to Nicholas Cruger, Nov. 12, 1771, *PAH,* 1:11.
9. Ibid., Jan. 10, 1772, *PAH,* 1:21.
10. AH to Newton, Feb. 1, 1772, *PAH,* 1:24.
11. AH to H. Cruger, Feb. 24, 1772, *PAH,* 1:25–6.

12. N. Cruger to Thomas Thomas, May 25, 1772, *PAH*, 1:33.
13. *Princetonians*, 1:103.
14. *Boston Post-Boy*, Sept. 28, 1741.
15. Quoted in Mitchell, *Youth*, 488, n20.
16. *PAH*, 1:81; Knox, *Select Sermons*, 34–35.
17. Mitchell, *AH, Youth*, 665.
18. Hugh Knox to AH, Oct. 27, 1783, *PAH*, 3:474–75.
19. *Royal Danish-American Gazette*, Oct. 17, 1772, *PAH*, 1:38–9.

Five: "A Wandering Guest in Worlds Unknown"

Prep School Days: *PAH*, 1:40–44; Mitchell, *AH, Youth*, 36–53; McDonald, *AH*, 10–12; Flexner, *Young Hamilton*, 45–63; Hendrickson, *Hamilton* 1:37–56; Kalm, *Travels in North America*; Sabine, *Loyalists*, 1:302–35; O'Brien, *Hercules Mulligan*, 41–47; Mulligan and Troup, "Narrative," *WMQ* 3rd series, 4 (1947): 203–25; Green, *Life of the Rev'd John Witherspoon*; Brandt, *American Aristocracy*.

1. *Boston Gazette*, Oct. 12, 1772.
2. Ibid., Nov. 2, 1772.
3. Quoted in Flexner, *Young Hamilton*, 17.
4. *Massachusetts Gazette*, Oct. 1, 1772.
5. Kalm, *Travels*, 123.
6. *New York Gazette*, Jan. 1, 1772.
7. Quoted in Mitchell, *AH Youth*, 74–5.
8. Mulligan, "Narrative," mss., Hamilton Papers, LOC.
9. Green, *Life of the Rev'd John Witherspoon*, 128.

Six: "Americans Are Entitled to Freedom"

Student Revolutionary: *PAH*: 1:43–182; Mitchell, *AH, Youth*, 57–81; Mitchell, *AH: Revolutionary Years*, 4–6; Burrows and Wallace, *Gotham*, 191–230; O'Brien, *Hercules Mulligan*, 41–47; Flexner, *Young Hamilton*, 20–99; Hendrickson, *Hamilton*, 1:57–101; Mulligan and Troup, "Narrative," *WMQ*, 3rd series, 4 (1947): 203–25; Thomas, "King's College Building," *QN-YHS*, Jones, *History of New York*; Abbott, *New York in the American Revolution*; Flick, *Loyalists in New York*; Stokes, *Iconography of Manhattan Island*.

1. Mulligan and Troup, "Narrative," 219.
2. Abbott, *New York in the American Revoluton*, 15.
3. Quoted in Burrows and Wallace, *Gotham*, 217.
4. Thomas, "King's College Building," 24.
5. Livingston, *Independent Reflector*.

6. *New York Gazette*, Jan. 10, 1774.

7. Mitchell, *AH, Youth*, 501, n60.

8. Thomas, "King's College Building," 34-5.

9. Ibid., 36.

10. Mulligan and Troup, "Narrative," 213.

11. Mitchell, *AH, Youth*, 63-64.

12. *PAH*, 1:85.

13. Mitchell, *AH, Youth*, 63-4.

14. JJ to A. McDougall, Dec. 4, 1775, *LDC*, 2:437.

15. *New York Gazette*, Dec. 16, 1773.

16. AH to McDougall, *PAH* [1774], 26: 353-54.

17. *PAH*, 1:43-44.

18. Mitchell, *AH, Youth*, 67.

19. *PAH*, 1:46.

20. *New York Gazetteer*, Dec. 22, 1774.

21. Mulligan and Troup, "Narrative," 214.

22. Ibid., 211.

23. *PAH*, 1:47.

24. Burrows and Wallace, *Gotham*, 217-8.

25. Mulligan and Troup, "Narrative," 219.

26. Burrows and Wallace, *Gotham*, 224.

27. Ibid.

28. Ibid., 228.

29. Mulligan and Troup, "Narrative," 219.

30. Mitchell, *AH, Youth*, 75-76.

31. *New York Journal*, Dec. 28, 1775.

32. Ibid., Jan. 4, 1776.

33. AH to JJ, Nov. 26, 1775, *PAH*, 1:177.

34. JJ to McDougall, Dec. 4, 1775; *LDC*, 2:437.

35. AH to JJ, Jan. 4, 1776, *PAH*, 1:181.

36. Mulligan and Troup, "Narrative," 210.

37. Mitchell, *AH: Revolutionary Years*, 5-6.

Seven: "Men Go to Those Who Pay Them"

Artilleryman: PAH, 1: 182-210; *PGW*, Revolutionary War Series, vols. 4-7; Mitchell, *AH, Youth*, 74-99; *AH; Revolutionary Years*, 1-62; Burrows and Wallace, *Gotham*, 223-44; Hendrickson, *Hamilton*, I:91-117; Fleming, *1776: Year of Illusions*; Randall, *GW*, 287-330.

1. Mulligan and Troup, "Narrative," 210.

2. AH to New York Provincial Congress, May 26, 1776, *PAH*, 1:182.

3. AH to New York Convention, Aug. 12, 1776, *PAH*, 1:187.

4. AH to New York Convention, Sept. 14, 1776, *PAH*, 1:188.

5. J. C. Fitzpatrick, *GW Himself*, 22.

6. Quoted in Mitchell, *AH, Youth*, 86.

7. Quoted in Burrows and Wallace, *Gotham*, 231, 234.

8. Quoted in Mitchell, *AH, Revolutionary Years*, 15.

9. Ibid., 18.

10. GW to Lund Washington, Oct. 6, 1776, *PGW*, Revolutionary War Series, 6:495.

11. GW to John Hancock, Dec. 1, 1776, *PGW*, Revolutionary War Series, 7:245.

12. O'Brien, *Hercules Mulligan*, 87; Mitchell, *AH: Revolutionary Years*, 29.

13. William Howe to G. Germain, Dec. 20, 1776, Colonial Office Papers, 5/94.

14. J. Grant to J. G. Rall, Dec. 1776, Force, *Am. Archives*, 5:11, 1317.

15. Wilkinson, quoted in Stryker, *Battles of Trenton and Princeton*, 32.

16. Quoted in Mitchell, *AH: Revolutionary Years*, 55.

17. Mitchell, *AH: Revolutionary Years*, 55; Mitchell, *AH, Youth*, 105.

18. Mitchell, *AH, Youth*, 109.

19. Ibid., 112.

20. Mitchell, *AH: Revolutionary Years*, 58–59.

21. Oswald Tilghman, *Memoir of Lt. Col. Tench Tilghman*, 147.

22. Mitchell, *AH: Revolutionary Years*, 59.

23. Mitchell, *AH, Youth*, 112–13.

24. Mitchell, *AH: Revolutionary Years*, 62.

25. Mitchell, *AH, Youth*, 112.

EIGHT: "WE SHALL BEAT THEM SOUNDLY"

Aide-de-Camp: PAH, 1:195–411; *LDC*, vols. 6–8; Nelson, *General Horatio Gates*; *PGW*, Revolutionary War Series, vols. 7–10, *WW*, vols. 9–10; Mitchell, *AH: Revolutionary Years*, 63–121; Wilkinson, *Memoirs of My Own Times*; Mitchell, *AH, Youth*, 53–130; Flexner, *Young Hamilton*, 125–205; Hendrickson, *Hamilton*, 1:119–72; Randall, *GW*, 306–57; Carp, *To Starve the Army at Pleasure*; Busch, *Winter Quarters*.

1. GW to Archibald Campbell, March 3, 1777, *PGW*, Revolutionary War Series, 8:493.

2. GW to Benedict Arnold (hereafter BA), March 3, 1777, *PGW*, Revolutionary War Series, 8:495.

3. AH to New York Committee of Correspondence, March 22, 1777, *PAH*, 1:211.

4. Ibid., April 5, 1777, *PAH*, 1:219–22.

5. Ibid., April 20, 1777, *PAH*, 1:233–36.

6. AH to GM, May 19, 1777, *PAH*, 1:254–36.

7. Ibid., Apr. 28, 1777, *PAH*, 1:240–41.

8. Hugh Knox to AH, April 30, 1777, *PAH*, 1:244–45.

9. AH to GM, Sept. 1, 1777, *PAH*, 1:321.

10. AH to JH, Sept. 18, 1777, *PAH*, 1:326–28.

11. Quoted in Mitchell, *AH: Revolutionary Years*, 82–83.

12. John Adams to Abigail Adams, Sept. 30, 1777, *LDC*, 8:27.

13. Quoted in Mitchell, *AH: Revolutionary Years*, 82.

14. GW to JH, Oct. 30, 1777, *PAH*, 1:347–48.

15. Quoted in Plumb, "French Connection."

16. GW to AH, Oct. 30, 1777, *PAH*, 1:347–48.

17. AH to GW, Nov. 2, 1777, *PAH*, 1:349–50.

18. James Lovell to HG, Nov. 27, 1777, mss., HGP, NYHS.

19. AH to GW, Nov. 6, 1777, *PAH*, 1:353–55.

20. Hendrickson, *Hamilton* 1: 246.

21. AH to HG, Nov. 5, 177, *PAH*, 1:350.

22. HG to GW, Nov. 5, 1777, mss, HGP, NYHS.

23. AH to Israel Putnam, Nov. 9, 1777, *PAH*, 1:356.

24. AH to GW, Nov. 10, 1777, *PAH*, 1:357–60.

25. GW to AH, Nov. 15, 1777, *PAH*, 1:365.

26. Hugh Hughes to HG, Dec. 5, 1777, mss., HGP, NYHS.

27. HG to Thomas Conway, Dec. 3, 1777, in Sparks (ed.), *Writings of Washington*, 5:495, HG to James Wilkinson, in Wilkinson, *Memoirs*, 1:395, HG to GW, Dec. 8, 1777, mss., HGP, NYHS.

28. HL to GW, quoted in Massey, *JL and the American Revolution*.

NINE: "A SYSTEM OF INFIDELITY"

Army Reforms: PAH vols. 1–2; *LDC*, vols. 8–10; *WW*, vols. 11–12; McDonald, *AH*, 14–20; Hendrickson, *Hamilton*, 1: 210–259; Mitchell, *AH: Revolutionary Years*, 122–64; Mitchell, *AH: Youth*, 143–81; Flexner, *Young Hamilton*, 139–243; Massey, *JL and the American Revolution* 86–127.

1. AH to GW, [Jan. 29, 1778], *PAH*, 1:414–21.

2. GW to JH, Feb. 1, 1778, *WW*, 10: 414; AH to GC, Feb. 13, 1778; *PAH*, 1:426.

3. Freeman, *GW*, 4:566–68; AH to Steuben, [March–April 1778], *PAH*, 1:448.

4. GM to AH, May 16, 1777, *PAH*, 1:253–54.

5. AH to GC, Feb. 13, 1778, *PAH*, 1:425–28.

6. GC to AH, March 5, 1778, *PAH*, 1:436–37.

7. AH to GM, May 19, 1777, *PAH*, 1:254–56.

8. AH to GC, March 12, 1778, *PAH*, 1:440–42.

9. Quoted in Massey, *JL and the American Revolution*, 95.

10. JL to HL, Feb. 2, 1778; *PHL*, 12:367–68.

11. AH to JJ, March 14, 1779, *PAH*, 2:17–19.

12. AH, April 10–11, 1778, *PAH*, 1:460–472.

13. GW, "Commission," April 4, 1778, *PAH*, 1:493–94.

14. Fish, in Mulligan, "Narrative," AH Papers, LOC.

15. AH to GC, March 12, 1778, *PAH*, 1:442.

16. AH to William Duer, June 18, 1778, *PAH*, 1:497–501.

17. Council of War to GW, June 24, 1778, *WW*, 12: 115–17.

18. AH to EB, June 26, 1778, *PAH*, 1:505.

19. McHenry, *Journal*, mss., Emmet Coll., NYPL.

20. "Eulogium on Major-General Greene," July 4, 1789, *Works*, 8, 68.

21. Quoted in Mitchell, *AH, Youth*, 162.

22. AH to GW, [June 26, 1778], *PAH*, 1:504–05.

23. AH to GW, June 26, 1778, *PAH*, 1:506.

24. AH to Elias Boudinot, July 5, 1778, *PAH*, 1:510–14.

25. McHenry, *Journal*, mss., Emmet Coll., NYPL.

26. GW to John Sullivan, GW Papers, LOC.

TEN: "TREASON OF THE BLACKEST DYE"

Courtship and Perfidy: PAH, vol. 2; *WW*, vols. 13–20; Flexner, *Young Hamilton*, 244–48; Mitchell, *AH, Youth*, 182–221; Mitchell, *AH: Revolutionary Years*, 185–216; McDonald, *AH*, 14–23; Randall, *BA*, 513–70; Van Doren, *Secret History of the Revolution*; J. R. Maguire, "Self-Portrait."

1. GW to Gouverneur Morris, Oct. 4, 1778, *WW*, 13: 21.

2. AH to JL, [April, 1779], *PAH*, 2:34–38.

3. JL to AH, Dec. 18, 1779, *PAH*, 2:231.

4. John Brooks to AH, July 4, 1779, *PAH*, 2:90–92.

5. Francis Dana to AH, July 25, 1779, *PAH*, 2:108–09.

6. William Gordon to AH, Aug. 25, 1779, *PAH*, 2:141–43.

7. AH to Gordon, Sept. 5, 1779, *PAH*, 2:153–56.

8. AH to JL, Sept. 11, 1779, *PAH*, 2:165–69.

9. AH to Catherine Livingston, April 11, 1777, *PAH*, 1:225–27.

10. *PAH*, 2:261–62.

11. Quoted in Flexner, *Young Hamilton* 271.

12. Ibid., 277.

13. AH to Catherine Livingston and ESH, [Jan.–Feb., 1780], *PAH*, 2:262.

14. AH to ESH, [Mar. 17, 1780], *PAH*, 2:285–87.

15. PS to AH, April 8, 1780, *PAH*, 2:305–07.

16. Quoted in Flexner, *Young Hamiton* 278.

17. PS to AH, April 8, 1780, *PAH*, 2:305–07.

18. AH to Catherine Van Renssalaer Schuyler, [April 14, 1780], *PAH*, 2:309–10.

19. AH to JL, [June 30, 1780], *PAH*, 2:348.

20. AH to ESH, [June–Oct. 1780], *PAH*, 2:350.

21. Ibid., July 6, 1780, *PAH*, 2:353.

22. Ibid., Aug. 1780, *PAH*, 2:397–98.

23. Ibid., Sept. 3, 1780, *PAH*, 2:418.

24. Quoted in Burrows and Wallace, *Gotham*, 252.

25. Ibid., 252–54.

26. Quoted in Wallace, *Traitorous Hero*, 221.

27. BA to Nathanael Greene, quoted in Van Doren, *Secret History*, 310.

28. AH to JL, [Oct. 11, 1780], *PAH*, 2:460–70.

29. BA to Beverley Robinson, Sept. 18, 1780, Van Doren, *Secret History*, 483.

30. Mss., British Headquarters Papers, Lord Dorchester Coll., WLCL.

31. Richard Varick, *Court of Inquiry*, 189–93.

32. AH to GW, [Sept. 25, 1780], *PAH*, 2:438–9.

33. AH to Nathanael Greene, Sept. 25, 1780, *PAH*, 2:440–1.

34. AH to GW, [Sept. 25, 1780], Mss., NYPL.

35. Varick, *Court of Inquiry*, 189–93.

36. AH to ESH, Sept. 26, [1780], 441–42.

37. Ibid.

38. GW to Joseph Reed, [Oct. 18, 1780], *WW*, 20: 213–15; GW to William Heath, Sept. 26, 1780, *WW*, 20: 88–89; AH to JL, [Oct. 11, 1780], *PAH*, 2:460–70.

39. AH to ESH, Sept. 26, [1780], *PAH*, 2:441–42; Oct. 2, 1780, 2:448–49.

40. AH to JL, [Oct. 11, 1780], *PAH*, 2:467.

41. AH to ESH, Oct. 2, 1780, *PAH*, 2:449; Oct. 5, 1780, 2:455–56; Oct. 13, 1780, 2:473–75; Oct. 27, 1780, 2:492–44.

42. AH to JL, [Oct. 11, 1780], *PAH*, 2:465–68.

Eleven: "Then We Must Part"

Breaks with GW: PAH, vols. 2–3 McDonald, *AH*, 23–43; Hendrickson, *Hamilton*, 1, Mitchell, *AH, Youth* Mitchell, *AH: Revolutionary Years*; *WW*, vol. 20; Randall, *GW*, 389–99; Leake, I.Q. *John Lamb*, 270–80.

1. AH to ESH, Oct. 5, 1780, *PAH*, 2:455–56.
2. Marquis de Fleury to AH, Oct. 20, 1780, *PAH*, 2:481–82.
3. AH to GW, [Nov. 22, 1780], *PAH*, 2:509–10.
4. Marquis de Lafayette to AH, Dec. 9, 1780, *PAH*, 2:519.
5. Quoted in Mitchell, *AH: Revolutionary Years*, 220.
6. *PAH*, 2:520–24.
7. J. McHenry to AH, Dec. 16, 1780, *PAH*, 2:524.
8. Nathanael Greene to AH, Jan. 10, 1781, *PAH*, 2:529–33.
9. AH to Margarita Schuyler, Jan. 21, 1781, *PAH*, 2:539–40.
10. PS to AH, Jan. 25, 1781, *PAH*, 2:542–43.
11. ASC to ESH, quoted in Flexner, *Young Hamilton*, 329.
12. AH to PS, Feb. 18, 1781, *PAH*, 2:563–68.
13. AH to J. McHenry, Feb. 18, 1781, *PAH*, 2:569.
14. ML to GW, Feb., 1781, *WW*, AH to PS, Feb. 18, 1781, *PAH*, 2:563–68.
15. PS to AH, Feb. 25, 1781, *PAH*, 2:575–77.
16. AH to GW, [April 27, 1781], *PAH*, 2:600–01.
17. GW to AH, Apr. 27, 1781, *PAH*, 2:601–02.
18. Hume, *Philosophical Works*, 2:264; A. Smith, *Theory of Moral Sentiments*, 80.
19. AH to [SPS], Dec. 1779–March 1780, *PAH*, 2:236–51.
20. McDonald, *AH*, 39.
21. AH to JL, Sept. 11, 1779, Jan. 8, June 30, Sept. 12, 1780, ibid., 2:167, 255, 347, 428.
22. AH to RM, April 20, 1781, *PAH*, 2:604–35.
23. AH to ESH, [July 10, 1781], *PAH*, 2:647.
24. *PAH*, 2:658.
25. AH to GW, Aug. 7, 1781, *PAH*, 2:659–60.
26. AH to ESH, Aug. 22, 1781, *PAH*, 2:667.
27. Ibid., Aug. 25, 1781, *PAH*, 2:668–69.
28. Ibid., [Sept. 15–18, 1781], *PAH*, 2:675.
29. AH to ESH, [Oct. 12, 1781], *PAH*, 2:677–78.
30. Quoted in Mitchell, *AH: Revolutionary Years*, 275–76.
31. AH to ESH, Oct. 16, 1781, *PAH*, 2:682.

32. Mitchell, *Revolutionary Wars*, 283.

33. Ibid., 285.

Twelve: "The Art of Fleecing Neighbors"

Congressman Hamilton: Julius Goebel, Jr., ed., *Law Practice of AH*, vol.1 PAH, vol. 2 Mitchell, *AH, Youth*, 262–345; Hendrickson, *Hamilton*, 1:338–450; O'Brien, *Hercules Mulligan*, 106–16; McDonald, *AH*, 43–90; Massey, *JL and the American Revolution* 220–34; Burrows and Wallace, *Gotham*, 255–87; Randall and Nahra, *Thomas Chittenden's Town*, 1–9, 55–94, Gordon, *Hamilton's Blessing*, 1–14.

1. AH to ML, Nov. 2, 1782, PAH, 3:192.

2. JL to AH, July, 1782, PAH, 3:121.

3. AH to JL, Aug. 15, 1782, PAH, 3:144–45.

4. Capt. William McKennan and Nathanael Greene quoted in Massey, *JL and the American Revolution*, 227; John Adams to HL, Nov. 6, 1782, Kendall Coll., HL Papers, Kendall Whaling Museum, Sharons, Mass.; AH to Nathanael Greene, Oct. 12, 1782, Goebel, *Law Practice of AH*, 1:5–6; PAH, 3:183–84.

5. AH to Richard Kidder Meade, Aug. 27, 1782, PAH, 3:150–51; March, 1782, PAH, 3:69–71.

6. "Suspension of the Rule," April 26, 1782, PAH, 3:82–83.

7. RN to AH, April 15, 1782, PAH, 3:72; "Warrant to Receive Money as Continental Receiver," April 15, 1782, ibid., 74.

8. Quoted in McDonald, *AH*, 53.

9. Goebel, *Law Practice of AH*, 1: 128, 81, 82, 83, 109.

10. Vattel, *Law of Nations*, xli-xlii; PAH, 3:122; Blackstone, *Commentaries*, 1:161–62, 4:67, 1:125–26.

11. PAH, 3:75–82.

12. AH to Robert R Livingston, Aug. 23, 1783, PAH, 3:431, AH to GM, April 7, 1784, PAH, 3:528–29.

13. Benjamin Vaughan to Lord Shelburne, April 10, 1782, Mss., Lansdowne Papers, WLCL.

14. Undated mss., GW Papers, microfilm reel 84, LOC.

15. Van Closen, *Revolutionary Journal*, 199–200, 272.

16. AH to HK, June 7, 1782, PAH, 3:91–3.

17. Stryker, Capture of the *Blockhouse at Toms River*, 24–31; JCC, Oct. 15, 1782.

18. AH to RM, Aug. 13, 1782, mss., NYPL.

19. AH to [John Lawrence], Dec. 12, 1782, PAH, 3:212.

20. AH to ESH; Dec. 18, 1782, PAH, 3:226.

21. Randall and Nahra, *Thomas Chittenden's Town*, 6, 57–8.

22. GW to Thomas Chittenden, Jan. 1, 1782, *WW*, 23: 419–22.

23. "Motion on Vermont," Dec. 5, 1782, *PAH*, 3:205–06.

24. AH to [John Laurence], Dec. 12, 1782, *PAH*, 3:212.

25. Quoted in Mitchell, *AH, Youth*, 287.

26. GC to AH, Dec. 29th, 1782; AH to GC, Jan. 1, 1783, *PAH*, 3:236; Jan. 12, 1783, *PAH*, 3:240–41.

27. AH to ESH, Dec. 1782, *PAH*, 3:235.

28. AH to ESH, Jan. 8, 1783, *PAH*, 3:238.

29. "Report on Army Memorial," Jan. 22, 1783, *PAH*, 3:245–46.

30. "Remarks on Raising Funds," Jan. 27, 1783, *PAH*, 3:245–46

31. "Remarks on the Collection of Funds," Jan. 28, 1783, *PAH*, 3: 246–47.

32. "Motion on the Establishment of Permanent Funds," Feb. 12, 1783, *PAH*, 3:252–53.

33. AH to GW, Feb. 13, 1783, *PAH*, 3:253–5.

34. GW to AH, March 4, 1783, *PAH*, 3:277–79.

35. AH to GW, March 25, 1783, *PAH*, 3:306.

36. "Remarks on the Provisional Peace Treaty," March 19, 1783, *PAH*, 3:294–95.

37. GW, "Circular Letter," March 30, 1783, *WW*, 25:270–72.

38. GW to AH, March 12, 1783, *WW*, 26: 216–18.

39. AHGC, June 29, 1783, *PAH*, 3:407–8; AH to ESH, July 22, 1783, *PAH*, 3:413.

40. AH to ESH, July 22, 1783, *PAH*, 3:413.

41. AH to JJ, July 25, 1783, *PAH*, 3:416–17.

42. McHenry to AH, Oct. 22, 1783, *PAH*, 3:472.

43. *WW*, 27:255–590; Freeman, *GW* 5:451–68.

Thirteen: "Acquisition of Power and Profit"

Lawyer and Lawmaker: PAH, 3:476–701; Mitchell, *AH, Youth*, 1:330–88; Hendrickson, *Hamilton*, 1, 406–50; O'Brien, *Hercules Mulligan*; McDonald, *AH*, 62–94; *LDC*, vols. 9–11; Crary, *Price of Loyalty*; Randall, *A Little Revenge*, Necker, *Treatise on the Administration of the Finances of France*, vols. 1–3.

1. T. Jones, *History of New York*, 2:783.

2. Quoted in O'Brien, *Hercules Mulligan* 122–24.

3. Quoted in Burrows and Wallace, *Gotham*, 285–87.

4. AH to JD, Aug. 5, 1783, *PAH*, 3:430.

5. RRL to AH, Aug. 30, 1783, *PAH*, 3:434–35.

6. "Letter from Phocion to the Considerate Citizens of New York, January, 1784," *PAH*, 3:483–97.

7. *New York Journal*, January 1784.

8. McDonald, *AH*, 65.

9. Goebel, *Law Practice of AH*, 1:317–93.

10. AH to GC, June 1, 1783, *PAH*, 3:367–72.

11. "Second Letter from Phocion," April 1784, *PAH*, 3:530–58.

12. Robert L. Livingston to AH, Aug. 30, 1783, *PAH*, 3:434–35.

13. AH to John B. Church, March 10, 1784, *PAH*, 3:520–23.

14. Necker, *Treatise*, 1:xclvi–xclvii.

15. ML to AH, Oct. 8, 1784; *PAH*, 3:580–81.

16. AH to GW, Nov. 25, 1785, *PAH*, 3:635–36, 3:51.

17. AH to ESH, March 17, 1785, *PAH*, 3:589.

18. ASC to AH, 1785, quoted in Hendrickson, *H*, 1:530–34.

19. AH to ASC, Aug. 3, 1785, mss, ASC Papers, UVA.

FOURTEEN: "WHAT MAY THIS LEAD TO?"

Confederation Years: *PAH*, 3:617–701; *PGW*, Confederation Series, vols. 4–5; *PTJ*, vols. 9–10; McDonald, *AH*, 90–115; Mitchell, *AH, Youth*, 356–465; Hendrickson, *Hamilton*, 2: 442–559; Belleisles, *Revolutionary Outlaws*, 245–65; Szathmary, *Shays Rebellion*; Freeman, *GW*, 6; R. Scigliano, ed. *Federalist*; Randall and Nahra, *Forgotten Americans*, 103–20.

1. AH to Richard Varick, [Sept. 1, 1786], mss., NYPL; AH to ESH, Sept. 18, 1786; *PAH*, 3:684.

2. *WW*, 27: 340.

3. "Appointment as Commissioner," May 5, 1786, *PAH*, 3:665–66.

4. "Address," Sept. 14, 1786, *PAH*, 3:686–89.

5. Quoted in Belleisles, *Revolutionary Outlaws*, 245–47.

6. Ibid., 248–51.

7. "First Speech," Jan. 19, 1787, *PAH*, 4:12.

8. "Second Speech," Jan. 19, 1787, *PAH*, 4:13–17.

9. Quoted in Freeman, *GW* 6:15.

10. Belleisles, *Revolutionary Outlaws*, 252–3.

11. AH, "Remarks," Feb. 8, 1787, *PAH*, 4:39.

12. March 14, 1787; *PAH*, 4:115–18.

13. Belleisles, *Revolutionary Outlaws*, 253.

14. AH, "Address," June 18, 1787, *PAH*, 4:187–95.

15. Ibid., 207–11.

16. Quoted in McDonald, 105.

17. AH to GW, July 3, 1787, *PAH*, 4:223–24.

18. GW to AH, July 10, 1787, *PAH*, 4:225; *PAH*, 4:229–32.

19. AH, "Remarks," Sept. 6, 1787, *PAH*, 4:243.

20. AH, "Remarks," Sept. 17, 1787, *PAH*, 4:253.

21. AH, "Conjectures about the New Constitution," Sept. 17–30, 1787, *PAH*, 4:275–77.

22. AH to GW, Oct. 11, 1787, *PAH*, 4:280–81; GW to AH, Oct. 18, 1787, *PAH*, 4:284–85.

23. ASC to AH, Oct. 2, 1787, *PAH*, 4:279–80.

24. AH, Federalist No. 1, Oct. 27, 1787, Scigliano, *Federalist* 3.

25. Ibid., 4.

26. AH, Federalist No. 15, Dec. 1, 1787, Scigliano, *Federalist* 86–7.

27. AH, Federalist No. 85, Aug. 13–16, 1788, Scigliano, *Federalist* 560–61.

28. GW to AH, Aug. 28, 1788, *PAH*, 5:207.

29. AH, "Remarks," June 20, 1788, *PAH*, 5:16.

30. Mitchell, *AH, Youth*, 455, 642n.

31. AH, "Third Speech," June 28, 178, *PAH*, 5:124; Mitchell, AH, Youth 462.

32. Ibid., 463–4.

Fifteen: "The Compass of National Authority"

Federalist: PAH, 5:220–579; *PGW*, Presidential Series; *PTJ*, vols. 16–26; Hendrickson, *Hamilton*, 2; Mitchell, *AH, National Adventure*, 1–373; McDonald, *AH*, 117–307; McCullough, *John Adams*; Randall, *TJ*; Randall, *GW*; Randall and Nahra, *Forgotten Americans*, 103–20; Gordon, *Hamilton's Blessing*, 11–14; Burrows and Wallace, *Gotham*, 270–312.

1. AH to GW, Aug. 13, 1788, *PAH*, 5: 201–02.

2. GW to AH, Aug. 28, 1788, *PAH*, 5: 206–08; AH to GW, September 1788, *PAH*, 5: 220–22.

3. GW to AH, Oct. 3, 1788, *PAH*, 5: 222–24.

4. AH to JM, Nov. 23, 1788, *PAH*, 5: 235–7.

5. AH, "H.G. Letters," *PAH*, 5: 263–306.

6. AH to James Wilson, Jan. 25, 1789, *PAH*, 5:247–49.

7. Quoted in McDonald, *AH*, 128.

8. Randall, *GW*, 445–49.

9. AH to GW, May 5, 1789, *PAH*, 5: 335–37; 337–38.

10. Cash Book, *PAH*, 3:55–56.

11. JA to AH, July 21, 1789, *PAH*, 5:363–4.

12. Burrows and Wallace, *Gotham*, 276.

13. Quoted in Randall, *TJ*, 487.

14. AH to ML, Oct. 6, 1789, *PAH*, 5: 425–27.

15. Hamilton, *IL*, xx.

16. McDonald, *AH*, 145–49.

17. John Witherspoon to AH, Oct. 26, 1789, *PAH*, 5: 464–5.

18. William Bingham to AH, Nov. 25, 1789, *PAH*, 5: 538–57.

19. AH to ASC, Nov. 8, 1789, mss., ASC Papers, UVA.

20. AH to Henry Lee, Dec. 1, 1789, *PAH*, 5:1.

SIXTEEN: "A HOST UNTO HIMSELF"

AH's "Blessing": *PAH*, vols. 7–26; *PTJ*, vols. 18–26; McDonald, *AH*, 163–363; Miller, *AH: Portrait in Paradox*; Mitchell, *AH, National Adventure*; Hendrickson, *AH*, vol. 2; Randall, *TJ*; Randall, *GW*; McCullough, *John Adams*; Brookhiser, *AH, American*; Fleming, *Duel*; Stourzh, *AH and the Idea of Republican Government*; Syrett, *Interview in Weehawken*; Sharp, *American Politics in the Early Republic*; JCH, 4; Lomask, *Aaron Burr*, vol. 2; Gordon, *Hamilton's Blessing*; Rossiter, *AH and the Constitution*; Cooke, *AH*; Elkins and McKittrick, *The Age of Federation*.

1. AH to ASC, Jan. 7, 1790, Mss., ASC Papers, UVA.

2. AH, "Report on the Public Credit," Jan. 9, 1790, *PAH*, 6:51–168.

3. Maclay, *Diary*, 183–84.

4. TJ, "*Anas*," quoted in Cunningham, *In Pursuit of Reason*, 139.

5. A. M. Hamilton, *Intimate Life of AH*, 315.

6. AH, "Report on the Bank," Dec. 13, 1790, *PAH*, 7:236–342.

7. AH, "Opinion on the Constitutionality of an Act to Establish a Bank," Feb. 23, 1791, *PAH*, 8:63–134.

8. GW, May 1791, *PTJ*, 20:291–92.

9. "Report on Manufactures," Jan. 1791, *PAH*, 7.

10. "Draft of the Reynolds Pamphlet," Aug. 25, 1797, *PAH*, 21:226.

11. Maria Reynolds to AH, Dec. 26, 1791, and Dec. 28, 1791, *PAH*, 10:557.

12. Robert Troup to AH, March 19, 1792, *PAH*, 11:155–58; William Duer to AH, March 12, 1792, *PAH*, 11–126.

13. AH to William Seton, March 19, 1792, *PAH*, 11:154–55.

14. AH to Edward Carrington, May 26, 1792, *PAH*, 11:432–33.

15. *PAH*, 21:258.

16. Mss., Schuyler Papers, NYPL.

17. TJ to JM, June 30, 1793, *L&B*, 7:420–22, TJ to JM, July 7, 1793, *L&B*, 7:436.

18. *PAH*, 12:312.

19. TJ to JM, quoted in Elkins and McKittrick, 435.

20. JM to TJ, Oct. 20, 1797, *PTJ*, 18:684–85.

21. AH, N.Y. Court of Errors, Feb. 1804, quoted in Fleming, *AH in His Own Words*, 394–95.

22. T. Fleming, *Duel*, 325.

BIBLIOGRAPHY

———◆———

Except if otherwise indicated,
all books cited are the trade hardcover editions.

Abbott, Wilbur C. *New York in the American Revolution*. New York, 1929.

Adair, Douglas. "A Note on Certain of AH's Pseudonyms." *WMQ* 12 (1955): 284–5.

Allen, Ethan. "A Narrative of the Captivity of Colonel Allen." In *American Rebels*, edited by Richard M. Dorson. New York, 1953.

Ames, Fisher. *Works*. Edited by W. B. Allen. Indianapolis: Liberty Classics, 1983.

Atherton, Gertrude. *The Conqueror*. New York, 1902.

———. "The Hunt for Hamilton's Mother." *North American Review*, 175 (June 1902): 229–42.

Atwood, Rodney. *The Hessians*. Cambridge, England, 1980.

Augur, Helen. *Secret War of Independence*. New York, 1955.

Axelrod, Jacob. *Philip Freneau: Champion of Democracy*. Austin, Texas, 1967.

Bailyn, Bernard P. *Ideological Origins of American Independence*. Cambridge, Mass., 1967.

Bakeless, John. *Turncoats, Traitors and Heroes*. Philadelphia, 1959.

Balderston, Marion. "Lord Howe Clears the Delaware." *PMHB* 96 (1972), 326–46.

Banning, Lance. *The Jeffersonian Persuasion: Evolution of a Party Ideology*. Ithaca, N.Y., 1978.

———. *Sacred Fire of Liberty: James Madison and the Founding of the American Republic*. Ithaca, N.Y., 1995.

Barch, Oscar T. *New York City During the War for Independence*. New York, 1931.

Belleisles, Michael. *Revolutionary Outlaws: Ethan Allen and the Struggle for Independence on the Early American Frontier*. Charlottesville, 1993.

Bill, Alfred Hoyt. *New Jersey and the Revolutionary War.* New Brunswick, N.J.,
   1964.

Billias, George Allan, ed. *GW's Opponents.* New York, 1969.

Blackstone, William. *Commentaries on the Laws of England.* 4 vols. London, 1765.

Bliven, Bruce. *Battle for Manhattan.* New York, 1956.

———. *Under the Guns: New York, 1775–76.* New York, 1972.

Boldt, David R., and Willard Sterne Randall, eds. *The Founding City.*
   Philadelphia, 1976.

Bolles, Albert S. *The Financial History of the U.S. from 1774 to 1789.* 4th ed., New
   York, 1896.

Bonomi, Patricia U. *A Factious People: Politics and Society in Colonial New York.*
   New York, 1971.

Bonsal, Stephen. *When the French Were Here.* New York, 1945.

Boudinot, Elias. *Journal.* Philadelphia, 1894.

Bowling, Kenneth R. "Politics in the First Congress, 1789–91." PhD diss.,
   Univ. of Wisconsin, 1968.

Boyd, George A. *Elias Boudinot, Patriot and Statesman.* Princeton, N.J., 1952.

Boyd, Julian. *Number 7, AH's Secret Attempts to Control American Foreign Policy.*
   Princeton, N.J., 1964.

Bradford, S.S. "Hunger Menaces the Revolution." *MHM* 61 (1966), 1–23.

Brandt, Carol. *An American Aristocracy: The Livingstons.* Garden City, N.Y., 1986.

British Head Quarters Papers. Mss., in WLCL.

Brod, Howard. "Hamilton's Great Invention." *Financial History* 17 (1999) 26–27,
   31.

Broglie, Duc de. *Memoirs of the Prince de Talleyrand.* 5 vols. New York, 1891.

Brookhiser, Richard. *AH, American.* New York, 1999.

Brown, Wallace. *The Good Americans, The Loyalists in the American Revolution.*
   New York, 1969.

Burnaby, Andrew. *Travels Through the Middle Settlements in North America, 1759–60.*
   London, 1775.

Burnett, Edmund C. *The Continental Congress.* New York, 1941.

———, ed. *Letters of the Members of the Continental Congress.* 8 vols., Washington,
   D.C., 1921–36.

Burr, Sam Engle. *Burr-Hamilton Duel & Related Matters: A Statement.* Aledo,
   Texas, 1971.

Burrows, Edwin G. and Mike Wallace. *Gotham: A History of New York City to
   1898.* New York, 1999.

Busch, Noel. *Winter Quarters*. New York, 1974.

Bush, Martin H. *Revolutionary Enigma: A Reappraisal of General Philip Schuyler of New York* Port Washington, N.Y., 1969.

Bushman, Richard L. "A Calculation of Ordnance and Ordnance Stores Wanted for the Army of the Northern Dept." *FTMB* 3 (1934), 190–91.

Butterfield, Lyman H. *John Witherspoon Comes to America*. Princeton, 1953.

Callahan, North. *Flight from the Republic: The Tories of the American Revolution*. New York, 1967.

———. *Henry Knox: GW's General*. New York, 1968.

Carp, E. Wayne. *To Starve the Army at Pleasure*. Chapel Hill, N.C., 1984.

Calhoon, Robert M. *The Loyalists in Revolutionary America, 1760–1781*. New York, 1973.

Callendar, James Thomson. *Letters to AH, King of the Federalists*. New York, 1802.

Cantor, Milton. *Hamilton*. Englewood Cliffs, N.J., 1971.

Chambers, William N. *Political Parties in a New Nation*. New York, 1963.

Charles, Joseph. *The Origins of the American Party System*. New York, 1961.

———. "Hamilton and Washington: The Origins of the American Party System." *WMQ* 12 (1955): 217–67.

Clinton, Sir Henry. *The American Rebellion: A Narrative of His Campaigns, 1775–82*. New York, 1949.

Cooke, Jacob E. *Alexander Hamilton: A Biography*. New York, 1982.

———. "Dinner at Jefferson's: A Note on Jacob E. Cooke's 'The Compromise of 1790.'" *WMQ* 28 (1971) 637.

Crary, Catherine. *Price of Loyalty*. New York, 1973.

Crosby, Richard Wheeler. "AH's Political Principles: Natural Rights, Democracy and the Good Regime." Ph.D. diss., Cornell University, 1970.

Culbertson, William S. *AH: An Essay*. New Haven, Conn., 1911.

Dakin, Douglas. *Turgot and the Ancien Regime*. New York, 1965.

Daniels, Jonathan. *Ordeal of Ambition: Jefferson, Hamilton and Burr*. Garden City, N.Y., 1970.

Davis, Joseph S. *Essays in the Earlier History of American Corporations*. New York, 1965.

Dawson, Henry B. *The Sons of Liberty in New York*. New York, 1969.

DeConde, Alexander. *Entangling Alliance: Politics and Diplomacy Under GW*. Durham, N.C., 1958.

Dietze, Gottfried. "Hamilton's Federalist—Treatise for Free Government." *Cornell Law Quarterly* 42 (1957): 307–28, 501–18.

Dillon, Dorothy R. *The New York Triumvirate*. New York, 1949.

Dix, Morgan, ed. *A History of the Parish of Trinity Church in the City of New York*. New York, 1898.

Dodds, Harold W. *John Witherspoon*. Princeton, N.J., 1944.

Doerflinger, Thomas M. *A Vigorous Spirit of Enterprise: Merchants and Economic Development in Revolutionary Philadelphia*. Chapel Hill, N.C., 1986.

Duane, James. *Papers*. Mss. in NYHS.

East, Robert A. *Business Enterprise in the American Revolutionary Era*. New York, 1938.

East, Robert, and Jacob Judd, eds. *The Loyalist Americans: A Focus on Greater New York*. Tarrytown, 1975.

Edwards, Byran. *The History, Civil and Commercial, of the British Colonies in the West Indies*. New York, 1972.

Egnal, Marc. "The Changing Structure of Philadelphia's Trade with the BWI." *PMHB* 99 (1975), 156–79.

Elkins, Stanley, and Eric McKittrick, *The Age of Federation*, New York, 1993.

Einstein, Lewis. *Divided Loyalties: Americans in England during the War of Independence*. London, 1933.

Emery, Noemic. *AH: An Intimate Portrait*. New York, 1982.

Farrand, Max. *Records of the Federal Convention*. New Haven, Conn., 1937.

Ferguson, E. James. *The Power of the Purse: A History of American Public Finance, 1776–1790*. Chapel Hill, 1961.

Fitzpatrick, John C. *GW Himself*. Indianapolis, 1933.

——, ed. *Writings of GW*. 38 vols., Washington, D.C., 1931–44.

Fleming, Thomas. *Duel: AH, Aaron Burr and the Future of America*. New York, 1999.

——. *1776: Year of Illusions*. New York, 1975.

——. *The Forgotten Victory: The Battle for New Jersey, 1780*. New York, 1973.

Flexner, James Thomas. *The Young Hamilton*. Boston, 1978.

Flick, Alexander. *Loyalists in New York During the American Revolution*. New York, 1901.

Foner, Philip S., ed. *Democratic-Republican Societies, 1790–1800*. Westport, Conn., 1976.

——. *Tom Paine and Revolutionary America*. New York, 1976.

Forbes, Duncan. *Hume's Philosophical Works*. Cambridge, England, 1975.

Force, Peter, ed. *American Archives*. 9 vols. Washington, D.C. 1837–1853.

Ford, Corey. *A Peculiar Service*. Boston, 1965.

Ford, Henry Jones. *AH*. New York, 1920.

Fort Ticonderoga Museum. *Bulletin*. Fort Ticonderoga, N.Y., 1927–.

Freeman, Douglas Southall. *GW: A Biography.* 7 vols. New York, 1948–57.

Freeman, Joanne B. *Affairs of Honor: National Politics in the New Republic.* New Haven, 2001.

———. "Dueling as Politics: Reinterpreting the Burr-Hamilton Duel." *WMQ,* 3d per., 53 (1996) 290–318.

Gates, Horatio. *Papers.* NYHS.

Gaylord, Irving C. *Burr-Hamilton Duel.* New York, 1889.

Gerlach, Don R. *Philip Schuyler and the American Revolution in New York.* Lincoln, Neb., 1964.

Gerlach, Larry R. *Prologue to Independence: New Jersey in the Coming of the American Revolution.* New Brunswick, N.J., 1976.

Gilbert, Felix. *To the Farewell Address.* Princeton, N.J., 1961.

Gipson, Lawrence Henry. *British Empire Before the American Revolution.* 16 vols., New York, 1966–1970.

Glover, Michael. *General Burgoyne in Canada and America.* London, 1978.

Goebel, Julius, Jr., ed. *Law Practice of Alexander Hamilton.* 5 vols. New York, 1964–81.

Gordon, John Steele. *Hamilton's Blessing.* New York, 1997.

Green, Ashbel. *Life of the Rev'd John Witherspoon.* New Brunswick, N.J., 1973.

Gruber, Ira D. *The Howe Brothers and the American Revolution.* Chapel Hill, N.C., 1972.

Gunderson, Joan R., and Gwen V. Gampel. "Married Women's Legal Status in Eighteenth-Century New York and Virginia." *WMQ,* 3rd series, 39 (1982): 114–34.

Halleck, Henry W. "Military Espionage." *American Journal of International Law,* 5 (1911), 590–603.

Hamilton, Alexander. *Writings.* Edited by Joanne B. Freeman. New York, 2001.

———. Edited by Harold C. Syrett, et al. *Papers.* 27 vols. New York, 1961–87.

Hamilton, Alexander, John Jay, and James Madison. *The Federalist.* Edited by Robert Scigliano. New York, 2000.

Hamilton, Allan Maclane. *The Intimate Life of Alexander Hamilton.* New York, 1910.

Hamilton, John Church. *Life of Alexander Hamilton.* 2 vols. New York, 1834.

Hammond, Bray. *Banks and Politics in America from the Revolution to the Civil War.* Princeton N.J., 1957.

Hatch, Robert McConnell. *Major John André.* Boston, 1986.

Henderson, Herbert James. *Party Politics in the Continental Congress.* New York, 1974.

————. "Congressional Factionalism and the Attempt to Recall BF." *WMQ* 3rd series, 27 (1970): 246–67.

————. "Constitutionalists and Republicans in the Continental Congress, 1776–86." *PH* 36 (1969): 119–44.

Hendrickson, Robert A. *Hamilton* 2 vols. New York, 1976.

————. *Rise and Fall of AH*. New York, 1981.

Higgenbotham, Don. *War and American Independence*. Boston, 1983.

Hofstadter, Richard. The Idea of a Party System: The Rise of Legitimate Opposition in the U.S., 1780–1840. Berkeley, Calif., 1969.

Hume, David. *Philosophical Works*. Edited by Thomas H. Green and Thomas H. Grose. 4 vols. 1964 reprint of London, 1886 edition.

Jefferson, Thomas. *Papers*. Edited by Julian P. Boyd, et al. 29 vols. to date. Princeton, N.J. 1950–.

Jellison, Charles A. *Ethan Allen, Frontier Rebel*. Syracuse, N.Y., 1983.

Jenson, Merrill. *The Articles of Confederation*. Madison, Wisc., 1940.

Jones, Thomas. *History of New York During the Revolutionary War*. 2 vols. New York, 1879.

Kalm, Peter. *Travels in North America, 1753–1761*. Reprint: 2 vols. New York, 1937.

Kammer, Michael. *Colonial New York, A History*. New York, 1975.

Ketchum, Richard M. *Winter Soldiers*. New York, 1972.

Klein, Milton. "The American Whig: Wm. Livingston of New York." Ph.D. diss., New York University, 1958.

Kohn, Richard H. *Eagle and Sword*. New York, 1975.

Konefsky, Sam J. *John Marshall and Alexander Hamilton, Architects of the American Constitution*. New York, 1964.

Lafayette, Marquis de. *Memoirs, Correspondence and Manuscripts of General Lafayette*. 3 vols. London, 1837.

Larson, Harold. "Alexander Hamilton: The Fact and Fiction of His Early Years." *WMQ* 91 (April 1952): 139–51.

Lenke, Isaac Q. *Memoir of the Life and Times of John Lamb*. Albany, 1850.

Leiby, Adrian C. *Revolutionary War in Hackensack Valley*. New Brunswick, N.J., 1962.

Lind, Michael. *Hamilton's Republic*. New York, 1997.

Lindsay, Merrill. "Pistols Shed Light on Famed Duel." *Smithsonian*, November 1976, 94–98.

Livingston, William. *The Independent Reflector*. Edited by Milton Klein. Cambridge, Mass., 1963.

Lodge, Henry Cabot. *AH*. New York, 1909.

Lomask, Milton. *Aaron Burr.* 2 vols. New York, 1979.

Lundin, Leonard C. *New Jersey: Cockpit of the Revolution.* Princeton, N.J., 1940.

McCormick, Richard P. *Experiment in Independence.* New Brunswick, N.J., 1950.

McCullough, David. *John Adams.* New York, 2001.

McDonald, Forrest. *AH: A Biography.* New York, 1979.

———. *The Presidency of George Washington.* New York, 1974.

———. *We the People: The Economic Origins of the Constitution.* Chicago, 1958.

Maclay, William. *Diary.* Edited by Edgar S. Maclay. New York, 1890.

McNamara, Peter. *Political Economy and Statesmanship.* DeKalb, Ill., 1998.

Maguire, J. Robert. "A Self-Portrait by Major John André." *Bulletin of the Fort Ticonderoga Museum* 16 (2000) 201–50.

Marshall, Douglas, and Howard H. Peckham. *Campaigns of the American Revolution.* Maplewood, N.J., 1976.

Mason, Alpheus Thomas. "The Federalist—A Split Personality." *American Historical Review* 57 (1952): 625–43.

Massey, Gregory D. *JL and the American Revolution.* Columbia, S.C., 2000.

Middlekauff, Robert. *The Glorious Cause: The American Revolution, 1763–1789.* New York, 1982.

Miller, John D. *AH: Portrait in Paradox.* New York, 1959.

Mitchell, Broadus. *AH: Youth to Maturity.* New York, 1957.

———. *AH: The National Adventure.*

———. *AH: Revolutionary Years.* New York, 1970.

———. "The Man Who Discovered Hamilton." *PNJHS* 69, no. 4 (1951): 88–114.

Monaghan, Frank, and Marvin Lowenthal. *This Was New York.* Garden City, N.J., 1943.

Monroe, James. *An Examination of the Late Proceedings in Congress Respecting the Official Conduct of the Secretary of the Treasury.* Philadelphia, 1793.

Morris, Richard B. *Alexander Hamilton and the Founding of the Nation.* New York, 1957.

———. *Witnesses at the Creation.* New York, 1985.

———, Ed. *John Jay: The Winning of the Peace.* New York, 1980.

Mulligan, Hercules, and Robert Troup. "Narrative." *WMQ,* 3 ser., 4 (1947), 203–25.

Naval Documents of the American Revolution. Edited by William Ball Clark. Washington, D.C., 1964–73, 10 vols.

Necker, Jacques. *A Treatise on the Administration of the Finances of France.* Trans. by Thomas Mortimer. 3 vols., London, 1785.

Nelson, Paul David. *General Horatio Gates*. Baton Rouge, La, 1976.

Nettels, Curtis P. *The Emergence of a National Economy, 1775–1815*. New York, 1962.

Nott, Eliphalet. *A Discourse Delivered in the City of Albany Occasioned by the Ever to Be Lamented Death of Gen. AH*. Greenfield, Mass., 1805.

O'Brien, Michael J. *Hercules Mulligan: Confidential Correspondent of GW*. New York, 1937.

Oliver, Frederick C. *AH: An Essay on American Union*. New York, 1923.

Otis, Harrison Gray. *Eulogy on Gen. AH*. Boston, 1804.

Pancake, John S. *1777: Year of the Hangman*. University, Ala., 1977.

Pares, Richard. *A West-India Fortune*. Hamden, Conn., 1968.

———. *War and Trade in the West Indies*. London, 1963.

Pearson, Michael. *Those Damned Rebels: The American Revolution as Seen Through British Eyes*. New York, 1972.

Peckham, Howard H., ed. *Sources of American Independence*, 2 vols. Chicago, 1978.

———. *The Toll of Independence: Engagements and Battle Casualties of the American Revolution*, Chicago, 1974.

———. *The War for Independence: A Military History*. Chicago, 1958.

Pell, John. *Ethan Allen*. Lake George, N.Y., 1929.

Pennypacker, Morton. *General Washington's Spies*. Brooklyn, N.Y., 1939.

Plumb, J.H. "The French Connection." *AH* 35 (1974): 27–57.

Postlethwaite, Malachy. *Universal Dictionary of Trade and Commerce*. 2 vols. London, 1757.

Potter, Janice. *The Liberty We Seek: Loyalist Ideology in Colonial New York and Massachusetts*. Cambridge, Mass., 1983.

Princetonians: A Biographical Dictionary. Edited by James McLochlan, et al. 5 vols. Princeton, N.J., 1976–.

Rake, Paul. *Republic Ancient and Modern*. Chapel Hill, N.C., 1994.

Randall, Willard Sterne. *A Little Revenge: BF and His Son*. Boston, 1984.

———. *BA: Patriot and Traitor*. New York, 1990.

———. *GW: A Life*. New York, 1997.

———. *TJ: A Life*. New York, 1993.

———. "The Fighting Federalist." *MHQ: The Quarterly Magazine of Military History*, 15 (2002): 15–32, 64–75.

Randall, W.S. and Nancy Nahra. *Forgotten Americans*. Boston, 1998.

———. *Thomas Chittenden's Town: A Story of Williston*, Vermont. Burlington, Vt., 1997.

Risch, Erna. *Supplying Washington's Army*. Washington, D.C., 1981.

Roche, John F. *AH*. Morristown, N.J., 1967.

Rogow, Arnold A. *A Fatal Friendship: AH & Aaron Burr.* New York, 1998.

Rossie, Jonathan G. *Politics of Command in American Revolution.* Syracuse, 1975.

Royster, Charles. *A Revolutionary People at War.* Chapel Hill, N.C., 1979.

Sabine, Lorenzo. *Biographical Sketches of the Loyalists of the American Revolution.* 2 vols. Boston, 1864.

Schachner, Nathan. *AH.* New York, 1946.

———, ed. "AH Viewed by His Friends: The Narratives of Robert Troup and Hercules Mulligan," in *WMQ,* 3rd series, 4 (1947): 203–25.

Schuyler, Philip. *Papers.* NYPL.

Sharp, James Roger. *American Politics in the Early Republic.* New Haven, Conn., 1993.

Slaughter, Thomas P. *The Whiskey Rebellion.* New York, 1986.

Smith, Adam. *An Inquiry into the Nature and Causes of the Wealth of Nations.* New York, 1937.

———. Edited by Dugald Stewart. *Theory of Moral Sentiments.* New York, 1960.

Smith, Jean Edwards. *John Marshall, Definer of a Nation.* New York, 1996.

Spaulding, E. Wilder. *His Excellency George Clinton, Critic of the Constitution.* New York, 1938.

———. *New York in the Critical Period, 1783–89.* New York, 1932.

Stinchcombe, William C. *The American Revolution and the French Alliance.* Syracuse, 1969.

Stokes, J. N. Phelps. *Iconography of Manhattan Island, 1498–1909.* New York, 1967.

Stourzh, Gerald. *AH and the Idea of Republican Government.* Stanford, Calif., 1970.

Stryker, William. *Capture of the Blockhouse at Tom's River.* Trenton, N.J., 1883.

———. *Battles of Trenton and Princeton.* New York, 1898.

Swiggert, Howard. *The Extraordinary Mr. Morris.* Garden City, N.Y., 1952.

Syrett, Harold Coffin. *Interview in Weehawken.* Middletown, Conn., 1960.

Szathmary, David. *Shays' Rebellion: The Making of an Agrarian Insurrection.* Amherst, Mass., 1980.

Thayer, Theodore. *As We Were: The Story of Old Elizabethtown.* Elizabeth, N.J., 1964.

Thomas, Milton H. "The King's College Building." *New York Historical Society Bulletin* 39 (1955): 23–61.

Tilghman, Oswald. *Memoir of Lieutenant Colonel Tench Tilghman.* Albany, 1876.

U.S. Continental Congress. *Journals of the Continental Congress, 1774–1783.* 10 vols. Philadelphia, 1775–1785.

———. *Papers of the Continental Congress, 1774–1789.* 204 Reels U.S. National Archives, microfilm ed., 247.

———. *Letters of Delegates to Congress*. Edited by Paul Smith, et al. 15 vols. to date. Washington, D.C., 1976–.

Van Doren, Carl. *Secret History of the American Revolution*. New York, 1938.

Van Ness, William Peter. *A Correct Statement of the Late Melancholy Affair of Honor Between General Hamilton and Col. Burr*. New York, 1804.

Vattel, Emmerich de. *The Law of Nations*. Reprinted, 1817. London, 1797.

Ver Steeg, Clarence L. *Robert Morris, Revolutionary Financier*. Philadelphia, 1954.

Wallace, Willard M. *Traitorous Hero: The Career and Fortunes of BA*. New York, 1951.

Ward, Christopher. *The War of the Revolution*. 2 vols. New York, 1952.

Wertenbaker, Thomas Jefferson. *Father Knickerbocker Rebels: New York City During the Revolution*. New York, 1948.

Wilkinson, James. *Memoirs of My Own Times*. 3 vols. Philadelphia, 1816.

Wright, Esmond. *Red, White and True Blue: The Loyalists in the Revolution*. New York, 1976.

Yoshpe, Harry B. *Disposition of Loyalist Estates in the Southern District of New York*. New York, 1939.

Young, Alfred F. *The Democratic Republicans of New York*. Chapel Hill, N.C., 1967.

INDEX

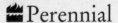
Perennial

Books by Willard Sterne Randall:

ALEXANDER HAMILTON
A Life
ISBN 0-06-095466-3 (paperback)

Orphaned at eleven and apprenticed to a counting house, the young Alexander Hamilton learned the principles of business that helped him, as the first Secretary of the Treasury, create the American banking system and invent the modern corporation. In his twenties, he lived through the American Revolution, primarily as aide-de-camp to General Washington, and went on to build a successful legal career, co-write *The Federalist Papers*, and build a life in politics. In *Alexander Hamilton: A Life*, what emerges is a totally fresh Hamilton, his contributions and what they mean today, all told in a highly readable style.

"The life of Alexander Hamilton, vividly re-created. . . . A fine biography."
—*Boston Globe*

THOMAS JEFFERSON
A Life
ISBN 0-06-097617-9 (paperback)

Drawing on firsthand scholarship as well as ongoing literary detective work on the Jefferson papers, Randall calls on his skills as an investigative journalist to unearth new material and to challenge long-held assumptions about the reasoning, motives, and works of this sage, philosopher, politician, and romantic. Revealing both Jefferson's inner and outer struggles, Randall sheds new light on Jefferson's thoughts on slavery and his alleged relations with the slave Sally Hemmings—as well as Revolutionary and diplomatic intrigues.

"A welcome, one-volume biography that strikes a balance between Jefferson's personal and public life." —*New York Times*